500

Voluntary Action
Research: 1972

This book is part of the "Voluntary Action Research Series" of the Center for a Voluntary Society (1507 M St., N.W., Washington, D.C. 20005), under the General Editorship of David Horton Smith. This series will not only include future annual review volumes like the present one, but will also include research and theoretical monographs on specific projects/topics contributed by scholars in various fields and countries. The Center for a Voluntary Society is organized for charitable, scientific and educational purposes to promote and expand the awareness, understanding and effective utilization of volunteers and voluntary associations in coping with human and social problems in the United States and elsewhere, and to evaluate the quality and effectiveness of the voluntary sector in making our society more humane, just, open, participatory, nonviolent and uncoerced.

Voluntary Action Research: 1972

Edited by
David Horton Smith
Center for a Voluntary Society
and Boston College

Richard D. Reddy
State University of New York
at Fredonia

Burt R. Baldwin
Boston College

Lexington Books
D.C. Heath and Company
Lexington, Massachusetts
Toronto   London

This book is gratefully dedicated by the editors

To Alex Inkeles

for a decade of moral support and practical help, and in recognition of his contributions to the integrated study of the impact of personal and social systems in social science—toward which the editors hope Part Two of this volume makes some additional contribution;

And to Amitai Etzioni

whose theoretical work on compliance structures in complex organizations and on the nature of an "active society" have had a more salutary and pervasive influence on Part One of this volume than could be easily guessed.

339298

Contents

List of Figures

List of Tables

Foreword

It is surprising that the term *voluntary association* is still a somewhat esoteric one, unfamiliar in popular parlance. For twenty-five years I have had the repeated experience, even on college campuses, of being asked, "But what is a voluntary association?" As soon as a brief definition is supplied the immediate response is, "Oh yes, of course." The response is something like that of the bourgeois gentlemen who discovered that without knowing it he had been speaking prose all his life.

The unfamiliarity of the term is the more surprising, then, since voluntary action in associations has long been a characteristic feature of Anglo-American democracy. We recall, for example, the memorable statements about voluntary associations in the United States which were made long ago by three distinguished foreign observers. Alexis de Tocqueville in his work on *Democracy in America* (1832) wrote:

Americans of all ages, all conditions, and all dispositions, constantly form associations. They have not only commercial and manufacturing companies, in which all take part, but associations of a thousand other kinds—religious, moral, serious, futile, general or restricted, enormous or diminutive. The Americans make associations to give entertainments, to found seminaries, to build inns, to construct churches, to diffuse books, to send missionaries to the antipodes: they found in this manner hospitals, prisons, and schools.

Toward the end of the century Lord Bryce in *The American Commonwealth* observed: "Associations are created, extended, and worked in the United States more quickly and effectively than in any other country." We can readily understand why Max Weber in 1911 spoke of the United States as "the association-land *par excellence.*"

In this country today there are millions of formal voluntary associations, not to speak of the countless social and hobby clubs and the informal associations concerned with leisure-time, recreational activity. Nevertheless, many books on American democracy, and even some books on civics and political science, make no reference to voluntary associations and their place in "the democratic way of life." Moreover, few courses in colleges, and none in the high schools, are available on this topic. Except for scattered articles in learned and popular journals, appropriate curriculum materials are almost nonexistent. We should note, however, that a number of volumes on special aspects of voluntary associations in past and present have been published, including two or three volumes of collected essays. Yet nothing so comprehensive or analytical as the volume before us has previously appeared.

This volume is projected as the first in a continuing series that will include studies from a wide range of disciplines such as sociology, political science, social psychology, social work, anthropology and cross-cultural studies, law, social philosophy, religion, and history. An area of research which is of recent vintage is the study of voluntary organizations in lesser developed countries. The present volume includes a number of papers delivered two years ago at the annual meetings of the American Sociological Association, papers revised for the present purpose.

Representatives of this variety of disciplines have been brought together (from the United States and other countries) in the Association of Voluntary Action Scholars. The president of this Association is the indefatigable and resourceful sociologist David Horton Smith, one of the most systematic scholars and bibliographers in this area of research. The Association has enjoyed the collaboration and support of the Center for a Voluntary Society under the direction of John Dixon. The Association will publish monographs on voluntary associations, and it has already initiated the publication of the new *Journal of Voluntary Action Research*. These studies will range from concern with conceptual and typological framework and the history of concepts to incentive theory and institutional processes and pathologies.

Taken altogether, these studies and associations, it is hoped, will help to form a community of scholars which will build up an interdisciplinary, interprofessional, international cooperation that can give shape to a new discipline. This new discipline should have the vocation of continuously taking stock of research in both theory and practice in the whole field of "voluntary action."

The comprehensiveness of this enterprise is presented in a compact, highly suggestive way in Chapter 1. Viewing the enterprise in this fashion, we can see that these studies will not only identify and illuminate what is involved in the constitutional right of "freedom of association"; they can serve also to increase our understanding of man as a social entity, as "an associating being," not overlooking to be sure the perversions and antisocial activities of certain types of association.

But here a word must be said regarding the limitation of all such studies. Formal associations are by no means confined to what is here understood as "voluntary action," the action of volunteers. Society is made up of nonvoluntary as well as voluntary organizations. Indeed, voluntary associations have been defined by Max Weber as intermediary associations, as the structures that lie between the politically organized or recognized powers on the one side—the state and its subsidiaries—and "the natural community" of the family on the other.* That is, voluntary associations lie in between the nonvoluntary associations that are the major institutional means of social nurture, continuity and

*This aspect of association theory and practice will be taken more emphatically into account in later volumes in the series. Involved here in the sphere of associations, voluntary and nonvoluntary, is a separation of powers in a pluralistic society which is somewhat analogous to the separation of powers within the political order, and in both cases a dispersion of power within an embracing unity.

control. Inevitably, however, mutuality of influence (as well as tension) obtains between the voluntary and the nonvoluntary sectors. Voluntary associations in this context are a constant source of experiment and innovation. Today we can see, for example, attempts to increase the voluntary element in the family by bringing together nuclear families under the same roof in a new sort of extended family. Voluntary associations also provide the youth with a means of achieving autonomy in face of the parents. Moreover, one of the major influences impinging upon the state is exercised by voluntary organizations concerned with public policies. These influences are countered of course by the great pressure groups, the lobbies of special interest groups (with affluent expense accounts) which threaten to make Congress into little more than a clearinghouse for industrial and financial powers. Many of these special interest groups scarcely belong under the rubric of voluntary associations as ordinarily defined, for they are instruments whose principal purpose is to enhance the economic benefits of the membership.

In any event, since the voluntary organizations exist in the interstices between the nonvoluntary associations, any appropriate concern with the former should not distract attention from the intrinsic concerns of the family or the political order. The current drive towards privatization in America is probably more detrimental to the common welfare as represented by the state than it is to voluntary organizations. If government is left to its own devices without effective criticism, more harm can be done than through the neglect of smaller associations. Political apathy in the United States is in large measure the consequence of an "emigration" from the political sphere into the narrow and private enclaves of the family, and especially of the middle-class family where the idols of the tribe engender the worship of the bitch-goddess Success (measured in terms of economic prestige). We recall the Platonic maxim that the family is the enemy of justice in the City.

Likewise, any exclusive and narrow concern for voluntary associations can be detrimental to the values and responsibilities attaching to the political order and its more comprehensive constituency. The promotion of voluntary associations by attempting to derogate the functions of the state is often only an ideology in the sense of being a concealed effort to protect special economic or ethnic interests against control at the hands of the state as an instrument of the general welfare of the community. We might call this the ideology of discrediting the state. On the other hand, in a technological society where concentrated economic power is greater than the power of the state, the latter becomes in large measure the manipulated puppet of this economic power. In this syndrome (of disease) voluntary associations can be rendered almost impotent. The blacks and other ethnic minorities are especially aware of this phenomenon. Here they encounter the ideology of "the rule of the majority."

For these reasons the problem of the relation between voluntary organizations (concerned with public policy) and the state takes on paramount significance today. It is axiomatic that both the state and voluntary associations are vital components in a viable democratic society. A major function of voluntary associations is to expose and instigate the correction of the state and other associations—especially to correct their violations of law and order, and to broaden the conceptions of justice and equality. Hence, in this area the characteristic vocation of authentically democratic voluntary organizations is to influence the government (through the medium of public opinion and other means) to do its job in representing and promoting the concerns of the commonweal. Ultimately, the state as well as voluntary associations are creatures of the total community, and in principle they are in a democratic society accountable to that community. Every citizen has potentially a contribution to make. The problem of all associations is to get him to make it. A major enemy of democratic society is the government that tries to frighten and stifle human freedom manifest in freedom of association.

The present volume must be understood in the context of this larger framework of the ecology of associations which, as long as man is a free being, offers vistas of peril as well as of opportunity. The mass man, the dehumanized man, is the passive, apathetic man who is indifferent to the opportunities and responsibilities and perversions of associations, whether they be voluntary or nonvoluntary. Human freedom is effectively defined or protected or manifested only in the institutional framework of associations. Here, as Walter Bagehot has reminded us, "strong beliefs win strong men, and then make them stronger."

James Luther Adams

Preface

After several years of effort, perseverance, and patience by the various authors of chapters in this book, the practical and intellectual hurdles to beginning this new annual series of review volumes have finally been surmounted. We are "off and running" at last. The editors are deeply grateful to all of those authors, typists, critics and others who have played a part in making this particular volume possible. Aside from the secretaries of various chapter authors, the greatest practical debt is due Bonita McCormack for careful typing of many of the chapters.

But where are we "off and running" *to*? This first volume has two simple aims.

First, we attempt in Part One to broaden and deepen our general understanding of what is meant by the term "voluntary action" and various related terms like "voluntary society," "voluntary association," "volunteer," etc. We also attempt in Part One to explore the dimensions and kinds of phenomena (and their sub-types) that might be included in the category of "voluntary action." For an adequate new field of research on voluntary action to emerge and grow, we must first have some better understanding of what the intellectual content of this field might be and why certain empirical phenomena should be seen as part of some larger intellectual whole.

Second, we attempt in Part Two to examine what is known (especially, but not exclusively, from the standpoints of sociology and psychology) about *who participates* in organized voluntary action *and why they do it*. From a very basic practical point of view, there would be little importance to voluntary action in society if a substantial number of individuals did not participate in many types of voluntary organizations, programs, and groups. Therefore, it is perhaps fitting that the substantive or empirical (vs. conceptual, theoretical) portion of this first volume of the series should focus on the root reality of individuals participating in groups. In a sense, this is the root reality of all of social science.

Why have we collectively written this book at all? What is the point of a series of review volumes on a field that is just beginning to emerge? One answer is that this book is itself largely a product of voluntary action. The individuals who have collaborated in writing and editing this volume have done so mainly because they believed an increased understanding of voluntary action phenomena to be important. This increased understanding, barely but well begun here, will have two important consequences, we hope. On the one hand, this volume, if successful, *will spur further and more fruitful research and theory on voluntary action phenomena from an interdisciplinary, interprofessional, and international perspective*. The field of research and theory on voluntary action will emerge just a bit faster and more consciously than would have happened otherwise. On the other hand, theoretical and research reviews such as this volume, if successful, *also will foster greater application of existing social science knowledge to the on-going voluntary action of individuals, organizations, and societies.* If we scholars and scientists are clearer on what we think we know and what we really do *not* know, we shall make it easier to put knowledge into practice and to apply social science to social action.

With these twin purposes in mind, then, we invite readers from among the broad social science scholarly research community; from history and the humanities; from the "human," social, and helping professions (including volunteer administrators and association officials); from the advanced undergraduate and graduate student community in all of these fields; and even from the "general reading public." Not all of these kinds of readers will find all of this volume interesting; but all should find *some* of it to be of interest, even though there is a great deal in the book that the general reader will correctly view as "technical" and "jargon."

We suggest the potential reader look first at Chapters 1 and 16, together with the Introductions to Parts One and Two. On the basis of the latter two introductory sections, a better decision can be made which chapters might be worth reading. Furthermore, each of the first four chapters of Part Two has a final summary section that draws together what the authors believe to be the major conclusions and findings of the empirical research reviewed in their chapter; the reader who is less interested in the details and more interested in a simple statement of what we think we know and what we still need to know should find these helpful. (Their implications for practice, in crude form, have been summarized in *Occasional Paper No. 1* of the Center for a Voluntary Society, a document entitled "Improving Voluntary Action.") Chapter 15 tries to draw the various threads of these chapters of Part Two together into a consistent overview. Because of the wide variety of intellectual positions taken, Part One is less easily summarized. Nevertheless, both Chapters 2 and 10 attempt a kind of useful overview of concepts of voluntary action at different system levels, without claiming to be summaries or products of "consensus" among the various authors of Part One.

Yet when all is said and done, we hope most readers will at least dip into all of the chapters of this volume. With one exception, they were all prepared originally for this volume and we think they make a useful and coherent whole, without claiming to exhaust the topics they deal with. We hope you will find that our collective labors have been as worthwhile for you as for all of the authors and editors.

1 Voluntary Action Theory and Research: An Introduction

DAVID HORTON SMITH

This is the first of a series of books attempting to review and synthesize the literature on voluntary action theory and research from an interdisciplinary and interprofessional perspective. The initiation of this series coincides generally with the formal beginning of voluntary action theory and research as a special interdisciplinary and interprofessional substantive field of inquiry in its own right. The Association of Voluntary Action Scholars was incorporated as an independent nonprofit scholarly organization in June of 1971, and the quarterly *Journal of Voluntary Action Research* began publication a few months later with the January 1972 issue. Yet, as we shall see in a moment, there have been groups of scholars working largely in isolation from each other on voluntary action topics in many established disciplines and professions for a good many years. The present types of activities—the Association, the *Journal*, and this series of books, among other activities—differ from related previous activities largely in their attempt to begin drawing together the threads of all kinds of intellectual inquiry on aspects of voluntary action into a more coherent whole.

We are interested in voluntary action phenomena for a variety of reasons, both intellectual and practical. The matter of the impact and effectiveness of voluntary action of various kinds will be taken up in detail in a subsequent volume of this series. For the present, it may suffice to note briefly that voluntary organizations (as *one* major structural form of voluntary action) take on importance in some of the following ways:

1. Voluntary organizations are the predominant organizations in several important societal areas such as religion, science, sociability, art, recreation, and leisure, while having widespread if secondary impacts in other fields such as health, welfare, education, politics, and the economy.
2. As leisure time increases in "post-industrial society," volunteer organizations and participation in them will command an increasing amount of the waking hours of most people.
3. Irrespective of the number of hours spent in fully remunerated activities, volunteer and nonprofit organizations in general (as contrasted with work organizations) tend to command the greatest personal commitment from large numbers of people—people *care* more about them.
4. Volunteer participation in many cases contributes meaningfully to individu-

1

als' positive mental health, satisfaction, and sense of happiness, thus counteracting the trend toward anomia, personal isolation, and alienation that in many cases tends to accompany the increasing urbanization, industrialization, and bureaucratization of society.

5. Certain kinds of nonprofit organizations, notably interest groups and pressure groups, are thought to be vital for the maintenance of a democratic society insofar as they facilitate a pluralism of power bases and the participation of a variety of individuals in the political process in ways other than by voting and office-holding.

6. Voluntary organizations and social movements are usually in the vanguard of social change and innovation, having in most cases less to lose and more to gain from such changes than do the more established, profit-making organizations or governmental bureaucracies.

7. On the other hand, certain voluntary organizations also play a major role in preserving cultures, artifacts, ideologies, values, and symbols of the past, thus contributing to the maintenance of our cultural heritage of diversity, the "many" from which we have become in some sense "one."

8. Finally, even if none of the foregoing functions of voluntary organizations were currently important in a given society, such organizations should still be worthy of study as vital manifestations of the fundamental freedom of association—a freedom that must be jealously guarded and carefully nurtured in a world where such freedom is by no means universal nor permanent in any sense. (See Smith, 1966, for an elaboration of some of these points.)

Because voluntary action has been seen as important to human life and society in all of these and still other ways, scholars in a variety of disciplines and professions have for a long time given attention to some aspects of voluntary action, broadly conceived. In the case of other fields (especially the recently emergent and developing fields like urban studies, black studies, and future studies), attention to aspects of voluntary action is a more recent phenomenon—occurring mainly in the last decade or so. It may be surprising to most readers to see the breadth of current scholarly interest in voluntary action as indicated by the fact that no less than thirty disciplines, professions, and fields have so far been identified as containing at least some scholars with a serious interest in aspects of voluntary action.

To give a clearer idea of the range of interest in voluntary action, we have prepared a preliminary listing of both the established fields of study relevant to voluntary action and the phenomena in each field that might well be viewed as part of, or directly related to, voluntary action. Although extensive, the following listing is meant to be illustrative—a "working document"—rather than exhaustive and complete. As the emerging field of voluntary action theory and research develops greater self-consciousness and internal organizational structure, and as more and more scholars begin to examine how aspects of *their* established field of study fit with the foci of this emerging field, the listing given below will grow and change correspondingly in its details. (The listing was first published in Volume 1, Number 1 of the *Journal of Voluntary Action Research*, and is reprinted here with permission.)

Phenomena Relevant to Voluntary Action as Studied by Various Fields

Accounting: Human resource accounting; value of *contributed* goods and services to an institution (as reflected in a balance sheet); cost-effectiveness of voluntary action (vs. work done by paid professionals or employees).

Agriculture/Rural Sociology: Peasant movements; cooperatives; farmers' associations; farm laborers' unions; 4-H and other rural youth groups; informal voluntary action in rural areas (barn raisings, mutual sharing, posses, vigilante groups, etc.).

Anthropology: Common interest associations; secret societies; mutual aid and cooperation; age grading groups; caste and clan associations; modern marriage as a "voluntary association"; adoption and fictive kinship; voluntary associations in developing countries; revolutionary movements.

Architecture/City Planning/Physical Planning: Citizen groups; advocacy planning; area planning councils; participatory democracy; citizen participation; demonstrations.

Black Studies: Civil rights groups; black power, black caucuses in professional organizations; slave revolts and uprisings; black churches and fraternal organizations; sit-ins, teach-ins, and demonstrations.

Business/Management: Corporate philanthropy; corporate volunteer programs; stockholder resistance movements; corporate community relations and urban affairs; pressure groups and corporate decision making; campus dissent and corporate recruitment; businessmen's clubs; trade associations; Chambers of Commerce; impact of National Association of Manufacturers; generating voluntary commitment in a business organization; the role of *pro bono* time in recruiting and holding high quality executives.

Community Development: Community involvement and decision making; citizen participation; community organizational structure; local initiative; community leadership; volunteer committees, councils, and groups; democratic small group processes; community self-study groups and surveys; client or target area participation in decisions; community action groups; mass meetings (neighborhood and community meetings).

Criminology, Penology, and Deviance: Deviant associations; juvenile gangs; adult criminal gangs; criminal associations (Cosa Nostra, etc.); conspiracies; underground groups; covert associations in prisons and reformatories; wife swapping groups; orgiastic groups; covert para-military groups; volunteers in courts and other correctional settings.

Demography: Demography of voluntary organizations and programs; voluntary birth control programs; voluntary sterilization; voluntary migration (individual and collective).

Economics: Non-market activities; the "grants economy"; uncoerced grants; nonprofit organizations; imputed values of contributed goods and services; flow of philanthropic money; total philanthropic giving, both organizational and individual; effect of voluntary activity on labor markets and prices; trade-offs between higher income and more time for voluntary activity; effects of Internal Revenue and taxation policies on voluntary action and voluntary donations.

Education, Training, and Human Development: Training volunteers, volunteer coordinators, and officials or staff of voluntary organizations and programs; human relations skills required for effective leadership in voluntary action; encounter and sensitivity groups; socialization and voluntary action; moral development; volunteers in schools (teacher aides, etc.); adult education participants ("volunteers for learning"); Teacher Corps; school committees and school boards; NEA; PTA; etc.

Future Studies: Possible alternative futures of the voluntary sector and voluntary action; probable impact of general future trends (in society and the natural environment) upon voluntary action of various kinds; probable impact of specific future events on particular voluntary organizations or movements (e.g., effect of a cancer cure on the American Cancer Society, etc.).

Geography: Spatial distributions of voluntary action; participation gradients in relation to the geographical distribution of other human activities and resources; spatial diffusion of specific types of voluntary action or voluntary associations; tourism and vacation-recreational travel (nationally and internationally); patterns of location of and attendance at national and international conventions, congresses, and meetings of voluntary organizations; patterns of location of the headquarters of voluntary groups.

History: Social movements in history; the history of voluntarism and voluntary organizations; the role of "great men" in founding major social movements or voluntary organizations; the role of voluntary organizations in political change, revolutions, and coups in various times and places; the first historical appearance of various kinds of organized voluntary action—political parties, professional associations, labor unions, women's liberation groups, etc.; the impact of political change (e.g., the rise of a totalitarian state) upon voluntary action in a country; voluntarism and the social order.

International Relations and International Organizations: History and activities of the U.N. and its component agencies; impact of the U.N. on international relations, economic development, political change, peace and war; international governmental organizations other than the U.N.; international *non*-governmental organizations (INGOs); role of INGOs in the international exchange of ideas, values, culture, technology, etc.; impact of INGOs on worldwide economic and political development.

Labor and Industrial Relations: Trade and craft unions; rise of labor unions and their impact on the economic status and working conditions of workers; impact of strikes; union participation and membership; union leaders, their selection and their background; relations between local unions and their national organizations; farm labor unions and peasant movements; role of communism and other political ideologies in the rise of trade unionism in various countries; impact of unions in politics and other institutional realms.

Law: Constitutional law and rights of free association, free speech, free assembly, orderly dissent, etc.; administrative regulations and laws fostering voluntary associations or programs; abridgement of rights of voluntary groups and voluntary action by laws, regulations or policies; legal status of voluntary groups; *pro bono publico* volunteer legal aid to the poor or powerless; class action suits on behalf of voluntary consumer or environmental groups; American Civil Liberties Union and other groups protecting through legal action the boundaries of voluntary action, individual and collective; "Nader's Raiders."

Leisure, Recreation, and Sports: Leisure time; recreational and sports voluntary groups; hobby groups; individual and family recreational activities; spectatorship and attendance at sports events, entertainment, etc.; informal participation in games, sports, and other recreation; amateur sports leagues; informal interpersonal relations; growth of the "leisure society" and its relation to the "voluntary society."

Medicine and Psychiatry: Psychiatric and psychodynamic roots of individual voluntary action of all kinds; effects of childhood experiences on the development of individual leaders and participants (or non-participants) in voluntary action; psychopathology and voluntary action or apathy; impact of physical health and illness conditions on individual voluntary action and participation in voluntary groups; role of American Medical Association and similar medical professional associations in affecting political decisions; hospital volunteers; ex-mental patient clubs; voluntary groups of handicapped, diabetics, etc.; voluntary medical aid to the poor, etc.

National Resources, Forestry, and Ecology: Environmental protection and conservation groups; volunteers in forests; environmental clean-up campaigns; voluntary professional monitoring of the extent businesses and industrial plants comply with antipollution regulations; defacement and pollution of the environment through individual voluntary action (littering, carelessness, etc.); maintenance and restoration of natural ecological balance through voluntary action of individual hunters, wildlife groups, etc.

Philanthropy, Foundations, and Fund Raising: Nature and types of philanthropy; changes in patterns of philanthropy over time; major individual philanthropy vs. mass, collective philanthropic donations vs. major organizational philanthropy; corporate philanthropy; philanthropic foundations vs. "tax dodges"; rise of major foundations and variations by country; impact of foundation giving on other forms of voluntary action (advocacy groups, service voluntarism, etc.); fund-raising techniques; mass canvass fund-raising by volunteers (United Funds, March of Dimes, etc.).

Philosophy: Liberalism, libertarianism, civil liberties and their philosophical roots; philosophy and ideology of freedom vs. control, free will vs. determinism, individual wishes vs. state demands; anarchy, democracy, autocracy and their philosophical underpinnings; axiology, morals, and value theory as related to altruistic voluntary action; selfishness vs. altruism as a philosophical problem; epistemology and definitions of reality as bases for individual and collective voluntary action, or resistance to same.

Political Science and Government: Pressure groups; lobbies; interest groups; pluralism, political parties; social movements, student movements, demonstrations, and political power; underground voluntary organizations and revolutions; the impact of voluntary action on government decision making; the power structure of voluntary organizations; political influence and political leadership in voluntary groups and social movements; voting, helping in political campaigns, writing your legislators, attending public hearings, demonstrations, volunteer participation in local or county governments, etc., as voluntary political action; abridgment of freedom of association and other civil rights by political decisions, laws, regulations, military or police power, etc.

Psychology/Social Psychology: Altruism and helping behavior; psychology of social movements; psychological factors (attitudes, personality, capacities, etc.) in individual voluntary action; learning and socialization as roots of voluntary participation; social psychology of mobs, panics, crazes, mass hysteria, mass revolts; the psychology of conscience, morals, and values as related to voluntary action; the psychology of "volunteering" for anything—voluntary groups, special tasks, experiments, riots, arduous or dangerous duties, etc.; the psychology of will, persistence, determination, and commitment in relation to voluntary action; reference groups and "significant others" as determinants of participation in voluntary action; small group processes and informal, interpersonal relations in the context of voluntary organizations or social movements; voluntary action and the psychology of meaning, perception, and interpretation of situations.

Public Administration: Citizen participation; citizen advocacy groups; community groups; voluntary action and public policy; impact of voluntary action on the staff of public agencies (local, county, state, national); rights of participation of public officials and staff in voluntary action on their "own time."

Rehabilitation and Counseling: Volunteers in courts; volunteers and the handicapped; volunteer half-way houses or programs for ex-addicts, ex-convicts, ex-mental patients, amputees, etc.; problems of setting up, staffing, funding, operating and evaluating volunteer rehabilitation and/or counseling programs; recruiting, training, and supervising volunteers; Alcoholics Anonymous; Synanon; volunteer draft counseling, career counseling, educational counseling, family planning counseling, etc.

Religion and Theology: Churches, denominations, and sects as voluntary organizations; religio-social movements; theological and moral bases of various kinds of voluntary action; the history and development of particular sects or religious groups; religious limitations on freedom of association; *local* churches (synagogues, etc.) as stimulators and sponsors of voluntary social service and advocacy groups in the community; *national* churches as supporters of service- and advocacy-oriented voluntary action; minority caucuses within existing national church bodies; the transition from volunteer to paid religious leaders in the development of a church or sect; religious affiliation as a voluntary choice in contemporary "poly-religious" society; attendance at religious services; participation in church business, operation and service committees; fund raising.

Social Work/Social Welfare: Community groups and community action; voluntary associations; citizen participation; client or consumer groups; welfare rights groups (e.g., N.W.R.O.); tenants' rights groups (e.g., N.T.O.); the origins of charity and social work as a profession (from volunteer to paid social welfare and service roles); settlement houses.

Sociology: Voluntary associations; formal voluntary organizations (FVOs); social movements; collective behavior; mobs; riots; demonstrations; marches; interest groups; utopian communities; communes; the voluntary society; recruitment and selection of individuals to voluntary action; relations among voluntary groups or between voluntary groups and economic, governmental, or other institutional agencies; the impact of voluntary action on society and decision making; the incidence and prevalence of voluntary associations; the role of voluntary associations and programs in the community; informal organization within large bureaucratic voluntary associations; individual participation in voluntary groups; the internal organizational structure and functioning of voluntary associations; voluntary action and social change; organizational change in voluntary associations and social movements; leisure behavior and recreational voluntary groups.

Urban Studies/Urbanology: Citizen participation; community control; participatory democracy; decentralization of power in large cities; citizen protests and demonstrations; community groups; mass meetings; area planning councils; citizen advisory boards (e.g., Model Cities, CAP); individual and group participation in city council (or equivalent) meetings and hearings; neighborhood citizen representatives; citizen advocacy planning groups and consultants; administrative regulations dealing with citizen participation in government programs.

Volunteer Administration: Volunteer programs associated with larger institutions such as corporations, prisons, hospitals, churches, schools, etc.; paid professional coordinators of volunteers; non-autonomous voluntary groups; development of volunteer administration as an emerging profession; recruitment, training, placement, motivation, supervision, recognition, and evaluation of volunteers; problems of sharing control and responsibility with volunteers in non-autonomous volunteer programs; the cost-effectiveness of volunteers for larger institutions (i.e., what outputs are obtained for inputs of paid staff and facilities, etc.).

Major Analytical Areas of Voluntary Action Theory and Research

The foregoing listing is an attempt to see how our conventional disciplines and professions, including some newly emergent fields—the conventional ways of compartmentalizing our perspectives on the world and human behavior—catch glimpses of or focus on parts of the subject matter of the emerging field of voluntary action theory and research. Such a list is important if we are to know where we have been and where we must start in our new interdisciplinary, interprofessional, intellectual endeavor. However, it is even more important to look to the future, to determine where we should be going and how we might get there. A significant amount of work has already been done in trying to do just this, to prepare, as it were, an "intellectual roadmap" of the field of voluntary action theory and research as it *might* be. This schema is also a living, growing thing, continually subject to revision, expansion, deletion, and improvement as more and more inputs are received from interested scholars in various relevant disciplines, professions, and fields.

The schema regarding the major analytical areas of voluntary action theory and research will serve in large part to guide the choice of broad content areas for review and synthesis in the present series of volumes. The present *version* of the schema has already come through two separate phases of interprofessional and interdisciplinary consideration and revision. A brief original version was prepared by the editors of this volume in early 1970. Then, using this earlier schema, a series of papers aimed at reviewing the literature (especially the sociological literature) on each of the component topics was solicited for a Seminar Session on "Voluntary Action Theory and Research: Steps Toward Synthesis" held at the 1970 Annual Meeting of the American Sociological Association in Washington, D.C. Some degree of interdisciplinary-interprofessional participation was obtained for that series of more than twenty papers, although, because of the auspices of the seminar, most participants were sociologists.

The Seminar Session discussed the solicited papers as well as discussing, to a lesser degree, the whole schema and the notion of an interdisciplinary-interprofessional review and synthesis of the literature on voluntary action. A primary conclusion that emerged was that the Seminar should be followed up by a more clearly interdisciplinary meeting-discussion dealing with the nature of voluntary action theory and research as a field of inquiry. With the joint sponsorship of the Center for a Voluntary Society (Washington, D.C.) and the Institute of Human Sciences of Boston College, such a meeting was held on October 31, 1970. Called "An Interdisciplinary Voluntary Action Task Force Planning Conference," this meeting was attended by about fifteen scholars representing about a dozen disciplines and professions.

The October 31 Conference had two main purposes. Its primary purpose was to create a general interdisciplinary and interprofessional conceptual framework that would encompass all major facets of voluntary action. This aim was accomplished, and resulted in a greatly expanded "Version 2" of the analytical schema that had been originally prepared in early 1970 by the present editors. The secondary aim of the Conference was to discuss the mobilization of a "Task Force" of scholars from various disciplines who would be sufficiently interested in voluntary action to participate in a variety of knowledge generation and synthesis activities. The discussion of this latter issue led to the conclusion that something like an Association of Voluntary Action Scholars would be both a fruitful and a feasible undertaking. In the ensuing year the Association became a reality, drawing on the support of most of the participants at the Oct. 31 Conference, as well as numerous other scholars. (For a brief overview of the Conference, see Smith, n.d.)

Version 2 of the general conceptual framework for voluntary action theory and research was published in its entirety in Volume 1, Number 1 of the *Journal of Voluntary Action Research* (pp. 6-19). For present purposes, it will be useful simply to present a brief summary of the main outlines of that scheme. (The following section quotes or paraphrases, with permission, from the original source just noted). We present this brief version of the scheme here because it is essential to an understanding of where the present series of volumes will be trying to go and how the contents of this first volume fit into the larger scheme of reviewing and synthesizing the literature on voluntary action from various fields, professions, and disciplines.

Some fifteen separate but related areas of inquiry seemed to emerge at the October 31 Conference as the "Major Analytical Areas of Voluntary Action Theory and Research: Version 2" (Smith and the Participants of the Interdisciplinary Voluntary Action Task Force Planning Conference, 1972). They may be summarized as follows:

1. *Definitions, theory and conceptual issues in voluntary action*

This topic raises the basic definitional, conceptual, and theoretical issues, such as: What is included and what is excluded by the term "voluntary action"? What are the necessary and sufficient criteria for terming some phenomenon "voluntary action"? What is the role in defining voluntary action of such dimensions as the degree of remuneration involved in an activity (including reimbursement for expenses or subsistence), the degree of coercion involved, the degree of selfishness or self-orientation (vs. altruism or other-orientation), the degree of aggregation of individuals (i.e., is voluntary action first and foremost a characteristic of individuals or of groups?), the degree of formalization of the social context (i.e., are socially unstructured and informal actions of individuals or groups to be considered voluntary action under appropriate circumstances, or must voluntary action be formally organized?), the degree of involvement of meaning-ideology-values, the degree of social change orientation, etc.? What makes an act, organization, group, or society really "voluntary?" How restrictive or broad do we want to make this latter term? What are the consequences of various definitional stances or approaches?

2. The nature and development of voluntary action from early times to modern society (history of voluntary action)

This analytical category emphasizes total, integrative description and understanding of some particular type of voluntary action for some given period and sociocultural context. Usually focusing on the history of a particular time, place, and type of voluntary action, scholarly work representing this category may also be comparative or deal with very long time spans. Any of the other analytical topics dealt with in the present scheme might well be involved in such integrative historical description-explanation, but attention to any particular analytical topic is generally subordinated to a desire for a wholistic description and appraisal over time. This analytical topic is *not* the same as special concern with the *conditions* for the development, growth, or dissolution of voluntary organizations or voluntary action of other types (see topics #4 and #5), although the present analytical topic may include such concerns. Further, the history of theories, concepts, and ideas about voluntary action is singled out for special attention as category #3, rather than including this form of "intellectual history" with the history of voluntary action per se.

3. History of Theory, Concepts, and Ideas of Voluntary Action and Related Topics

Where the preceding topic deals with an integrative account of the development of voluntary action over time (what might be considered part of institutional history, social history, or interpretive-historical sociology), the present analytical topic focuses primarily upon intellectual history and the sociology of knowledge regarding voluntary action ideas and concepts. Under the present rubric such questions may be raised as the following: When did the concept or idea of a "voluntary association" first arise? Is the notion of a "volunteer" a middle- and upper-class concept? Do all modern contemporary societies have a concept of voluntary associations? Of voluntary action? Of volunteers? How do national character, national traditions, cultural ethos, zeitgeist, and related phenomena and ideas affect the development of voluntary action ideas and voluntary action itself in various forms?

4. The nature and determinants of the incidence, growth, change, and cessation of voluntary activity in territorially based social systems

This analytical category is concerned with questions about what levels of voluntary activity exist and why voluntary action of various kinds begins, grows, spreads, declines, or ceases in given territorially based social systems. The emphasis here is on *comparative* explanation and description of voluntary activity rates for large social systems as units, in contrast with category #2, which places more emphasis on a totally integrative description and understanding over time for a *single* society or social system, in general. Another way of putting this distinction between category #2 and the present category is to note that the former approach tends to be more humanistic and descriptive, seeking to understand the uniqueness of a particular society and time period, while the present category is more positivistic (scientific) and explanatory in a statistical sense, seeking not only to describe and understand but also to account for similar events across social systems and time periods.

5. *The nature and determinants of
the incidence, growth, change, and
dissolution of voluntary groups
and organizations*

Where the previous analytical category dealt with the dynamics of voluntary activity for territorially based social systems as units of analysis, the present category focuses on the dynamics of voluntary groups or organizations themselves as units of analysis. Instead of being interested here in *rates* of voluntary activity of various kinds, we instead emphasize observable regularities in the birth, growth, and death of *particular groups* and organizations of various types, attempting to explain these dynamics both in terms of internal and external conditions of the organizations in question.

6. *The nature and determinants of
relationships between voluntary
groups and other groups and
individual affiliates*

The central focus of this topic is on what is often called "interorganizational relations" in current sociology, but with special attention here to voluntary groups as foci. Emphasis is placed upon understanding how a voluntary group or organization relates to other voluntary groups of the same or different kinds, as well as how it relates to groups and organizations that are not voluntary in nature. In addition, the present category deals with external *individual* affiliates of voluntary groups (e.g., with client populations, publics, donor populations, potential member populations, etc.). For both group and individual affiliates with a given voluntary group or type of group, we are interested not only in describing the usual nature of the relationships involved but also in explaining why these relationships occur and how they affect the structure and functioning of the group itself.

7. The nature and determinants of the effectiveness of voluntary groups and their impact on social processes, social institutions, the larger society and the bio-physical environment

The matter of impact is a crucial one in the area of voluntary action. Many social observers view voluntary action as both ephemeral and/or ineffectual, while others see voluntary action as the source of all workable good ideas in society and the very backbone of democracy. The impact of voluntary action may be divided into several analytical categories. The present category focuses upon the impact of voluntary *groups* (rather than *individual* voluntary action) upon their social-biological-physical *environment* (rather than upon their *members*).

8. The nature and determinants of the internal structure and functioning of voluntary groups, organizations, and related collectivities

The focus of this analytical category is on how voluntary groups operate internally and why they operate that way. Together with the foregoing analytical category, the present category is of great practical interest to leaders and administrators of all kinds of voluntary organizations, as well as being of interest to students of organizations and groups. Some of the major questions to be answered under the present rubric include the following: What are the usual sizes of voluntary groups, organizations or movements and what determines this size? What is the member composition of various kinds of voluntary groups, and what determines this mix (in terms of age, sex, socio-economic status, capacities, beliefs, attitudes, values, desires, needs, habits, etc.)? How formalized is the structure of various voluntary groups and their boundaries? What is the power structure, bureaucratic structure, informal influence structure, compliance structure, etc., of voluntary groups, and how is this determined? What are the goals of the organization or movement: as stated officially, as inferred from the activities of members, as inferred from the activities of elected leaders, as inferred from the activities of professional staff, etc.? What is the ideology of the group, its accepted values and beliefs? What are the major economic aspects of the group— its budget, productive performances, distribution and consumption of goods and services as a group, the division of labor and task specialization within the group, etc.?

9. *The nature and determinants of
individual voluntary activity and
role selection*

The focus of this analytical topic is on the voluntary action of individuals as
units of analysis, rather than on groups or territorially based social systems as
units of analysis. On the one hand we are interested in the kinds and amounts of
voluntary action in which individuals engage, but more importantly we are interested in explaining the motivation, etc., for these levels and kinds of participation. Among the types of individual activity included here are overall participation in various kinds of formal voluntary organizations, in informal voluntary
groups, as well as voluntary activity in non-group and solitary settings. For each
of these kinds of settings we are interested in understanding an individual's decision to found a voluntary group or organization, join a voluntary group or enter
a voluntary action setting, actively participate in voluntary activity of one or
another kind within a given setting or group (e.g., committee work, recreational
activity, service activities to outsiders, general meeting attendance, etc.), take on
a leadership role, and leave the group or setting in question.

10. *The nature and determinants of
the impact of voluntary action upon
individual participants*

Under category #7 we considered the impact of voluntary groups on *external*
persons, groups, and objects. By contrast, the present analytical category focuses
upon the *internal* impact of voluntary action—how it affects individuals who are
involved as participants (e.g., the members of a voluntary organization or group,
the person who tries to help another in an altruistic behavior episode, etc.). On
the one hand we are interested here in what impact, if any, various kinds of
voluntary action tend to have on various kinds of individuals. On the other hand,
we would also like to know why some kinds of voluntary action have a greater
impact than others on some people more than others.

11. *The nature and determinants of the
impact of exceptional individuals upon
and through voluntary action of various
kinds*

This category turns around the focus of the previous category. Instead of asking
how voluntary action affects its participants, we ask how individual participants
affect voluntary action. We are not interested in the obvious relationships here—

that voluntary action, voluntary groups, and voluntary societies could not exist without individuals. Rather, we are especially interested here in the impact of *exceptional* individuals upon voluntary action in various realms and at various system levels.

12. *The values of voluntary action*

The questions that arise under this topic deal with evaluating various kinds of voluntary action in terms of various standards of value. A complete description of the value of voluntary action would indicate how each of the many kinds of voluntary action (individual, group or societal voluntary action aimed at all kinds of purposes using all kinds of means and having all kinds of effects) is good, bad or indifferent relative to major kinds of alternative value standards of interest. To make this task more manageable, it is probably wise to select a few major value systems or standards and then to determine how voluntary action contributes to, hinders, or is neutral with respect to the achievement of the goals implied by each of these value systems. For instance, if one wants a maximum of governmental control over citizen behavior, then certain kinds of voluntary action (e.g., of the sort found in Red China and the U.S.S.R.) are most "valuable" while others are "bad" or "dangerous." On the other hand, if one wants to optimize the freedom, equality of opportunity, and the quality of life of all individuals, then quite different kinds of voluntary action may tend to be most "valuable," while contrasting kinds of activity will be "bad." Under the present analytical category of interests will fall also concerns with the "normal" vs. "pathological" in voluntary action, at least insofar as these terms are defined in terms of values rather than in terms of empirical frequency of occurrence. (*Empirical* frequency-based definitions of normality and deviance will emerge once adequate survey data is available on a broad scale for the various topics listed earlier in the present scheme.)

13. *The futures of voluntary action*

Under this category come all manner of speculative questions, descriptions, and projections regarding possible alternative futures for voluntary action of various kinds. In part, this category is included to make it clear that concern with voluntary action should very much be a part of the emerging field of future studies and that experts in that field should not overlook this important aspect of human and social behavior in their work. In another sense, the present analytical category is complementary to category #2, which deals with the history of voluntary action, and category #3, which deals with the history of concepts of voluntary action.

14. *The development of methods for
studying voluntary action*

Theories, concepts, definitions, and ideas about voluntary action have been relevant to all of the foregoing analytical categories, with special emphasis being
present in categories #1 and #3. Methods of study, analysis and evaluation have
likewise been relevant to most of the foregoing categories, yet our analytical
scheme as a whole would be incomplete if we were to omit a special category
that highlights concern for methods of studying voluntary action. Under the
present category fall all manner of specific and comparative questions regarding
how to study, reconstruct, understand, explain, predict, and project voluntary
action of all kinds.

15. *The development of voluntary action
theory and research as a professional and
scholarly field of interdisciplinary study*

This final category of our analytical scheme indicates our self-consciousness
about the professional, scholarly study of voluntary action. Here we wish to
raise all of those questions about where we have been as professionals in the
scholarly study of voluntary action and where we might be going. Matters of
ethics, value assumptions, and connections with practice are all appropriate to
raise here, as are questions about how best to organize ourselves and to operate
in the future.

**The Plan and Aims of the Current
Volume**

The foregoing review of major analytical topics of voluntary action theory and
research makes it simple to point out where the contents of the present volume
fit into the overall "analytical" picture of reviewing what is known about voluntary action. *Part One* of this volume deals with the kinds of definitional and
conceptual issues that fall into category #1 of the analytical scheme. *Part Two*
deals with the determinants of individual participation in organized voluntary
action, a set of issues that fall into category #9 of the analytical scheme. Neither
Part One nor Part Two purports to be a complete and exhaustive treatment of its
subject, nor to exhaust the contents of the analytical category each represents.
Subsequent volumes of this series will continue to deal with definitional and
conceptual issues, since they are so central to our enterprise. Similarly, other
volumes in the series will return to the matter of individual participation in voluntary activities, especially participation in less organized forms of voluntary
action.

Parts One and Two of the present volume do not purport to be optimally interdisciplinary and interprofessional. The editors of this volume happen to be sociologists, and, by virtue of access, organized the Seminar Session referred to earlier at the American Sociological Association Convention in September 1970. Some papers from that session were revised and appear in the present volume, while some others of those papers will appear in revised form in a subsequent volume. In addition, other relevant definitional and conceptual papers were solicited for this volume, mainly from the community of sociological scholars. This "overemphasis" on sociological perspectives comes, then, mainly from practical considerations, *not* from an assumption that sociologists "have all the answers." In future volumes of this series, we expect to achieve a much broader representation and balance of disciplinary and professional contributions now that we have gotten started. We had to start somewhere!

References

Smith, David Horton
1966 "The Importance of Formal Voluntary Organizations for Society." *Sociology and Social Research* 50: 483-92.
n.d. "The Interdisciplinary Voluntary Action Task Force Planning Conference, October 31, 1970: Brief Report." Mimeographed. Chestnut Hill, Mass.: Institute of Human Sciences, Boston College.
Smith, David Horton and the Participants of the Interdisciplinary Voluntary Action Task Force Planning Conference
1972 "Major Analytical Topics of Voluntary Action Theory and Research: Version 2." *Journal of Voluntary Action Research* 1 (1): 6-19.

Part One: Definitional, Conceptual, and Typological Issues in Voluntary Action

Introduction to Part One

DAVID HORTON SMITH

There are many interesting conceptual and theoretical issues relating to voluntary action that need to be taken up as integral parts of our ongoing attempt to review and synthesize knowledge in the field. Of this broad range of issues, the questions that deal with definitions and types of voluntary action seem most *fundamental*. Hence, we have chosen to focus on definitional issues in Part One of the present volume. Chapter 2, by James Shultz, takes up the broad question of what is a *voluntary society* and how we should define its major components—the voluntary sector, voluntary organizations, voluntary roles. This chapter provides *one* kind of overview of the *several* distinct system levels of voluntary action that are dealt with in the rest of Part One. However, in emphasizing *altruism* throughout, Shultz takes a special definitional stance with which not all scholars of voluntary action would agree—nor need they agree.

The next three chapters (3, 4, and 5) deal with conceptual and typological issues regarding *voluntary associations*. Palisi's chapter was published previously in a journal a few years ago, but his analysis and critique fit so well with the present section that the editors have had it reprinted here. The Bode chapter carries the analysis of the voluntary association concept still further, indicating some of the key dimensions or considerations that any adequate definition of this concept must deal with. Warner's chapter provides a complementary perspective by suggesting a series of major conceptual elements that tend to characterize *all* voluntary associations in some significant degree. Some of these elements may be viewed as *defining* or essential characteristics, while others are simply *usual* characteristics. A clear delineation of *both* types of elements is necessary for an adequate understanding of how voluntary associations differ from *other* major kinds of formal organizations and other types of voluntary action.

The next four chapters (6, 7, 8, and 9) deal with a variety of kinds of voluntary action *other than* voluntary associations. The broad aim of these chapters is to show *the variety of phenomena that may be seen as forms of voluntary action*. Each paper discusses the ways in which a particular social phenomenon may be defined as a kind of voluntary action. In nearly all preliterate and perhaps most peasant societies, as well as in more developed societies that have "mandatory state churches," religions and religious groups tend to have only minor "voluntary" components. Yet *churches and denominations* in most contemporary societies are very much "voluntary organizations," as made clear by Scherer in chapter 6.

Many scholars, like Shultz in chapter 2, prefer to define voluntary action in terms of altruism. Such an approach precludes much of the field of *leisure behavior* from being included in the category of "voluntary action." Yet, as Bosserman and Gagan point out, there are many points at which the study of leisure and the study of voluntary action overlap. It is hard to define a thoroughgoing "voluntary society" without viewing it also as a "leisure society" in some substantial degree, and vice versa. Chapter 7 thus helps to make the point that voluntary action can at times be purely *self-expressive*, not only *service oriented* and altruistic—all without denying the importance of altruistic forms of voluntary action.

Chapters 8 and 9 focus on still another facet of voluntary action—*social change oriented and advocacy groups*. Theodore, in fact, suggests that relevance to social change be taken as the *central* defining element of voluntary action. She views voluntary action as nearly synonymous with social change—as collective attempts to deal with or produce social change. Landsberger, in chapter 9, is more specifically concerned with labor unions and peasant movements as examples of change-oriented voluntary action. However, he is mainly concerned with how the study of such working class groups overlaps with the study of voluntary action in general, rather than trying to define voluntary action as including *only* these or other kinds of social change oriented collective behavior. Landsberger's paper is further quite helpful in discussing some of the relationships between the concept of voluntary action and various broad kinds of "collective behavior"— mobs, crowds, panics, and social movements of various kinds.

The last chapter of Part One, written by the editors of this volume, attempts to present an overall definitional scheme for the field of voluntary action. It focuses on nearly all of the major system levels of voluntary action—the voluntary society, voluntary sector, voluntary community, voluntary organizations, voluntary roles, and voluntary acts. Yet the approach taken is by no means one that attempts to summarize and synthesize the approaches of the other chapters of Part One. Instead, chapter 10 presents *one* coherent and fairly comprehensive set of definitions that may be found useful by other scholars—if only as a stimulus for further thought and discussion focused on the conceptual issues raised.

These several chapters comprising Part One only *begin* the in-depth discussion of definitional, conceptual, and typological issues in the field of voluntary action. In subsequent volumes a number of other kinds of phenomena that may in part or whole be defined as "voluntary action" will be explored. For instance, there are a number of types of *individual activity* that may be considered under this broad category—individual religious participation, individual political activity, individual altruism and helping behavior, individual adult education, and individual philanthropy and giving. Perhaps even informal interpersonal relations, marriage and adoption in modern society, and the whole question of "vocation" (commitment to a "calling" vs. a "mere job") should also be discussed in the context of defining the nature and limits of voluntary action.

There are also a number of kinds of *collective or group voluntary activity* that need to be dealt with conceptually as aspects of "voluntary action." In addition to voluntary associations and social movements, dealt with in Part One of this volume, subsequent volumes will consider the conceptual issues involved in viewing "voluntary action" as including other social phenomena such as collective dissent (riots, demonstrations, revolts, coups, revolutions, etc.); politically deviant underground groups and conspiracies; collective citizen participation in regulatory and military activities (vigilante groups, "raising the hue and cry," "citizen militias," para-military groups in modern society, etc.); cooperatives; volunteer local government boards and committees; organized philanthropy in *nonvolunteer* settings (foundations, corporate philanthropy); nonprofit, nongovernmental, non-volunteer organizations (consulting, informational, research, expressive, and service organizations of the independent or voluntary sector); and even collective responses to disaster.

At a still higher social system level, there will be good reason to discuss *voluntary communities,* utopian communities and contemporary "communes" as kinds of voluntary action. Similarly, at the societal level, it will be important to deal with the conceptual issues involved in defining various types of extremely *non-voluntary societies* as contrasted with ideal types of voluntary societies. Finally, consideration must also be given to definitional-conceptual problems of *voluntary action at the intersocietal or international level.* Conceptually, the U.N. may be seen as a voluntary organization with sovereign nation states as members. In addition, there are numerous other kinds of international "voluntary groups" of governments, or agencies of governments. Then there is the whole realm of *non*-governmental international voluntary organizations to be discussed as components of voluntary action.

All in all, there are still many kinds of definitional and conceptual issues regarding voluntary action to be discussed in future volumes. Yet even if these discussions were complete, we would only have just begun our larger task of seeking broad theoretical linkages between the various disparate social and individual phenomena that are "voluntary action." One ultimate goal—now a long way off—is to create a unified theory (theories?) of voluntary action. Such a theory will specify in detail the similarities and differences among the kinds of voluntary action we deal with in Part One here or have just touched on as an agenda for treatment in future volumes of this series. In addition, such a theory will indicate how structural similarities and differences have implications for the processes, functioning and impacts of various kinds of voluntary action. The discussions begun in Part One of this volume are important first steps toward such a unified theory (or theories).

2

The Voluntary Society
and Its Components

JAMES SHULTZ

The Elements of Voluntarism

This chapter attempts to arrive at a definition of a "voluntary society" and to explore the implications of this definition for individual and organizational action.

The Voluntary Society

The voluntary society, as an ideal type, is a society which achieves a high level of social integration, but does this with minimal reliance on force and money as organizing principles. It is *a relatively nonviolent, noncoercive, and nonmaterialistic society.* It relegates force and money to a secondary causal role in human affairs. Voluntarism is one of the goals of such a society, as it is also a means which is employed to establish and accomplish societal priorities, and to define and solve social problems.

A voluntary society is not simply one with minimal reliance on money and force, though such autonomy is its prerequisite. Voluntariness must be defined also as a positive societal attribute, a force for societal action. The positive definition begins with the notion that *a voluntary society is organized by tapping and encouraging the service ideal*—the norm that all individual and organizational units should autonomously make a societal contribution. In a voluntary society, the service ideal is pervasive.

In the voluntary society the service ideal enables two system levels—the individual and the organizational—to integrate with each other for the overall good of a society, without the society's use of money and force to bring about this integration. Such a society would not preclude the use of force in its government (mandatory taxes, jails) or the use of money as a part of its system of exchange of goods and services. However, it would reduce the usual extent of the reliance on money and force to a secondary and supportive role, in contrast to their common dominant role.

The Organizational Component
of Societal Voluntarism

A service orientation in organizations is the organizational embodiment of the societal level service ideal. Organizations high in the service ideal are *autono-*

25

mous, contributive, cause organizations, or more briefly, contributive organizations. Autonomous contributive cause orientation is a quality which all organizations may possess to some degree. *Autonomy* is the element of organizational independence. An autonomous organization is a decision-making entity; its goals and how they are achieved are determined by its membership and leadership. A *contributive* organization is fundamentally pro-societal. It adapts to social changes, yet it also creates social changes since it engages in moral entrepreneurship on behalf of certain segments of society. The *cause* element is present in that organizational functioning depends on the believable appeal to participants and other constituencies regarding the moral quality of endeavor. An autonomous contributive cause needs that quality in individuals which we will term *the discretionary service orientation.*

The definition of organizations as autonomous, contributive causes assumes someone or some process is providing a tentative answer to the question: which causes are contributive? The answer is full of value judgments about society. An autonomous contributive cause organization is protected from too great a gap between perceived social needs and the set of "real" social needs by a significant degree of discretionary service orientation in its individuals and by reasonable sophistication of its mechanisms for assessing society and the organization's place in societal planning and goal setting. The corrective mechanism of autonomy (relatively unconstrained by money or force) functions to let the organization's self-analysis and the discretionary service orientation of its members operate freely according to the service ideal.

*The Individual Component of Societal
Voluntarism*

Discretionary service orientation is the individual component most consistent with societal voluntariness and contributive organizations. Its presence in individuals reduces the need for reliance by organizations and by the society on coercion and remuneration as organizing tools. Discretion implies the presence of choices, plus social consciousness to exercise the choices. Discretion points to the availability of a *free, educated, informed citizenry*. Service orientation is a concept often used in describing professionals. It implies intentional concentration on benefits to other units for which one bears some responsibility. Though not necessarily without remuneration, individual service orientation is often a strong enough force to neutralize both coercion and remuneration when commercial gain and/or legal concern conflicts with the well-being of the object of service. The discretionary service oriented individual is the essential individual component of the voluntary society. He is the effective citizen.

Manifest and Latent Forms of the
Service Ideal: The Need for
Voluntarization of the Non-voluntary
Sector

Voluntarization is a "subtle" societal process which is not confined to categorically defined sets of organizations or of individual acts. Voluntarization is more
than volunteers and voluntary associations. Social science has often attempted to
focus its studies on categorically defined types of institutions: religion, occupation, the family. This approach is not well suited to the above definitions, which
provide us with a pervasive abstract variable—degree of voluntarism. The degree
of voluntarism is directly related to the presence of the service ideal as an organizing principle and its prerequisite, autonomy. At the individual level, we have
termed this attribute "discretionary service orientation." At the organizational
level we have termed this attribute "autonomous contributive cause orientation." We will subsequently use the terms *volunteer* and *voluntary organization*
for the sake of conventionality and simplicity as we continue to explore the
functioning of the service ideal as manifested to a significant and self-conscious
degree in certain individuals and organizations. However, it is important to note
that, while the primary manifest locus of the service ideal in this society has
been in voluntary associations, volunteer programs, philanthropy, and social
movements, other systems may be the locus to some degree. Autonomous contributive cause organizations—systems oriented to the service ideal officially or
unofficially—will differ from society to society and from one historical period to
the next.

Combining the individual and organizational levels into a more global level of
analysis, the *voluntary sector* is defined as the sum total of the *formal and
official* presence of the service ideal in a society, including the individual level
(volunteering) and the organizational level (voluntary associations, etc.). The
non-voluntary sectors are the remainder of society after the voluntary sector is
subtracted. These non-voluntary sectors are usually the commercial and the
governmental sectors. The voluntary society is defined by the voluntariness of its
non-voluntary sectors as well as by the importance of its voluntary sector. A
society has high voluntariness when it has *general voluntarization*, involving an
effective voluntary sector and a relatively high level of voluntariness in the
non-voluntary sectors. Societies with medium voluntariness fall into two types:
latent voluntarization involves a weak voluntary sector but an optimal level of
voluntariness in the non-voluntary sectors; *manifest voluntarization* involves a
strong voluntary sector but low voluntariness in the non-voluntary sectors. The
fourth option, low voluntariness in the society as a whole, is termed *general
devoluntarization*. These four options are presented graphically in figure 2-1.
When nations are compared, it is suggested that the United States is closest to
manifest voluntarization, though Israel may be closest to general voluntarization.

Figure 2-1. Types of Voluntarization or Devoluntarization of Societies

Voluntariness of Non-Voluntary Sectors	Presence of Voluntary Sector	
	Strong	Weak
Strong	General Voluntarization (Israel)	Latent Voluntarization (Cuba)
Weak	Manifest Voluntarization (U.S.A.)	General Devoluntarization (Nazi Germany)

Nazi Germany is an example of general devoluntarization, while Cuba is an example close to the latent voluntarization type.

Devoluntarization probably is unlikely in American society, owing to the high and increasing levels of education, social consciousness, affluence, mobility, norms of self-determination, and interdependence with the world at large. Yet it could happen here. The emphasis in the United States on philanthropy, volunteering, and "charitable" organizations (the voluntary sector) does not imply that the United States has general voluntarization. Manifest voluntarization is equal in voluntariness to latent voluntarization. Both manifest and latent voluntarization have strengths and weaknesses. The voluntary sector, by making the service ideal official, serves as the carrier of important cultural symbols and meanings. This has occurred especially in religion, charitable organizations, and social movements. This carrier function is more effective when the service ideal is embodied in a number of collective forms, however, imperfect, rather than being present only as an individual attribute in the population as the discretionary service orientation (the courage, integrity, and social dedication of specific individuals).

On the other hand, the value of the carrier function of the voluntary sector is balanced by the sheer social mass of the *non*-voluntary sector. Much more is at stake in human terms; one more degree of voluntariness in the *non*-voluntary sector, because of sheer mass, usually outweighs a change of several degrees of voluntariness in the voluntary sector. When, as in U.S. society, there is a strong voluntary sector but the service ideal is weak in the non-voluntary sectors, this tends to discredit the service ideal and to create cynicism, culminating in an attack upon or co-optation of the voluntary sector.

Changes in Volunteers and Voluntary
Organizations Over Time

The following analysis employs the concept of procession[1] —a flow from altruistic service organizations toward quasi organizations; from altruistic volunteers to pseudo volunteers; and from dedicated to selfish professionals. The analysis assumes that the best individual example of the service ideal—described above as the discretionary service orientation—is found in certain *altruistic volunteers* and *dedicated professionals.* The best organizational example of the service ideal—described above as the autonomous, contributive, cause organization—is found in the *altruistic voluntary organization.* The altruistic volunteers, dedicated professionals, and altruistic voluntary organizations form the vanguard of the service ideal as a force in society.

The Individual Procession

Altruistic volunteers are defined as the cutting edge of the service ideal as embodied in the individual. They are the most idealistic elements—people most socially conscious and most willing to subordinate their own material rewards and personal safety to service ideals. The *average volunteer* is a supporter and follower of the altruist. He blends a primary concern for the service ideal with a secondary concern for the factors of force and money and tends to lend some stability to the service ideal and usually forms the majority of the volunteer force. The *pseudo volunteer* puts primary concern on matters of force and material gain, but has a secondary concern for the service ideal. He is dysfunctional if he becomes the dominant societal type; however, he is functional in his responsiveness to the impact of the service ideal and its implications, thereby broadening the strength of the service ideal.

The *dedicated professional* takes the service ideal into the employment arena. He is primarily service oriented, putting service above coercion, self-advancement, and material gain when there is a conflict. His service orientation is often not in terms of the general service ideal but rather is a manifestation of the specific service mandate and service ideals of his profession. The *average professional* has a primary concern with his own material and social situation but a substantial secondary concern for the service ideal. The *selfish professional*, on the other hand, is essentially out for himself and his family, giving little or no concern to the service ideal supposedly at the root of his profession. He is dominated by materialistic and often legal considerations.

Figure 2-2 presents the two varieties of the individual procession schematically. The two-headed arrows indicate the movement can occur in either direction between adjacent categories, although the trend in a given society or situation may be markedly in one direction or the other.

Figure 2-2. The Individual Procession

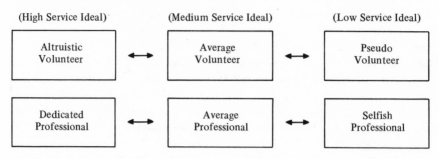

The Organizational Procession[a]

Altruistic voluntary organizations are defined as the cutting edge of the service ideal as embodied in organizations. They are the most idealistic organizations in seeking the general welfare of society or of broad groups within it that are presently "have-nots" in some realm. The *established voluntary organization* is a supporter and a follower of the altruistic, a modified organization attempting to blend the service ideal with the realities of money, bureaucracy, and force, and their correlates. Such established voluntary organizations are hampered in their functioning; yet, unless they lose the service ideal altogether in actual and official operation and lose touch with altruistic voluntary organizations, they serve to widen the overall power base and effectiveness of the service ideal.

Quasi-voluntary organizations, by sheer social mass, constitute an important expression of the service ideal. In a voluntary society the largest institutions would be of this type. An increasing role for quasi-voluntary organizations at the expense of non-voluntary organizations would reduce compartmentalization of the service ideal in specialized "voluntary" organizations, and would increase the application of the service ideal to massive economic institutions and to major aspects of government. To some extent, all organizations would become voluntary organizations. The present compartmentalization of the service ideal has led to a loss of the overall strength of the ideal, giving it a role very much secondary to money, bureaucracy, and force in those organizations which perceive themselves not to be involved, even when the service ideal has strong institutional expressions and is a powerful element of the culture.

Figure 2-3 presents the "Organizational Procession" schematically, again indicating the possibility of change in either direction along the procession. However, for organizations, the *general* trend is from left to right. Organizations that were once in the vanguard of the service ideal rigidify and gradually fall away

[a]It should be noted that for purposes of presentation we are assuming national organizations and categorizing them as one type. In a more refined analysis it could be shown that such organizations have various types within them—as in the case of religious groups with formal sub-units of different types.

Figure 2-3. The Organizational Procession

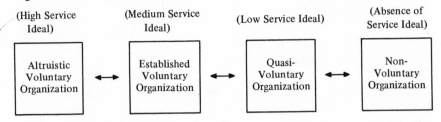

from the ideal to become established or even quasi-voluntary organizations. Thus, altruistic voluntary organizations tend to be recently founded.

*The Individual-Organizational
Interaction in the Voluntary
Sector*

There is a high correlation between the individual and organizational levels in the presence of the service ideal. Altruistic volunteers tend to be found in altruistic voluntary organizations and to maintain dominant roles in them. Conversely, pseudo volunteers are most likely to be found in quasi-voluntary organizations.

If one type of discretionary service oriented individual is working in a type of organization incongruent with his *own* orientation, he will tend to become congruent, will have other congruent organizations as primary reference groups, will attempt to make over his own organization to his own type, or will move to a more congruent organization.

The more altruistic an organization is, by definition, the more it depends on discretion. Thus, the increasing predominance of a lower degree of discretionary service orientation (e.g., more pseudo volunteers) will be quickly translated into organizational devoluntarization. Altruistic organizations tend to be more vulnerable to "downward" influence from pseudo volunteers than quasi-voluntary organizations are vulnerable to "upward" influence from altruistic volunteers. To resist a decline in orientation to the service ideal, an established voluntary organization needs a strong contingent of altruistic volunteers and dedicated professionals as well as its typical contingent of average volunteers and professionals.

The greater the incongruency between the individual and organizational levels, the greater the cost at both levels. The altruist in a quasi-voluntary organization will tend to become a martyr, but he can deal a blow to the service legitimacy of that organization by repeatedly pointing to the secondary role of the service ideal. Conversely, the pseudo volunteer in an altruistic organization is likely to become a cynic, suffering from the scorn of his peers.

The Contemporary Role and Functioning of Voluntary Organizations

Altruistic Voluntary Organizations

Compared to the nineteenth or early twentieth century, late twentieth century altruistic voluntary organizations have tended to be self-help and social action groups rather than charitable service groups. They often have a political or economic focus. They are less likely to be oriented to direct service to needy individuals outside the organization. They are more likely to be explicitly secular, even if support for them is being provided by religious groups.

The religious, benevolent, direct service model of voluntarism refers to the classical charity, while the secular, self-help, system-change model of voluntarism refers to the contemporary cause group. The long-term global trend has been for cause groups to replace classical charities as the prototypical altruistic voluntary organizations. The contemporary relevance of the service ideal as expressed in older voluntary organizations and programs is being questioned—at least as they relate to present day social needs and problems. *In other terms, the mantle of being "a worthy cause" is being transferred from traditional direct service charity to a different type of social action group.* Even when one voluntary group helps another, the help is increasingly couched in the self-help idiom—helping others to help themselves. The tendency of altruistic volunteers to found new associations has not diminished; yet the content of the service ideal expressed in these organizations has changed.

Not all "cause" groups are altruistic. Classification is based on analysis of the presence of "discretion" and "service orientation" in individual participants and on the presence of autonomous social "contributiveness" in the organization. However, our analysis of the present direction of the service ideal in our society would suggest that appeals to anger and minority group mobility have as much or often more right to moral legitimacy than the older appeals to self-righteous benevolence and charity.

Because of the organizational process effect, the quasi-voluntary organizations and some business and government organizations are trying to do today what altruistic voluntary organizations did yesterday. The average professionals are doing today what only the altruistic volunteers did yesterday. Many of the highest status voluntary organizations are only quasi-voluntary, having weakened the service ideal in their operations and holding on to out-of-date forms of the service ideal. Many volunteer service programs promoted today by and within business and government rely heavily on the kind of one-to-one personal service helpfulness characteristic of classical charity. In one sense, *business-and-government-related voluntary action is just now catching up with where the voluntary sector vanguard was active many decades ago.*

The organizing style of contemporary altruistic voluntary organizations may be as important as the content of their service ideal. Their style tends to be relatively *non*-institutional and *non*-bureaucratic. It is more like a cadre than an organization as we usually think of it. The formal organization provides support mainly in areas where society is less likely to back up the organization with money and force. There is often a very low overhead—few buildings, salaries, or other fixed costs. When money is spent, it is most likely to be spent on communication—newsletters, media advertising, telephones, or travel. Altruistic volunteers are plentiful. Altruistic voluntary organizations can command donated professional talents (e.g., the public relations and media experts available to peace groups). Altruistic volunteers tend to expect and often demand the expendability of the organization. They think cause organizations should have a high turnover rate as they accomplish or fail to accomplish specific tasks and purposes. The worst thing would be *organizational survival as an end in itself.* In fact, such organizations are often defined by an event, or even by a specific date—the April 22 Earth Day Teach-In, for instance.

The cause group *style* of organization does *not* in itself mean that the organization using it is on the cutting edge of the service ideal or is attracting altruistic volunteers. What seems to be high ego involvement of altruistic volunteers can be "ego tripping." Often, so-called cause groups are simply too weak to be relevant. Again, the drama and sense of moral crisis of a cause group can be engineered mainly to maintain a leadership clique or to raise money.

There are things the society could do to decrease the waste of talent, money, and moral energy in certain groups. Such groups function best when they have access to resources and legitimation from established voluntary organizations. Beyond that, there is little need for philanthropic machinery or even tax exemption. The groups are more likely to be prevalent and genuine when there is freedom of speech and association, but even official harassment is not decisive in destroying them, due to the organizing style of such groups.

Established Voluntary Organizations

These are the "relevant," yet established, voluntary organizations. They have the ability to tap altruistic volunteers, though their main constituency is dedicated professionals and average volunteers. One difference between established and quasi-voluntary organizations is their openness to the service ideal as expressed in contemporary altruistic voluntary organizations. *Established* voluntary organizations get their "renewal" from *altruistic* voluntary organizations. Given the present message of altruistic organizations about the service ideal, established organizations—if they are to maintain their "integrity" in terms of the service ideal—will increasingly have to engage in action to affect business and government on behalf of the service ideal. Also, elements of the contemporary altruistic organizing style will have to be adopted, by established organizations, especially the explicit critique of organizational survival orientation, the contrasting orientation to system change, and the movement away from a high overhead operating style (multilevel bureaucracies, buildings, high fixed salaries).

There is much tension in the life of an established voluntary organization. It has vulnerability to the incessant moral entrepreneuring of cause groups and their perpetual discrediting of the relevance of earlier programs and causes. Established voluntary groups embody governmental and commercial organizing principles but attempt to keep those secondary to the service ideal. These tensions lead to a difficulty in organizational self-definition which results in two usual organizational characteristics: (a) vague generalized goals and (b) democratic proceduralism (committees, constitutions, etc.). Thus the frustration of altruistic volunteers in established voluntary organizations is often focused in their sense of organizational cumbersomeness. The vague goals maintain integration of diverse parts, but don't facilitate comprehensive, up-to-date analyses of concrete results and effectiveness. The emphasis on elections, offices, levels, and proper procedures maintains control and is modeled after the democratic governmental principle, though there is a placating element since voluntary organizations are usually lacking in the element of force which is present in actual government. Democratic proceduralism does not facilitate rapid social action as does the looser contemporary task oriented style of organization. It does insure an element of stability and legitimacy.

The data are not available here to do a thorough analysis of voluntary organizations. However, one obvious distinction between *established* and *quasi*-voluntary organizations is the former's ability to follow the leadership of contemporary altruistic organizations. This rule of thumb would suggest that the mainline Protestant denominations in America tend to be established voluntary organizations (Presbyterian, Episcopal, Methodist, etc.) as are the League of Women Voters, Southern Christian Leadership Conference, the Sierra Club, the American Civil Liberties Union, etc.

Quasi-Voluntary Organizations

The quasi-voluntary organization, like the established voluntary organization, is usually a private, nonprofit organization with stated goals of charity or social betterment for some specified constituency. Quasi-voluntary organizations tend to be more highly governmental or commercial in operation than established voluntary organizations and less responsive to the leadership of altruistic voluntary organizations. Typical features include (1) a majority of members may be salaried employees of the group, especially high influence members; laymen are involved only for fund-raising, ceremony, and public relations or for routine, low-skill jobs; (2) business and governmental models of organization permeate the thinking of the "managers" or "officers" of the organization; (3) the organizations rely on income sources other than altruistic volunteer contributors—government funds, endowment, *quid pro quo* services, foundations, etc.; (4) the size of the budget and the growth rate rather than social relevance is used as the major measure of effective organizational functioning; (5) the organizations define themselves as non-political yet rely on tax exemption and conventionality of goals; they tend to be as controlled by governmental policy as are intra-governmental units; and (6) there is heavy or exclusive reliance on pseudo volunteers and average or selfish professionals—to the exclusion of dedicated professionals and altruistic or average volunteers.

The key defining element in quasi-voluntary organizations is that the service ideal is present but only as a secondary variable to the governmental and commercial principles. A quasi-voluntary organization is more like a governmental or commercial organization than like an altruistic voluntary organization. They are almost invariably highly bureaucratic. They almost always express an out-of-date service ideal. Such organizations tend to assume no conflict between the service ideal and governmental or commercial organizing principles. Such organizations are especially prevalent in fields of service which have ceased to be so new and controversial as to require or evoke altruistic activity. Such services are now a socially acceptable part of the commercial and governmental realms (e.g., hospitals, museums, and colleges). The family service aspect of churches has the same kind of acceptance, as expressed in the developer's creation of standard churches in new towns. A high percentage of the 18 to 20 billion dollars in total American private philanthropy goes into capital fund expenditures for quasi-voluntary organizations.

Quasi-voluntary organizations experience much more difficulty than established and altruistic organizations in using the service ideal to mobilize volunteers. They are more likely to rely on the leftover time and money of individuals. Lacking dramatic and cause features, their only practical alternative is to rely on explicit reciprocity *(quid pro quo)* combined with calculated efforts to engineer the sense of generosity. They tend to justify themselves by superficial appeal to an out-of-date but conventional version of the service ideal.

Some quasi-voluntary organizations are the mature stages of formerly altruistic or established voluntary organizations. Other quasi-voluntary organizations are created and heavily supported by business and government to be their voluntary, charitable arm, as in the case of many foundations. An impressionistic classification suggests that the Red Cross, PTA, corporate volunteer programs, Scouts, YMCA, etc., tend to be quasi-voluntary organizations, as do many foundations, private colleges, private museums, and hospitals.

While quasi-voluntary organizations are not as high in autonomous contributive cause orientation as altruistic or even established voluntary organizations, they still have the service ideal as their official organizing principle (private nonprofit status, goals, and language). In reality, the service ideal is present as the *secondary* actual organizing principle. Although not on the cutting edge of the service ideal, quasi-voluntary organizations play useful roles in the society. *They are clearly preferable to non-voluntary organizations* in which the service ideal plays almost no role at all. Further, although the organization may be only quasi-voluntary, it may have established or altruistic sub-units within it. Dedicated professionals and altruistic volunteers who call for stricter attention to the service ideal can "reform" a quasi-voluntary organization.

In an increasingly interdependent society, the full and responsible exercise of the mandate of a voluntary organization in either the altruistic or established category requires some influence on the public policy process, including legislation, and some influence on business enterprise. When voluntary organizations leave out controversial and change-oriented political or para-political activities, they begin to betray or parochialize their mandate. This turns such organizations into lost causes or artificial causes and leads to a weakening of their voluntaristic and humanitarian style (i.e., leads to a quasi-voluntary style of organization). This loss of credibility results in a decreased relevance of the mission of the organization and leads to a declining appeal to altruistic volunteers. The governmental and bureaucratic features, such as voting and officers, and the business procedures, such as balancing the budget, maintaining the facilities and attaining a specified growth rate, gain ascendance over altruistic purpose and direction. In fact, such organizations tend to find increasing utilization of business and governmental organizing principles to be an organizational necessity, having weakened their reliance on the service ideal. The effect, even while the organizations are officially private and nonprofit, is to decrease their capacity to be volunteer-utilizing, humanitarian organizations. The process of maintaining the service ideal in such organizations is the reassertion of the mandate by altruistic volunteers and by dedicated professionals.

Whereas a *decline* in the service ideal moves an altruistic or established voluntary organization toward becoming a quasi-voluntary organization, many business organizations move toward quasi-voluntary organizations from the opposite direction by an *increase* in the service ideal. They set up, as sub-units, organizations or programs devoted to "public service" rather than profit. Many firms donate significant amounts of employee time to community activities (e.g., United Fund drives). In some cases, businesses choose to delay or forego some profits in order to be consistent with the business leaders' sense of the public good. To this degree, some businesses have "voluntary action" components, and some business sub-organizations are quasi-voluntary organizations.

Many governmental programs grant, by law, a significant degree of local program autonomy and attempt to involve volunteers (citizen participation) in pursuing their common interests in specified social goals. In addition, there are government run or government controlled volunteer programs like VISTA, the Peace Corps, Foster Grandparents, the Senior Core of Retired Executives, 4-H, etc. To the degree that business and government have such "voluntary action" characteristics or sub-units, they are part of the service ideal movement of the society and contribute to the voluntariness of the non-voluntary sector of society.

The tendency for business and government to appeal to volunteers is probably less important for societal voluntarization than the growing voluntarization of employment itself. Studies of recent college graduates and present students have shown a trend toward greater service orientation or idealism, which leads students to require autonomous and service-oriented jobs. This has led to corresponding organizational adaptation (e.g., the legitimization of *pro bono publico* or community service time as an incentive to counterbalance lucrative but less satisfying work).

The concept of the organizational procession suggests that as general voluntarization of the society occurs in future years even more businesses and governments may be expected to operate like established voluntary or quasi-voluntary organizations than now do.

Another aspect of the quasi-voluntary organization is the attempt by altruistic organizations, especially radical groups, to infiltrate the most established organizations with "caucuses" or councils. For instance, Campaign GM attempted to develop leverage with university stockholders to vote in line with social concerns. Most professional associations have caucuses or sub-units which are attempting to increase the service orientation as compared to economic vested interests in the operation of the associations. Among other things, these caucuses try to develop more dedicated professionals and fewer selfish professionals.

There is a tendency for quasi-voluntary organizations which are created by or part of business and government to regress to their official operating principle (e.g., either remuneration or control by force) when pressured by events. The presence of dedicated professionals inside, plus confrontation by altruistic organizations from outside, modifies and limits this trend.

Conclusion and Summary

It is apparent that the movement toward integrating the service ideal with society as a whole involves a wide variety of phenomena. The separation between the socially conscious and the economically- and coercion-oriented must evolve into a joint movement toward a voluntary society involving the coalescence of individual and institutional aspirations. The service ideal must be continually redefined and increasingly injected into societal functioning. The catalytic force behind this movement entails the involvement of *every* component of voluntarism: altruistic volunteers, average volunteers, pseudo volunteers, dedicated professionals, average professionals, altruistic voluntary organizations, established voluntary organizations, and quasi-voluntary organizations. The key test is the combined impact of the vanguard (altruistic volunteers, dedicated professionals, and altruistic voluntary organizations) on other volunteers, professionals, and voluntary organizations and ultimately on all aspects of governmental and economic functioning. In having this impact, the service ideal assumes a primary role in society rather than a rhetorical, compartmentalized, or residual role.

Thus, the older concept of the separate, narrowly based voluntary association or volunteer program, working toward narrow goals for a limited constituency, has been redefined and elaborated as a societal movement expressing the contemporary service ideal on a broad scale.

Notes

1. This model is an adaptation of the model used by David Riesman in "The Academic Procession" for analyzing the flow of innovation and standard setting in U.S. higher education. See David Riesman, *Constraint and Variety in American Education* (Garden City, N.J.: Doubleday Anchor Books, Doubleday and Co., 1958).

3

A Critical Analysis of the Voluntary Association Concept[a]

BARTOLOMEO J. PALISI

Literature on formal voluntary organizations (hereafter abbreviated FVOs) has been extensive, but with rare exceptions has narrowly focused on the extent of membership within a given population as the dependent variable (Teele, 1965). Demographic and social-class variables have been most often employed as independent variables in explaining the amount of FVO activity. Some studies have focused on kinds of FVOs people join, but there have been few adequate conceptualizations of these organization types (Gordon and Babchuk, 1959). Little effort has been allocated to comparing FVOs with other kinds of formal organizations, and to considering how the FVO fits into the general category "organizations." Furthermore, there has been no attempt to measure whether FVOs are, in fact, voluntary. The result is that studies of FVOs are not standardized. Organizations included in the voluntary category in one study are not included in other studies. At some time or another groups ranging from churches, labor unions, some types of profit-making organizations and kinship groups, to fraternal groups, civic groups, and athletic teams have been considered voluntary (Axelrod, 1956; Wright and Hyman, 1958). These diverse types of groups are often classified together in analysis. This is not necessarily an undesirable condition as long as one is aware of the basis of a classification, and knows how the classification will affect the findings and their interpretation. But one does not know this.

Since the voluntary nature of FVOs is an unknown quantity, one wonders whether the concept of FVO is an objectively verifiable category, a value determined judgment, or simply a convenient label which has no sociological basis. Are sociologists justified in classifying various groups as voluntary, or are they creating a myth perhaps because American society's orientations toward the values of democracy, individualism, and free will predispose them to accept the existence of FVOs (and voluntary behavior in general) without empirical verification? Even if voluntariness of groups does not exist, the concept may be a useful one if people believe they, or others, are behaving voluntarily, and if this belief significantly affects their behavior in an objectively verifiable manner. But one must be able to measure this subjective dimension if it is to be useful. This chapter attempts to define and analyze the concept FVO, to identify the components of the concept, and to suggest some problems in making the concept operational and useful for sociology.

[a]This chapter is reprinted with permission from *Sociology and Social Research* 52 (July 1968): 392-405.

39

Some Unanswered Questions
about FVOs

A close look at FVO literature demonstrates the elementary nature of our knowledge of this important dimension of organizational behavior. Many studies of FVOs are by-products of larger studies, and most studies are descriptive (Hausknecht, 1962). Except for a few attempts to link FVO literature to functionalism there has been little effort to relate FVO behavior to sociological theory (Rose, 1954; Smith, 1966). The great percentage of studies focus on rates of participation. However, there is not even wide agreement on the rates of participation in FVOs of people with different age, sex, rural-urban background, and occupation characteristics (Axelrod, 1956; Bushee, 1945; Komarovsky, 1946; Dotson, 1951; Warner and Lunt, 1941). It is also assumed by almost everyone that FVOs are different from the non-voluntary type of organization and that participation in FVOs is selective of certain types of people [(middle class, Protestant, white, urban, males) Hausknecht, 1962)]. But who participates in non-voluntary organizations? Are these people any different from their voluntary association counterparts? Is there really such an entity as a voluntary organization? It is the contention of this chapter that the concept of FVO is meaningless for the study of organizations and for the discipline of sociology.

A number of organizational characteristics have been attributed to voluntariness in the literature, but there is little empirical verification of the relationship between these characteristics and voluntariness. Let us look at some of these characteristics. Various functions have been attributed to FVOs (Rose, 1954; Gist and Fava, 1964). Are these "functions" different from those of so-called non-voluntary groups? Do FVOs have fewer, or a greater number of difficulties in achieving these functions, or in reaching goals (whether goals are functional or not)? Some major ideas about organization goal achieving have hinged on the voluntary criterion. For instance, Sills suggests that some FVOs do not have as great a problem of membership apathy as do other organizations because people "freely" choose to join FVOs (Sills, 1957). But, where is the evidence to show how freely people choose to belong to any organization?

At least one major typology of FVOs has classified organizations on the basis of differences in their intended functions or goals. Gordon and Babchuk classify instrumental FVOs as having activities which are means to achieving ends for the benefit of groups other than the organizational membership. Expressive FVOs have activities which are ends in themselves. According to Gordon and Babchuk these types of FVOs may have different structure, problems, and significance for society. They also have different amounts of accessibility (Gordon and Babchuk, 1959). This classification appears to be aimed entirely at FVOs. To what extent is the above classification based upon the voluntary-non-voluntary distinction?

Sociologists have suggested basic differences in the structures of FVOs and non-voluntary organizations. For example, Etzioni states that "all voluntary associations have a similar structure: they are primarily social, using, in addition, varying degrees of pure normative power" (Etzioni, 1961). On the other hand researchers indicate that FVOs differ from each other in structure. Sills differentiates between FVOs which have corporate types of hierarchical structures and those with federation types of authority structures (Sills, 1957). He suggests that different problems and behaviors are related to these types. Is the concept of FVO really significant for the study of organizational structure?

Criteria Used to Define and
Classify FVOs

When sociologists have defined FVOs they have typically seen them as being private, nonprofit, and having members who join and are free to leave by their own choice (Maccoby, 1958). Although the definition has become widely accepted, the rationale behind it has not been adequately, nor explicitly stated. Furthermore, the definition is rarely utilized when classifying organizations as voluntary or non-voluntary.[b]

Sociologists have based their definition and classification of FVOs upon common-sense and somewhat "obvious" criteria. These criteria fall into four categories, each assumedly specifying a type of force or pressure influencing organization voluntariness.[c]

The first and most common criterion used is the presence or absence of economic force. Profit-making (economic) organizations are not usually considered voluntary because they are seen as essential for man's need to earn a living.[d] Yet, not all economic organizations are considered non-voluntary, and

[b]The author reviewed much of the available literature on voluntary associations and although some authors define voluntary organizations, none indicated how they measure voluntariness, nor did they state that they tried to measure this concept. Most sociologists operationalize voluntary by simply asking respondents to list organizations they belong to.
[c]This statement is based on an extensive review of the literature on voluntary associations. It must be recognized, however, that sociologists have rarely, if ever, specifically stated the type of force which was the basis of their classification. Force may originate from a number of places. One source might be the organization itself (especially after the person has become a member of the group). However, most sociological treatments of FVOs imply (but again do not specify) that an organization is not voluntary if the members were forced to join because of their needs, or because of certain forces which have origins in society (but outside of the organization being considered).

For the purposes of this chapter the concepts "force" and "pressure" are defined as any factors which influence a person to behave in a certain way, and are not the product of rational choice. Also, "voluntariness" is defined as the ability of a person or group to act without the influence of force or pressure.

[d]The obvious conclusion about classifying economic organizations as non-voluntary because members are influenced by economic force (need to earn a living) is that there is a congruency between the type of forces affecting the individual (economic) and the kind of organization (economic). This overlooks the possibility that people may join economic organizations for non-economic reasons.

there is little agreement among researchers as to which ones are non-voluntary. Business and professional organizations, groups formed by farmers to regulate prices of crops, and labor unions have from time to time been considered voluntary (Dackawich, 1966; Hay, 1950; Hausknecht, 1962). The voluntariness of labor unions is particularly hazy from an economic view because although they do not have profits as organizations, a major goal is to secure higher wages for workers. Also, urban-industrial workers must belong to a union in order to keep their jobs and protect their right to earn a living.

It appears that some sociologists have dichotomized economic organizations into two categories. One category is composed of work organizations and are usually considered non-voluntary. The second type of economic organization is not primarily a work group. This type is considered voluntary by most sociologists. Labor unions, farmer cooperatives, and professional associations are examples of formal voluntary economic groups. However, they are economic, affect the profits of members, and therefore contradict the definition of FVOs as nonprofit. Furthermore, many sociologists do not classify all non-work economic organizations as voluntary (Dotson, 1951). In short, the lack of consensus about the classification of economic organizations as voluntary or non-voluntary suggests that this type of classification is arbitrary.

A second typical determinant of non-voluntariness appears to be ascribed status. Membership in a religious faith (e.g., belonging to a church) is usually considered non-voluntary because a person is "born into" that faith. However, groups affiliated with a religion (e.g., the Catholic Rosary Society) are often classified as voluntary even though these groups are not usually open to individuals of different religions. Ethnic and racial groups (e.g., Black Muslims, Ku Klux Klan) are sometimes considered voluntary, although membership is obviously influenced greatly by ascribed status (Axelrod, 1956; Wright and Hyman, 1958; Gordon and Babchuk, 1959). The ascribed criteria of age and sex are rarely if ever used in determining the voluntariness of organizations. The Boy Scouts and Daughters of the American Revolution are considered FVOs by virtually all sociologists. Why have sociologists seen religion as a determinant of non-voluntariness, but not most other ascribed criteria?

A third type of force used by sociologists in determining voluntariness of organizations is physical and legal force or coercion. Prisons, concentration camps, mental hospitals, and the military are obviously seen as non-voluntary by virtually all sociologists.

A fourth type of force deals with functions in society which are judged to be essential for that society. This may be the rationale behind classifying FVOs as privately owned and not public or governmental. Consequently educational, medical, protective, and legislative organizations are not voluntary. Although almost all sociologists agree that public and governmental organizations are not voluntary they do not include private hospitals and private schools as voluntary. Private groups such as the John Birch Society and the Minutemen are rarely, if ever, included in studies of FVOs, but the Young Republicans as well as other groups affiliated with major political parties are voluntary. The rationale behind these classifications is not clear.

A final thought about the nature of the four "obvious" criteria identified above is that any given organization may have more than one of these types of forces. For example, some organizations which attain members through physical coercion (prisons) serve the public, or are government operated.

Not only have sociologists used the four criteria inconsistently, but they have not demonstrated that these forces are stronger than other possible forces. Is profit-making a stronger force than non-economic factors; are public institutions more necessary than private institutions; is physical coercion stronger than other kinds of pressure and are ascribed characteristics stronger influences on behavior than achieved criteria? It is suggested here that free choice vs. force are the crucial determinants of voluntariness. It is further suggested that the major forces which usually limit voluntariness are not the above four forces. A person may change his religious membership, hide his racial identity, refuse to enter the military service, or resist going to prison. The key to whether a person has choices (or has choice to some degree) is a fifth type of force—social pressure. The strength of the four forces may come largely from group factors—from the structure and values of society and its subgroups.

Social Forces and FVOs

Sociologists have recognized that people having different social characteristics have differential rates of FVO participation. In fact most studies of FVOs try to explain participation in these groups by using social variables (Hausknecht, 1962; Axelrod, 1956). Yet few if any researchers treat these variables as representing possible kinds of social force. How does one explain the higher rates of FVO participation for middle-class people than for working-class persons, or for married people rather than for single people, for urbanites as opposed to rural people and for white collar workers than for unskilled laborers without accounting for possible social forces? One could propose that some categories of people join more FVOs because they desire to (thus voluntarily), but why do some categories of individuals consistently "wish" to join FVOs while other types of people do not? Would differential opportunities, family structures, values of roles, etc., affect the desires of individuals? If so, then are not these social conditions types of social force? It could also be reasoned that such categories as middle-class people can financially afford to belong to FVOs better than can working-class individuals. This type of economic orientation is not completely valid because working-class persons often have higher wages than middle-class individuals, but continue not to participate in FVOs.[e] Furthermore, social class

[e]The question now being considered concerning economic influence on FVO participation goes beyond the earlier contention that classification of organizations on the basis of economic criteria have been arbitrary. The present position is that even if such classifications were not arbitrary, economic factors only have significance via social force.

is not entirely determined by economic status. Middle-class people are not only influenced or forced to participate in FVOs by virtue of their social position but the working class is often prevented from participating in FVOs (forced not to participate) because of their social characteristics.

Similarly, sex is an ascribed characteristic. Yet, in some social situations men participate in FVOs more than do women. In other situations women participate more frequently than men (Hausknecht, 1962). It appears that the social situation in which men and women find themselves (e.g., type of community, their social class, family structure, role definition, differential norms) are the forces behind their differential participation.

Finally, perhaps coercion and functional necessity must be understood by knowing the social situation. For example, someone can only be physically or legally forced to go to prison or belong to a labor union if society, or some group within society, demands it. Coercion is simply the means of exercising social force. In a similar vein, assuming that functional necessity can be demonstrated, the functional necessity of certain organizations can only be determined by society. An organization which is necessary in one society may not be required in a different type of social system.

The possibility that social force not only limits voluntariness, but often underlies other apparent forces suggests that social forces of various types may have escaped analysis when not manifested in economic, ascribed, coercive, or functional patterns. With this in mind one can ask what the major types of social force are. Social pressure or force can be classified into three general categories: (1) the opportunity structure which affects choice by presenting limited alternatives to the group or individual; (2) direct social pressure via interaction with other people; and (3) value orientations and group norms which bias choices of individuals.

There are two ways in which the opportunity structure affects alternatives: (a) in terms of the number of alternatives presented to the actor, and (b) by limiting the range (variety) of alternatives open for the actor to choose from. A person having only two alternatives does not have the same degree of choice as if he had numerous possibilities open to him. Also, the variety of, or degree of differentiation between, available alternatives affects choice. The entire question of alternatives has rarely been spelled out in sociological inquiries about FVOs. For instance, as indicated earlier, few if any studies have considered colleges as voluntary organizations but some researchers have considered labor unions voluntary. But limiting our focus to the presence of and range of alternatives open to potential members, does not the person usually have a number of colleges to choose from (even if one determines he must attend college), whereas once a person's occupation is established does he have a choice of which union to join (especially in a closed-shop situation)? In a similar vein, do some people have fewer alternatives to select from in choosing a college (because of social class status or family pressure, etc.) than do other persons?

The number of alternative choices made available to the actor by society is also influenced by structural limitations on awareness of the individual. For example, high school graduates have the opportunity to attend college. However, if the individual has a social background which blocks his perception of, or motivation to obtain these opportunities, he does not, in reality, have the alternative of attending college. Thus, it is difficult to separate awareness of from actual availability of a FVO to the person.

With respect to the second type of social force, members of groups to which the individual belongs and who are important to the individual may directly influence or even compel him to participate in FVOs. For example, members of the family influence each other to become involved in FVOs, (husbands influence their wives to participate in civic groups, parents influence children to join scout groups, and parents may join the PTA or church groups for their children's benefit). Friends influence each other to join FVOs. Many studies suggest that new members of organizations are recruited through the influence organization members have on them as friends (Sills, 1957). New members of organizations are also recruited via contact with other organizations which may vary in type from civic, political, and recreational to business and industrial (Sills, 1957). Direct social influence upon the individual may come from almost any group to which the individual belongs or hopes to belong.

A third type of social pressure exerted upon individuals originates from the culture and values of society. In making a choice, the merits of alternatives may be judged in terms of beliefs and thus are relative to the values of the individual and group. Individuals assimilate the values and culture of society and subgroups to varying degrees and are aware of group norms and sanctions (even if they have not internalized values). Therefore, they judge the relative merits of alternatives within the context of beliefs, norms, and sanctions. But, do beliefs and norms merely serve as frames of reference for choosing alternatives, or do they force choices to be made? Can one meaningfully distinguish between these two possible roles of beliefs and norms? Sociological approaches to human behavior have often stressed the important affects which norms, culture, and values have on human actions. For instance, Sumner noted that the norms of society can make any behavior right (Sumner, 1906). If norms have so much influence on behavior, can any act related to dominant norms be considered voluntary? People often join "volunteer" groups because they think it is the right thing to do, because it is their duty or because it is important (Sills, 1957). They join whether they realize or not the affects cultural values have on them. Values do not have to be recognized by the individual in order to greatly affect him. Women often participate in philanthropic and civic groups because they feel certain causes are important for society and the community and that it is their "duty" to further these causes. Students attend college because they believe that education is valuable for its own sake and for success in life. Yet, sociologists have not spelled out whether the activities of organizations are highly valued by members of these organizations, and, if so, how compelling or necessary participation in the organization is to people who value its objectives.

The Non-Voluntariness of FVOs

From the above discussion it may be concluded that social forces have been neglected in classifying organization voluntariness. Norms, values, the opportunity structure of society, and personal influence are types of social pressure which may limit the voluntariness of organizations. Since individuals and groups are always influenced by social group pressures there is no free choice, there is no voluntary behavior, and finally, there are no FVOs. Any person who participates in any group does so because of some type of social pressure. Sociologically, we have to assume that the social pressure was great enough to influence him to participate since he is, in fact, doing so. It is the purpose of sociology to understand and predict the influence of social structure, interaction, values, and norms, etc. (in other words, social relationships or social pressures) upon individual and/or group behavior. Nonsocial variables (e.g., psychological, economic, biological) are only of concern to sociologists when these variables are related to the social dimension. When the sociologist has such interests, however, he is not acting as a "pure" sociologist. Therefore, it is the contention here that, sociologically, there are no degrees of voluntariness of organizations, and that it is impossible to measure degrees of voluntariness because the group and social pressure are two sides of the same coin.

However, there are obvious differences between a special interest group such as the Rose Growing Society and a prison or military organization. I contend that a key to these differences is the absence of one or more types of social force (but never all of them) acting upon an individual or a group. Thus, organization members may be influenced by normative force or by differential opportunities or interaction.

Forces which are usually implied to have an effect on voluntariness of organizations (economic, ascribed, coercive, functional) are perhaps manifest occurrences of latent social force. The relationship between these so-called "manifest forces" and social force can be demonstrated by table 3-1 which gives examples of situations in which types of latent social forces occur as manifest forces.

Table 3-1 also has examples of organizations in which members are likely to experience the specified situation. The table does not include all possible types of manifest forces (e.g., psychological and physical needs). It is not implied that categories shown are exclusive of each other. The examples of organizations (shown in parentheses) may actually have a number of manifest and latent social forces combining to influence member participation.

Sociology must develop empirical measures of the types of force influencing

Table 3-1
Examples of Situations in Which Latent Social Forces Are Likely to Be Seen as Types of Manifest Forces

Manifest Forces	Types of Latent Social Forces		
	Opportunity Structure	Interaction Structure	Culture (values, norms)
Economic	Community organizations recruit business executives (Boards of Organizations)	Senior executives influence junior executives to join organizations (Civic Groups)	Wealth is valued (Investor Groups)
Ascribed	Religious groups accessible only to members of that faith (Rosary Society)	Peers influence each other to join groups (Boy Scouts)	Black racial beliefs (Black Muslims)
Coercive	Induction into military is selective of class (United States Army)	Differential Association as a cause of crime (Prison)	Anomie causes mental illness (Mental Hospital)
Functional Necessity	Urban complexity increases public organizations (School, Police, Government)	Relations between workers and managers (Labor Unions)	The values of health and personal welfare (American Cancer Society)
Social	differential opportunity for self expression (Upper Class Cultural Groups)	increased personal contacts increase organization activity (Philanthropic Organizations)	Professional values of sociologists (American Sociological Association)

48

persons to participate in organizations. Hopefully, such measures may help us to understand individual behavior within different kinds of organizations because they focus on the type of force acting upon the individual and group rather than upon the kind of organization being studied. For example, it is possible that people may join an economic organization because of social pressures rather than for economic reasons. Attention to social forces acting upon individuals may reveal differences between members who do not participate actively in organizations and active members. For example, do high ranking executives of business corporations experience different types of social pressure to be active in the corporation than do junior executives, or foremen? Are persons who join, but are not active in civic organizations influenced to participate by different forces than are individuals who are very active in civic groups?

Another value of measuring the types of force influencing organization participation is that it would allow us to study the way in which organization structure (hierarchy, communication, division of labor, etc.) is affected by types of pressure influencing members. It also would enable sociologists to analyze problems organizations may have in achieving goals because of forces acting upon individuals. For example, turnover in membership usually has a negative influence on goal achievement and may be influenced by certain types of social forces which originate either from within the organization, or from groups outside of it.

Finally, consideration of the forces affecting membership participation in organizations would allow sociologists to link meaningfully organization behavior, structure, goal achievement, etc., to society, the community, and other groups. This is possible because the social forces may originate in different groups and levels of society. The source of a force may provide a link between the individual, the organization and other society or community groups.

In conclusion, it may not be possible or useful to measure the degree of voluntariness of social organizations (Rose, 1967). The concept of voluntary should be replaced by a concept of differential social force and an attempt should be made to measure empirically types of social force or pressure influencing members of groups to participate in their groups. The basic question which needs further analysis and investigation is whether there is a relationship among types of pressure influencing people to join organizations, the kind of people these various types of pressure act upon, and the types of organizations with which different people and pressures are associated.

References

Axelrod, Morris
1956 "Urban Structure and Social Participation." *American Sociological Review* 21: 13-18.

Bushee, Frederick
1945 "Social Organizations in a Small City." *American Journal of Sociology* 51: 217-26.
Dackawich, S. John
1966 "Voluntary Associations of Central Area Negroes." *Pacific Sociological Review* 9: 74-84.
Dotson, Floyd
1951 "Patterns of Voluntary Associations Among Urban Working Class Families." *American Sociological Review* 16: 687-93.
Etzioni, Amitai
1961 *A Comparative Analysis of Complex Organizations.* New York: The Free Press, A Division of MacMillan Co.
Gist, Noel P. and Sylvia Fleis Fava
1964 *Urban Society.* New York: Thomas Y. Crowell Co.
Gordon, Wayne C. and Nicholas Babchuk
1959 "A Typology of Voluntary Associations." *American Sociological Review* 24: 22-29.
Hay, Donald G.
1950 "The Social Participation of Households in Selected Rural Communities of the Northeast." *Rural Sociology* 15: 141-48.
Hausknecht, Murray
1962 *The Joiners.* New York: The Bedminster Press.
Komarovsky, Mirra
1946 "Voluntary Associations of Urban Dwellers." *American Sociological Review* 11: 686-98.
Maccoby, Herbert
1958 "The Differential Political Activity of Participants in a Voluntary Association." *American Sociological Review* 23: 524-32.
Rose, Arnold
1954 *Theory and Method in the Social Sciences.* Minneapolis, Minnesota: University of Minnesota Press.
1967 *The Power Structure: Political Process in American Society.* New York: Oxford University Press.
Sills, David
1957 *The Volunteers.* New York: The Free Press, A Division of MacMillan Co.
Smith, David Horton
1966 "The Importance of Formal Voluntary Organizations for Society." *Sociology and Social Research* 50: 483-94.
Sumner, William Graham
1906 *Folkways.* Boston: Ginn and Company.
Teele, James E.
1965 "An Appraisal of Research on Social Participation." *The Sociological Quarterly* 6: 257-68.

Warner, Lloyd W. and Paul S. Lunt
1941 *The Social Life of a Modern Community.* New Haven: Yale University Press.
Wright, Charles and Herbert Hyman
1958 "Voluntary Association Membership of American Adults: Evidence From National Sample Surveys." *American Sociological Review* 23: 284-294.

4

The Voluntary Association Concept in Twentieth Century American Sociology

JERRY G. BODE

This chapter is written with three purposes in mind. First, an attempt is made to trace the development of current general definitions of the concepts "formal voluntary organization" (or "voluntary association") and "voluntary participation." The discipline of sociology has been primarily responsible for both the theoretical development and the empirical work with regard to these concepts. However, we will also deal briefly with the uses of these concepts in political science and economics.

Secondly, and as a natural outgrowth of the first point, we will explore the general lines of research effort engendered by early and more current concept-ualizations of these two phenomena. Perhaps more importantly, an attempt is made to assess the strengths and weaknesses of the definitions used. This is done by pointing to avenues of research which have been "closed," or at least obscured, by the apparently uncritical acceptance of definitions to be found in the literature.

Finally, several points are raised concerning the refinement of current definitions and the development of new definitions.

Historical View

General

In the search for evidences of study on the subject of voluntary associations, one looks nearly in vain through almost the first three decades of twentieth century American sociological literature. Ross, Cooley, Ward, Small, and others simply did not distinguish voluntary organizations as a separate category of social phenomena. It was apparently not until the latter 1920s or early 1930s that voluntary organizations were considered important enough to become an object of study. Earlier than this, only passing references to "clubs" may be found, and the participation of individuals in their community and society was viewed as largely undifferentiated in type.

Two historical aspects might be considered accountable for the fact that voluntary organizations and participation were not studied much prior to 1930. First, voluntary organizations were few in number and limited in scope. Sieder

51

(1966) points out that while voluntary associations of the benevolent type began to appear first in about 1840, it was not until after 1900 that there was any significant proliferation of other types of voluntary associations, de Toqueville to the contrary notwithstanding. Glaser and Sills (1966) also note that:

In order for voluntary associations to flourish, a society must have certain characteristics. There must be a tradition of limited central power and of performance of social functions by numerous smaller units. . . . The government must not have a tradition of closely controlling and manipulating private organizations. The country's religion and national philosophy must to some extent preach the duties of the community and of community elites to help the less fortunate. . . . The upper and middle classes must have enough time and money to spare for association activity. . . . (p. 3)

Second, sociology itself only began its rapid expansion as a discipline in the United States during the 1920s. Although established as a field of study in this country around the turn of the century, it had grown slowly until after World War I. Likewise, it was during the 1920s that sociology became empirically oriented. Probably this growth and change of direction in sociology, and the immediately preceding expansion of voluntary participation, are together responsible for "setting the stage" for voluntary organization studies.

What becomes most apparent in the search for an early, and theoretically-grounded, definition of formal voluntary associations in sociology is that, like many sociological concepts, the definition "just grew."[a] A thorough search disclosed not a single source in which voluntary associations were set in any kind of larger theoretical framework, developed from a set of related concepts, or even set forth as a logically-derived meaningful category distinctly apart from other types of human organization.

It is obviously impossible to construct an exhaustive chronology of the various definitions of voluntary associations, and the following examples have been selected for the way in which they are believed to represent the mainstream of development of the modern concept(s) of voluntary associations, rather than as examples of the entire range of possible definitions that might be found.

Influential Factors in the Period
1925-1935

Apparently there were also three contemporary sources for the rise of interest in voluntary associations which took place in the early 1930s. First, sociologists

[a]Throughout this chapter, the terms "voluntary organization" and "voluntary association" are used interchangeably. Although the author's personal preference and habit is "voluntary association," no conceptual differences between the terms are apparent in the literature, and none are implied here.

had been cognizant of the fact that Americans were often characterized in the popular press and by political observers as a nation of "joiners." Charles and Mary Beard, in an influential book, had subscribed to this common notion and cited de Tocqueville's comment of nearly a century before that Americans had a pronounced propensity to join in many associations (Beard and Beard, 1927).

Second, the 1920s were a time of rising affluence and the rapidly expanding use of machines both in industry and private life. One result was increasing time and opportunity for leisure pursuits, as the work week shortened and personal resources increased. In turn, this produced a marked rise in interest in the uses put to leisure by people in general, an interest both within and outside the field of sociology.

Third, and more specifically within the field of sociology, the emphasis on community studies was strong. As one aspect of this "social anthropological" focus on total communities, voluntary associations were generally explored, though the terminology and conceptualization were variable. These three influences, at least, seem apparent in examining the early community studies.

Early Definitions

One of the earliest attempts at a definition was that of the Lynds (Lynd and Lynd, 1929). In keeping with the thought of the time, they cast their consideration of voluntary groups in terms of these being leisure-time activities, and called them "clubs." Their definition was, " . . . an organized group having at least one meeting a month which is entirely or partly social." Such clubs were categorized as follows: Athletic; Benevolent (and auxiliary); Business and professional; Church and other religious; Civic; Literary, musical, and study; Military and patriotic; Social; Trade unions; and Miscellaneous (Lynd and Lynd, p. 527).

In keeping with the preoccupation with social class, or occupational prestige category, common to studies of the time, the Lynds present data on differential club activity by occupational level and sex. Their conceptualization, again representative of the sociology of the time, was empirical and entirely atheoretical. Associational (or "club") activities were noted with regard to various aspects of community life, and a significant part of their study is devoted to the uses of leisure time.

If any claim can be made to the systematic development of the concept of formal voluntary associations, the credit should probably go to Komarovsky. Her definition, in 1933, was that these included all formal associations, " . . . except economic concerns (stores, corporations), governmental agencies, and schools," and that, "Their functions are characterized by explicit regularity and standardization—such as being identified by a name, or having officers, or having a written constitution, or having regular meetings." (Komarovsky, 1933, p. 84.)

Shortly thereafter, in a chapter she wrote in a co-authored book, Komarovsky also suggested that voluntary associations should be classified as "instrumental," "mixed," and "leisure," according to their function for the individual member (Lundberg, Komarovsky, and McInery, 1934, ch. 5). In making such a classification, she cites MacIver (1931) as a source, but modifies his definition. Komarovsky also followed previous trends in the literature in that she measured amounts and types of participation or membership according to social class, community type or area of community, and sex.

The most specific early definition to be found is in a Report of the Urbanism Committee to the National Resources Committee (1937), and is as follows:

The term 'voluntary association' is used in this report to denote those groups which are private (as distinguished from public or governmental bodies) and entrance into which rests on the choice of the individual (as distinguished from involuntary formations such as family, church, and nation into which the individual is born). The term 'voluntary association' is also restricted in this report to non-profit voluntary associations (as distinguished from profit-making corporations, partnerships, etc.). More specifically, then, this section deals with such groups as fraternal orders, civic and reform societies, cooperatives, trade unions, trade associations, youth associations, and recreation and leisure-time groups. (p. 24)

This definition is cited by Axelrod (1956), and was widely accepted in its essential characteristics by a good many researchers from the middle 1940s to the present time.

Conceptual Development After 1940

In the subsequent few years, additional refinement or modification of the concept of formal voluntary association is not to be found. Queen (1941) suggests that social participation may be employed as a means of studying social problems, along with a study of social disorganization. His perception of social participation is that, "This concept is made to include membership and activity in social groups, sharing in a culture through various media of communication and engaging in 'expressional' activities, and 'acceptance' by other individuals." Queen suggests that participation be studied in terms of degree of participation, types available to individuals, and several "characteristics," among which he includes mental, physical and economic.

Mather (1941), in the same issue of *American Sociological Review*, reports findings on income and social participation. He alludes to no theory at all, and categorizes organizations into churches, fraternal, service clubs, recreational, patriotic, political, and cultural. *Mather was, apparently, among the first to exclude trade unions from the general category of voluntary associations*. However, like the Lynds and Komarovsky up until that time, he still considered that churches should be included as voluntary associations in measures of social participation.

Warner and Lunt (1941) constructed a relatively elaborate scheme for classifying associations in Yankee City. While too complex to explain in detail here, their system revolved around two major classifications, called the "simple or single" and the "complex or multiple or integrative." The former had, supposedly, four recognizable sub-types, and the latter, three. Warner and Lunt cite no previous sources, or existing theory, for their description of associations. Associations were defined as:

. . . a mechanism which helps place the members of a society in a class hierarchy. It is a type of grouping highly favored in our society, and arranges individuals in an organization which characteristically includes some and excludes others.

The association differs from kinship institutions in that it is a voluntary group rather than one into which the individual is born. . . . Again, the association differs primarily from economic structure because ultimate control rests with all of the members; . . . (p. 301)

Churches, schools, and governmental bodies *were excluded from the Warner and Lunt classification*, but trade unions were included.

Warner and Lunt devote considerable attention to two basic themes with regard to associations. In keeping with their major focus on social class, associational behavior is rather elaborately analyzed in terms of social class as a determinant of that behavior. Also, a major theme is the integrative function of associations. This integration is both in terms of the individual with his community, and the various elements of the community with each other. *In this work, perhaps for the first time, the integrative function of voluntary associations is given equal or greater emphasis than the earlier idea that voluntary associations were important chiefly in terms of their function with regard to leisure time.*

Bushee (1945) wrote that "A study of social organizations is instructive for two reasons: First, inasmuch as these organizations are purposive, it indicates the major social interests of the population. Second, it furnishes a measure of one form of social life." Bushee uses the same categories of organizations as did Lynd and Lynd; with two exceptions. He excluded unions, and his definition of "churches" and "other religious" were somewhat different. The Lynds combined these two categories, and used another called "religious other than church," which Bushee did not.

One of the most frequently cited pieces of research in the study of voluntary associations is that of Komarovsky (1946). The reason for later citations probably have to do with the focus of this paper on *urban* participation rather than that in rural or small town. Certainly the paper was neither methodologically strong nor conceptually or theoretically rigorous. *Komarovsky, with no reasons given, specifically excluded churches as associations, but included church-related groups.* In the study, Komarovsky used eighteen categories plus one residual category to classify the participation of her respondents. Her rationale for these classifications was, "Associations were classified on the basis of their explicitly stated objectives, as inferred from their names or remarks of the respondents" (p. 692). Number and type of associations were dependent variables, with the major independent variables being social class (actually, occupational category), sex, and religion.

It was at about this point in time that the formal voluntary association, and correspondingly, the concept of "participation" seems to have been consensually defined. Significantly different parameters of this category of organizations have not appeared since, and *about the only inconsistency of note is that of whether or not unions were to be included in the category of voluntary associations.*

Recent Typologies

There were few suggestions for simplifying or categorizing concepts around which to organize the heterogeneous grouping of associations until Gordon and Babchuk (1959) presented their "instrumental-expressive" typology of voluntary associations. One exception was the set of classifications proposed by Fox (in Sills, 1957), who suggested a classification according to which groups they serve; *majoral* for major institutions, *minoral* for those serving important minority categories in the society, and *medial* for those which mediate between major parts of the population. Apparently, this proposed scheme has not received much attention. Among the many writers who used what was essentially the "1933 Komarovsky definition" were Dotson (1951), Axelrod (1956), Greer (1956), Bell and Force (1956), Wright and Hyman (1958), Zimmer (1955) and many others.

In presenting their typology, Gordon and Babchuk observed, in what must surely be ranked as a classic piece of understatement, that "While modern sociology provides an integrated body of theory and empirical data on formal organization, comparable knowledge in the study of voluntary associations is lacking." Their typology employs two functional dimensions and the dimension of organization accessibility to persons. They refer, as have others in a less systematic way, to the status-conferring or status-defining function of voluntary associations. Also, as one function they adopted the dimension of *instrumental-expressive* to describe the degree to which the organization is oriented toward influencing the larger society, or some segment of it. In a sense, this function of the organization also corresponds to an "impersonal versus person" orientation of the member, or perhaps more nearly a "pleasure-only versus influence-by-association" orientation of the members.

The Gordon/Babchuk typology has been employed in several pieces of research, with a fair amount of predictive success; especially with regard to the instrumental-expressive dimension or classification. Jacoby and Babchuk (1963), Jacoby (1965), Babchuk and Edwards (1965), and others have used this approach.

A somewhat similar, but much more social-psychologically oriented typology has been proposed by Warriner and Prather (1965). They suggested, and carried out research using a classification according to the single criterion of "assumed value function" of the voluntary association for the members of it. That is, what members see as the important characteristic of the organization. The four categories of functions used were: (1) *pleasure in performance*, (2) *sociability*, or the desire for communion with others, (3) *symbolic*, or activity which evokes or reaffirms a valued belief system, and (4) *productive*, or activities which produce goods, services, or a change in some object.

Rather than offer a specific definition of voluntary associations, Warriner and Prather take the position that "Although there have been periodic discussions of the criteria for the category 'voluntary associations,' the term primarily designates a set of interests and questions rather than a special kind of organization." They do, however, note that in general the organizations in the category of voluntary associations have usually been those that are "smaller, local, and institutionally less significant," than those focused upon by students of organizational analysis. Moreover, the organizations which Warriner and Prather studied conformed to such criteria. They did include churches in their study.

Another article which appeared in the same issue of *Sociological Inquiry* (Morris, 1965) uses this definition: "voluntary associations are groups in which membership is in no sense obligatory, which have a formal constitution, but which do not have paid officials at the local level." Morris notes that such a definition excludes "peripheral groups" such as churches, labor unions, and small primary or laboratory groups. He also arbitrarily excludes national level political pressure groups even though these fit his definition.

Rose and Rose (1969) make several perceptive observations concerning the general problem of definition. They say:

Voluntary associations are presumably those into which an individual may freely choose to enter and from which he may freely choose to withdraw. But such a statement is a tautology: voluntary implies free choice. "Voluntariness" may be placed on a continuum and thus "voluntary" and "involuntary" become polar terms in an ideal-typical dichotomy. There is no clear-cut, realistic line of division between the two ... The assumption is that man, a rational creature, in certain circumstances weighs the advantages and disadvantages of joining a certain group or participating in a collective enterprise ... Such a group would be a "voluntary" association. Conversely, an "involuntary" organization would be one in which the individual is compelled to be a member because of external pressures ... those an individual is born into or must join to survive in the society: the state, the family, the economic system, the school system, the church, the army (where conscription is the law), and perhaps others.

Ignoring the metaphysical implications, there is seldom free will in the psychological sense considered above. Formal and informal means of social control, or social forces, in effect dictate that certain individuals are going to join certain "voluntary" associations. In those cases when the individual does reflect on the advisability of joining an association . . . he may not be "free" in his choice because there are overwhelming advantages to one choice or another, which dictate his decision . . . it is possible, at least in principle, for anyone to withdraw from any involuntary association except a jailhouse.

The discussion of the logical meaning of "voluntary" and "involuntary" is really not essential to an analysis of voluntary associations. The reason is that the "voluntary" association is a concept (however lacking in precise formulation it might be) in sociology, and in that universe of discourse it has a meaning that cannot be understood from its constituent words . . . there are certain universal criteria of involuntary associations (though not of voluntary ones). Thus "voluntary" acquires a residual meaning . . . The term is merely a concept determined both by conventionality and usefulness." (pp. 296-297)

Just what can be made of the several kinds of definitions, both implicit and explicit, and the latter suggestions that definition is irrelevant, impossible, or possible only as a residual category is unclear. *It is apparent that most researchers have not paid a great deal of attention to the development of a definition of their object of study, and those who have made the effort either adopted existing (and arbitrary) categorizations or evade the issue by appeals to a common-sense or consensual definition which is not explicated.* None of these approaches seems entirely satisfactory, but we, too, will temporarily put off the problem until we have made an examination of what this state of affairs has meant for research.

What the previous and existing definitions of formal voluntary associations have meant in the way of directing research efforts is the object of the next two major sections of this chapter.

The Concepts as Used in Political Science and Economics

To this point, the development of the concepts of formal voluntary organization and voluntary participation has been treated exclusively from the standpoint of sociology. We should at least briefly examine these concepts from the viewpoint of political science and economics.

Before doing so, however, the author wishes to caution readers that his knowledge in both fields is much more limited than in sociology. The statements made here regarding these two disciplines are a result of rather distinct impressions gained by considerable reading in the fields, but not of extensive training or of the same degree of personal scholarly endeavor as is true for him regarding sociology.

Among the several impressions gained from reading in these fields, the following are most prominent. First, in neither field is there a particularly careful distinction made among varying kinds of social amalgamations. "Group" is used as a term to apply to such diverse phenomena as statistical, or political aggregates and to small, informal friendship groups. Thus, *while "voluntary associations" is occasionally found as a term in both fields, its referent is often vague and variable.*

Second, economists in particular are more concerned with formal organizational structure and function than with the origins, types, and prevalence of organizations in general; or the distinguishing of one type of organization from another. There is no apparent unwillingness to grant the existence and influence of informal groups and networks within formal organizational structures, but little attention is directed toward separating one kind of social participation from another.

Political scientists and economists seem, in general, to prefer to regard individuals as primarily political animals or computers. That is, a basic and usually unstated assumption is that a given set of political or economic conditions will induce individual reactions in the form of opinions or decisions. Further, on the basis of these opinions or decisions, associations or groupings of individuals will occur, given only some opportunity to do so and the means of communicating. The problems of interest in these disciplines then become those of specifying size, general organizational structure, external effects, life cycle, and the like of these spontaneous amalgamations. Economists are more often concerned with either numbers of individuals or formal organizations, while political scientists deal more often with "interest groups" which are usually (from a sociologist's point of view) simply statistical aggregates. In fact, Hagan (1958) states that, " . . . the interest and the group are the same phenomena viewed from slightly different positions, and an interest group is a tautological expression."

Among the problems which are seldom dealt with in economics and political science are the social forces leading to the formation of associations, the variable individual opportunities and propensities to become members of associations, types and degrees of individual participation, and the range of varying organizational functions outside of the political or economic spheres.

It seems a fair, and not surprising, generalization to say that in economics, political science, and other disciplines attention to voluntary organizations is much more sharply focused on a few aspects of such organizations than is true in sociology. At the same time, in disciplines other than sociology both individual-organizational relationships and organizational types are much less carefully differentiated.

Previous Lines of Research

Some indications of the directions that research on voluntary associations has taken have already been mentioned. In general terms, these will be reviewed here, together with some evaluative observations of that research by students of this area of study.

In early community studies, the principal focus of attention on voluntary associations primarily had to do with two functions. These functions were that of occupying the time, primarily leisure time, of members of the community and their role in integrating persons into their larger community and linking, or integrating, different parts of the community with each other. In keeping with the integrative frame of reference, then, it is not surprising that organizations such as churches and labor unions were included within the general category as separate sub-categories.

Another major theme, which has been more thoroughly explored than any other, is the link between occupational category or social class and voluntary participation. Almost invariably, participation type and amount have been treated as dependent variables. Other demographic characteristics which appeared early as determinants of voluntary association participation, and have shown up consistently in the literature over the past forty years, are those of ethnicity, sex, race, and religion.

The special attention to the role of voluntary associations in leisure activities has been less explicit in studies since about 1945.

Other themes which have appeared, but received only limited attention from sociologists are as follows:

1. Examinations of the voluntary association as supportive of, or contributing to, the community power structure. (Warner and Lunt, 1941; Goldhamer, 1942; Laskin and Phillett, 1965).
2. Attention to the organizational growth of the association itself (e.g., Chapin, 1951). This characteristic has been explored to a much greater extent by both economists and political scientists.
3. The correlates of leadership in voluntary associations (Rose, 1962). This aspect has received greater attention from political scientists.
4. Differences in patterns of participation according to area of residence (Zimmer, 1955; Wright and Hyman, 1958).

Depending on the criteria one might employ to identify "themes," there are probably others that could be found; but in any case these would not be major foci.

More recently, there has been some renewal of interest in the integrative nature of voluntary associations, a theme which has recurred, implicitly or explicitly, since the earliest community studies. Babchuk and Edwards (1965) suggest that the integrative function should be viewed from both a social-psychological level and a strictly sociological level, with the latter being viewed as a number of separate kinds of research problems. Jacoby (1965) and Laskin and Phillett (1965) also report research on the topic of the integrative role of voluntary associations.

Babchuk and Warriner (1965) identify three theoretical concerns which have been common in the study of voluntary associations. One of these "focuses on the nature and structure of *society*, especially industrial society." Under this heading they include considerations of associations as contributors to society, as integrating mechanisms, and their role in societal processes such as decision-making and socialization. A second concern is primarily social-psychological, in which the focus is on personal satisfaction of needs of various kinds. A third perspective they identify is one in which associations are viewed from the standpoint of organizational theory; that is, in terms of their structure and internal and external relationships. Again we note that this aspect of voluntary associations has been the subject of more attention by political scientists and economists than by sociologists. Babchuk and Warriner also note that "Despite these variant theoretical interests, there is common to all voluntary association studies the phenomenon of *participation* and it is through this phenomenon that all of these interests can be given empirical relevance to one another." (p. 136)

Some Unexplored Research Areas

The manner in which researchers have defined voluntary associations and participation, implicitly or explicitly, has undoubtedly had something to do with the fact that many questions relevant to this area of study have never been asked, let alone answered. In spite of the fact that Babchuk and Warriner can identify three major areas of research concern which rather nicely span the field, there are significant gaps in the total research effort. Some of these gaps have been indicated, and others apparently have been overlooked. We can speculate that at least part of the problem is that we have been "prisoners of our language," specifically our definitions.

Rose and Rose (1969) identified one major problem, but did not explore it. Curiously, one, if not *the* major defining characteristic of voluntary associations has been the tautological one of the act of volunteering. At the same time, the categories used have quite arbitrarily excluded organizational ties which are quite as voluntary as those included. For example, one is surely as much a "volunteer" in establishing his link to a family of procreation (spouse and children) as he is in joining a professional association allied with his occupation, perhaps more so. If there is a dimension involved in the act of volunteering to participate that distinguishes volunteering in one kind of organization from volunteering in another, such a dimension has never been made clear.

If there is no dimension of volunteer behavior that allows distinguishing one kind from another, then it seems logical that we should study the *total* participatory behavior of individuals. That is, *we ought not to deal only with participation in a "residual category" of organizations, but the sum and separate parts of individual voluntary participation in all of society.* Babchuk and Warriner suggest that participation is the single aspect of voluntary association study that links the various kinds of study to each other. It is here suggested that this is one major area for research that has not been adequately explored.

In a parallel kind of inquiry, some attention should probably be given to the reasons individuals feel "compelled" to "volunteer." Here again, few examples of such research interests can be found.

Morris (1965) identifies another area that has lacked the attention of researchers, and one which is very close to a topic that has received much attention. Few have attempted to assess the significance of voluntary association membership and participation as causal variables in social mobility, or as status-enhancing or status-defining modes of behavior. Perhaps the early emphasis on social class as a determinant of voluntary association behavior created a bias in viewing the direction of causality. Whatever the reason, we have neglected this area for research, and should be reminded that causal connections among social variables are seldom one-way propositions.

Further, the study of voluntary association and participation has been a curiously "bounded" kind of study. That is, findings from this segment of the discipline have seldom been applied to other kinds of social organizations, by researchers either within or outside the area. This lack is all the more singular considering the vague limits of the category labeled "voluntary associations."

Also implicit in some studies, but never carefully considered, are some seemingly obvious causal variables in explaining the nature and type of voluntary participation. Even controlling for social class, age, sex, and other commonly researched variables, there are obviously differences in both opportunity and propensity to engage in voluntary association participation. What about family size (or obligations), time available, type of employment, financial obligations, career phase, and many other "enabling factors" as determinants of amount and type of participation?

Likewise, what of several social-psychological factors, such as socialization experience, personality type, intelligence, and the like as determinants of participation? In a field of inquiry which seems obviously social-psychological in nature, there has been little serious attention to social-psychological variables in any part of our studies. One significant exception is the work of Smith (1966). What about simply asking people why they join various kinds of organizations, what they expected to derive from participation, and whether their expectations were met? All too often the reasons for participation and the personal (or psychological) derivatives of such participation are simply *assumed* in studies of formal voluntary associations.

Also neglected has been any study of the perceptions participants have about the effect of their activities, which seems to be particularly appropriate in studies of instrumental associations. Perhaps the question ought to be expanded to one of attempting to determine the perceptions of individuals of the way in which they are linked to society; that is, how, and to which parts. Clearly, voluntary associations must be becoming more important for individuals as intermediary organizations between themselves and a society that grows ever larger and more complex. For example, organizational "identity" is probably unimportant for a small-town banker, since occupation and position are so apparent to others. But for an assistant vice-president of a branch bank in a metropolitan area; personal identity is no longer a matter of occupation, family, or any other direct institutional tie; and quite probably voluntary associations are more important. (This argument is only slightly different than that of Wirth [1938]).

Toward a Definition

At this point, a completely satisfactory definition of voluntary associations seems less possible than a set of considerations for developing a definition, or several definitions.

One major kind of decision involved in the development of definition is whether there shall be one all-encompassing definition or several particularistic definitions, depending upon the research problem, a partitioning of the current category of voluntary associations, or some other consideration. Each course is subject to criticism, and each has its advantages. Briefly, these are considered below.

Undoubtedly, a decision to develop a single definition could lead to its having either of two kinds of inadequacies. First, a definition intended to encompass all kinds and conditions of voluntary associations to include all their attributes could become so detailed, vague, or abstract as to preclude its effective operationalization. Second, a sort of "least-common-denominator" approach would run the risk of not effectively delineating voluntary associations as a category (if indeed they are). Such a definition almost necessarily would be strongly social-psychological in nature, hence probably open to criticism as being reductionist.

On the other hand, it seems important that some minimum set of defining characteristics be developed for both "voluntary associations" and "participation." The limits of these need not necessarily be co-terminal. That is, participation (which seemingly must be "participation in the society around one") would be, in my view, inclusive of more kinds and conditions of behavior than that included in the category of voluntary associations. Thus, the suggestion here is that a definition is needed for voluntary associations, but that this definition may be simply a set of minimum essential characteristics.

I would also argue that such a definition must necessarily be at least in part a social-psychological one, and that this requirement is not undesirable. The term "voluntary," as well as the range of previously studied organizations, strongly implies that an individual, conscious decision is made regarding participation. Such being the case, there is an obvious disjunction with social organizations or amalgamations wherein no such decision is made, as for example the family of orientation (parents and siblings), the state, the grade school, or a military organization composed of draftees. Ignoring the implications for behavior occasioned by the act of volunteering seems to be "rigidly sociological" at the expense of completeness of understanding.

It is further suggested that "volunteering" must not be treated as either a dichotomous variable, or as a unidimensional variable. Obviously, an individual is very often coerced, cajoled, or conned into "volunteering." Individuals also join organizations enthusiastically, half-heartedly, or do not join them at all when afforded the opportunity. None of this is to suggest that we cannot study voluntary associations as social units, focusing primarily on group or organizational attributes. Rather, the suggestion is that "psychologizing" a bit in the definition of the object of our study may serve to alert and remind us of its unique characteristics.

Using several definitions, depending on the research problem or some other criterion, is a course fraught with problems. One attraction is that a unique, fragmentary, or less abstract definition is easier to operationalize. Hence, the researcher is less obviously open to criticism for failure to make the theory-research, or conceptual-empirical, link clear. Further, a bit of astute "shopping" in the resulting literature would undoubtedly establish precedent for almost any kind of research focus.

The disadvantages, however, are numerous. Among such disadvantages are the lack of a unifying focus (or central theoretical schema), the license for proliferation of varying definitions which inevitably lose all resemblance to one another, and the further fragmentation of an already diverse field. *There is nothing intrinsically wrong with the development of special definitions for particular research interests, but if these cannot be subsumed under some kind of general definition of voluntary associations this would seem to be indicative of a serious failure to maintain focus and direction in our research.*

A definition should, like the typologies employed by some researchers, take into account (although not necessarily name) several dimensions of voluntary associations. The characteristic of "voluntary," with its myriad meanings, is quite insufficient as a singular defining charcteristic no matter how significant as *a* characteristic. The following are some characteristics of organizations which seem to be particularly relevant in our consideration of voluntary associations. No claim is made that this represents a complete list, or that all are equally necessary for our consideration.

Each of the "dimensions" identified below is presented as though it could be considered a continuum, though in fact we may have oversimplified by such a presentation.

1. Relationship of the association to individual interests:
   (direct . . . . . indirect)
   This dimension might be particularly appropriate with instrumental associations, since presumably expressive associations are all immediately related to member satisfaction. Professional associations seem directly related to individual interests or benefits, while something like the Young Republicans seems less directly related (at least in its manifest functions) to member interests.

2. Nature of link to community or societal structure:
   (integrative . . . . . alienating)
   Most associations furnish an identifiable avenue of approach to a larger societal unit, especially instrumental voluntary associations. Some, however, serve to "pull away" their members. An example might be the SDS Weathermen.

3. The instrumental . . . . . expressive dimension.

4. Coercive power of organization over member:
   (high . . . . . low)
   Some voluntary associations severely restrict only one sphere of member behavior, such as the American Medical Association. Others, such as a traditional college fraternity or the SDS "Weathermen," may almost totally order member behavior, at least for short periods of time. Other voluntary associations have little or no control over actions of its members.

5. Closeness of association to an institution:
   (close [or part of] . . . . . remote)
   This dimension is akin to the categories proposed by Fox (p. 79 in Sills, 1957). Church laymen's organizations or PTAs are very nearly part of the institutions with which they are allied, while bowling teams or bridge clubs are often quite independent of any institutional link.

6. Degree of "voluntariness":
   (high . . . . . low)
   Many organizations within the current category of voluntary associations are completely voluntary, but others (as Rose notes) are much less voluntary.

   Finally, a definition must not be simply a residual category, which necessarily implies a lack of regularity or internal consistency. *In one sense, previous definitions of voluntary associations have been like those of collective behavior. Voluntary associations have been all organizations not otherwise designated for study by sociologists, or specifically conceptualized. Collective behavior, covering the somewhat incredible range from individual actions in natural disasters to social movements, seems to have been all that behavior otherwise unaccounted for by sociologists.* It may be that there are threads of consistency running throughout each of these heterogeneous categories, and if such is the case with voluntary associations perhaps these can be ordered into a definition. More likely, however, we must reexamine the traditional boundaries of our study before we can produce an acceptable definition.

66

In any event, it is imperative that the problem of definition and conceptualization be faced. If sociologists are studying something that is undefinable, then we are closer to theology than science, and the possibilities for genuine progress are greatly diminished.

Voluntary associations seem to represent a kind of filling and connecting tissue between major social structures, and between individuals and these structures. Thus it is essential that they be more accurately understood. Otherwise our picture of society is more an impressionistic sketch than a faithful portrait.

References

Axelrod, Morris
1956 "Urban Structure and Social Participation." *American Sociological Review* 21 (February): 13-18.
Babchuk, Nicholas and John N. Edwards
1965 "Voluntary Associations and the Integration Hypotheses." *Sociological Inquiry* 35, 2 (Spring): 149-62.
Babchuk, Nicholas and Charles K. Warriner
1965 "Four Types of Voluntary Associations." *Sociological Inquiry* 35, 2 (Spring): 135-37.
Beard, Charles and Mary Beard
1927 *The Rise of American Civilization*. Vol. II. New York: MacMillan.
Bell, Wendell and Maryanne T. Force
1956 "Urban Neighborhood Types and Participation in Formal Associations." *American Sociological Review* 21 (February): 25-34.
Borgatta, Edgar F. and Henry J. Meyer (eds.)
1959 *Social Control and the Foundations of Sociology*: Pioneer Contributions of Edward Alsworth Ross to the Study of Society. Boston: Beacon Press.
Bushee, Frederick A.
1945 "Social Organization of a Small City." *American Journal of Sociology* 51 (November): 217-26.
Chapin, F. Stuart
1951 "The Growth of Bureaucracy—An Hypothesis." *American Sociological Review* 16 (December): 835-36.
Correy, J.A. and H.J. Abraham
1964 *Elements of Democratic Government*. New York: Oxford University Press.
Dotson, Floyd
1951 "Patterns of Voluntary Associations Among Urban Working Class Families." *American Sociological Review* 16 (December): 687-93.
Erbe, William
1964 "Social Involvement in Political Activity." *American Sociological Review* 29 (April): 198-215.

Glaser, William A. and David L. Sills (eds.)

1966 *The Government of Associations*. Totowa, N.J.: The Bedminster Press.

Goldhamer, Herbert

1942 "Some Factors Affecting Participation in Voluntary Associations." Unpublished Ph.D. thesis, University of Chicago.

Gordon, C. Wayne and Nicholas Babchuk

1959 "A Typology of Voluntary Associations." *American Sociological Review* 24 (February): 22-29.

Greer, Scott

1956 "Urbanism Reconsidered: A Comparative Study of Local Areas in a Metropolis." *American Sociological Review* 21 (February): 19-25.

1958 "Individual Participation in Mass Society." In Roland Young (ed.), *Approaches to the Study of Politics*. Evanston, Illinois: Northwestern University Press, 329-43.

Hagan, Charles B.

1958 "The Group in a Political Science." In Roland Young (ed.), *Approaches to the Study of Politics*. Evanston, Illinois: Northwestern University Press.

Hausknecht, Murray

1962 *The Joiners: A Sociological Description of Voluntary Association Membership in the U.S.* New York: The Bedminister Press.

Hodge, Robert W. and Donald J. Treiman

1968 "Social Participation and Social Status." *American Sociological Review* 35 (October): 722-40.

Jacoby, Arthur P.

1965 "Some Correlates of Instrumental and Expressive Orientations to Associational Membership." *Sociological Inquiry* 35 (Spring): 163-75.

Jacoby, Arthur P. and Nicholas Babchuk

1963 "Instrumental and Expressive Voluntary Associations." *Sociology and Social Research* 47 (July): 466-68.

Komarovsky, Mirra

1933 "A Comparative Study of Voluntary Organizations of Two Suburban Communities." *Publications of the Sociological Society of America* 27 (May): 686-98.

1946 "The Voluntary Associations of Urban Dwellers." *American Sociological Review* 11 (December): 686-98.

Laskin, Richard and Serena Phillett

1965 "An Integrative Analysis of Voluntary Associational Leadership and Reputational Influence." *Sociological Inquiry* 35 (Spring): 176-85.

Lundberg, George A.; Mirra Komarovsky; and Mary Alice McInery

1934 *Leisure:* A Suburban Study. New York: Columbia University Press, 126-69.

Lynd, Robert S. and Helen M. Lynd

1929 *Middletown*. New York: Harcourt, Brace and Company.

MacIver, Robert M.
1931 *Society: Its Structure and Changes*. New York: Long and Smith, Inc.
Mather, William G.
1941 "The Concepts of Social Disorganization and Social Participation." *American Sociological Review* 6 (October): 380-83.
McCloskey, Robert G.
1958 "American Political Thought." In Roland Young (ed.), *Approaches to the Study of Politics*. Evanston, Illinois: Northwestern University Press, 155-71.
Morris, Raymond N.
1965 "British and American Research on Voluntary Associations: A Comparison." *Sociological Inquiry* 35 (Spring): 186-200.
Palisi, Bartolomeo J.
1965 "Ethnic Generation and Social Participation." *Sociological Inquiry* 35 (Spring): 219-26.
Queen, Stuart A.
1941 "The Concepts of Social Disorganization and Social Participation." *American Sociological Review* 6 (October): 307-16.
Rose, Arnold M.
1962 "Alienation and Participation: A Comparison of Group Leaders and the 'Mass'." *American Sociological Review* 27 (December): 834-38.
Rose, Arnold M. and Caroline B. Rose
1969 *Sociology:* The Study of Human Relations. New York: Alfred A. Knopf, 295-320.
Ross, Edward A.
1940 *New-Age Sociology*. New York: D. Appleton-Century Company Incorporated.
Sieder, Violet M.
1966 "The Historical Origins of the American Volunteer." In Glaser and Sills (eds.), *The Government of Associations*. Totowa, New Jersey: The Bedminster Press.
Sills, David L.
1957 *The Volunteers*. New York: The Free Press.
Smith, David H.
1966 "A Psychological Model of Individual Participation in Formal Voluntary Organizations: Application to Some Chilean Data." *American Journal of Sociology* 72 (November): 249-66.
Warner, William Lloyd and Paul S. Lunt
1941 *The Social Life of a Modern Community*. New Haven: Yale University Press.
Warriner, Charles K. and Jane Emery Prather
1965 "Four Types of Voluntary Associations." *Sociological Inquiry* 35, 2 (Spring): 138-48.

Wirth, Louis

1938 "Urbanism as a Way of Life." *American Journal of Sociology* 44 (July): 1-24.

Wright, Charles R. and Herbert Hyman

1958 "Voluntary Association Membership of American Adults: Evidence from National Sample Surveys." *American Sociological Review* 23 (June): 284-93.

Young, Roland (ed.)

1958 *Approaches to the Study of Politics.* Evanston, Illinois: Northwestern University Press.

Young, Ruth C. and Olaf F. Larsen

1965 "The Contribution of Voluntary Associations to Community Structure." *American Journal of Sociology* 71 (September): 178-86.

Zimmer, Basil G.

1955 "Participation of Migrants in Urban Structures." *American Sociological Review* 20 (April): 218-24.

(No Author Given)

1937 "Our Cities, Their Role in the National Economy." Report of the Urbanism Committee to the National Resources Committee. Washington, D.C.: U.S. Government Printing Office.

5 Major Conceptual Elements of Voluntary Associations[1]

W. KEITH WARNER

It is difficult to describe the major conceptual elements of voluntary associations for two elementary reasons. One is that there has been no conventionally accepted definition of what is meant by this kind of organization. The second reason, consequently, is the lack of an inventory and classification of the organizations in society meeting the accepted definition.

Even the labels vary considerably. Voluntary association, voluntary organization, formal voluntary organization, special interest group, common interest association, community organization (or association), and social group are just some of the labels that have been used more or less interchangeably by various students of the subject. Some persons do *not* use these terms interchangeably. Therefore, we cannot be sure that different people are referring to the same organizations in society when they use a given label.

Because of the foregoing, it is useful to delineate some of the prominent themes generally apparent in much of the past study. What have people meant by the type of organization that has been called a voluntary association (or one of the other labels named above)? Trying to answer this question may provide a useful step in advancing our understanding of some of the major conceptual elements in this kind of organization.

The purpose of the following discussion is to describe briefly ten of the characteristics attributed to voluntary associations in many past studies. In doing this, the objective will not be to define the concept,[2] nor will it be to put forward an "ideal type" idea of what voluntary associations ought to be, or to develop criteria for distinguishing one kind of voluntary association from another. Instead, *the objective is to suggest the primary characteristics that have been thought to indicate notable distinctions between voluntary associations and other kinds of organizations.*

The ten attributes seem to be generally characteristic of organizations that have been called voluntary associations, although there are important exceptions, and such organizations vary substantially along these dimensions.[3] No doubt there are other important attributes not included among these ten that merit close attention. Those to be discussed are interrelated in many ways that need specification in the future.

71

Ten Characteristics of Voluntary Associations

1. *Voluntary Involvement*

The label "voluntary associations" has been applied to those organizations in which affiliation, activity, and disaffiliation are "voluntary"—but not much progress has been made in defining what "voluntary" means, or in measuring degrees of it. (See Palisi, 1968.) Most of the empirical studies have gone forward on either implicit or ad hoc resolutions of this problem. Studies of voluntary associations have not paid much attention to measuring voluntariness of involvement as a central variable in contrast with other kinds of organizations. Rather the term has designated an imprecise set of organizations around which a large, somewhat distinctive, and as yet uncodified body of literature has developed. (In fact, the present series of volumes constitutes one of the first comprehensive attempts at codification of this literature, perhaps the first with an interdisciplinary approach.)

Much of the distinction between voluntary and non-voluntary seems to have been based on economic remuneration or legal coercion. If a person is *not* paid for his involvement (in direct economic terms) or legally required to take part, presumably his participation is optional. That is what the implicit assumption seems to have been in most cases. Thus, persons were recruited as members, were free to refrain from affiliation or active involvement, and could discontinue membership if they wished. Particularly salient has been the consideration as to whether the person's livelihood was based on the organizational activity.

The degree to which these options have been available, in fact, has varied a good deal. Conditions such as contractual membership for specified periods, membership as an occupational necessity, and membership commenced during youth as a family tradition (in churches, for example) affect the degree to which involvement is optional. And informal social pressures of all kinds can affect membership and participation in most kinds of "voluntary associations."

The general voluntary character also varies substantially with the number or proportion of the personnel who are paid. Many organizations that are called voluntary associations have paid staffs. Some of these staffs are large in number and carry on extensive business and administrative operations. The number of paid personnel in this kind of organization tends to be small, however, in proportion to the total size of the membership.

The more membership is voluntary, in the general sense implied above, the more problematic is the viability of the organization. The reason is that "organization" implies coordination and control. Thus, the more the members exercise their option to disengage from coordinated and controlled organizational activity, the less viable is the organization.

Presumably, most or all of the other nine characteristics discussed below interact with the "voluntary involvement" variable in the development and operation of voluntary associations. The nature and extent of such interactive relations remain to be explored adequately.

2. *Secondary Importance*

Compared with occupational and family concerns, voluntary associations traditionally have been said to be of secondary importance (Barber, 1950, pp. 486-487). They are usually relegated to leisure-time activity, and to competition for leftover time and other resources.

This secondariness of importance, or degree of importance, varies in relation to several conditions. One is relation to vocational interests. Some voluntary associations represent interests that are substantially extensions of the members' occupational or professional enterprise, whereas others are largely avocational interests for most members.

A second condition influencing degree of importance is the relation to social movements. Social movement organizations attempt to mobilize their members to give an unusual amount of salience to the organization and the "cause" for which it is working. This can become a primary concern for some members, but usually even social movement organizations are relegated to leisure time.

A third consideration is the extent to which personnel in the organization are paid. Voluntary associations are obviously less secondary for the full-time paid staff members than for most volunteer participants.

One general implication of this secondary importance is that voluntary associations typically operate with a relative scarcity of resources, especially in relation to the scope of their avowed objectives and in comparison to the resources of the public agencies and business enterprises with which they sometimes try to compete or cooperate in pursuing specific goals.

3. *Normative Inducements*

Voluntary associations tend to be predominantly normative in the inducements with which they obtain member participation (Etzioni, 1961, pp. 5-6). Even in professional associations seeking to advance the occupational aims of their membership, normative inducement appears typical.

Voluntary associations vary in the dominance of normative inducements according to such conditions as the existence of paid staff, the existence of indirect utilitarian (monetary) benefits from the organization, the use of utilitarian negative sanctions (such as fines), and contractual or other (legal or quasi-legal) membership obligations that constrain voluntariness of entry, exit, or performance.

A general implication is that voluntary associations tend to be less successful than public agencies and business enterprises in achieving disciplined involvement, commitment, and adherence to organizational policy positions among their members.

4. *Specialization of Interests*

Voluntary associations tend to be relatively specialized in the interests they address. This does not mean they seek single interests; relatively few may be that narrowly focused.

Specialization proceeds along two lines. One is in the range of member interests to which the association is addressed. The groups tend to represent considerably less than all of their members' interests. This means that if a person is to have several or all of his interests represented, he must have multiple affiliations.

A second line of specialization is in addressing only pieces of major societal problems. Voluntary associations often aim at only segments of broad problems like "conservation." Therefore, the programs of several different associations would have to be added together somehow if voluntary association mechanisms were to be available for the total range of components of such societal problems.

A major problem for voluntary associations is matching member interests, organizational objectives, and societal problems. A second problem is taking into account the cross-pressures resulting from membership in multiple special interest groups.

5. *Segmental Membership Participation*

Deriving partly from specialized interests and partly from secondary importance, is the variable of segmental membership participation (Selznick, 1951, pp. 325-326). Members tend to be only partially involved in any given organization, first because it is of relatively secondary importance, and second because it is only one of those needed to advance the range of their interests. This varies with the number of affiliations, and with the quality and intensity of involvement in the organizations.

The necessity of affiliation with several special interest associations if one is to have his diverse interests represented by voluntary associations, and the segmental participation in each, point to some important considerations. One is that there are limits both to the number of associations into which persons can be mobilized and organized, and to the quantity and quality of involvement that can be given to each. These limits may well fall short of encompassing enough organizations to account for all of the average person's interests. Thus, for example, mobilization into the ecology-environment movement must have some effect on involvement in prior or simultaneous movements such as civil rights and "women's liberation."

Moreover, the use of "public demand" as a gauge for the necessity of political action must take into account the extent to which the present modes of organization accurately reflect demand rather than only limits on mobilization in leisure time.

6. *Avocational Operation*

Another variable that characterizes what is usually meant by voluntary associations is the avocational operation of the organization by volunteers. This varies, of course, with the existence and size of a paid staff, and also by the expertise that may be voluntarily donated by members. For example, lawyers may donate legal expertise to voluntary associations in their representational efforts before administrative agencies or in the courts. Nevertheless, such associations tend to be operated by leaders, particularly at *local* levels, whose primary training, occupational expertise, and experience are in some other line of work.

One implication of this is that voluntary associations have the problem of using part-time, "amateur" personnel in tasks that must compete, conflict or deal with organizations having full-time professional personnel. An example is the lobbying efforts of some conservation groups competing with the professional lobbyists of industry.

7. *Intermittent Activity*

Consistent with expectations deriving from the foregoing, voluntary associations tend to meet or come together and operate as an organization intermittently (Etzioni, 1961, pp. 288-295). Some meet as often as several times each week, whereas others meet as seldom as once a year or less. Intermittency also varies with extra-meeting activities, such as field projects or services, and of course by the existence of a full-time paid staff who may carry on the work of the association between the meetings by the general membership.

In advancing the interests of members, instrumental voluntary associations are probably more handicapped by this intermittency than expressive-interpersonal ones, because the former must compete with agencies and business enterprises that are not so restricted in problems of time and schedules. At the same time, it is intermittency that helps members with multiple affiliations to carry on activity in their several associations. Intermittent activity would not appear to be an equally potential handicap for consummatory or expressive associations.

8. *Oligarchical Control*

Oligarchy is the one variable in this set that appears least peculiar to voluntary associations. Indeed, oligarchy in the sense of centralization of power and authority is fundamental to the nature of organization (Michels, 1959).

Two aspects of oligarchy are important to note. One is the extent to which those who control the association represent the general membership (Perrow, 1964, p. 415). The other is the extent to which the general membership may take advantage of the leadership by abdicating the work to them, while still receiving many of the benefits (Warner, 1964, pp. 11-12; Olson, 1965, p. 35; and Barber, 1950, p. 487). Segmental membership in specialized organizations of relatively secondary importance facilitates leaving the responsibility, and control, to those willing to do the work—especially when benefits can still be obtained by doing so. Thus, oligarchy cannot be considered simply a result of membership apathy.

One general implication is that official positions of organizations cannot be taken uncritically as representing the interests of all members; the degree of representativeness is a problematic variable. Voluntary associations seldom have very adequate systematic provisions for minimizing oligarchy, or for being accountable to their members for that problem (McConnell, 1966, pp. 152-154).

9. *Low Degree of Organization (formalization)*

Voluntary associations are characterized by a relatively low degree of organization in comparison with most other types of organizations. That is, the degree of formality (formalization) is relatively low, as is the degree to which coordination and control of member activities is effectuated. This is somewhat masked by the rhetoric of organization—by objectives, policies, programs, and structures that exist in name and sound real, but that are relatively seldom implemented in coordinated actions and group products. Often the structure and programs are ad hoc (Warner, 1965, p. 226).

The low degree of organization lessens the demands on the members, but also lessens the instrumentality of the association for many tasks, including those requiring interdependent member actions. So long as the organization mainly wants large numbers of members on the rolls in order to "carry political weight" in dealing with political leaders, or seeks uncomplicated expressive goals, little formal organization may be required of the general membership. But when the group seeks to accomplish other tasks, the degree of formalization of the organization can become a more salient variable.

10. *Private Organization*

Finally, voluntary associations at least implicitly have been considered private organizations in two senses. One is that this term is not intended to describe governmental agencies. The second is that there is generally no substantial external, especially public, accountability for the policies, programs and accomplishments of the organization. Neither is there presumed to be a public mechanism for control or accountability regarding the entry, performance, and exit of the members.[4]

Little sociological study of the private-public variation in voluntary organizations appears to have been done. Yet voluntary associations differ in the extent of their sponsorship and assistance by various governmental agencies, and in the extent they carry out governmental program interests in cooperation with such agencies. They also differ in the performance of other public or quasi-public functions not closely related to particular governmental agencies. For example, philanthropic fund raising is an activity resulting in much more public concern over accountability of the organization's procedures and accomplishments than is some expressive recreational activity.

Many of their functions are aimed at serving "the public interest," and thus the public has a concern about what they are doing and how they are going about it. Other functions of voluntary associations seek to mediate between the individual and public agencies, and in doing this the association seeks to act in the public arena to serve important, sometimes vital, interests of both members and nonmembers. Nevertheless, considering voluntary associations, implicitly or explicitly, as private organizations sets the context for seeing their internal control systems as "private governments."[5]

An important question, then, becomes what is the relation between private governments in voluntary associations and the performance of functions aimed at serving a public beyond the membership of the association. The characteristic of oligarchy, for example, takes on a different meaning in private governments serving public or quasi-public functions than in expressive social groups.

Another dimension of variation in the private aspect of voluntary associations is revealed by consideration of those kinds of organizations that are composed of governmental agencies.[6] Presumably, the private character of voluntary associations diminishes as they encompass either public functions or public agencies, or both. Volunteer "programs" in connection with public courts, hospitals, schools and other government operated organizations are examples of what might be called non-autonomous voluntary groups, rather than voluntary associations per se.

Discussion

The foregoing ten characteristics seem to be generally recognized or implicitly assumed in the designation of organizations as voluntary associations. They have not been used as an integrated set of criteria that taken together "define" what has been meant by voluntary associations. Rather, it appears that one or more of them have generally been characteristic of many studies, and that all of them seem fairly general to the studies of organizations of this type (even if they have been only implicit).

They indicate "working criteria" that have been used to distinguish between these organizations and other kinds. Such distinction has been used not so much to compare this type of organization with other types as to label organizations for study or discussion. Following from such studies is a large and fairly distinctive body of literature that is not yet sufficiently codified to reveal how adequate these characteristics are as definitional criteria, or how analytically important they are as "major conceptual elements."

Examination of differences among types of voluntary associations would no doubt show some interesting variations in these ten conceptual elements, and in the configurations of their interrelations. For example, there might be some stable patterns of difference between instrumental and consummatory or expressive voluntary associations regarding these variables. Similarly, differences in whether or not an association is part of a social movement will likely be related to important differences in these variables and their interrelations.

In addition to variations among types of voluntary associations, there are likely to be important differences related to stages of development or life cycle of the organization, and to conditions in the environment such as resistance or support or geographical dispersion.

A Suggestion

The foregoing discussion has been retrospective. But what of the future? One possibility would be to seek an empirical reconciliation between a careful attempt at defining voluntary associations, and some of the characteristics traditionally attributed to such organizations.

For example, in chapter 10 of this volume, Smith, Reddy, and Baldwin offer a detailed and systematic essay defining voluntary action and voluntary associations. In terms of the present discussion, their focus relates to the first characteristic, voluntary involvement (as it is called above), and the definition appears to be based essentially on the "normative inducements" variable that both they and this present discussion have borrowed from Etzioni (1961).

For voluntary associations, as defined by Smith and his associates, it would be very useful to have empirical descriptions of the other eight characteristics discussed above (assuming two of the ten are included in their definition). This would be one way of obtaining some empirical basis for reconciling traditional conceptions of voluntary associations with current efforts to advance definition, classification, and codification of knowledge in this area.

The results should indicate the extent to which: (1) traditional characteristics are indeed distinctive, compared with non-voluntary associations (as defined by Smith and his associates), and (2) types of voluntary associations differ in stable ways with respect to their variation on the eight characteristics. But perhaps most important, such results might further encourage and facilitate an organization of the knowledge from past studies within a systematic framework. If so, future studies could be much more productive.

Notes

1. This is an expanded section of a paper titled "Voluntary Associations and Public Involvement in Resource Policy Making and Administration," prepared for the seminar on Volunteer Action Theory and Research: Steps Toward Synthesis, at the annual meeting of the American Sociological Association, Washington, D.C., 1970.

2. Current works on this problem of definition are Smith, Reddy, and Baldwin, chapter 10 in this volume; and Bode, chapter 4 in this volume.

3. Several of these characteristics have been sketched in Warner, 1965: 224-226; and Moore, 1963: 104-114.

4. For several insights regarding voluntary associations and the private-public dimension, see Pennock and Chapman, 1969. Lack of public control and accountability has been challenged recently, for example by city governments in deciding whether to grant liquor licenses to organizations that discriminate racially in their criteria for membership.

5. For example, see McConnell, 1969; Lakoff, 1969; and Miller, 1969.

6. An example of this can be seen in Scott and Bollens, 1968: 11-12.

References

Barber, Bernard
1950 "Participation and Mass Apathy in Associations." In Alvin W. Gouldner (ed.), *Studies in Leadership: Leadership and Democratic Action*. New York: Harper, 477-504.
Etzioni, Amitai
1961 *A Comparative Analysis of Complex Organizations: On Power, Involvement, and Their Correlates*. New York: The Free Press of Glencoe.
Lakoff, Sanford A.
1969 "Private Government in the Managed Society." In J. Roland Pennock and John W. Chapman (eds.), *Voluntary Associations*. New York: Atherton, 170-201.
McConnell, Grant
1966 *Private Power and American Democracy*. New York: Knopf.

1969 "The Public Values of the Private Association." In J. Roland Pennock and John W. Chapman (eds.), *Voluntary Associations*. New York: Atherton, 147-60.

Michels, Robert
1959 *Political Parties*. New York: Dover.

Miller, Arthur Selwyn
1969 "The Constitution and the Voluntary Association: Some Notes toward a Theory." In J. Roland Pennock and John W. Chapman (eds.), *Voluntary Associations*. New York: Atherton, 233-62.

Moore, Wilbert E.
1963 *Man, Time, and Society*. New York: Wiley.

Olson, Mancur, Jr.
1965 *The Logic of Collective Action: Public Goods and the Theory of Groups*. Cambridge, Mass.: Harvard University Press.

Palisi, Bartolomeo J.
1968 "A Critical Analysis of the Voluntary Association Concept." *Sociology and Social Research* 52 (July): 392-405. Reprinted as chapter 3 in this volume.

Pennock, J. Roland, and John W. Chapman (eds.)
1969 *Voluntary Associations*. New York: Atherton.

Perrow, Charles
1964 "The Sociological Perspective and Political Pluralism." *Social Research* 31 (Winter): 411-22.

Scott, Stanley, and John C. Bollens
1968 *Governing a Metropolitan Region: The San Francisco Bay Area*. Berkeley: University of California, Institute of Governmental Studies.

Selznick, Philip
1951 "Institutional Vulnerability in Mass Society." *American Journal of Sociology* 56 (January): 320-31.

Warner, W. Keith
1964 "The Benefit-Participation Relationship in Voluntary Organizations." Madison: University of Wisconsin, Department of Rural Sociology (mimeographed).
1965 "Problems of Participation." *Journal of Cooperative Extension* 3 (Winter): 219-28.

6 The Church as a Formal Voluntary Organization

Ross P. Scherer

A review of voluntary action theory and research could hardly proceed without some attention to the church as a structure for voluntary action, for throughout Western history the churches have provided motivation and manpower for much individual and joint voluntary activity. Only recently, however, has the church been viewed as an organization among other organizations. While the sociology of religion since its inception has been concerned with group religious forms, the concepts and thinking have tended to be particularistic to religion and incapable of application to other sectors. These concepts have also probably been tainted with theological biases preventing their use in a purely descriptive way. Fortunately, the last twenty years have seen a phenomenal growth of theorizing and research in the field of formal organizations. While religious organizations have certain special features, religious self-understanding can be considerably enhanced by applying to religious organizations the *same* concepts and understandings which are being applied to organizations in general.

It is the thesis of this chapter that religious associations were one of the earliest forms of association in history and that innovations in religious organization have been formative, directly or indirectly, for the modern contractual formal voluntary organization. Religious impulses, of course, have been in interactive dialogue with other social, economic, and political forces, and have been affected by as well as affecting other forces. The influence of developing religious forms upon political and voluntary structures has often been indirect and unanticipated; and both the nature of church and religion has been inextricably linked with other sociopolitical forces in the course of social evolution. Our thesis follows that of Max Weber (1930), who held that religious impulses assisted in changing the course of history but were also conditioned and influenced by that same course of history.

The definition of voluntary action broadly followed in this volume is that voluntarism is not action which can be compelled either by the physical or legal coercion of government (as the possessor of a monopoly on the legitimate exercise of force and violence), or by the utilitarian exchange process of the economic sector. *Voluntary actions and voluntary associations, in their pure forms, are completely free and uncoerced. Actually, however, most historic manifestations of the voluntary are mixtures of the coerced and uncoerced.* Religious groups have had a long history of involvement with governmental and even

81

utilitarian compulsions. But the genius of religious action is the combination of the unavoidable and compelling with a willed response to a call from on high. Paradoxically, the religious impulse can be freely willed yet linked to near possession by a higher power. *The present chapter's concern is with collective or corporate voluntary action, not individual religious action.* In an ideal sense, religious actions are distinguished by a concern with powers that are ultimate, transcendent, and superhuman.

Our discussion is focused on Christianity and, primarily, its religious forms as they have emerged in the United States, especially the denomination. Most world religions had their emergence in pre-industrial societies; most, except for Christianity, lack much in the way of organizational elaboration (Wilson, 1966). Relatively few are as missionizing as Christianity and Islam have been. Most are lay religions and lack professional clergies, which have been a potent force for organizational differentiation and elaboration.

Our review begins first with a tracing of the "covenant" idea through the Old and New Testament periods, establishment of Christianity in the West, and the Reformation period into the emergence of modern denominational pluralism in the United States. We then review the distinctive typologies which have been applied to religious organizations, narrow and particularist as they are; then, we turn to the applicability of current organizational typologies to religious structures. We follow this with a brief profile of the variety of voluntary religious organizations from the international to the local church level; an examination of the ways in which religious organizational processes are like and unlike those of other formal voluntary organizations; and finally, a summary of social factors affecting continuing organizational development and possible directions.

Historical Background

Throughout the history of human society, religion has played different roles in relation to the development of social complexity. Sometimes it has assisted, sometimes it has hindered the breaking off of separate units of social structure from the general undifferentiated social matrix. Some of these epochal breaks are veiled in the dim past—the emergence of the city-state and the separation of citizenship from kinship obligations. The course of history has not been linear, and the actual fact has been a cyclical pattern of emergence, merging, and again emergence. So it has been with the nature of religious association. *The jump from ascriptive to achieved religious status, from kin-related to voluntary forms of religion has been a critical one.* In many ways, it was unexpected and needs to be explained in terms of specific historical circumstances. Weber regarded religious *attitude* as an important innovating determinant of the modern world. Later writers suggest that he was on the right track but that he underestimated the importance of new and concomitant forms of religious *association.*

The Old Testmant

The Old Testament contains several examples of a covenant between man and God, the Children of Israel and Yahweh. Probably the most famous is that between God and Abraham (Genesis 17). *This covenant was distinguished in that it was initiated by God; yet, it was voluntary in that man was understood as being free to depart from it.* The Old Testament Jewish God was a universal God, yet the covenant was only for a particular people; hence, it was in reality not open to all. In practice, admission to the covenant became ethnic and ascriptive by birth. Parsons (1964, pp. 277-278) points out that, despite the depoliticizing effects of the Jewish exile and the consequent elevation of religion as a collective bond, Judaism could not divest itself from cultural accretions. While the Diaspora synagogue undoubtedly served as a model for the early Christian congregation, the latter was to carry social evolution a step further.

The New Testament

Early Christianity started out sociologically as a sectarian variant of Judaism. While Christ's Disciples engaged in missionizing, some of them defined their mission to be the conversion of the Jews and, when directed at the Gentiles, the keeping of the Mosaic code. Conflict over policy culminated in a famous meeting between the Judaizing Peter and the non-Judaizing Paul (Acts 15). Peter was inspired to divest his evangelizing efforts of the particularities of Judaism (Acts 10). The more universal Pauline formula became the ultimate pattern of Christian organizational expansion: "There is neither Jew nor Greek, there is neither slave nor free, there is neither male nor female; for you are all one in Christ Jesus" (Galatians 3:28). This meant a fundamental differentiation of the essence of Christianity from particular cultural patterns, even though the Christian Church was to link itself with the state some three hundred years hence in an alliance which was to create a Christian synthesis lasting for thirteen centuries. With the establishment of Christianity in the fourth century, the religious group returned to its essentially ascriptive basis.

The Protestant Reformation

The sixteenth century phase of the Protestant Reformation, while it produced drastic changes in theological understanding and worldly outlook, did not radically change the nature of religious organization—it certainly did not make it voluntary. The Lutheran Reformation did produce conflict and competition between the Roman Catholic and evangelical branches; it also defined a new relationship between church and state; but it did not abandon the basic alliance between the church and the society (Holl, 1959). As the Reformation became routinized, Pietist movements humanized and renewed life with good works; but they seemed not to change the basic structure.

More significant for religious structure were concomitants of the Calvinist, Reformed branch of the Reformation, but again not the early Genevan Calvinism but rather the English and Germanic Reformed variations. Calvin's theocratic concepts, rather than leading to greater religious organizational complexity, actually propounded a return to a more primitive organizational fusion. Calvin's attempt to build a community on the divine model via law failed.

The "second wave" of Calvinism, specifically its English Puritan form, was more significant for voluntary innovation. The Puritans emerged, sectlike, out of the Church of England to "purify" it of Catholic remnants. A major idea was a neo-Israelite concept of covenant with God, involving "nonconformity" and implications of being a chosen elite group. In exile away from England for a time, these English Puritans implemented a medieval but seldom practiced idea of a preexisting social contract for their congregational organization. Thus, there developed in parallel ways ideas of civil, contractual parliamentary government and also a voluntary religiously covenanted group (Trinterud, 1964, p. 60). As with Weber's "elective affinity" between Protestant and capitalist "spirits," so also there was an emerging compatibility between political and ecclesiastical concepts of association (Eisenstadt, 1969, pp. 303, 309; Little, 1969, pp. 81-131, espec. 126-131). The Puritan congregation became the manifestation of the new consensual order—an independent standard for secular institutions. This new church-form did not emerge where the Puritans were dominant, but rather where they were in a minority (Little, 1969, pp. 222-223). While the work of the Puritans never abolished the privileged position of the Church of England, new psychological consciousness as well as structure were institutionalized in the successive terms by which these early "voluntarists" were known—Puritans, Dissenters, Nonconformists, Free Churchmen (Williams, 1966, p. 77).

New World Denominational Pluralism

The English dissenters eventually had toleration and the right to organize their own "free churches"; but they did not live to see disestablishment in the mother country. The New World saw not only a continuance of toleration but the institutionalization of nonestablishment or a "secular" state. The American pattern of church-state separation came about at least in part by accident. In nine of the thirteen original American colonies, the territorial (Anglican) church was the original pattern (Garrison, 1948; Handy, 1966). Denominational pluralism arose from an unwitting collusion of some of the founding fathers, who didn't want European religious divisions to divide the new country, and the transplanted sects who didn't want a European-type state church to be established

(Mead, 1954). The "denomination" thus emerged as the new church form of the modern world:

The familiar distinction between "church" and "sect" largely loses its force and clarity in the American scene, for the "denomination," a voluntary association of men united by common general beliefs for the purposes of accomplishing certain specified purposes, an association combining both churchly and sectarian motifs, quickly became the dominant church form under the new conditions (Handy, 1966, p. 132).

The denomination thus became an accommodationist form. "Denominationalism is thus a curious combination of intolerance and tolerance" (Pauck, 1952, p. 49)—intolerance within, tolerance without. Because of this ambivalence, ". . . voluntarism operated to allow Protestants to stand fast for liberty in principle and yet take it away in practice" (Handy, 1966, p. 37). That is, few were really comfortable with the new design as a principle, but they welcomed it as a lesser of evils. Forever after, the "will to belong," not territory, defined the new form (Gustafson, 1966, p. 300).

Various writers have pointed to seemingly detrimental side effects of the denominational form on the frontier. The denomination was activist and evangelizing as it attempted to church the frontier. It was pragmatic, atheological, proprietorial, lay-dominated, exclusivist, and class-selective. All denominations on this new frontier were forced to develop mechanisms by which to extend themselves. The "free churches" or sect-originated groups were more successful. In their beginnings, they were largely conglomerates or "holding companies" of various newly founded, purposive voluntary societies for missions, welfare, etc. (Gustafson, 1961). Many of these (e.g., Disciples, American Baptists) were later reorganized and consolidated into denominations as we now know them, in successive stages. Thus, many of our leading denominations are mergers of clusters of separate purposive voluntary associations. The local congregations, the special-purpose boards, and any overall coordinative apparatus thus comprise the American denomination (Winter, 1968, pp. 40-46).

Summary

We can trace a note of voluntarism throughout Christian history beginning with the Old Testament covenant, reaching a peak in the New Testament Pauline ideal of a church separated from ethnic ascription. While the church never became submerged in the state in the West, voluntarism disappeared for more than a thousand years (except in the founding of numerous religious orders). With the break-up of the medieval fusion at the Reformation, coupled with the influence of the Enlightenment and economic freedom, new contractual forms emerged both in the civil and religious areas. Puritan contractual forms became a prototype for the emergence of a new voluntary form in the new world—the denomination. The new form became both cause and effect of new social differentiation. Though explicit in America for almost two centuries, the new form received belated but formal legitimacy in the Constitution on Religious Liberty of the Roman Catholic Vatican Council II in the early 1960s.

Typology

Interspersed throughout the preceding historical review have been various type concepts—sect, church, denomination. These are specifically religious concepts. While some of the ideas underlying them could be generalized for application to all kinds of organizations, the particularism inherent in them has barred wide usage in other organizational areas. Given this limitation, they can still be used. However, more fruitful scientific understanding is likely to be gained from application of more general concepts in the new field of formal organizations. We will first review organizational typologies drawing from the sociology of religion; then we will briefly examine the utility of some recent general typologies of organizations for better understanding religious organizations.

Specifically Religious Types

Joachim Wach (1944) has developed the most detailed treatment of "natural" and "specifically religious" groups. Under "natural" cults, he lists family-kinship, community (village, city, nation), and racial and age-sex religious groups. Under specifically religious groups, he lists the (primitive) secret society; the mystery society of Greece and Rome; the "sampradaya" of Hinduism; the circle, brotherhood, and ecclesiastical body of founded religions; the protest group within ecclesiastical bodies (including monastic orders); and more radical protests, including the relatively accommodationist "independent group" (free church) and sect (Wach, 1944, chaps. IV, V). In later work, Wach adopts the term "denomination" for the independent group.

Simple pre-industrial societies lack much social differentiation, so the secret society and natural religious groups pretty well sum up the situation. Complex pre-industrial societies can have primitively differentiated religious groups like mystery societies, along with state cults. The founded and world religions tended to emerge in such societies too. During the Middle Ages of the West, countless religious orders emerged as quasi-voluntary associations. In the latter Middle Ages as well as in the Reformation period, countless sects and schismatic groups were spawned both as consequence and as affirmation of the break-up of the medieval fusion.

Up until the modern period, the sect and church (sometimes called ecclesia) types were the major types of religious organization. The sect has been viewed as an exclusivist group in conflict with or withdrawl from its host society and church. Depending upon its aims, whether to attempt conversion of its surrounding society or to put it under symbolic judgment, the sect may settle down and become an accommodated group (denomination), maintain itself if isolation is possible, continue as a conflict group, or splinter and die (Wilson, 1959). While all sects in seceding from a host "church" must obviously embody some voluntary features, they normally are not concerned to institutionalize any new pattern of voluntary organization, except under the special circumstances referred to in connection with the English Puritans. That is, *the concept of sectarianism does not necessarily seem creative of new social organization.* In the Middle Ages, at least, sectarian impulses tended to be channeled into forms (religious orders) that were connected to an umbrella organization, the mother church; in the succeeding period, some sectarian strivings appear to have been dissipated in an aimless manner. As Novak (1966, p. 105) points out, "the Free Church tradition . . . has so far been better able to cope with the Constantinian establishment than with the secular, democratic establishment."

The typical sectarian movement did not, in principle, seek to institutionalize a new form. However, as mentioned in the historical section of this chapter, a third concept emerged which sought to institutionalize freedom for religious organization but without the ephemeral character of the sect. Hudson (1955) points out that the word "denomination" was first used by the Evangelical Revival movement within the Church of England to denote a new kind of enduring religious structure.

The basic contention of the denominational theory of the church is that the true church is not to be identified in any exclusive sense with any particular ecclesiastical institution. . . . No denomination claims to represent the whole of Christ. No denomination claims that all other churches are false churches. No denomination claims that all members of society should be incorporated within its own membership. No denomination claims that the whole of society and the state should submit to its ecclesiastical regulations. Yet, all denominations recognize their responsibility for the whole of society and they expect to cooperate in freedom and mutual respect with other denominations in discharging that responsibility (Hudson, 1955, p. 32).

Thus, Independent-minded clergy in the Church of England in the seventeenth century opposed both Anglican and Presbyterian concepts of establishment. They were concerned to find a formula which would allow for both unity and disagreement. "Separation" must not itself be considered "schism." The Independents failed in their dream but they did live to see the Act of Toleration, which in effect created "free churches" or denominations alongside the established church.

The new form, as explained previously, was destined to reach fruition in pluralistic America. *DeJong (1938) gives three conceptual sources for the new concept: (1) the congregationalist concept of the church as a covenant of true believers in a minority situation; (2) the concept of a purposive, subjectivist voluntary society of Locke, Madison, and Jefferson seeking the salvation of souls (Methodism is a prototype); (3) separation of church and state as enunciated by Roger Williams, who was expelled from the New England theocracy. In sum,*

the American denomination is a voluntary organization with a religious purpose—the salvation of souls and moral improvement, loosely knit, on a democratic basis, without a central legal authority, an organization which gives the layman a large share in determining its policy and emphasizes the autonomy of the local congregations; a form of visible church without absolutistic or universal pretensions, but still including large groups of the population and dividing them for various reasons, either religious (emphasis on certain aspects of Christianity), or if secular reasons (social standing, racial divisions, and historic prejudices); and a free organization in a free state, exerting its influence by persuasion only (DeJong, 1938, p. 372).

In the situation of pluralism, various transformations took place. Over the period of time, some sects became denominations (Methodism); transplanted state churches had to become denominations (Episcopal, Lutheran bodies); some, because of an inability to accept pluralism, exhibited some sectarian features (Roman Catholicism). Even today, it is highly important when studying American denominations to determine if the body in question is sect-originated, church-originated, or an original denomination (Unitarianism).

The concepts of sect, church, and denomination are useful in contrasting and comparing European and American societies and their types of religious organization. They are also useful in keeping us aware of the weight of historic tradition in the activity of today. However, these concepts do not carry us very far in the detailed study of contemporary denominations since the criteria are vague and overlapping. Before we turn to more general organizational typologies, there is one which, while specifically religious, stays close to the self-interpretations of religious groups. The following seem to be ideal types: (1) *the medieval cultic church*—faith is conformity to liturgical truth; history is replaced with a transhistorical body (pre-Vatican Catholicism and Anglicanism); (2) *the confessional assembly*—the church comes into being in hearing the message of forgiveness via preaching, acknowledgment of what has been done (Lutheran, Presbyterian); (3) *the prophetic fellowship*—a servant church avoiding escape into superhistory and concerned with responsibility for world around it (Winter, 1963, p. 72 ff.). Winter's own preference is for the third type, since he regards the first two as out of date.

General Organizational Types

Logically there is no limit to the number of typologies which can be elaborated, beginning with organizations' relationships to environment and continuing to the nethermost parts of their internal structures. A more limited number are referred to in common use. A number of typologies in current use will be presented, followed by their application to the primary formal voluntary religious organization, the denomination. While the creator of the type does not always specify its structural rationale, most appear to be ideal types, meaning that actual organizations usually embody mixtures.

1. Downs (1967) makes much of *the market/non-market character of organizations.* The American denomination would appear to exist in a market (vs. the Pentagon, for example, which does not seem to do so); however, the nature of feedback and the competitive decisions have been little studied.

2. MacIver (1937, p. 14) and Lenski (1961, pp. 10-22) speak of *groups as "communal" and "associational."* Communal ties tend to be ascriptive, indelible, related to primary group affiliation, particular yet extensive, and somehow implying the sharing of a common life. Associational ties on the other hand are more contractual, achieved, limited, transferable, universal but segmental, being based on common but impersonal interests. Lenski considered religious groups to be communally based when the members tended to be born in the area, had spouses, relatives, and friends of the same faith; others were associationally based when they lacked these characteristics but showed high organizational participation. Undoubtedly, the communal and associational dimensions are matters of degree. The first generation sect can consist of adult converts and so be associational; on the other hand, it can involve a good deal of sharing and primary fellowship. Lenski (1961, p. 37) maintains that Jews lack strong ties to the synagogue (associationally weak) but are communally strong; Catholics have strong associational ties and medium communality; white Protestants are medium in both; and black Protestants are medium in associational ties and strong in the communal.

3. Blau and Scott (1962, pp. 42-57) *categorize organizations according to the "prime beneficiary": members, owners, clients, public.* They term an organization oriented to the benefit of members a *mutual-benefit* association; one oriented to owner benefit a *business* concern; one where client benefit is a major concern a *service* organization; and one primarily benefiting the public-at-large a *commonweal* organization. *Generally speaking, most formal voluntary organizations, including religious ones, would fit the mutual-benefit model* (although service and commonweal voluntary organizations are also common). This is especially true on the level of the local congregation. Up until recently, the Roman Catholic Church has exhibited characteristics of the service model, according to which the interests of the professionals (the clergy) have been most normative. In fact, one way of interpreting Roman Catholic *aggiornamento* or "renewal" since Vatican II is to say that this Church is shifting from a service to a mutual benefit model. Many churchmen, especially those working on the national denominational level, tend to conceive of the religious organization as also having a commonweal function, as existing for the good of society-at-large. *In summary, while churches exist*

primarily to serve their own members, religious groups have at various times stressed their service to client groups and to the public-at-large.

4. *Weber's types of authority or domination* (Weber, 1947)–*charismatic, traditional, and rational-legal*–are perhaps the best known of all attempts at typology. Sects have exhibited charismatic domination most purely. Established churches have operated by heavy mixtures of traditionalism and pre-industrial legal codes. The Puritan church concept undoubtedly ushered in the first emphasis upon purely rational-legal forms of legitimacy. Charisma remains, however, as a latent and potential force within religious groups possessing a prophetic tradition, even where charisma became the official charisma of preaching and the sacraments. Under conditions of pluralistic voluntarism in the United States, where domination came to be conditioned by persuasion, Harrison says it is necessary to add another category to Weber's line-up: he calls this *"rational-pragmatic" authority* (1959, p. 209). Furthermore, political movements today are as much the locale for explosions of inspired, non-traditional leadership as is the formal religious body.

5. Sills (Glaser and Sills, 1966, p. 22) *distinguished the corporate from the federated type of voluntary association.* He holds that the corporate form centralizes decision making in a central headquarters and is equivalent to episcopal government in the churches; while the federated form involves only an advisory relation to local chapters, being equivalent to congregational church government. Sills may be correct; however, the traditional labels for church government—episcopal, presbyterian, and congregational—are often more ideological than descriptive of how religious organizations actually operate.

6. Etzioni (1964, pp. 59-60) has developed one of the most fruitful approaches to the study of organizations in his *types of compliance structure–coercive, utilitarian, and normative,* since these signify aspects both of group structure and of personal motivation. Goffman's concept of the "total" organization (1961, pp. 4-12) seems akin to Etzioni's coercive type. While Goffman does not specify a polar opposite of the total organization, the notion of "detotalization" can be applied to his concept, especially in connection with what has been happening to Catholic religious orders since Vatican II. The opposite and complement to Goffman's total organization would appear to be the formal voluntary organization. That is, *the religious order in being detotalized becomes, in effect, a voluntary association.*

Etzioni's types of compliance are ideal types; thus, all three forms are likely to be present in any one religious organization. There certainly have been mixtures of the coercive form in pre-Vatican II "totalized" religious communities; there have been and are elements of the utilitarian where monetary contributions and distribution have been prominent. But Etzioni is correct in his classification of religious organizations under the normative, in view of the way in which such groups have been able, by the use of symbolic means, to win the trust and allegiance of millions to religious causes through-out history. Where voluntary pluralism prevails, the individual is most free to attach himself or to leave a group of his own accord, the hallmark of Etzioni's normative compliance.

Summary

The denomination in distinction from other organizations exists within a market and receives feedback; it involves communal characteristics deriving from wide family inheritance, as well as contractual aspects; it exists primarily for member benefit; it tends to operate by a combination of traditional and rational-prag-matic types of authority, punctuated occasionally by charismatic outbursts from within; it most often is a federation of semi-autonomous local congregations and agencies; and more than most other organizations attaches people to it by means of normative (symbolic) compliance. The above are not the only ways for classi-fying organizations—only a few out of the many possible.

Denominational Structure and Process

In this section we take a brief overview of the range of denominational struc-tures from the international to local levels and across denominational lines. Then, using a model of major organizational processes, we examine how denomi-national organizations in the United States tend to operate in the same way. Finally, we specify some of the factors which condition denominational oper-ation and possible directions of religious organizational development.

Range of Denominational Jurisdictional Structures

If you compose a matrix of the jurisdictional levels and the religio-cultural groups into which the major American religious groups are divided, a widely varying picture is revealed (see table 6-1). Roman Catholic structure is the most centralized by virtue of policy initiation from the Vatican. There are also strong elements of communality in the local, non-mobile character of the clergy attached over a lifetime to a particular diocese (religious order clergy and the bishops themselves are exceptions). The U.S. Catholic Conference appears to be mainly advisory and coordinating; thus, American Catholicism lacks strong national executive arms. Individual dioceses vary in terms of the particular style of the bishop-in-charge (Deegan, 1970; Winter, 1968).

Table 6-1
The Suggested Range of Denominational Levels and Structures in the U.S.A.[a]

Jurisdictional Level	Roman Catholic	Protestant	Jewish	Interdenominational
International	Vatican Council Pope and Curia	World Methodist Council Lutheran World Federation Baptist World Alliance World Alliance of Reformed Churches, etc.	Agudoth Israel (Zionist) World Union for **Progressive** Judaism	World Council of Churches
National Legislative	National Conference of Catholic Bishops National Federation of Priests Councils	Annual, biennial, triennial assembly, convention, conferences, etc. according to denomination Lutheran Council in the U.S.A. (includes 3 major bodies)	Synagogue Council of America (includes rabbinical and congregational councils by Orthodox, Conservative, and Reform)	National Council of Churches Coordinative federations of denominational agencies
Executive	U.S. Catholic Conf.	General secretariats boards, etc., and staffs	B'nai B'rith, ADL American Jewish Comm.	
Regional	Province (religious orders)	State synod, conference, district, etc.	Board of Rabbis	State councils
Metropolitan	Diocese, deanery	Presbytery, district, cluster	Local affiliates of national bodies	Metropolitan Councils, urban training centers; "clergy fellowships" intercongregational clusters
Paraparochial	Semiautonomous service, welfare-health, educational groups, etc. Religious orders Priests' associations	Local ministers' associations	Welfare federations and defense agencies (ADL)	Conferences of community organizations
Local churches & sub-units	Parish Men's, women's, youth, liturgical, educational, service, etc. units	Congregation	Congregation	

[a]Some of the material in this table was drawn from various portions of Frank S. Mead, *Handbook of Denominations in the United States* (Nashville, Tenn.: Abingdon Press, 1970). Other material comes from Margaret Fisk, ed., *Encyclopedia of Associations, Vol. I* (Detroit: Gale Research Co., 1970).

Jewish structure is avowedly pluralistic, said currently to involve a decline of the synagogue and the ascendancy of brotherhood, welfare, defense agencies (Elazar, 1970; Winter, 1968, pp. 66-96). Its pluralism and diffusion of authority probably represent the polar opposite of the Catholic hierarchial model. It undoubtedly works as well as it does because of the highly communal character of Jewish people, the lack of missionary expansion, and the high level of education of Jews.

Protestantism, on the other hand, is "radically congregationalized" (Gustafson, 1966, p. 299). Protestant bodies tend to be coalitions, federations, conglomerates of national, regional, and local agencies and congregations. Protestant policy has strongly legitimized the principle of local autonomy (Norgren, 1970). The notion is that the local church delegates some of its powers upward to higher units, if this is done at all. Protestant financing proceeds by a process of trickling funds upward from the congregation to the regional jurisdiction and through it to the national body. Generally, Protestant congregations tend to be relatively small in size, and many are rural. Most clergy are free to move anywhere (except for the Methodists). Congregations are organized not by geography but by "interest" or social class self-selection. Thus, Protestant bodies tend to be less communal and more associational than the Roman Catholic. The geographic character of the local Catholic Church means greater inclusiveness possibly than the Protestant congregation but more ascriptiveness. These together with the large size of Catholic churches and the lower degree of parliamentary decision making probably give Catholic structure a more communal character. Intermediate voluntary associations and movements within Protestant bodies function to keep Protestant policy close to the grassroots also.

Conciliar and interdenominational structures are currently in flux. They originally grew to coordinate individual denominational efforts and hence to reduce duplication, but also to focus power in relation to government and the public sector. The National Council of Churches and also state and local councils are currently undergoing restructure in order to co-opt Catholic and conservative Protestant bodies. Whether such restructure will strengthen or weaken the conciliar movement is presently not clear.

The above discussion has omitted specifically black religious groups, "third force" groups, sects, groups with strong ethnic overtones (e.g., Eastern Orthodox bodies), and groups still defining their relationship to the rest of organized religion in the United States (e.g., Latter Day Saints, Christian Scientists). Most of these are strongly "lay" oriented and tend to be locally autonomous. Black self-consciousness is currently becoming quite strong (Williams, 1970). While most wholly black religious bodies have come out of Protestant traditions (Methodist, Baptist), the emerging pattern of black religious organization in metropolitan areas may resemble the Jewish pattern of federationist pluralism. As Lenski's findings (1961) indicate, black religious structure is highly communal; it seems to be breaking out of the "Protestant sector" and becoming a loose federation of various congregational, welfare, and economic movements across denominational lines. Black pride and an ideology of localism will probably make for continuation of black separatism for some time to come. Nonetheless, the black churchmen who teach in integrated seminaries or who are members of predominantly white denominations and their ministerial bodies will provide some linkage between the black and white religious worlds.

Denominational Organizational Processes

Now let us present the range of organizational processes of the denomination as the main prototype of the religious voluntary organization. The following observations should probably best be regarded as hypotheses, some of which may be empirically verifiable. *Our concern will be to illustrate not only how the denomination operates like other voluntary organizations (unions, political parties, veterans groups, philanthropic, and social action movements) but also how religious bodies are unlike other voluntary units in their behavior.* This treatment will follow the general categories of system tasks as outlined by Parsons and Bales (Parsons, 1959). We will look at each of the major forms of organizational process, then at their interrelationships. One problem is that denominations fluctuate between voluntariness and involuntariness—some have strong communal characteristics; some are church-originated European transplants which reluctantly have had to accommodate to pluralism. Some, on the other hand, are settled down sects which revel in their pluralist minority position. Some have become hybrids of the two through merger.

a. External Relations. The primary task of all organizations today is adaptation to the social milieu—structural, economic, interpersonal. Several tasks emerge in connection with adaptation to the external situation. The first one is *the problem of legitimacy or organizational security.* Along with other voluntary organizations, American denominations stand detached from the official community structure. The official public dogma is that the churches are on their own. In America, a "service" ideology means that organizations must perform service to justify the blessing and support of the community. Today it is apparent that the "public legitimacy" of religious denominations is in danger. It is not clear what they contribute to the community as a whole; there are cries within the churches to abandon tax exemptions, to get out of profit-making activities (if there are any); many costly activities have been taken over by the state (hospitals, welfare functions, education). Thus, there has been a great deal of "organizational secularization" of religion. Probably the only strategy by which churches can reclaim their legitimacy over against the community is through a joint voice—interdenominational councils. But this poses problems.

There is a great deal of ambivalence within the churches whether their function should be primarily "priestly," providing sanction for the status quo in the community; or "prophetic," providing a critical and innovating role; or be neutral toward present social arrangements and divisions, yet trying somehow to be an enabler for reconciliation between man and man, group and group, class and class, etc. In a democratic society, where persuasion is the mode of influence, application of informal power is not necessarily weaker than formal. A recent Gallup poll, however, illustrates the cleavage currently found among churchmen:

Protestant ministers by the ratio of 4 to 1 say churches should be mainly concerned with the spiritual life of the individual rather than problems of society as a whole, although many say "both." Catholic priests are evenly divided in their views, while rabbis are nearly 3-to-1 on the side that problems of society as a whole should be the primary concern of churches and synagogues. (Gallup and Davies, 1971).

A second problem of adaptation is funding. Like other organizations, churches must gather funds for sustenance on a voluntary basis. Religious organizations are one of the most numerous and ubiquitous form of voluntary association—there are over 300,000 local units in over 250 religious bodies in the United States (National Council of Churches, *Yearbook of American Churches*). The "religion business" is quite large (Balk, 1968). Sociologists have pointed out how the pluralist situation makes for a denomination's having to "sell" itself in a "market" (Berger, 1969, p. 138) with consumer-dominated tastes. With financial turndowns, churches tend to receive smaller proportions of the discretionary dollar left after payments for food, clothing, housing, insurance, and leisure activities. National denominations, in particular, receive the short end after the contributions trickle up from the congregation and through the middle level jurisdictional unit.

Churchmen point to another powerful resource which, officially at least, other organizations lack—the supernatural. While secularization of attitude in America may be only partial, divesting of function is more complete on the religious organizational level. This means in the public mind that churches no longer have a monopoly of "charisma" vis-à-vis social and political movements of various kinds. Challenges to the social order come just as frequently (or more frequently) from various contemporary minorities—youth, women, blacks, etc.—as from formal churches.

A third major task with regard to environment is co-optation of a social base or constituency. All organizations must co-opt or develop the allegiance of such a base or die; and like other organizations, denominations run the risk of becoming prisoner of that base (Niebuhr, 1929). This captivity is considered the great "scandal" of American denominationalism, that such bodies become identified with a particular class, race, region, or ethnic group. On the other hand, with the definition of structure that religion has been given in America, what other result could have been possible? An additional problem is that most denominations try via missionary expansion to become "popular" organizations and so broaden their intake. This results in their becoming "domesticated" through basis of membership in family groups of parents and children, resulting frequently in bland and conservative outlooks on important social issues (Glock and Stark, 1965, pp. 135-138; Broom and Selznick, 1963, pp. 386-387). Other studies of parish clergy show that, given the present decentralized tactics of hiring and funding of ministers' salaries in the local church, local clergymen tend of all clergy to be least capable of radicalism (Hadden, 1970, p. 193; Demerath and Hammond, 1969, pp. 188-195). A survey of the social origins of Protestant clergy shows that the clergy of some denominations tend to have much higher rates of occupational inheritance and to be more "home-grown" (American Lutheran Church, Lutheran Church—Missouri Synod, Presbyterian Church in the U.S.); while others (e.g., Episcopal, United Church of Christ) have lower rates of inheritance and "borrow" their clergy much more from other denominations (Scherer, 1966, pp. 49, 52-53). Again, this means some embody communal elements to a larger degree.

b. Internal Differentiation, Goal-attainment, and Problem-solving. Regarding authority structure, earlier it was pointed out that, while denominations vary a good deal, all probably operate on the basis of Harrison's "rational-pragmatic" authority pattern which relies very heavily upon persuasion (1959, p. 209). Wood (1970, p. 1065), however, maintains that the greater the legitimacy of *formal* authority, the more effective the religious leaders can be in a crisis, since they can fall back on formal definitions of power. As mentioned previously, American Protestant and Jewish bodies utilize parliamentary mechanisms of decision; these, however, are very often infused with tradition and an emphasis upon seniority. Most such parliamentary church assemblies include a balance of clergy and lay representation. Proportionally, of course, and professionally in terms of expertise and commitment, the clergy are generally much more power-ful (cf. the theses of Michels, 1962; and Lipset, 1954). As with other organiza-tions, large-scale denominations are frequently beset by member apathy. The authority pattern of some denominations is further beset by ambiguity of final authority in critical decisions—a parliamentary assembly, theological experts, or an officially defined charismatic authority (e.g., the New Testament).

When it comes to "program" and the setting of goals, denominations have only recently begun to view themselves as "goal-attaining" organizations; and the local congregation has done so even less. Demerath and Hammond say that one of the blights of churches is "goallessness" (1969, pp. 173-180). One prob-lem with ambiguity of goals is that goal *displacement* becomes easier. In fact, however, the history of denominations in the New World has given evidence of their pursuing many specific goals—evangelizing or churching the continent, building edifices, indoctrinating the next generation, marrying, burying the dead, etc. Churches formerly talked of "missions," now they speak of "mission." With the decline of frontier religious areas and with economic turndown, denominational stance shifts from the establishment of new congregations to renewal and salvage of existing ones. Because of the local proprietarial concept of church structure, regional jurisdictions can only intervene if there is a money flow down to the congregation. If subsidies to congregations in trouble grow, then the higher jurisdictions may exercise more control over the lower.

If churches are considered to carry out expressive rather than purposive functions for their members, then the possibility of goal-displacement does not look so bad. No other organization probably is so invested with value as is the church. Clergy and laity tend to disagree over objectives of the church as an organization—the laity seek comfort and tend to see the church from an internal viewpoint only; the clergy tend to see a much wider role for challenge and tend to view the church much more in relationship to the external environment (Hadden, 1970, pp. 115-181; Kersten, 1970, passim). The local clergyman is caught as the man-in-the-middle in his role of interpreter of the denomination down to the layman.

Search mechanisms tend not to be very institutionalized within denominations. Research and planning departments came into denominational organization tables with the wave of survey techniques in the 1940s and 1950s; some entered as a result of management studies and reorganizations of headquarters' staffs through mergers of denominations and consequent updating. (See Kloetzli, 1960; Schroeder, 1971). But such units have had an insecure future, and some were wiped out with fiscal retrenchment in the late 1960s. Thus, religious organizations have lacked the research and development potentialities of our military-industrial complex. This results in lack of adequate and systematic feedback. Some churchmen were never really very much sold on the utility of research for church process; hence, they could rationalize the demise of research units by means of traditional theological formulae according to a "closed systems" model.

Staff specialization is a topic receiving some study of late. Winter (1968) studied the elaboration of headquarters and agency structure over against the congregational-pastoral structure. He points to the growth of fund-raising, welfare, the Sunday School movement, publications, missionizing. All these were given impetus by the dislocations and modernization produced by two world wars. Staff selection in denominations beyond the local level is not wholly ascriptive—the jobs do not tend to be sought as patronage; they don't pay that well. Yet, they are not very much rationalized either (Harrison, 1959, p. 211). Some headquarters jobs require graduate training (e.g., in education, welfare); but most clergy job-holders are probably generalists. Because of the uncertain authority conferred by such positions and the need to persuade clergy peers and the laity, political savvy becomes a more important qualification for church executives than an advanced technical degree (unless it is in business management). Today, there is more and more co-opting of laymen to such positions, and these usually have specialized training. Probably few national denominational headquarters have rationalized job structures in the Weberian bureaucratic sense; that is, very few job-holders can transfer laterally from one denomination to another. But such job-systems are probably not as feudally structured as are the systems of local and county government offices in the United States. Middle-management positions (regional bishops, superintendents, conference secretaries, etc.) probably involve a combination of honorary and executive criteria, depending upon the degree to which the office is symbolic or executive. Regional supervisory personnel are currently having to shift their attention from the initiating of new congregations to the conservation of the old; in many ways, the latter is more complex and requires greater skills in human relations. A study done in 1965 (Scherer, 1966, p. 46) shows that the proportion of active clergy of the major American Protestant denominations in local congregational work varies from 71 percent to 89 percent. The difference from 100 percent is made up by the clergy engaged in specialized ministerial work, executive positions, and teaching. The Methodists had the most in parish work and the United Church of Christ the least.

c. **Internal Cohesion.** Few organizations in the modern world or in any period have had greater symbolic sources for cohesion than the churches. Religious groups are unique in the rich panoply of rites, liturgies, and sacramental processes available to them. Few organizations are as ideological and possessed of transcendent "definitions of the situation" as are the churches. These serve to insure loyalty and firm absorption of the "decisional premises" of the organization. Durkheim's great thesis on the role of religion in group cohesion developed as no great surprise. But simultaneously, such strengths can also prove to be liabilities when it comes to goal attainment. The infusion of historically conditioned forms with ultimate value can be a barrier to change when demanded by the environment; this is "ritualism," the affirmation of "institutionalized means" together with the rejection of "cultural goals" (Merton, 1957, pp. 149-153). Religious-theological language, when it takes on "doxological" overtones, can also be a barrier to communication. Implicit in religious discussion frequently are biases to harmony, concord, and aversion to the possibility of creative conflict.

A related problem is that, when conflict over economic, ethnic, and other social differences is coupled with religious difference, it becomes more intense (e.g., "ethnic Protestant" vs. "ethnic Catholic" in Northern Ireland). Such conflict is harder to solve via mediation; its intensity results from greater investment of self (Coleman, 1956, pp. 44-56).

Judicial powers are possibly not as fully differentiated and developed in religious structures as in modern civil ones. Where religious groups have involved large numbers of people with heavy communal components, and where ethical outlooks of church groups have provided defined patterns for daily living, religious denominations have in effect served as "private governments." While voluntary associations are private from the viewpoint of the state and the entire community, *denominations have frequently spawned numerous sub-voluntary associations of their own which have performed mediating or "brokering" functions for different strata of their constituencies.* Such associations have given representation and voice to disaffected groups. Religious orders, for example, in the history of the Catholic Church have provided this function. Voluntary groups beget further voluntary groups.

d. Replenishment and Maintenance of Personnel. All organizations must replenish their supply of members, induct them into the system, and provide for their psychosociological nurture. To do this, denominations must develop programs of recruitment, socialization, and education, and systems of rewards and sanctions—hence, the proliferation of systems of honorific office. As with organizational integration, here also religious groups have greater resources for motivating and rewarding the individual—a system of supernatural sanctions. Religious groups have not only richer resources for socializing the individual, through a wide network of religious education classes and primary groups in the congregation, but also through co-optation of the family as a socializing agency. Denominational membership tends more to be inherited than wholly chosen anew in the United States (Stark and Glock, 1968, pp. 185, 195). The combination of family nurture with the powerful symbolism of the church makes for stability in the individual. Increasingly, as local churches have grown larger in size, they have had to work harder at involving the individual in a primary group way.

On the other hand, groups with such powerful resources as the churches must also face the problem of "oversocialization." An earlier view in sociology proposed that religious groups disproportionately draw the closed-minded and the bigots to themselves and further comfirm them in their bigotry (e.g., Rokeach, 1969, pp. 33-37). Other studies qualify this by stating that only a particular kind of religion—primarily an ethnic or communal type—is correlated with bigotry; that purely associational religion can actually be moderately liberating (Kersten, 1970, pp. 80-85). This problem obviously needs further research. Gibbs and Ewer (1969) hold that a low degree of education combined with a communal orientation makes for a narrow orientation.

Again, the nurturing function of the local church may be in conflict with its assisting its members to take a more radical stance in their social roles. The co-optation of the family and the consequent domestication of the local church help the wider society to sustain itself by means of recharging the individual, providing him a transcendent and clear identity, relieving his guilt and being a shock absorber. On the other hand, an overemphasis upon other worldliness and eternal comfort may produce too much inwardness and myopia. The local congregation in America has tended to be proprietarial; it is where the individual parishioner has his investment and where his "privacy" is most evident and resistant to what he considers intrusion (Winter, 1962, pp. 67-92; Smith, 1965).

Summary

The traditional role assignment of churches in the pluralist society—by police, judges, journalists, frequently intellectuals—is priestly. The church should attend to internal cohesion and sustenance and renewal of the individual believer. The church is frequently not seen as contributing to societal *adaptation*; it is not given much margin to be prophetic or to be involved in goal determination for society. Thus, churches have stressed cohesion at the expense of adaptation and goal attainment. Adaptation puts a strain on organizations, any organization; those which stress the facing of change get involved in internal conflict and strain (e.g., the National Council of Churches and its budget crisis of 1970). This choice, however, probably is not an either-or one. The question is how to achieve an optimum of both. Kersten (1970), for example, provides evidence of how the Lutheran Church in America has chosen the path of greater adaptation with consequent risk of less organizational loyalty; the Evangelical Lutheran Wisconsin Synod, on the other hand, has chosen the path of internal cohesion (which seems almost absolute) with the concomitant of closed-mindedness and prejudice toward most outgroups.

Determinants and Directions

There now only remains, in this treatment of the denomination as a formal voluntary organization, briefly to spell out what are some of the forces, the constraints, the determinants of religious structure, and also possible future directions as currently seen.

*Factors Affecting Denominational
Operation*

The following are some of the social forces which condition organizational process in the modern denomination. Most of these affect *all* organizations, not only religious voluntary associations of the denominational kind.

1. The role of state and federal governments is crucial. While many denominations have been preoccupied with internal problems, the vast majority are ultra-sensitive to the ways in which the courts, legislatures, and executive

leadership have on occasion broadened or contracted the defined role of churches in society.

2. Closely related to this is the common attitude toward religious organization and its public role as revealed in public opinion polls. As Berger (1969) points out, there can still be considerable *attitudinal "sacralization"* among the public simultaneously with *organizational secularization.*

3. Externally induced conflicts within the wider society necessarily disturb the inner tranquility of religious publics. The overriding public issue of our generation is the race problem, and this probably more than any other single issue has been the major environmentally induced catalyst of our time as far as the churches have been concerned. Social polarization, of course, presents severe tests for an organization whose major concerns have been cohesion.

4. The types of dominant organizational models extant in the host society ordinarily have a strong influence upon the development of religious structures. Most American denominations, of course, have had their origins in the past. Despite the dating of origins, American denominations have proved to be remarkably malleable and functional in relationship to pragmatic necessities. E.K. Francis (1950) presents an interesting discussion of the ways in which Roman Catholic orders have tended in their structural forms to embody the reigning organizational models at the time of the order's origination.

5. It was a leading thesis of Max Weber that the behavior of the leading elites in a society was a clue to its future direction. Certainly the outlooks of a John Kennedy, a Richard Nixon, a Nelson Rockefeller, or an Irwin Miller can be determinative of the future role or organized religion.

6. The level of economic development and of economic surplus can be very crucial for social innovation in voluntary associations, including religious bodies. Seemingly, whenever fiscal retrenchment occurs, prophetic or innovating programs are trimmed out of denominational budgets.

7. As was mentioned earlier, the kind of social base—its age distribution, educational level, degree of mobility, and emancipation—can importantly condition the capacity of large religious bodies to maneuver in the social arena.

8. The self-identity of religious bodies, although itself to some extent a product of historical interaction, is an important determinant of the body's outlook and manner of coping with its environment. As Winter (1963) points out, it makes a difference whether a religious body conceives of itself primarily as cultic, confessional, or prophetic. Wilson (1959) points out that if a sect's goals are society oriented it is more likely to accommodate itself eventually to cooperating with the "world" (in contrast to organizations with predominantly other worldly goals). Weber regarded a group's attitude to the world as crucial to meaningfully interpreting its actions.

9. Organizational size and ensuing increase in scale undoubtedly have a significant effect on internal ambience of churches, but this has been studied very

little. Organizations like churches, which make much of nurturing and restorative functions with regard to their members, should probably study the impact of increasing size on these functions more than they do.

10. Many writers regard technology as the prime agent of change in our time. In some respects, denominations, of all types of organizations, might seem most removed from the influence of technological change. On the other hand, an organization like the church, which in essence is a system of communicative persuasion, could be greatly affected by the contemporary communicative-information revolution.

New Directions for Religious Organization

It may be foolhardy to comment about possible future directions for organized religion in view of the constancy of current social change. There is some evidence for the following hypothesized directions, although it may be hard to document them.

1. There may be a simultaneous surrendering of public legitimacy by those churches which take a non-controversial stance on public issues (although they may buy constituents' good will), along with a new search for legitimacy and increased public respect by those groups who adopt a stance which is prophetic and critical of the status quo. Groups which seek to surrender the tax-exempt status of churches, clergy discounts, etc., emphasize giving to, rather than receiving from, the host society. The Berrigan brothers and Martin Luther King exhibit the newer prophetic form of legitimacy.

2. The last decades have witnessed an increase in ecumenical consciousness and frequency of organic mergers among Protestant denominations. Observers argue whether such movements and mergers arise from a position of strength or weakness; theological vision and market weakness, however, need not necessarily be opposites. Mergers probably do make for organizational rationalization in the task of updating structures; they also probably lessen the need for informal systems as forms become adapted to changing functions.

3. An obvious problem of the late 1960s and early 1970s is financial retrenchment and consequent shock to programs and staff personnel, especially on the national denominational level. Since innovation is more likely to proceed from the top down in voluntary organizations, this retrenchment may present a significant loss in long-run adaptation to environmental change.

4. There seems to be an increasing awareness that churches carry their "treasure in earthen vessels," and that organizations are more effective if

they clearly spell out their assumptions, goals, strategies, and tactics and then make some evaluation of the overall process. The present seems to be a period of great interest in "evaluation" research, although few studies have yet been done (e.g., Metz, 1967). There is growing awareness that the task of the denominations may no longer simply be the churching of society but the reconciliation of a society which is already churched.

5. The trend toward decentralization of decisions has already been commented upon.

6. Related to the last point is the "detotalization" of religious professionals in the Catholic Church. One thrust of this is the trend toward professionalization and professional awareness among the clergy. Whether clergy in the United States can ever develop the kind of public legitimacy achieved by other professionals (physicians, academics, etc.) may be questioned, in view of the clergyman's attachment to a particular private constituency (Gannon, 1971).

7. Some denominations are likely to experience greater internal conflict and polarization as they seek to broaden their social base and become more responsive to and attract new constituencies on the outside. Unfortunately, this process has not been studied to the extent that it has for political parties and their factional processes, although some of the same hypotheses probably apply.

Summary

This chapter has attempted to describe the nature of the modern American denomination as a formal voluntary organization in terms of modern organizational theory. The focus has been confined primarily to the United States. Contractual concepts have been seen as latent throughout Judaeo-Christian history in the notion of a sacred "covenant" between God and man. This idea reached its fullest development in the seventeenth century Puritan notion of the voluntary assembly, particularly where Puritanism was in a minority position. Structurally speaking, the concept reached its implementation in the non-establishment of denominational pluralism in the new world.

Previous sociological thinking about religious organization has been confined by ideas too exclusively related to religion (e.g., sect, church). It seems more fruitful to examine the ways in which religious organizational processes are like those which occur in other organizations—e.g., the need to adapt to external environment, to define and attain goals, to maintain internal cohesion, and to provide nurture and support for members. Religious organizations, however, must face the problem of meeting several tasks *at the same time*, rather than exclusively maximizing the need for cohesion to the exclusion of adaptation.

Churches, on the other hand, claim to be different from other organizations in their access to transcendent resources; this is embodied in theologically-derived statements of purposes and tactics. The basic dilemma, however, confronts churches in the American situation: how much of an emphasis upon the prophetic is compatible with a membership structure which rests upon a basically decentralized and federated basis?

References

Balk, Alfred
1968 *The Religion Business*. Richmond, Va.: John Knox Press.
Berger, Peter L.
1969 *The Sacred Canopy:* Elements of a Sociological Theory of Religion. Garden City, New York: Doubleday.
Blau, Peter M. and W. Richard Scott
1962 *Formal Organizations:* A Comparative Approach. San Francisco, Calif.: Chandler.
Broom, Leonard and Philip Selznick
1963 *Sociology.* (3rd ed.) New York: Harper and Row.
Coleman, James
1956 "Social Cleavage and Religious Conflict." *Journal of Social Issues* 12: 44-56.
Deegan, Arthur X. III
1970 "Directions in Catholic Organization." Unpublished paper presented to Society for Scientific Study of Religion, Chicago, Ill., December 28, 1970.
DeJong, J.M.
1938 "The Denomination as the American Churchform." *Nieuw Theologisch Tijdschrift* 27: 347-88.
Demerath, Nicholas J. III and Philip E. Hammond
1969 *Religion in Social Context, Tradition and Transition.* New York: Random House.
Downs, Anthony
1967 *Inside Bureaucracy.* Boston, Mass.: Little Brown.
Eisenstadt, S.N.
1969 "The Protestant Ethic Thesis." In Roland Robertson (ed.), *Sociology of Religion: Selected Readings*, Baltimore, M.D.: Penguin, 297-317.
Elazar, Daniel J.
1970 "Directions in Jewish Organization." Unpublished paper presented to Society for Scientific Study of Religion, Chicago, Ill., December 28, 1970.
Etzioni, Amitai
1964 *Modern Organizations.* Englewood Cliffs, N.J.: Prentice-Hall.
Fisk, Margaret (ed.)
1970 *Encyclopedia of Associations, Vol. I National Organizations of the United States.* Detroit: Gale Research Co.

Francis, E.K.
1950 "Toward a Typology of Religious Orders." *American Journal of Sociology* 55 (March): 437-49.

Gallup, George Jr. and John O. Davies
1971 "Crisis in the Church, Optimistic Note for Religion." *Chicago Sun-Times, Section 2:6* (April 11, 1971).

Gannon, Thomas M., S.J.
1971 "Priest/Minister: Profession or Non-Profession?" *Review of Religious Research* 12 (Winter): 66-79.

Garrison, William E.
1948 "Characteristics of American Organized Religion." *Annals* 256 (March): 14-24.

Gibbs, James O. and Phyllis A. Ewer
1969 "The External Adaptation of Religious Organizations: Church Response to Social Issues." *Sociological Analysis* 30 (Winter): 223-34.

Glaser, William A. and David L. Sills (eds.).
1966 *The Government of Associations: Selections from the Behavioral Sciences.* Totawa, N.J.: The Bedminster Press.

Glock, Charles Y. and Rodney Stark
1965 *Religion and Society in Tension.* Chicago, Ill.: Rand-McNally.

Goffman, Erving
1961 *Asylums.* Garden City, New York: Doubleday.

Gustafson, James
1961 *Treasure in Earthen Vessels: The Church As a Human Community.* New York: Harper and Row.
1966 "The Voluntary Church: A Moral Appraisal." In D.B. Robertson (ed.), *Voluntary Associations: A Study of Groups in Free Societies.* Richmond, Va.: John Knox Press, 299-322.

Hadden, Jeffrey K.
1970 *The Gathering Storm in the Churches.* Garden City, N.Y.: Doubleday.

Handy, Robert T.
1966 "The Voluntary Principle in Religion and Religious Freedom in America." In D.B. Robertson (ed.), *Voluntary Associations: A Study of Groups in Free Societies.* Richmond, Va.: John Knox Press, 129-39.

Harrison, Paul
1959 *Authority and Power in the Free Church Tradition.* A Social Case Study of the American Baptist Convention. Carbondale, Ill.: Southern Illinois U. Press.

Holl, Karl
1959 *The Cultural Significance of the Reformation.* New York: Meridian.

Hudson, Winthrop
1955 "Denominationalism as a Basis for Ecumenicity: A Seventeenth Century Conception." *Church History* 14 (March): 32-50.

Kersten, Lawrence K.

1970 *The Lutheran Ethic. The Impact of Religion on Laymen and Clergy.* Detroit, Mich.: Wayne State U. Press.

Kloetzli, Walter

1960 "The History and Present Situation in Research and Planning." In Perry L. Norton (ed.), *Search: A National Consultation on Personnel Needs in Church Planning and Research.* New York: National Council of Churches, 20-41.

Lenski, Gerhard

1961 *The Religious Factor.* A Sociological Study of Religion's Impact on Politics, Economics, and Family Life. Garden City, N.Y.: Doubleday.

Lipset, Seymour M.

1954 "The Political Process in Trade Unions: A Theoretical Statement." In Monroe Berger, Theodore Abel, and Charles Page (eds.), *Freedom and Control in Modern Society.* New York: D. Van Nostrand, 82-124.

Little, David

1969 *Religion, Order, and Law.* A Study in Pre-Revolutionary England. New York: Harper and Row.

MacIver, Robert M.

1937 *Society, A Textbook of Sociology.* New York: Farrar and Rinehart.

Mead, Frank S.

1970 *Handbook of Denominations in the United States.* Nashville, Tenn.: Abingdon Press.

Mead, Sidney E.

1954 "Denominationalism: The Shape of Protestantism in America." *Church History* 23: 291-320.

Merton, Robert K.

1957 *Social Theory and Social Structure.* Glencoe, Illinois, The Free Press, 149-53.

Metz, Donald L.

1967 *New Congregations: Security and Mission Conflict.* Philadelphia, Pa.: Westminster.

Michels, Robert

1962 *Political Parties.* New York: Free Press-Macmillan.

National Council of Churches

1915 Since 1916 annually and biennially. *Yearbook of American Churches.* New York, N.Y.

Norgren, William A.

1970 "Directions in Protestant Organization." Unpublished paper presented to Society for Scientific Study of Religion, Chicago, Ill., December 28, 1970.

Novak, Michael

1966 "The Meaning of 'Church' in Anabaptism and Roman Catholicism: Past and Present." In D.B. Robertson (ed.), *Voluntary Associations: A Study of Groups in Free Societies.* Richmond, Va.: John Knox Press, 91-107.

Niebuhr, H. Richard
1929 *The Social Sources of Denominationalism.* New York: Meridian.

Parsons, Talcott
1959 "General Theory in Sociology." In Robert K. Merton, Leonard Broom, and Leonard S. Cottrell Jr. (eds.), *Sociology Today: Problems and Prospects.* New York: Basic Books, 3-38.
1964 "Christianity and Modern Industrial Society." In Louis Schneider (ed.), *Religion, Culture, and Society*, A Reader in the Sociology of Religion. New York: John Wiley, 273-98.

Pauck, Wilhelm
1952 "Theology in the Life of Contemporary American Protestantism." *Shane Quarterly* 13 (April): 37-50.

Rokeach, Milton
1969 "Religious Values and Social Compassion." *Review of Religious Research* 11 (Fall): 24-39.

Scherer, Ross P.
1966 "Some Statistics on Church Personnel." Ross P. Scherer and Theodore O. Wedel (eds.). In *The Church and Its Manpower Management.* New York: National Council of Churches, 45-57.

Schroeder, W. Widick
1971 "The Development of Religious Research in the United States: Retrospect and Prospect." *Review of Religious Research* 13 (Fall): 2-12.

Smith, Charles M.
1965 *How to Become Bishop Without Being Religious.* New York: Pocket Books.

Stark, Rodney and Charles Y. Glock
1968 *American Piety: The Nature of Religious Commitment.* Berkeley, Calif.: Univ. of California Press.

Trinterud, Leonard J.
1964 "The Origins of Puritanism." Sidney A. Burrell (ed.). In *The Role of Religion in Modern European History.* New York: Macmillan, 55-65. (Originally published in 1951.)

Wach, Joachim
1944 *Sociology of Religion.* Chicago, Ill.: Univ. of Chicago Press.

Weber, Max
1930 *The Protestant Ethic and the Spirit of Capitalism.* New York: Charles Scribner's Sons.
1947 *The Theory of Social and Economic Organization.* New York: Oxford Univ. Press.

Wilson, Bryan
1959 "An Analysis of Sect Development." *American Sociological Review* 24 (February): 3-15.

108

1966 "Religious Organization." In volume 13, *International Encyclopedia of the Social Sciences.* New York: Macmillan, 428-37.

Williams, George H.

1966 "The Religious Background of the Idea of a Loyal Opposition." In D.B. Robertson (ed.), *Voluntary Associations: A Study of Groups in Free Societies.* Richmond, Va.: John Knox Press, 55-89.

Williams, Preston B.

1970 "Directions in Black Religious Organization." Unpublished paper presented to Society for the Scientific Study of Religion, Chicago, Ill., December 28, 1970.

Winter, Gibson

1962 *The Suburban Captivity of the Churches.* New York: Macmillan.

1963 *The New Creation as Metropolis.* New York: Macmillan.

1968 *Religious Identity, A Study of Religious Organization.* New York: Macmillan.

Wood, James R.

1970 "Authority and Controversial Policy: The Churches and Civil Rights." *American Sociological Review* 35 (December): 1057-69.

7

Leisure Behavior and Voluntary Action

For those who do like that future, the next thing is to lean back under a tree, put your arms behind your head, wonder at the pass we've come to, smile, and remember that the beginnings and ends of man's every great enterprise are untidy.

Sebastian DeGrazia (1964, p. 416)

DeGrazia's epigrammatic statement characterizes where we're at in the present chapter of contemporary society. "The beginnings and the ends. . . are untidy." This suggests a discontinuity, a break in societal continuity. Concretely, we are at the end of the modern (industrial) society and emerging into the post-modern (post-industrial) society. Another way of characterizing such a post-modern society is to call it the "leisured society" or the "voluntary society."

The flow of sociocultural history has been characterized at many points by breaks or leaps in its continuity. Kenneth Boulding (as presented in Winthrop, 1968, p. 1) refers to these points as system breaks. Society moves according to a dominant cultural theme, which releases a profusion of symbolic forms and material characteristics in the process of adaptation to the environment. Such a proliferation of forms may generate a state of conflict between new and old features formerly taken for granted. Such a conflict may distract the system from a balanced goal-state. Such breakpoints are then characterized by a shift to a new dominant theme, which reorders the cultural process toward the goal-state. Thus, the system takes advantage of negative feedback to orient itself morphogenetically to a new system state (Buckley 1967, pp. 58-62 and passim). In the transition from an industrial to a post-industrial state the technological fact of cybernation has released human energy which enhances a movement from scientific-technical dominance to an aesthetic-ethical dominance (Bell 1970; Dumazdier 1970). This transition has ramifications for the nature of voluntary action in society, especially as it relates to leisure.

Through cybernation, the scientific-technical base has freed man from working 3,500 hours per year in 1870 to working less than 2,000 hours in 1970. In table 7-1 we can see the prospective growth in productivity and the possible uses of freed time.

The main notion which emerges from the U.S. Senate hearings on *Retirement and the Individual* (U.S. Senate, 1967, pp. 58-61) is the idea of *alternatives or options. Increasing freed time opens up a wide possibility of directions, most of which involve some kind of voluntary action.* Even though the forty hour week

109

Table 7-1
Prospective Growth in Productivity and Possible Uses of Released Time

| | Possible Increases in Real GNP (1960 dollars) | | | Alternative Uses of Potential Nonworking Time | | | Education and Training | |
| | | | | | | | | |
Year	GNP (billions)	Per Capita GNP	Total Number of Years	Retirement Age	Length of Workweek (hours)	Vacation Time (weeks)	Labor Force Retrained[1] (percent)	Years of Extended Education
1965	$ 627.2	$3,181		65 or over	40	3		
1966	655.6	3,280	2,245,542	65	39	4	2.9	1.2
1967	635.6	3,382	4,655,526	63	38	7	5.0	2.4
1968	707.1	3,490	6,910,648	61	36	7	8.7	3.4
1969	745.3	3,578	8,880,092	59	36	8	11.1	4.2
1970	779.3	3,690	11,263,301	57	34	10	13.8	5.1
1975	973.4	4,307	23,135,642	50	30	16	26.2	9.4
1980	1,250.2	5,050	35,586,729	44	25	21	37.2	13.8
1985	1,544.5	5,902	47,200,158	38	22	25	45.2	17.5

[1]Figures are in addition to the number of workers now trained in public and private programs.

Source: GNP projections and employment data from National Planning Association, Report No. 65-1, March 1965. Labor force data for other computations taken from Manpower Report of the President, March 1965, p. 248, table E-2.

This table is reproduced, with permission, from Hearing: Retirement and the Individual, U.S. Senate Special Committee on Aging, Washington, D.C., June 7-8, 1967.

remained dominant during the decade of the '60s, the expansion of the three day weekend increased. Currently, growing numbers of firms are trying the four day, forty hour week at the request of the employees themselves (Poor, 1970). Workers want the additional time off; they want it in bulk periods which give them more options. Shorter periods are significantly more limiting. This desire for longer weekends is in direct contrast to responses workers made in the late 1950s (Riesman 1958, pp. 368-369). Then they were unsure about it; they sought second jobs, or said they would, when surveyed; their wives were anxious about having the husband around the house another day; the husband feared it would be an extended, lost "honey-do" weekend. ("Honey do this, and honey do that.") The shift in attitude is dramatic. Instead of leisure being a problem in terms of what to do with it, just the opposite is true: the desire is for bulk periods of freed time, the majority of which is to be spent in leisure activities.

The new technology has expanded to social organizations. Bureaucracy is being augmented by cybernetic programing. Organizations are becoming more efficient, less dependent on human labor at many levels, and hence more impersonal. Cybernetics offers startling new forms of control. The individual senses himself increasingly manipulated and more profoundly alienated from the fruits of his labor. This new technology means that "potentially unlimited output can be achieved by systems of machines which will require little cooperation from human beings" (The Ad Hoc Committee on the Triple Revolution, 1964, p. 6). Such a productive system includes programed bureaucratic organization. Man feels "out of control," powerless, a cipher. In the face of production without human beings, unemployment and dependency upon minimal and unrelated government measures such as unemployment insurance, social security, and welfare payments are the bleak future of increasing millions. Such means "are less and less able to disguise a historic irony: that a substantial proportion of the population is subsisting on minimal incomes, often below the poverty line, at a time when sufficient productive potential is available to supply the needs of everyone in the United States" (The Ad Hoc Committee 1964, p. 6). Permanent poverty is not the only result. An environmental crisis faces the nation, the direct result of an economic system based on a technology run rampant. A ten year war in Vietnam, increasingly cybernetically programed, suggests the human subservience to technique. At least, these are the perceptions of many.

The aesthetic-ethical mutation is thus a response to the new technology and its new forms of social control (Marcuse, 1964, pp. 1-19). The scientific-technical society threatens the individual and his happiness. *The aesthetic-ethical society represents a renaissance of the individual and voluntary action, voluntary choice.* It proclaims the individual person's *right* to enjoyment, to dream, to love, to celebrate, to express himself through his body, through all forms of art. *It is an affirmation of the quality of life.* Such a mutation represents a revolt against a sense of coercion and repression, against a one-sided productivity emphasis, against outmoded taboos and an antiquated puritanism. It is also a fundamental questioning of the technique of the scientific-technical mutation. Cybernetics is a tool which is strictly amenable to the positivistic aspects of science and our world. It allows for the efficient manipulation of operationally definable concepts, numbers, and physical tasks. But it does not handle the interpretation of *meanings* of abstract symbols. Cybernetics and technology free man from the former so that he may be challenged by the latter.

Technology has created the freed time, of which leisure is the greatest component. *Leisure is the cultural model of the post-industrial society. Leisure time not only gives man freedom for psychic release but also allows him to be the agent for criticism of his own culture.* In this sense, the two mutations—scientific/technical *and* aesthetic/ethical are in conflict.

In another way they are complementary. These two mutations accelerate the elementary processes of industrial production creating at one and the same time more wealth and more free time. The increase in mass wealth and free time makes possible, indeed stimulates, the consumption of leisure on a mass scale. This is the "natural" direction for consumption to take after the basic felt needs are met, such as building a new home, buying furniture, appliances, etc. After a time *things* begin to satiate. The desire moves on to self-expression, i.e., leisure activities.

Indeed, the "leisure class" is gone. The mass consumption of leisure is a reality. According to Merrill Lynch, Pierce, Fenner & Smith (1970, p. 2), discretionary income (the amount left after buying the necessities) "increased at a compound annual rate of 7% during the 1960's . . . that indicator should grow at a faster rate during the 1970's. As a result, spending on recreation should account for a greater proportion of the total. Between 1955 and 1968, consumer spending increased from 5.5% of total personal expenditures to 6.3%." The desire to consume leisure activities means a demand for those goods and services related to leisure.

Moreover, *the technological mutation increasingly frees man from production and frees him for consumption.* The extent of this process is seen in the recent birth of the tertiary economy: Wealth is measured more in services than in goods. By 1958, more than one-half of the U.S. working force was in the tertiary sector of services. Put another way, this means less than half was in mining, agriculture, and manufacturing (Fuchs 1965, pp. 5-16). Services are there to meet the needs of *consumers*—services for the appliances and the new homes (the "necessities"), and now, expanding services for leisure. *In short, leisure is becoming more and more valued as a thing in itself; it is becoming institutionalized and legitimate on a broad scale in our society.*

A predominant feature of a tertiary economy is that it deals more in symbols than in things. Services are people related. Interaction becomes central (e.g., public relations). Social interaction is carried out through symbols. The primacy of symbols and symbol-making produces greater flexibility and malleability, an important quality of the post-industrial society. This creates, among other things, alternatives (options) in life styles translated through how income is spent, where one lives, and how one lives. (There is not only discretionary income, but discretionary time, mobility, and life style.) *The technological mutation plus the aesthetic-ethical value orientation at once make these alternatives possible and necessary, and move us toward a "voluntary society."*

Such options are the means of *individual* expressions. In industrial society "time off" or *leisure* was "used" to recuperate, to regain strength to return to the central activity, *work*. Now that the work week is forty hours or less with sometimes a three day weekend, and a year of less than 225 work days, leisure is no longer simply a time to recuperate or recover from work. *Leisure has become a means of personal expression and self-fulfillment; leisure is that time away from the obligations (if any) of family, religion, work, schooling or politics when relatively unconstrained individual choices lead to a variety of voluntary actions.* It is the setting for the aesthetic-ethical response to technology and bureaucracy. The industrial, technical, scientific world is oriented towards the rational; rationality and efficiency are the key goals of economic and governmental organization, and of all bureaucracy, by definition. Human relationships are thus ordered around these purposes. They are contractual, objectified, associational or secondary. The leisure world's orientation is one of freedom of the individual to realize himself—limited by the ethic of social responsibility—through relationships which are mutually supportive, based in whole or in large part on affect, the paradigm being the love relationship. These two views confront each other in the contemporary period.

This confrontation, revealing a sharp "systems break" or discontinuity in societal types and the emergence of new forms, has immense import for voluntarism and voluntary associations.

However, self-expression still comes generally within a social context. While we have pointed to the discontinuities in social structure that arise with the emergence of a post-industrial era, this does not imply that social organization is eclipsed by anarchy. Organization is the substance of society. Ultimately it defines the limits of individual freedom. What we are suggesting is that with the transition between major societal states, especially a transition growing out of a scientific-technological base, comes a greater latitude of organizational forms. This generates a broader freedom of choice for the individual.

We might conceive of "organization" as a property of social systems which naturally evolves to counter the entropic tendencies of the environment. Whether they automatically emerge or are planned, values, norms, collectivities, and roles limit to a permissible sub-set the larger potential set of behaviors that conceptually *could* occur by random dispersion. Specifically, *collectivities (here equated to "organizations" and encompassing "associations") are sub-systems of society which formally define goals to be achieved and specify means by which these goals are attained.* The variation of types of goals and means is limited by values and norms that compose any culture. When cultures are stable in the sense that sets of values and norms are consistent, then the forms of collectivities tend to follow a homogeneous pattern. But when a social system is undergoing basic cultural change, competing values produce an inconsistency which is reflected in a growing diversity of collective forms, as exemplified in a greater variety of voluntary associations and social movements.

The trauma of moving from industrial to post-industrial society produces changes in collective forms in relation to the notion of voluntarism. Indeed the tumultuous movement into this new society is accompanied by a clash of ontological assumptions, both normative and epistemological. The guiding force may lie in a movement from an emphasis on the *material* to the *non-material* aspects of culture, or from the quantitative to the qualitative. To reiterate what we noted above, the fact of a tertiary economy emphasizes the place of symbols per se. Cybernation provides a super-efficient procedure for articulating symbols and exercising decisions. Instantaneous communication is diminishing the size of the globe. The more that non-material factors become central to a society, the more influential is speed. Speed is a prime characteristic of the post-industrial society. A bridge is being established between the seas of east and west. Clashes between oriental and occidental assumptions about reality burst into multifarious forms of ideas. In conjunction with the breakdown of predictability—a sign of the ontological and epistemological conflict—that comes with cultural change is a desire of innovation. Innovation is itself becoming institutionalized (Bell, 1970). This is perhaps one of the reasons for the fascination with psychedelic drugs. Another reason is the concern with the inner life. How does one see within? Such speed, such fundamental clashes of ontologies suggest the differences in the current generation gap may be multiplied in the next, as suggested by the lyrics of contemporary songwriters like John Sebastian, Paul Simon, Bob Dylan, and James Taylor.

A way of illustrating the cultural clash or conflict between the industrial and post-industrial societies, between west and east, between generations, is shown in table 7-2, which outlines much of what we have said thus far. What are the implications of all of this for voluntary associations and leisure? Just what is the notion of *voluntary association* in this new context of the post-industrial, cybernetic, leisure world?

Voluntary Behavior and Voluntary Associations

Before we take up voluntary behavior and voluntary associations in relation to post-industrial society, we should look at some definitional questions.

As to *voluntary behavior* we would accept the Smith, Reddy, and Baldwin definition in chapter 10 of this volume, "That voluntary action (at the level of the individual) is primarily motivated by the expectation of psychic benefits. . .

Table 7-2
Contrasting Emphases of Industrial and Post-Industrial Society

	Industrial	Post-Industrial
Economic:	Production oriented Primary and secondary sectors predominate	Consumption oriented The tertiary sector predominates
Structure:	Bureaucracy Formal rules and relationships Centralization	Face-to-face, primary relationships Internalized norms are more important Internal searching Decentralization
Epistemology:	Empiricism	Subjectivism
Logic:	Rationalism Reason and objectivity	Dialectical, mystical Emotion and affect
Other Factors:	Delayed gratification Alienation Empirical community Age is revered West-oriented	Immediate gratification Commitment Psychic community Youth is revered East-oriented

(it) includes all behavior (whether individual or collective) that is primarily a product of commitment to values other than sheer economic benefit, self-preservation, physical force, physiological need, and psychic or social compulsion. Voluntary action may involve helping others, helping oneself, or both. In any event, voluntary action tends to include all of those activities which most serve to give meaning and satisfaction to life from the standpoint of the individual."

In this definition we can see the reason for the close association between leisure time and voluntary action. All leisure time is spent in voluntary action, but not all voluntary acts are performed during leisure time. (Note that this does not imply that people enter leisure voluntarily all of the time.) Another reason for this close association is that voluntary action is done for psychic satisfaction. This fits well the notion that increasing freed time is being spent in leisure activities (leisure time) for purposes of self-expression of the individual. Leisure is becoming the cultural setting, the basic cultural model of the post-industrial society. Not only is leisure the model, it is a component of the cultural response to the technical/scientific revolution which threatens the survival of the individual. Hence, leisure activity is done for both psychic satisfaction and psychic survival.

"Associations" (or "organizations") are traditionally viewed as membership groupings in the form of a collectivity which functions as an articulator of desired goals through specified means. There is more than one facet to the notion of a "voluntary" association. We conceive of two ways in which an association may be voluntary. The first derives from the idea of whether or not basic social values obligate a person to membership in an association. This may

116

be labeled the *requisite-voluntary* continuum of membership obligation. The second follows from the notion of responsibility for goal attainment. Is the responsibility in the hands of government or its citizenry. Thus an association may be located along an *official-voluntary* continuum of responsibility for goal-attainment. Traditionally membership in an occupational association (business firm) for example, has been perceived as requisite. If one is to receive the sustenance goods basic to his existence he must be in the work force, or is perceived as deviant as far as society's standards are concerned.

A property space of voluntarism may be constructed by crossing the two dimensions of responsibility and obligations to membership:

Responsibility

	Voluntary (Private)	Official (Public)
Voluntary		
Obligations to Membership		
Requisite		

Thus we can speak of four polar types ranging from voluntary membership in private groups to requisite membership in public organizations. (An extreme case of the most voluntary is the situation where the individual chooses to join no group but to act or withdraw on his own.) While this paradigm is presented diagramatically for heuristic purposes, it should be kept in mind that both of the dimensions are continuous variables; therefore, there are many more than four possibilities because each of the options comes in degrees.

While some voluntary associations may be labeled general purpose organizations, that is to say, they provide organized energy which may be utilized to fulfill several disparate kinds of tasks, most associations are oriented toward specific ends. Therefore, it is convenient to consider voluntary organizations in relation to the specific institutional area for which they have a primary purpose. We might thus examine the way in which our paradigm of voluntariness relates to each institutional area.

Economy

The individual in industrial society finds his occupational role occupancy primarily as requisite and usually contained in private enterprises. It is requisite in the sense that men, and increasingly women, are expected to hold a job; it is private in the sense that government is not expected to provide that job (although in many cases government may do so). In a sense this is the traditional free-enterprise myth of industrial society. Although the welfare structure provides a "cure" for extreme cases of chronic joblessness, the recipient is still perceived as deviant and the system itself is probably perceived by the public as a temporary response to crises such as depressions and recessions. The current administration's welfare solution is aimed at requiring that a man work. Furthermore, the government still works largely on a private contract system for producing public goods. Relatively few enterprises are publicly owned, although the number has been growing with the expansion of government at all levels, especially the federal level.

Referring back to our discussion of the scientific-technical base for both advanced industrial society and the emerging post-industrial society, we note that the requisite nature of work is diminishing as the possibility of a guaranteed annual income increases, as the role of government in providing goods and services expands, and as the interchangeability of men and women in work roles increases. *The stigma of non-work, we suggest, will decrease under these new conditions.*

Moreover, with the cultural clash of the transition comes the questioning of the meaning of work. We find especially in youth the feeling that if the job is not meaningful, then there is very little impetus for taking it on. This is supported by recent surveys conducted by the Columbia Broadcasting System (1969), *Fortune* magazine (1969), and a Harris Poll (1970) for *Life* magazine. It might be suggested that the movement to "cooperative artisan communes" is less an *escape* on the part of youth, than it is a *search* for meaningful occupational commitment. Whereas jobs in industrial society have been protected by membership in labor and professional associations, the importance of occupational associations may be declining relative to other types of organizations in transitional society (Harp and Gagan 1966, p. 39) and replaced by an individual's assessment of whether or not doing "his own thing" is where he wants to be.

Two new and disparate patterns of economic association thus seem to be emerging in the transition to post-industrial society. One is the surfacing of *an awareness that there may be a public responsibility for the provision of sustenance (minimum annual income)*. The other is *the emergence among youth of the notion that it is one's own responsibility to decide what kind of job he will hold, if any. In either case there appears to be a movement away from the notion of occupational role occupancy as a requisite to more of a voluntary option*. But a central question for future post-industrial society still remains.

This is with regard to the private-public dimension. Will the responsibility for providing work be fulfilled more and more by public organizations, or by private associations, by activity groupings (such as communes), or by individuals alone? Or will a dualism of both remain in operation?

It appears at this point that, if one form is to gain ascendency over another, it will be that form which is most conducive to establishing or maintaining individual commitment to action. We have suggested above that alienation appears to be one dysfunctional product of the technical age. The emergence of alternative institutional activity groupings may be a feedback mechanism which will rechannel individual commitment of energy in the post-industrial era. A growing popularity of work in the context of voluntary associations of the social change and social service variety is one of many emerging trends here.

Family

In an attempt to arrive at a definition of the family, Zelditch (1964, p. 680) has pointed out that there appear to be no necessary properties which hold universally. He suggests that four traits do often cluster: provision of sexual access, legitimation of reproduction, responsibility for child-rearing, and acting as a unit of consumption. The family is a system into which a great deal of value has apparently been infused. It is thus one of the basic institutions of society and we choose to examine its scope in relation to voluntarism for that reason.

In industrial society, the family is a highly private and requisite system. Although extramarital promiscuity, illegitimate children, foster parentage, and failure to provide for family members may be as old as man, we suspect in an industrial society all of these are perceived as deviant acts outside of family membership. Thus, except for consumption in industrial society, it is requisite to be in a family in order to achieve the first three goals Zelditch outlined. Furthermore, the decision to take responsibility for attaining these goals has been a strictly *private* one. In addition to this, the satisfaction of the intrinsic love relationship between people has been paradigmatically a function of the family.

However, it appears many of these functions are becoming extra-familial in the transitional period. Rollo May (1969, chaps. 2 and 3) in his provocative and sensitive study of the contemporary nature of *love* and *will*, notes the sickening of *eros* through making the love relationship one that is based on the technique of "love-making," in other words, seeing the other individual as a thing, an *object* to be used and manipulated. This objectification appears in some way to be a product of late industrial society and could well be one reason for the change in family form as seen in serial polygamy (cf., Becker, 1968; Laing, 1969).

New forms of the family are developing in this transitional period. Primarily such examples as trial marriage, living together, and cooperative living (communes) seem to be a skeptical response to the proposition that contractual, legal bonds are sufficient to make a relationship. An assumption of the transitional period is that the *meaning* of sex, childbearing, and child-rearing derives from love.

Therefore it appears in the transitional period, while the family functions remain a private responsibility, membership in the traditional family is becoming less requisite and more voluntary. Divorce is increasingly prevalent and less stigmatizing. New forms of marriage and family relationships are being explored, pointing to both the transitional nature of the current situation and the existence of alternatives.

In post-industrial society we would expect that norms governing voluntary family membership may become even stronger. On the other hand, concerning the private-public dimension, two extremes appear to be equally likely: although we see intrinsic relationships essentially a private phenomenon, the distinct possibility of a global population crisis could mean adoption of public responsibility for determination of family life patterns (Ehrlich and Holdren, 1971, p. 56).

Education

The central tasks of education as an institution are those of socialization, training, and providing a buffer for the labor force. Youth membership in educational institutions has been required by law, and the fulfillment of educational functions have primarily been a public responsibility.

In pre-industrial society a person moved directly from childhood to adulthood. Education was the responsibility of the extended family-kinship-village system. Industrial society required training in totally different kinds of skills, which meant the development of formal education outside the family-kinship-village complex. Thus, the period of preparation for adulthood was dramatically extended, creating the stage of development we call adolescence. Advanced industrial society and the transitional type require even more sophisticated training. The period of education is once again extended, creating what Kenneth Keniston calls "youth," a separate stage of development towards adulthood. We suggest this last stage will become more widespread, extending to more and more strata of young persons. *Thus through the late industrial period educational associations (elementary and even secondary schools) have not been voluntary in either sense, to wit: they are both requisite and public.* However, as we are suggesting in Roszak's words (1969, p. 28), "Youth is becoming a long-term career," and the young are seeking a freedom to decide just how that career is to be structured. In fact, the Black Panthers recently held a liberation day to attempt to free children from their "classroom prisons." The *New Schools Exchange Newsletter* (n.d.) documents many locations of free schools, associations which are both private and voluntary.

As a case in point, the life style of youth appears to be pursuing the notion of freedom beyond the idea of educational associational membership and towards a rebirth of individualism. "You decide what you want to learn, what your curriculum is to be. You define the meaning of your education in terms of how well you can apply it in *praxis* in the community. You stay in, not because you are a member denoted by a registration, but only as long as you feel you are doing something which is meaningful." It is a personal definition of role and extremely non-organizational in a sociological sense. Given that organization is seen as a more efficient way to adapt to one's environment, one might ask whether or not this *non-associational* life style will have the power to maintain itself, once post-industrial society has settled in. *Will educational organization membership continue to be more voluntary and private in the future, or will the force of bureaucratic organization cause it to rigidify along requisite and public lines?*

Religion

The American traditions of separation of church and state and of religious pluralism make church group membership a private and moderately voluntary activity. The 1950s saw a curious revival of *interest* in religion. "Interest," Martin E. Marty (1958, p. 10) suggests, "is a rather limp and non-commital word to be using about discussion of ultimates. It carries overtones of self-advantage and self-concern more than other-advantage and God-concern. It need imply little more than curiosity." This interest tended to move religious associations somewhat toward the requisite end of the scale, or about in the middle of the voluntary-requisite continuum. It was almost un-American not to believe in God and not to proclaim membership in a church. Church sponsored associations proliferated in the United States during the 1950s and early 1960s. However, the nature of those religious associations—even church membership itself—was primarily social or expressive. Will Herberg (1960) characterized American religion and related associations as celebrating "the American way of life." Religion seemed to lack its historical concern with ultimate meaning. Churches were hard to distinguish from country clubs; likewise, associations like a men's club showed little distinctiveness from Kiwanis or Rotary groups. This lack of specificity, focus, and involvement in the profound existential questions of human life began to show up in the statistics on church attendance and the attitudes of Americans about the influence of religion.

Other factors which may have influenced this decline in organized religion are (1) the scientific-technological component which gives a legitimation to atheism, and (2) the growing understanding of the workings of the natural world making it less important to seek theological explanations or rely on a transcendental faith.

Whatever the causes, the decline in support of organized religion is apparent and, consequently, there is a concomitant decrease in the requisite aspect of religious voluntary associations (churches). Hadden (1970, pp. 25ff.) cites figures from national polls that show average church attendance to have declined by about 5 percent in the period 1955-66. More strikingly, 43 percent more people viewed religion as losing its influence on American life in 1967 than in 1957. This view of the declining importance of religion was 10 percent more frequent among youth 21-29 years old than among people 50 and over, and was 8 percent more frequent among college educated people than among people with only a grade school education.

Transitional society reveals the startling increase in non-requisite cultic, mystical (based often on eastern religions), and magical religious groups, or perhaps more accurately, voluntary associations. The very existence of these groups and their widespread character suggest the transitional nature of the contemporary era. Also, the experimentation with different types of religious experience brought on by the meeting of east and west—hence, the clash of ontologies—is still another indicator of a period of transition. Probing deeper, organized religion has tended to adapt itself to the ascendency of science by placing emphasis on the social function of the church over the theological function (Troeltsch 1931). The cultural clash brought on by the confrontation of the scientific-technological and aesthetic-ethical mutations raises serious questions about whether science really has all the answers. The terrifying social problems which advanced industrial society has produced also raise serious agonizing doubts. Will this lead to a return to mysticism in post-industrial society?

These emerging mystical cults are sectarian and, hence, more voluntary and private in nature. However, they will probably tend towards a more organized, church type over time, thus becoming more requisite and ascriptive by birth rather than a matter of individual voluntary choice. Some of these new religious associations seem to be the vanguard for introducing the structure, ideas, and ritual of eastern religions into American society, while other new religious associations move away from transcendental, mystical concerns, placing an emphasis on social ethics and social action.

Even more interesting, from the standpoint of voluntary action, is the formation of groups with a very loose and open concept of membership, or no membership concept at all. If such groups grow in prevalence, religious commitment may well become more personal and less social, perhaps supporting Alfred North Whitehead's definition that "religion is what a person does in his solitariness."

Polity

The primary political organizations of industrial society are the various levels of government, most notably the national government. Such organizations are public and largely requisite in industrial society. They are requisite in the sense that various levels of government insist on their control over those individuals and groups that fall within their jurisdictions. Conscription of youth into the armed forces and enforced payment of taxes of various kinds are only two examples of many that could be given.

In the transitional period toward a post-industrial society, governments are being increasingly resisted. Both individuals and groups are challenging the fundamental right of governments to conscript and to tax at will for purposes selected by a small elite (however selected). *More and more people are pushing for a view of the individual's relation to government that emphasizes voluntary choice by the individual of where and on what terms he will deal with, or submit to, government laws, rules and regulations.* Finding the appropriate middle ground between totalitarianism/Big Brother on the one hand, and total anarchy, on the other, is a challenge now faced increasingly by governments as never before.

Another important type of political organization in industrial society is the voluntary-private association such as the political party or political interest group or club. It is the individual's *private* responsibility to join those political pressure and interest groups that best represent him, and to work for or against those candidates or pieces of legislation that are selected *for* him. However, growing dissatisfaction with the nature of the selection process for both laws and candidates has led to increasing withdrawal of many people in our transitional society, especially youth, from the traditional political process.

The transitional period seems to be leading to a situation in which both voluntary and requisite aspects are merging. On the one hand political associations seem to be becoming more voluntary, as the SDS illustrates with its emphasis on non-organizational, individual responsibility. On the other hand, the radical left seems to underscore the requisite quality of political involvement with its familiar slogan, "If you're not *part* of the solution, you're part of the problem."

Again, the voluntary aspect is reasserted in the *Yippie* stress on non-membership and a parallel affirmation of life style as the most important emphasis. Some segments of the youth culture propound anarchy as the solution which is a radical profession of voluntariness.

At the other extreme are black separatists who demand involvement on the part of black people, making their associations highly requisite in nature.

The voluntary side is reaffirmed in the purposive rebellion on the part of some groups among the young who see *doing* more important than *belonging*. However, they follow by contending that if one doesn't do *something*, he's being irresponsible; therefore, activity is becoming requisite, even if belonging is not.

In post-industrial society we can only ask some leading questions. Will political life and political parties be under greater public control with membership required? Will public control of the party mechanisms obtain and membership be allotted only to a privileged group? Or will there be a free-flowing voluntary-private polity operating which is based on responsibility and meaningful action? As bulk leisure time increases, will there be a waning in political interest on the part of the citizenry? Recent data from the Soviet Union and France suggest this is the case (Strumilin, 1961). What does this portend for democratic polity? Is direct, informal political influence and pressure becoming more important? Are television and street politics changing the democratic pluralism so long considered a basic attribute of American politics? Are the masses increasingly subject to totalitarianism as voluntary associations become manipulated by those in political and economic power? (Mills, 1956; Kornhauser, 1959; Litwak, 1961; Dye and Zeigler, 1970).

Leisure

We have noted above many aspects of this institutional pattern. We would make some additional observations. First, in industrial society we note the existence of many expressive hobby groups, recreational associations, social clubs, etc. This indicates that man still does not wish to stand alone even in his leisure. David Reisman, et al. (1953) in *The Lonely Crowd* and William H. Whyte (1957) in *The Organization Man* give perceptive descriptions of advanced industrialized man. Freed bulk time was a problem to many in the 1950s. The four day forty hour week was tried out then and both husbands and wives were uneasy with such blocks of freed time on their hands, as noted earlier. Though a wide choice of options for the use of freed time was being rapidly developed, there was lacking the basic orientation and value structure to accept leisure activity as normal, expected behavior rather than deviant. It simply took time to get adjusted to this new reality of larger and larger blocks of freed time. The trend over the past twenty years has been to use that freed time for leisure (see United States Senate, 1967). Such time is becoming increasingly more valuable than money in the eyes of workers and professional people. There is a limit to the uses of money (e.g., what it's worth if there is no time to enjoy one's wealth through psychically and physically enjoyable activity?). Hence, unions, for example, have often placed as much emphasis on negotiating for more freed time as on more economic benefits. The 1970 round of negotiations between the automobile workers (UAW) and the companies hinged on arrangements for early retirement with full benefits. Likewise, negotiations are underway at this writing between Chrysler Corporation and the UAW to institute some form of the four day, forty hour week.

The transitional society shows a return to the family for leisure expression, such as in TV viewing and all aspects of tourism, camping, etc. Loose associational membership groupings abound serving those who seek the open road (e.g., Airstream Trailer owners, American Automobile Association (AAA), and travel clubs). Tourism is the single biggest industry on a worldwide scale.

The transitional society comes into sharpest focus among youth. They seek ways to express themselves as individuals. Rock festivals provide such an outlet. They underline private freedom, non-membership, open groups, and extremely tolerant life styles. Daniel Bell (1970, p. 20) notes how widespread this movement is in that it makes little difference what one's socioeconomic background happens to be. The "counter-culture" is being recruited from every stratum. The life style of this "counter-culture" values non-conflict, but whether this will last over time is a crucial question. To wit: the outside threat to such a way of life may be too much, as happened at Altamont, California, when the Hells' Angels went on the rampage at a Rolling Stones Concert and killed one of the spectators.

What seems to be suggested for post-industrial society from these trends in leisure patterns, coupled with the intensifying environmental crisis, and the growth of centralized power and bureaucracy, is for leisure to move further down the requisite scale as freed bulk time becomes more and more a reality. *Man will increasingly work to have time for leisure as self-development and self-fulfillment and not the reverse of using leisure simply for recuperation to go back to work.* Also, increased interdependency, brought on by population density and the systematic destruction of land, water, and air, will mean that *the public sector must enter more fully into protecting the consumers of leisure.* More control and more planning seem to be imperatives. Hence, the interdependency of all institutions is entering a new chapter where a new form of social and political order is emerging to meet the demands of post-industrial society. What that new order is we can only conjecture. A continuing study and analysis of voluntary action and voluntary associations is one way of determining what the shape of the future order will be.

References

Becker, Ernest
1968 *The Structure of Evil.* New York: George Braziller.
Bell, Daniel
1970 "The Cultural Contradictions of Capitalism." *The Public Interest* 21 (Fall): 16-43.
Buckley, Walter
1967 *Sociology and Modern Systems Theory.* Englewood Cliffs, New Jersey: Prentice Hall.
Columbia Broadcasting System
1969 *Generations Apart*: A Study of the Generation Gap. Conducted for CBS News by Daniel Yankelovitch, Inc.
DeGrazia, Sebastian
1964 *Of Time, Work and Leisure.* New York: Anchor Books.

Dumazedier, Joffre
1970 "Post Industrial Society." Unpublished manuscript.
Dye, Thomas R., and Harmon Zeigler
1970 *The Irony of Democracy*. Belmont, California: Wadsworth Publishing Co.
Ehrlich, Paul, and John Holdren
1970 "Avoiding the Problem." *Saturday Review*. 54 (March 6): 56.
Fuchs, Victor
1965 "Some Implications of the Growing Importance of the Service Industries." *The Task of Economics*. Forty-fifth Annual Report of National Bureau of Economic Research. New York, New York.
Fortune
1969 January, vol. 79 (see especially pp. 180-81).
Hadden, Jeffrey
1970 *The Gathering Storm in the Churches*. New York: Anchor Doubleday.
Harp, John, and Richard Gagan
1966 "Voluntary Organizations in Small Communities of New York State: A Preliminary Report." Ithaca, New York: Cornell University Press.
Harris, Louis and Associates, Inc.
1970 "Youth Attitudes" for Life Magazine. Unpublished.
Herberg, Will
1960 *Protestant, Catholic, Jew*. New York: Anchor Doubleday.
Kornhauser, William
1959 *The Politics of Mass Society*. New York: The Free Press of Glencoe.
Laing, R.D.
1969 *The Self and Others*. New York: Random House.
Litwak, Eugene
1961 "Voluntary Associations and Neighborhood Cohesion." *American Sociological Review* 26 (April): 258-71.
Marcuse, Herbert
1964 *One Dimensional Man*. Boston: Beacon Press.
Marty, Martin
1958 *The New Shape of American Religion*. New York: Harper Row.
May, Rollo
1969 *Love and Will*. New York: W.W.,Norton & Company, Inc.
McLuhan, Marshall
1964 *Understanding Media*. New York: Signet Books.
Merrill Lynch, Pierce, Fenner & Smith, Inc.
1970 "A Look at the Leisuretime Industry." New York: Merrill Lynch, Pierce, Fenner & Smith, Inc. Brochure.
Mills, C. Wright
1956 *The Power Elite*. New York: Oxford University Press.
New Schools Exchange Newsletter. 2840 Hidden Valley Lane, Santa Barbara,
n.d. California, 93103.

Poor, Riva
1970 *4 Days, 40 Hours*. Cambridge, Massachusetts: Bursk & Poor Publishing.
Riesman, David
1958 "Leisure and Work in Post-Industrial Society." In Eric Larrabee (ed.), *Mass Leisure*. Glencoe, Illinois: The Free Press, 363-85.
Riesman, David, Nathan Glazer, and Reuel Denney
1953 *The Lonely Crowd*. New York: Anchor Doubleday.
Roszak, Theodore
1969 *The Making of a Counter Culture*. Garden City, New York: Anchor, Doubleday.
Strumilin, S.G.
1961 *Problemy Socialisma: Kommunizma USSR* (Problems of Socialism and Communism in USSR). Moscow.
The Ad Hoc Committee on the Triple Revolution
1964 *The Triple Revolution*. Santa Barbara, California: Printed by the Committee.
Troeltsch, Ernst
1931 *The Social Teachings of the Christian Churches*. London: Allen and Unwin.
United States Senate
1967 *Retirement and the Individual, Hearings by the Subcommittee of the Special Committee on Aging*. 90th Congress, 1st Session, Part 1, June 7-8.
Whyte, William H.
1957 *The Organization Man*. New York: Anchor Doubleday.
Winthrop, Henry
1968 *Ventures in Social Interpretation*. New York: Appleton-Century-Crofts.
Zelditch, Morris
1964 "Family, Marriage, and Kinship." In R.E.L. Faris (ed.), *Handbook of Modern Sociology*. Chicago: Rand McNally, 680-733.

8

Social Change and Voluntary Action

ATHENA THEODORE

This chapter addresses itself to the following two points. First, is voluntary action distinctly different from other kinds of social behavior? Second, if it is, how can it be defined and empirically examined within some unifying theoretical framework? Bode (in chapter 4 of this volume), Palisi (1968, also, chapter 3 of this volume), and Smith, et al. (in chapter 10 of this volume) have discussed these points. We would like to present here an alternative perspective.

Voluntary action would be unique behavior only insofar as it could be distinguished from other kinds of social behavior. If such a distinction cannot meaningfully be made, there is no point in using the term "voluntary action."

There are five distinctive features of some kinds of social behavior that should lead such behavior to be included in a special category called voluntary action:

1. Voluntary action involves non-coercive participation;
2. Voluntary action is non-remunerative;
3. Voluntary action is organized activity performed collectively;
4. Voluntary action is temporary or, at most, semi-permanent;
5. Voluntary action consists of rational, purposive action oriented toward effecting (or controlling) social change.

It is suggested that the concept of voluntary action as a general sub-category of social behavior has utility only insofar as *all* the foregoing features are included in its definition. By the same token, other aspects which have been included in various other definitions should be excluded. In combination, the five features identify a normative and highly institutionalized pattern of social behavior in our society, clearly distinguishable from other patterns of social behavior. What is especially to be emphasized is that *voluntary action is synonymous with organized structures for, or related to, social change. In a sense, it is the embodiment of social change.* Viewing voluntary action within the framework of social change may eliminate some of the definitional difficulties of this phenomenon (Rose, 1969).

Voluntary Action and Social Change

How can we support the view that voluntary action should be defined as organized structures for social change?

127

First of all, change itself has been institutionalized in the Western world from the eighteenth century onward. Thus, although technical innovations have occurred haphazardly in all societies, in the West such changes have been deliberately sought and institutionalized. Underlying technology is science, with its philosophy and ideology of progress and humanitarianism. Change-agent roles have been structured around change: the research engineer, for example, has the specific task of constantly seeking ways to improve existing commodities or invent new products so that social relationships in the productive system can never become traditionally stabilized.

Secondly, change is the very essence of a democracy. In free societies, all citizens of legal age can vote to change whatever they consider to be undesirable about the system. Voting behavior is thus an important type of voluntary action, not only because it has the greatest potential for change by generating and distributing power in the society but also because it is shared by the greatest number of citizens and because it can produce immediate changes. However, all societies, even those which are pre-literate, have some amount of voluntary action. The totalitarian society, however, can never have more than a minimal amount of voluntary action because change is controlled by the state.

A closer look at the distinctive meaning and functions of voluntary action reveals that the dimension of social change is central to this concept and should be included in its definition. Two aspects of social change may be distinguished in voluntary action: one effecting social change; the other controlling social change.

1. *Voluntary Action as Effecting Social Change*

In a complex, urbanized, and highly industrial society such as ours, the existing social structures and social institutions may become too rigid or too weak to provide for urgent social needs which arise. *Voluntary action constitutes an important first step toward getting something done in a society.* It may do nothing more than start the ball rolling, so to speak, thus providing a launching pad for needed action in some direction, be it social, economic, or political. Voluntary action quickens the social processes needed to introduce the necessary societal changes, thus closing the gap between science and its awesome social consequences. Thus, *voluntary action is temporary.* It is inconsequential as to whether or not the goals are *fully* achieved; what matters is that voluntary action provides the initial collective impetus for change. Definitions which emphasize the goals themselves as the ends of action fail to consider this temporary dimension of voluntarism. In addition, the means used to effect change may vary, the means to be used may be unknown, and specific goals may also change. Political action comprises the most powerful sources of social change when its outcome is expected to change laws. Examples to be included under this aspect of social change are all kinds of change-oriented pressure groups and social improvement or social reform groups.

2. *Voluntary Action as Controlling Social Change*

On the other hand, when social change occurs too fast for the existing institutions to cope with it, voluntary action may function as a measure of social control. It is often a countermeasure which checks or delays the change or helps to cushion the impact of the change on the society's members. Thus, it may be the effective force in protecting and stabilizing the society by minimizing both personal and social disorganization, hence preventing undue disruption. It may also be the force preventing the extinction of the society. Voluntary action thus performs an important psychological function by allaying much of the emotional insecurity and alienation to be found in the impersonal, mass society. Examples here include conservative political groups, fraternal and ethnic groups, and mutual aid groups. Some groups, such as fraternal organizations and labor unions, may be classified under *both* aspects of social change.

These two aspects of voluntary behavior, viewed within a dynamic framework of change and counterchange, necessarily include some kinds of behavior not already mentioned and exclude others. Altruistic behavior is one important general type of social behavior to be included as worthy of mention, especially because of its institutionalization in the stereotyped volunteer role. However, many forms of non-altruistic behavior are *also* included under the present definition. What is clearly not included as voluntary action are such actions as fraternity hazing, picking up hitchhikers, shoplifting, listening to records, and drinking beer with friends.

When does the social behavior classed as voluntary cease being voluntary? In at least four instances: (1) when the voluntary group disintegrates through lack of commitment, leadership, etc., (2) when the changes sought by voluntary action are achieved, (3) when the undesirable or threatening situations are brought under control by voluntary action, or (4) when the action initiated by the voluntary effort becomes institutionalized through work organizations, professional associations, government sponsorship, the legal system, or even custom. For example, the National Foundation for Infantile Paralysis was forced to turn to other diseases to conquer in order to justify its existence after the discovery of the successful polio vaccine. Peace groups may disappear overnight as wars come to an end, and conservative political groups may lower their voices as the radical or liberal political groups lower theirs. Finally, when missionary roles in foreign lands become institutionalized through such government-sponsored programs as the Peace Corps, joining the Peace Corps can no longer be classified as voluntary action, although a quasi-voluntary designation might be appropriate in such a case. Monetary remuneration—even the most minimal reward or subsidization of expenses—comprises an important stage in the institutionalization process. How, for example, would the Peace Corps be designated if young males (and females) in the foreseeable future were compelled to select *either* military service *or* the Peace Corps as service to their country?

Voluntary Action as Collective Action

The fact that the proposed definition identifies voluntary action as change-oriented action in a collective structural form and not as an individual enterprise does not mean that the individual is unimportant or even unnecessary for this action to take place. The decision-making process begins at the individual level, a fact which explains why the role of the volunteer is highly institutionalized. However, in the realistic situation of the complex modern society, only rarely does the individual by himself have the power to effect change. Thus, although contributing money, goods, or services to some "cause" or social movement may be defined as voluntary action, it is only because people contribute these things in unison that any clearly observable change can take place. Social change in a modern society can be effected only through the joint effort of individuals.

Psychic Benefits

It has already been indicated that voluntary action performs functions for the individual as well as for the social system. Some of the difficulties encountered in defining voluntary behavior solely at the level of personality have been suggested by Smith, et al. (in chapter 10 of this volume), even though the expectation of psychic benefits is central to their definition. The most important argument against an explanation of all voluntary behavior within this framework is that individuals are always seeking psychic benefits, if for no other reason than because this is one important way in which the personality system can remain integrated. Personal meaning to life is gained not only by voluntary action but also by other experiences such as religion and through primary group relationships. Thus, by themselves, psychic benefits do not distinguish voluntary behavior from other kinds of behavior and the expectation of psychic benefits cannot constitute the sole criterion for defining such behavior. In addition, the fact that individuals will derive one kind of psychic benefit one day and another kind the next places psychic benefits on rather shaky ground as the basis for a definition of voluntary action.

However, social change may be sought for the express purpose of realizing psychic benefits. As the other side of the coin which defines voluntary action as seeking change, the social control may mean nothing more than the prevention of personality disorganization under conditions of anomie. Where primary groups are weak or non-existent, as often occurs in the urban situation with its mobile population and exaggerated self-interest, emotional support and personal security are often gained through the opportunities for social interaction afforded by the voluntary organization. Moreover, this support helps to reduce behavioral difficulties. Such groups as fraternal and ethnic organizations and mutual aid societies have already been mentioned; church fellowships also clearly belong to this category. Social clubs organized for the sheer purpose of fun, relaxation, and physical exercise do not fall within the scope of voluntary action unless they also serve as pressure groups or provide significant emotional and social support. However, even those groups whose expressed purposes are nonvoluntary (i.e., not oriented toward initiating or controlling social change) may at some time activate a voluntary enterprise or activity in some change-oriented direction. The term "leisure-time behavior," which implies that relaxation and other expressive and psychic benefits are being sought, can also conceivably include change-oriented action.

Formal Voluntary Organizations and Voluntary Action

Considerable attention has been given in the voluntary action literature to the nature and types of voluntary organizations and their size and membership. The concept of voluntary association, which appears to have the longest history of definitional acceptance, has been discussed by Bode (chapter 4 of this volume) and Palisi (1968, also, chapter 3 of this volume) as needing much explication to be scientifically precise and useful. I would agree, but for different reasons.

Emphasis on the organization (or association) itself fails to take into consideration the fact that the older voluntary organization loses its voluntary character as it becomes bureaucratized and institutionalized, either through more and more remunerative positions, through government sponsorship, or through greater social acceptance and implementation of its objectives in custom or in law. Voluntary action itself never becomes stabilized in an organizational context: its own institutionalization takes place only as it occurs outside the existing institutional structure of the society. But in its temporary state, it assumes an identity in some organized and rules-centered arrangement since some degree of coordination and administration of the voluntary effort is needed.

There is yet another reason for excluding the voluntary organization itself as necessary to the definition of voluntary action. In a rapidly changing society, voluntary action frequently occurs on the reference group level, where a high degree of isolated, yet predictable, collective conduct is possible. Sociologically, the reference group goes beyond any participation group: it is formed by the impact of the mass media—books, newspapers, magazines, and especially radio and television. It represents the individual looking out into an ever-widening, increasingly complex and mobile social universe needing urgent social changes.

To view voluntary action only in terms of participation in primary groups or in formal organizations is to overlook the fact that people do not always act in actual spatial clusters of primary groups or as functionaries of formal organizations: they act according to their own self-identification in relation to the world outside their immediate social system. Thus, some forms of mass behavior (referred to as "collective" behavior by social psychologists) are clearly to be included in the definition of voluntary action as, for example, mass demonstrations and activist groups with their demands for instant change. Both types of groups have been appearing with increasing frequency in present day social movements. In particular, the proliferation of the smaller, spontaneous, and sometimes leaderless type of voluntary action indicate a degree of flexibility and efficiency not present in the more formalized groups. *Perhaps if there were to be any "pure" type of volunteer organization, it would consist of this more loosely structured voluntary group.* Its significance for our purposes, however, is that it illustrates the necessity of attributing less importance to the organizational structure than has been the practice in the past.

The problem with using the organization (or association) as the basis of any definition is that *the organization itself is not the crucial element in voluntary action.* As already indicated, *what is important is the collective effort to get something done which needs doing and to which no one else is attending.* At most, those definitions which focus on the organization itself and its membership do nothing more than classify the voluntary organization in question as one sub-type of formal organization, necessitating an explanation for this distinction on the basis of remuneration versus non-remuneration (or part-remuneration), private versus public control, and different goals or orientation to goals—distinctions which must then be subjected to an infinite variety of exceptions.

Preoccupation with the formal voluntary organization or voluntary association and with the instrumental-expressive differentiation, on the one hand, and the notion of "joining" or "belonging" to this organization or association, on the other, serves only to add to the confusion as to what should or should not be included in a definition of voluntary action. The age of the organization, the size of its membership, and the number of remunerated or party remunerated positions all reflect the degree of institutionalization of the organization as it moves toward the fruition of its stated goals.

I submit that viewing voluntary action within a theoretical framework of social change establishes the foundation for a systematic study of this phenomenon. Exactly how one would proceed to conduct empirical studies and which studies should be made lies outside the scope of this paper. However, sociologists have been giving increasingly greater attention to the phenomenon of social change. Although known theories of social change have yet to measure such change in terms of the voluntary participation of the society's members, there is no reason to believe that this would constitute an insurmountable task. A typology such as that suggested by Smith, et al. (chapter 10 of this volume) certainly is one step in the right direction. A great deal of research has already been done on voluntary action: what is needed is to draw together all this research under a unifying theoretical scheme. The definition proposed here is sociological and offers such a unifying theoretical framework "without becoming so detailed, vague, or abstract as to preclude its effective operationalization" (Bode, p. 63 of this volume). In addition, this definition, because it views voluntary action in terms of social change, should have greater application to the various social agencies which are presently pressing for important social, economic, and political changes both for the benefit of their respective communities and for the nation at large.

Finally, the point must be made that we may expect to see a marked increase in the degree of voluntary participation, not only in our own society, but elsewhere. While the world continues to shrink and the social consciousness increases, we are joined by other nations as we face the threat of nuclear power, pollution of the environment, overpopulation, manipulation of life processes, and, in general, severe social imbalances caused by rapid technological change. The many social changes and counterchanges which will take place in the future will require an even greater voluntary effort than in the past. The disadvantaged classes already have begun to embrace the voluntary way as the new activists, and other patterns in voluntary action are emerging in terms of the sex and age composition of the population. In developed democratic societies where the voluntary groups mediate between the primary groups and the overall organization of the society, they can exercise a degree of social control not present in any other type of society. It is not inconceivable that the "active society" which Etzioni (1968) describes in terms of responsiveness to its changing membership and engagement in perpetual self-transformation may develop at least in part because of the voluntary effort of its citizens. It would be a tragedy indeed if the social scientist were not at least prepared to study this transformation for lack of a suitable definition!

References

Etzioni, Amitai
1968 *The Active Society: A Theory of Societal and Political Processes.* New York: The Free Press.
Gordon, Wayne C., and Babchuk, Nicholas
1959 "A Typology of Voluntary Organizations." *American Sociological Review* 24: 22-29.
Palisi, Bartolomeo J.
1968 "A Critical Analysis of the Voluntary Association Concept." *Sociology and Social Research* 52: 392-405. Included as chapter 3 in the present volume.

Rose, Arnold
1969 *Sociology: The Study of Human Relations*. New York: Alfred A. Knopf.

Trade Unions, Peasant Movements, and Social Movements as Voluntary Action

Henry A. Landsberger

Definition and Sociological Significance of Working-class and Peasant Movements

The vantage point of this chapter is in the first instance that of interest in a phenomenon other than "voluntary action" in the abstract. Our interest is in *the movements and organizations of peasants and industrial workers regardless, so to speak, of whether these do or do not meet the definition of voluntary action agreed upon by others!* Our conceptual interest is particularly in the field of *group mobility through collective action.*

Nevertheless, the scientific bond between the editors and myself is substantial. They are interested in discovering the kinds of problems raised when the attempt is made to apply to a specific kind of act, group or organization such as those of interest to us, the definitions they propose for phenomena such as "voluntary action," and "voluntary" or "volunteer organizations." From my side, the bond is based on the fact that the issues raised by Smith, Reddy, and Baldwin as well as by Bode and Palisi are of great importance in this particular field even though they are by no means the only important ones. For example, the differentiation between "economic" as distinct from "psychic" benefits which is central to the editors' thinking and the issue of the degree of "free will," "coercion," and "voluntarism" in joining groups and organizations which they discuss at length—both issues are critical to an understanding of the movements of industrial workers, of peasants, and of other similarly placed categories of persons. In this chapter the first of two related ones, we shall focus chiefly on the level of the individual and of the internal structure of these movements in exploring the problems and issues raised by Smith and his colleagues. In a chapter of Volume Two of the present series, we shall focus more on the relation of the organization to its environment.

Our interest in working class and peasant movements stems from the fact that these groups occupy (perhaps in the case of the industrial working classes in the developed countries, it would be better to say that they once *did* occupy) a position toward the bottom of any and all status dimensions one might wish to apply: material well-being, political and economic power, access to education, prestige, etc. Individuals belonging to these categories have often reacted *collectively* to their depressed status. That is, they have had *similar* reactions, *influ-*

135

enced (consciously or otherwise) by the reactions of others who are in the same situation (Landsberger, 1969, p. 8).

This is a broad definition. It includes not only formally organized, goal-oriented -trade unions and peasant organizations, but also, and even, individual migration insofar as it is influenced by the recognition of general, not just personal, misery; by the recognition of shared grievances; and by the awareness at some level that others, too, are migrating. This was the situation in the case of Russian peasant migrations in the nineteenth century and the three preceding centuries.

The concept of "movements of low status persons" includes also expressive reactions such as escapist *religious* movements, provided that, and only *to the extent that*, the analyst sees them as being a reaction to low status. (We will discuss below our preference for "more-or-less" measurement as against "either-or" categorization.) Expressive movements are included even if the movement neither will nor is intended to be instrumental in altering the low status of its participants, as was the case—disputed, admittedly—of working-class non-conformism in England (Thompson, 1964). The concept therefore includes both expressive movements of a hostile kind, like the French *jacqueries* of the fourteenth century, and instrumentally-oriented movements. It includes also movements which contain an anti-colonialist, and nationalist, or even a religious "Holy War" element, provided only that hostility toward foreigners or infidels is partly attributable to their being high status and not merely to their being infidels or foreigners as such. The militancy and ultimate triumph of the peasantry under Mao and Tito have been analyzed from this point of view (Johnson, 1962). In both cases, a nationalist element served to reinforce, in complicated ways, the struggle to elevate status. But a purely nationalist or religious movement is *not* defined by us as a peasant movement merely because peasants are involved.

The essence of all these working class and peasant "movements" then, is more-or-less: (1) a collective reaction, (2) expressive or instrumental, against low status per se, (3) sometimes fused with other reactions (nationalist, religious), at other times pure. In the case of instrumental movements, they are collective efforts to achieve upward mobility, or to prevent downward mobility along any or all status dimensions, particularly the political and economic. Figure 9-1 makes explicit the analytic dimensions touched on by the above highly condensed discussion. We are fully aware that despite a common root, the key dimensions are vastly different from each other and that these differences need to be systematically described.

We will first address ourselves to some formal characteristics which definitions in this field ought, in our opinion, to possess if they are to be fruitful, particularly with reference to unit level (individual, organization) and with respect to time or stage of development of the movement. We shall then discuss the problem of motivation, so central for Smith et al. (chap. 10 in this volume),

Figure 9-1. Schematic Representation of Key Dimensions of Peasant Movements

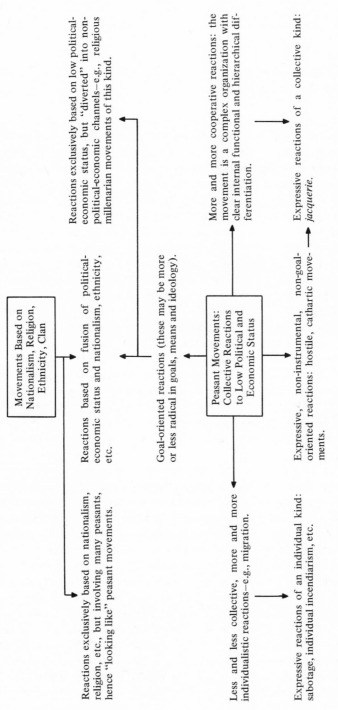

This chart is intended to portray the fact that, apart from fusion with movements not based on political-economic status, even "pure" peasant movements need to be described in terms of a three-dimensional space: (1) individualism versus cooperation, organization; (2) goal-oriented, instrumental versus expressive; and (3) radicalism versus acceptance of status quo (as applied to the goals, means and ideology of the movement). It is the analyst's task to explain the movement's position in this three-dimensional space by drawing on causal variables such as the state of, and preceding changes in, the larger political and social structure, the peasant community, technological level and changes, etc.

Source: Reprinted from *Latin American Peasant Movements*, edited by Henry A. Landsberger. Copyright 1969 by Cornell University. Used by permission of Cornell University Press.

and pass on by means of it to various critical substantive issues in the study of working class and peasant movements.

Each Level of Organization Merits Its Own Analysis

Smith et al. state explicitly that they wish to classify organizations and groups primarily on the basis of the motivations of participating individuals. We would like to advocate retaining the organizational level and, perhaps, too, that of the societal sector as appropriate ones for the analysis of goals and motives in their own right without, however, be it carefully noted, in the least downgrading the importance of also engaging in a psychosocial analysis of individual motivation.

Smith et al. discuss this issue on p. 173. They are reluctant to become involved in the problem of distinguishing, for example, between a foundation (which does not have profit as an organizational goal, but the employees of which may be about as much economically motivated as those of any other organization), on the one hand, and a cooperative for poor people run by priests, where the cooperative as an organization does have making a profit as its goal, but the staff is not economically motivated, on the other hand.

I am, of course, aware of the theoretical and even ideological dangers inherent in reifying an organization and endowing it falsely with goals. Some of the dangers are that unless some individual makes a certain organizational goal his own, it does not really exist; that benefit to individuals is too easily taken as equivalent to benefit to the organization as a whole; etc. Nevertheless, I think it is better to be aware of these dangers and seek to avoid them, than to give up analysis, at least in the case of labor and peasant movements, at the level of the organization.

A trade union, for example, despite unanimity among its leaders that, let us say, its goal is the organization of the unorganized, may not be able to afford to organize a certain small group of poor workers, however needy, if their collective dues would not exceed the cost of servicing them. There literally may not be money to pay the union official to do the organizing and servicing work. At this juncture (i.e., when the union is in financial trouble), the organization may begin to behave just like any commercial enterprise and enunciate a policy to that effect, assessing very carefully the cost of cultivating a certain "market" against the financial gains likely to accrue from doing so. And once this kind of cost accounting policy and mentality is acquired by the union or by a peasant organization (as it literally has to be if it is to survive), it may have all kinds of unintended effects on the behavior of individuals as well as on organizational policy. For example—and not only formal histories, but our own research here and abroad has furnished us with many cases of this—highly motivated, skilled, and otherwise valuable persons may have supported a certain movement at great personal sacrifice precisely because it was *not* profit (or loss-avoidance) oriented, but sought to "defend the poor whatever the cost." This kind of person may become disaffected, withdraw, and thereby damage the organization as severely as the pursuit of a too-costly organizing drive might have done. Note that in this important dilemma for the organization, no accusation is involved that *individuals* are seeking to profit, or that they are not willing to sacrifice themselves sufficiently. It is the organization, pushed by certain individuals, that is then quite meaningfully regarded as "cost conscious" or not.

For this reason, we suggest that in analyzing the kinds of organizations under consideration by Smith, et al., and specifically, the kinds of movements in which I am interested, the goals of the individuals involved, and the goals of the organizations should be kept separate, and analyzed separately. This injunction applies, indeed, not only to the analysis of goals, but to various other characteristics, some of which may be relevant to both levels of analysis.

Time Perpsective

A fruitful approach to the definition of movements such as those of interest to us requires at least one further characteristic: reference to the stage of development of the movement. The "natural history" or "stage" approach to social movements is, of course, quite old. It is today, rightly, not in high scientific repute. We do not wish to enter here into wide-ranging, detailed discussions of the merits and faults of that approach, and how it might be employed so as to maximize its advantages and minimize its disadvantages.

But the motivations of leaders and followers are among the characteristics of labor and peasant movements which may be expected to vary quite systematically depending not so much on time as such, as on the fate of the movement. And typically, in the case of the movements of low status persons, fate is harsh in the early days. Hence it is essential that there be available at that time a good deal of "collectivity orientation": that famous fifth "pattern variable," the use of which, most regretably, Talcott Parsons no longer employs widely, despite his assertion years ago (Parsons, 1951, pp. 132-136) (and we think it correct) that neither society as a whole nor its lower level units can survive without it.

"Collectivity orientation" is the taking by a lower level unit, of the survival and well-being of a higher unit quite specifically as one goal. It therefore limits not only the search for economic benefit, but also the satisfaction of other psychic needs such as that for power or acceptance, unless they coincide with the survival of the organization. It is present when the individual acts to maintain a group (cf., Smith, 1967), organization or societal sector; or when a small group acts to maintain a larger unit to which it belongs (e.g., when a union "local" or "branch" agrees to an industry-wide agreement even though its aspirations have not been satisfied but might have been at the expense of others). The pursuit of self-interest, even of the non-material kind (e.g., the quest for power or popularity) is eschewed. Parsons rightly maintained that it had to be on occasion if society were to survive. The history of labor movements is, of course, replete with persons moved at least in part by altruistic motives (Walter P. Reuther being perhaps the best known example to the man in the street), even though others may simultaneously have had, quite evidently, more self-seeking motives (e.g., John L. Lewis).

Returning to our main point: we believe that *in their early states, the organizations of low status persons have so little to offer—precisely because they are low in all reward-values—that they could not be established except by individuals who for some reason are "collectively oriented."* They are willing to put in and to invest time, career opportunities, perhaps family welfare, with no reasonable expectation of return of any kind. *However, as these organizations become better established, it is clear both that their need for such sacrificing behavior lessens and also that less of it is forthcoming.* Leaders who were originally self-sacrificing may, after a while, feel that the time has come when they may, in justice, and without danger to others, ask for some of the material benefits and psychic rewards which they have early sacrificed. Or, perhaps, a new wave of young leaders comes along which simply is not imbued to the same extent as were the first leaders with the ideals of self-sacrifice.

In any case, our concern here is not so much to draw attention to the vagaries over time of one particular motivation (which, however, does very definitely fall within the category Smith, et al. would call "voluntary"). Rather, our purpose is to establish that any quality describing an association—including the others referred to by Smith, et al., such as autonomy and formalization—are subject to change over time. Hence an association cannot be categorized once and for all as voluntary, formal or autonomous, nor can it be, with finality, placed on a certain point on a continuum measuring these dimensions (if a continuous rather than a categorical approach is used as we would, of course, advocate). We come now to a whole host of problems inherent in studying "motivation" in movements such as those of interest to us.

Multidimensionality of Motivations

First, as will be apparent from previous writings (see Landsberger, 1969, pp. 1-6), I strongly favor the use of multiple dimensions rather than a single one to analyze the "acts" or "behavior" which occur in the setting of a "voluntary association." Although for typological purposes Smith, et al. would place the search for material benefit *and* acceding to coercion *and* various other "nonvoluntary" motives into one category, and would place all other motivations in a second, calling the latter "voluntary," for empirical use they admit the utility of viewing these motivations as a set of separate dimensions. I do not see the substantive, psychological unity nor any conceptual similarity binding each of these categories together, nor can I see the heuristic value of utilizing the dichotomy they proposed, even as ideal types.

I therefore prefer strongly the more usual approach which envisages that any act (e.g., attendance at a union meeting, invading or repossessing a piece of land) may be motivated by the pursuit of several goals simultaneously: the quest for better income; the need to acquire a sense of efficacy and self-confidence; compliance with subtle group norms in order not to become an isolate; ideals of group loyalty; and support for basic, deeply felt values such as justice and equality. There are, then, operative in this kind of behavior as in all other behavior the usual (but not agreed upon!) list of possible human motives. Some scholars prefer Maslow's five basic needs (Maslow, 1954); I still like Henry Murray's twenty-six needs (Murray, 1938). But whatever one's preference is, I am not sure that much is gained by grouping all needs into merely two categories: one termed "voluntary," the other "non-voluntary." I am particularly dubious when the chief category, "voluntary" is de facto defined negatively and, at that, negatively in contrast with two motivations which are as different from each other as is the search for economic benefit, on the one hand, and the avoidance of coercion on the other hand. The latter, as Palisi (1968, also, Chap. 3 in the present volume) points out, is itself a very complex phenomenon which we will analyze later in this chapter.

There is one important logical implication of the above multi-motivation approach. It is that whole acts do not get placed, but that, instead, their qualities are measured. Smith, et al. have already recognized that neither whole persons nor whole associations can be categorized, but only acts. We prefer to think in even more analytical and conceptual terms: not acts, but their qualities are described and even these on several dimensions. Thus, the motives of the act of attendance are simultaneously described and located on various continua.

Recognition that any act may be prompted—even in one person—by different motives reinforcing each other or even opposing each other, enables us to handle more easily some well-known empirical facts about labor and peasant movements and, indeed, about all associations which Smith, et al. would call "voluntary." There is the fact, for example, that leaders are likely to have different motives than members, and that even members are likely to differ systematically from each other (Tannenbaum and Kahn, 1958). The "activist" is motivated differently from the "careerist"; the latter from the "politican," etc. (see, e.g., Seidman, et al., 1958). Indeed, even among the leaders, distinct sub-groups are likely to be found with clusters of motivations which are relatively similar, and which differentiate them from other sub-groups of leaders. Except in the roughest way, a single dichotomy of "voluntary" vs. "non-voluntary" acts is far too constricted to take care of the rich and complex panoply of motivations which we already know to exist.

The constellation of motives to join or, once a member, to be active in an organization may also differ *from one culture to another*. In the case of labor movements, Lipset (1961) has drawn attention to the fact that a relatively altruistic class loyalty is, or at least was, much more frequent in Europe than in the United States of America, and helped to motivate union activity there, whereas in this country, individual mobility aspirations among union leaders are more accepted than they are overseas. Let us explore these complexities a little more in connection with one issue raised by Smith, et al. which is of unusual interest in the study of working-class and peasant movements: that of coercion.

Coercion vs. Voluntarism

While the rhetoric of the movement of low status people is that they are by and for them, the practical requirements of unity, in order to exert sufficiently intense pressure on a hostile environment, are very frequently such that the degree of "voluntarism" is generally problematic. In times of crises such as strikes, for example, when interrupting supply is essential, "scabbing" (i.e., the act of working while others are on strike) is not tolerated. The potential for violence against (and by) strikebreakers is recognized to be so substantial that in all but the earliest phases in the establishment of labor-management relations (in this country and others) the employer, rather than risk bloodshed, will generally not seek to keep his plant in operation by attempting to use strikebreakers. In short, there has often been a great deal of doubt as to what was "voluntary," what mere acquiescence, and what downright coercion, and the precise mental state of those who are members of trade unions has been a constant subject of discussion and study among those concerned—practically as well as scientifically—with the labor movement. The fascination is due to the fact that a notable proportion of what ought clearly to be an eager, voluntary membership, motivated by broad social ideals or else attracted by the likelihood of satisfying personal interests, or both, even on brief examination turns out to be often far from enthusiastic. Yet describing the situation in terms of sheer "coercion" may not be appropriate either.

As an indication that the labor movement consists simultaneously both of supporters and of reluctant members, let us note that U.S. labor unions generally seek to obtain a "union shop" clause in their contracts with employers, at least in those states where "right-to-work" laws do not make it illegal. A worker, if he is not a member of the union, must join it as a condition of remaining in employment. In some countries, a worker may even be legally required to become a union member if a union has won an election in his plant or company, while in still other countries, such as the United Kingdom, social pressure is customarily used for the same purpose. Legislation had to be passed (e.g., the Labor-Management Reporting Act of 1959) to insure members' rights against their union, and even more significant is the fact that both landlords and employers have found it easy, throughout history and in all countries, to have "informers" among the membership. Acts of outright "treachery" and "selling out," even on the part of leaders, are a part of the early history of most movements of this kind.

All the above indicates that while a notable number of workers do want to be members of their organizations, others are relatively unenthusiastic or downright hostile. Coercion in one form or another, mild or strong, widespread or rare, is, then, by no means totally absent. But, of course, neither is enthusiasm on the part of other members absent, especially in the early days, else the union would never have become established.

Other groups at higher occupational levels, such as doctors, have of course always done precisely the same thing: controlling supply of services by requiring membership in the trade association. But since they have been able to claim, simultaneously, that they were certifying competence, upholding professional ethics, and maintaining standards of performance, they have been permitted to control supply without much restraint by the government. Trade unions in the construction trades have been able to make somewhat similar claims and have therefore also been permitted greater control over the supply of labor than have other unions.

The absence of enthusiasm seems to continue once the individual is a member of an established organization. For observers everywhere have noted that the vast majority of members, once in a union, are "apathetic"; a pejorative term which quite unnecessarily reflects on the total person instead of dispassionately describing the fact that a very low percentage of members attend and participate in union meetings and vote in union elections. The reasons for this are far from clear and use of the word "apathy" probably obscures them. Figures below 1 percent, and certainly below 10 percent, are quite usual for attendance at union meetings. These figures vary, of course, in predictable ways with the characteristics of the person, the nature of the issue, and certain structural variables of the union itself (Tannenbaum, 1964). But whatever the variation, it tends to be around a very low average. (For an expanded treatment of the entire issue of participation in movements of this kind at various organizational levels, see Landsberger, 1970.) Nevertheless, unions are not unique among "voluntary associations" in having active participation by only a small minority. Indeed, this very common fact of low member participation rates in *most* (but not all) kinds of union activities is one of the main reasons for viewing unions as at least a marginal (if not full-fledged) type of voluntary association.

Pressure to join the political emanations of the working class movement (i.e., Labor, Socialist, or Communist party, depending on the country) has been less strong. The positive consequences of having members, and the negative ones of having a smaller number, are far fewer and in any case far less certain. In societies permitting some degree of political competition between classes, what matters, usually, is voting at the polls (difficult to control in such societies) rather than size of party membership. Indeed, if the party's role is intended to be that of an efficient mobilizing agent, membership is sometimes deliberately limited rather than open, in order to include only the most dedicated individuals, and to attempt to avoid internal divisions. Though varying from country to country and time to time, this often has been the policy of the Communist party.

As for membership in consumer cooperatives—traditionally the third arm of the working class movement in northern and western Europe—there has been even less pressure to join and patronize co-op shops. For as long as one or a few such shops could survive in each area, one of the major purposes of the movement—that of deterring privately owned shops from setting exploitative prices—could be accomplished. One hundred percent membership was not necessary, as it is in the case of a trade union oriented toward bargaining with, and possibly striking against, an employer.

The degree of voluntarism as to membership permitted the potential member in each of the three branches of the working class movement therefore varies quite understandably with the degree to which inclusiveness—control of the "supply"—may or may not be necessary for the accomplishment of the organization's goal. It also varies with the possibility of succeeding in the effort to make membership inclusive. In the work place, success is clearly possible because much pressure can be exerted, and it is also very necessary; hence "voluntarism" of membership may be low. To influence voting and buying patterns in the larger community is much more difficult and is therefore not attempted; "voluntarism" of participation tends to be high.

These empirical facts concerning the mixture of voluntarism, apathy, and coercion to be found in interest groups which one would have expected to be based on eager voluntarism only, have led Mancur Olson (1965) to reason, more or less deductively rather than inductively, that the desire for personal benefit cannot be the motive for widespread engagement in collective action—at least, not if people weigh their cost and benefits accurately. For the *additional* benefit which any one individual obtains through his personal effort in a common enterprise is necessarily very small (particularly if the organization is large), while the cost to him (time, inconvenience, dues) is substantial. Olson maintains, therefore, that an organization such as a labor union consists partly (of a very small group) of persons who do receive rewards and gratifications from participating (i.e., benefits both material and other than material) and a much larger group who are apathetic and/or have to be coerced to belong. In any case, it is intriguing, but a fact, that organizations dedicated to improving the status of a certain group tend to be regarded for much of the time, and by many of its members, with apathy and even hostility.

Palisi (1968, also, Chap. 3 in this volume) has already commented on the looseness of the concept "coercion." He substitutes the word "forces" to make the very basic socio-psychological point that (a) all behavior is, in the end, the result of some internally felt motivational need, (b) but that these needs are more, or less, immediately related to the social environment: through having been internalized some time ago as motives or moral, superego values; through fear of social ostracism (relative to the internal motivation for group acceptance); or through manipulation of external opportunity structures so as to threaten some need with frustration.

This point should be taken one step further, to link the concept of "coercion" even more clearly with standard lists of psychological needs and motivations which we discussed earlier (e.g., a list such as A.H. Maslow's or Henry Murray's). Whenever we speak of "coercion," I believe we are simply referring to the *negative* half of a standard "human needs" continuum or to the reduction of some positive point already reached. Thus, the threat of a loss of a job if one does not join a union is simply use of the lower end of the "material deprivation—material well-being" continuum; and social ostracism is simply the lower end of the "disapproval," or "rejection-acceptance" continuum. There are some variables which do not go much beyond the neutral point (e.g., the need for physical survival or pain avoidance). But apart from these, I believe, the idea of "coercion" is best handled, and is best taken out of its unusual conceptual status, by regarding it as manipulation through threat of deprivation, whether still within the positive range, or already in the negative range, of a standard need dimension.

We see, therefore, a very complex and highly shaded motivational picture. Coercion, itself a complex phenomenon, economic motives, and very different kinds of psychic benefits (personal, altruistic) are blended together in ways which vary systematically from group to group and person to person, and which also vary over time: again, one presumes, systematically. The correlates, causes, and consequences of this complex motivational situation can and should be studied. But a simple division between "voluntary" and "non-voluntary" is probably not helpful except for communicating general areas of interest and focus, nor are a priori categorical assumptions as to "irrationality," "lack of institutionalization," and "collectivization" likely to be fruitful.

The Continousness of Variables: Three Special Applications

As will be clear from the above, I prefer to think in terms of continuous dimensions and variables rather than in terms of dichotomies and categorizations. It is more fruitful to think of the causes and consequences of the fact that an act may be *more or less* motivated by economic considerations or by the quest for power or by fear of loss of job, than to think of explaining what acts are "primarily" so motivated or else "not so motivated." *In practice*, we may have to dichotomize because we may not be able to measure more finely. Or we may have to dichotomize at times for simplicity of communication. But at the level of concept, we should think in terms of continua as does Bode (Chap. 4 in this Volume) when analyzing this kind of social movement. Yet historically, that has not been the case.

Perhaps because the fields originally developed out of the fascination of writers like Tarde and LeBon with how differently a crowd acts, feels, and believes when compared with individuals observed in isolation, the fields of collective behavior and social movements have continued a style of thinking which has emphasized that a phenomenon is either one thing or another, either a hostile act or a norm-oriented movement; either institutionalized or not; either a public or a mob. Nevertheless, Turner, at the end of the introductory section of his classic review of the field, speculates that *"It is altogether possible that further search will ultimately undermine all of the traditional dynamic distinction between collective behavior and organizational behavior and . . . . suggest that investigators should stress continuity rather than discontinuity with conventional behavior"* (italics supplied) (Turner, 1964. See also Killian (1964) for a review of "Social movements.").

Whatever may be true of other kinds of movements, we endorse this position heartily in the case of the collective behavior and social movements of low status groups. Indeed, we would wish to broaden Turner's suggestion by encouraging investigators to see, in addition, the continuity between different types of collective behavior, and to recognize the fact that they can be present simultaneously. Hostile outbursts may well accompany the existence of more permanent, norm-oriented movements, to use Smelser's (1963) categorization. These categories thereby become analytical abstractions and dimensions, and cease to be substantive, concretely existing entities. This style of thinking is very much the same as encouraging the investigator (in a very different but related field), not to think in terms of whether an organization is or is not a Weberian bureaucracy, but about the *degree to which* it has the characteristics of a bureaucracy. We will apply this style of conceptualization to three aspects of social movements, specifically working class and peasant movements: the degree to which they are (1) collective, (2) uninstitutionalized, and (3) irrational.

"Collectivization." Let us illustrate by imagining a group of persons of low status, say, factory workers at an early stage in the industrialization process. (1) Some will not even be aware as individuals that they might have grievances: low wages, long hours, job insecurity. (2) Some will be aware that they have grievances but their behavior will be little affected by it. (3) Others will react to their own grievance—through absenteeism, poor work, low productivity: the "strike in detail," as Kerr, et al. (1960) call it, but they may not be aware that others have the same grievances and that others are reacting in the same way. (4) Or they may be aware that others have the same grievances, but not be much affected by that awareness. (5) But others still will not only themselves engage in this kind of "strike in detail" but they will be encouraged, and to a greater or lesser degree affected, by the fact that others feel similarly and that others are reacting in the same way. At this point, a modest form of class consciousness is present. (6) Beyond this, there will be not only mutual awareness, but tentative, more or less explicit communication about shared grievances, and agreement about certain acts, at least among some knots of people here and there and even though both agreement and communication may be loose and informal. A larger group may be aware of that agreement without participating in it. Poor workmanship, amounting in part to sabotage, for example, will take on the quality of an informal norm. It will begin to be defined, at least by some, both as a legitimate expression of the group's resentment, and perhaps also as an appropriate instrument or pressuring mechanism. At this point, we are clearly beginning to deal with an incipient organization by individuals and groups. (7) A few workers may be conspiring very explicitly to commit such acts, or to strike, and may have reached a high level of internal organization (i.e., patterned communication, division of organizational labor, planning, etc.), though as yet without coordinating with other groups. In other words, the situation is at the level of a formal, but still *simple* organization. (8) Finally, there is coordination between groups and we have, in essence, the forging of complex "voluntary organizations."

There is no implication in the above that it constitutes a sequence nor a necessary progression. On the contrary, one of our points is that even in the same situation—the same factory, the same rural area—all these reactions may be simultaneously present. They *certainly* may be simultaneously present across the society at large.

The above, while put into rather homey terms, and hypothetical in the sense of not describing any specific situation, illustrates what we suggest be termed different degrees of "collectivization": of reaction to their low status by role occupants. These reactions range, then, from "zero," through awareness of one's own status, to awareness of others similarly situated but without this affecting behavior, to being influenced by others but without the influence being structured, to informal structure, to formal but simple organizational structure, to complex formal organization.

In the study of working class and peasant movements, two important measures involving this series can be obtained. (We are, we believe, merely formalizing what others have in fact had in mind.) It may be best to think separately in terms of *two* variables rather than in terms of a single variable, "degree of collectivization." First, it is useful to think in terms of *how many members of a certain low status group are at least at the point of being conscious of and influenced by the fact that others, too, have similar grievances and are reacting to them, as compared with the total number of members who potentially might be so conscious.* This can be thought of either in absolute numbers or in relative terms (i.e., in terms of the proportion of those in categories 5-8 to the entirety of the group). In Peru, while the Indians of some areas were already engaged in highly organized rent strikes and land invasions, others, even if aware of the fact, were totally unaffected by it. We might call this the *degree of extension* of the movement (which can clearly be more or less), thereby taking into account the long-standing tradition in the study of social movements of not regarding something as collective behavior or as a social movement unless a fairly substantial number of persons are involved. But by treating it as a continuum, we avoid the awkward problem of specifying some arbitrary number of individuals as a requisite to being called "a social movement."

Equally important, but quite different, are variations between one movement and another in the *degree of organization* within the sector which is at least conscious. One calculates, so to speak, a statistical "mean" *within* the sector denoted by points (5) to (8). Let us call this dimension "organization." It would measure the extent to which *those who are affected by being conscious of the similarity of their own position to that of others, are in categories (7) and (8) i.e., are to be found in simple or complex organizations designed to correct their grievances, as compared with the extent to which they are still in categories (5) and (6) of mere awareness or only informal coordination.*

Note that degree of "extension" and degree of "organization" are logically not correlated even though they may be empirically. Further, they do in fact (i.e., in the real world) exist independently, with important practical implications. (We would not bother to make logical distinctions for their own sake.) Peasant unrest may often be wide in extent, but one of its problems is that it is not formally organized. Working-class movements, on the other hand, may leave out many potential members (low "extension"), but those who are conscious, are well organized (high degree of "organization") and may gain much as a result: more than sheer numbers would lead one to expect. Figure 9-2 illustrates these possibilities.

Figure 9-2. The "Extension" and "Organization" of Low Status Movements

	Low Organization	High Organization
Low Extension	Only few are even aware of grievances	Working class movement in developing countries: "islands of strength"
High Extension	Generalized peasant discontent but little organization	Working class movement in N. Europe: Percentage of unionized workers very high

The above implies that we see no reason to exclude from a study of social movements one which has reached a high degree of organization. There seems to be some readiness to do so on the part of those who stress that the absence of formal organization is an essential characteristic of anything that can be right-fully called a social movement. We see the absence of formal organization as a matter of degree, and we regard as particularly interesting the study of why some groups, though aware of their shared grievances, cannot establish organizations while other groups, similarly situated, do establish them.

Is collective behavior "uninstitutionalized"? The literature is ambiguous about the precise referent of the concept: "uninstitutionalized." But it is usually ada-mant that this is an essential characteristic of collective behavior and social movements. "According to the degree of which it becomes institutionalized, it loses its distinctive character" (Smelser, 1963, p. 8).

Sometimes, the term seems to refer to the *situation*, not the movement, as being "undefined or unstructured" (Smelser, 1963, p. 9, quoting, and agreeing with, Blumer, 1951). But there is little that is "undefined or unstructured" about the declining wages and job opportunities about which the earliest craft unions complained at the beginning of the nineteenth century; nor about the lost rights to land and water which angered peasant communities in Mexico in the latter part of the nineteenth century.

At other times, "undefined" and "non-institutionalized" seem to refer to the *degree of organization* of the response. With this, we have just dealt. We see it as a variable, not a category, and we see no reasons for excluding the upper range of the scale from study.

Finally, "non-institutionalized" seems sometimes to refer to the kinds of behavior (in themselves, incidentally, two very different phenomena). But in behavior (in themeselves, incidentally, two very different phenomena). But in the case of low status movements, this comes perilously close to the social scientist's accepting the elite definition of what is "normative" and what is not. In the case of the civil rights movement of the early 1960s for example, neither the *goal* of achieving registration as voters and school integration, nor the *means* of queuing up at the courthouse to achieve it, or of sitting at a lunch counter asking to be served, would appear to be non-normative by more general Amer-ican values and norms. Indeed, such movements often claim to be defenders of existing values. They frequently base themselves on supposedly existing but non-observed values, and do so with as much as, or more justification than, their opponents.

As for the use of the term "non-institutionalization" in the statistical sense of a claim not having been made before, or the means not having been employed before, this, too, is clearly a matter of degree. At what time, for example, did collective bargaining become "institutionalized" in the United States? It certain-ly existed on quite a substantial, though spotty, scale throughout the nineteenth century. Should labor unrest in the 1930s therefore not be called a "movement"? It surely should be. In sum, we believe that the concept of "non-institutionalized" either does not apply at all, in many instances, to the movements in which we are interested; or that it applies only in a dimensional, more-or-less manner in the same way as it does to the conduct of established businesses.

We need, then, to recognize that an essential characteristic of many social movements, especially those of low status roles, is that many, if not all, goals being sought and many, if not all, means employed may clearly have been won and employed by others quite similarly situated (or may have been characteristic even of the same group in earlier times). Thus, it may be precisely this discrepancy which is the stimulant to collective action. "Non-institutionalization" is therefore at best exactly half the story.

Are the social movements of low status groups "irrational"? While the point has received surprisingly little comment, Smelser, in his *Theory of Collective Behavior* (1963, pp. 71-73), places the characteristic of "irrationality" at the very center of his definition, thereby not only continuing, but even strengthening and elaborating with more sophistication and elegance than ever before, an old tradition in the field.

As a matter of fact, we do not question that collective behavior *is* characterized by some "short-circuiting" in logic. There is something implausible in any theory which holds that "if only" (to use Smelser's term) industry were nationalized, after a proletarian revolution, all necessary steps could be taken to solve the world's problems, and no new and very massive problems would arise.

Our point—seemingly flippant but meant very seriously—is that *all* behavior, individual as well as collective, institutionalized and non-institutionalized, seems to be characterized by a good deal of illogic. No case has been made to show that irrationality is more characteristic of collective behavior than of other forms of behavior, and this needs to be done before we can accept it as a distinctive characteristic. It is not enough by itself to show that collective behavior is based on "short-circuiting . . . (by-passing) many of the specifications, contingencies, and controls that are required" (Smelser, 1963, p. 72). Neither more nor less irrational may be the generalized belief, underlying our institutionalized university system, to the effect that 40-50 percent of our youth benefits from higher education, especially higher education dispensed largely through reading and lectures; and neither more nor less irrational are many an individual's hopes that by using one rather than another method of child-rearing, the child will be happier and healthier.

With respect to the movement of low status groups in particular, we find it difficult to label their beliefs as necessarily "akin to magical beliefs" (Smelser, 1963, p. 8). Typical demands of peasant movements are that the number of compulsory workdays on the landowner's land in lieu of rent be reduced; or that there be written, long-term leases; or even that large estates be expropriated.

None of these demands, typical of a "norm-oriented movement," in Smelser's terminology, seem unusually bizarre. Nor, in the industrial sector, do demands seem unusually irrational for union recognition, better wages, nor even the demand that key industries be nationalized so that they be made more efficient, or that their investment (and therefore employment) be stabilized, and the political power of their owners reduced. We do not say that these steps would be sure to guarantee the coming of the millenium. All we assert is that they do not, on their face, strike us as a dramatically less realistic step toward the millenium than other steps proposed, such as that of continuing the system as it is at present. We have the impression that there may very well be a greater admixture of irrationality in movements other than those of low status groups, whose chief aim is that of improving that status. In particular, those movements in which this basic aim has been transformed into symbolic content (almost like "dream-work" in Freud's theories) may be highly suitable to Smelser's analysis. The "cargo cults" of the Pacific, and perhaps the movements of middle-class radicals whether right, left, or center, are of this kind. Some of the basic and rather mundane status defensive aims of these movements, as in the case of lower middle class National Socialism, may indeed be hidden underneath belief systems which appear patently irrational. But the movements of those of lower status (until permeated by ideologies from the outside?) are usually as down-to-earth and reasonable as any other average belief.

In sum: we regard the matter of the rationality-irrationality of the belief system associated with a social movement as a dimension, and see no a priori reason for thinking that the kinds of movements in which we are interested are necessarily all at one position of this continuum, and certainly no reason for thinking that they are all at an extreme position.

"Economic Benefits" as a Motive

The relation of labor and peasant organizations to "economic benefits" is a particularly complex one and this, of course, is the reason why these organizations have been placed sometimes within the category of "voluntary organizations" and at other times not, as both Bode (chap. 4 in this volume) and Palisi (1968, also, chap. 3 in this volume) well describe. The *ultimate* elevation of their members' economic (and political) status is a central goal of working class and peasant movements, and the relationship of the fact to the immediate and specific behavior of members, and of the organizations themselves, needs to be considered.

The following may be asserted: (1) Such organizations by definition have economic goals, whether in the "narrow" sense of fighting for higher wages, pressing for the return of land perhaps misappropriated by landlords in the past, fighting for more secure tenancy arrangements etc., or whether in the more profound sense of altering the entire economic and political system of their society. (2) However, unlike the goals of economic enterprises as more commonly understood, these economic benefits do not even transitorily go to the organizations, but directly to its members. Nevertheless, the differences between commercial organizations and trade unions should not be exaggerated. Companies, too, aim for profit primarily for the sake of shareholders. And unions tend to take on the same kind of nonprofit *and yet non-individual goals* as do companies: sheer growth, stability, etc. (3) The labor movement, or parts thereof, may have, however, other immediate goals *as well* as economic ones. Indeed, they may have *exclusively* non-economic immediate goals. Thus, the labor movements of western Europe toward the end of the nineteenth century and the beginning of the twentieth were in part composed of substantial sections who sought only political power in the intermediate future and eschewed bargaining with employers or pressing for better labor laws.

There is a parallel here at the level of the individual: he participates in the activities of the union without economic reward, but, perhaps, and depending on the individual, in the ultimate hope of improving his economic status, just as a labor movement, even if temporarily politically oriented, ultimately hopes for economic improvement for its members. Smith, et al. would then regard the individual's acts (e.g., in attending or not attending union meetings) as "voluntary" insofar as they are not prompted by immediate economic goals (i.e., pay for attending the meeting). Similarly, the labor movement may participate in the political life of the country without direct economic "remuneration" either for itself or for its members, but in the hope that ultimately both its own position as an organization and that of its members will be improved.

To complicate the situation further: (4) as we have already noted, the ultimate goals of the labor movement, in Europe at least, may be far broader than mere economic benefits and may have to do with the entire social, political, and moral reorganization of society. This would make the movement, *at the level of analysis of the movement as such*, "voluntary." Finally, (5) and at the level of the individual, the individual certainly gets no immediate economic reward for attending a union meeting. But then, neither does the shareholder for attending a shareholder's meeting.

How one classifies the labor movement according to the system proposed by Smith et al. is, therefore, a matter of what level and time-span of the movement one focuses on. This is the sense in which they refer to unions as "marginal examples" of voluntary associations. It is no wonder, given the above complexities, that classification of unions has in fact been highly unstable.

We see no particular reason to draw a single line at the act itself and its remuneration in order to classify it once and for all as either economically motivated or not. If an act is engaged in because its consequences are seen as ultimately resulting in economic benefit, then it would be best to classify it as such at least for some purposes, even if not for others. Similarly, it should be classified according to whatever other gratification may be its ultimate aim or aims. Such an approach makes it easier to deal with the well-known fact, to which we have already drawn attention, that attendance at specially called union meetings at which contract negotiations and employers' offers are discussed, is much higher than attendance at regular monthly union meetings. At neither kind of meeting is the act of attendance directly rewarded with economic benefits. Hence, the difference in attendance cannot be explained on the basis of differences in immediate economic reward. It can be explained if we regard benefit which is "once, or twice removed from the act" as being the incentive for that act (i.e., if we look at the act as instrumental). I suggest that the motive or motives of an act be described in accordance with whatever means-ends chains, long or short, are taken into account by the individual performing the act, or which can be reasonably be ascribed to him, and not only in accord with whatever immediate rewards the act may bring with it objectively.

Motivational Causes of Instability in Movements

There are interesting implications for the stability of working class and peasant movements in the twin facts that the quest for "more" (i.e., for mobility along various dimensions) is the ultimate goal of these movements on behalf of their members and that collective action and individual action are alternative routes to that goal. These two facts are of importance in understanding—at the level of the individual, and particularly of the leader—variations in his willingness to devote himself to the movement, including the existence of corruption. They are also of importance in understanding a phenomenon at the level of the organization: the very widespread existence of "parochialism," of not cooperating with other groups, particularly groups even more unfortunately situated and deprived.

At the level of the individual, the author and a colleague first became acquainted with corruption in low status movements through our field work in Latin American peasant movements, and our knowledge of large-scale financial mismanagement in the U.S. trade union movement as made public in the so-called McClellan Senate Hearings in the mid-1950s, as well as through recent revelations about black militant movements. One interpretation is to attribute such phenomena to culture: the emphasis on materialism and individual initiative in the United States, for example.

But reading British labor history, it is clear that succumbing to the temptation to increase one's material status through direct misappropriation of union funds was very widespread there also and attempts were made early to guard against it. Moreover, both in these and other countries (France, for example) corruption was also present in other perhaps even more harmful, but more subtle forms: leaders who would drift over into the camp of the enemy, so to speak, "bought" (according to his detractors at least) by flattery and the power and material rewards of a new position (as distinct from the more obvious monetary bribery while maintaining the old position).

Yet another pattern is that of the leader who separates himself from the movement to make his fortune alone. If we realize that it is aspirations to improve status—shared, but ultimately nevertheless individual—which is the source of the movement of low status persons, it is highly understandable that if a much easier road than collective action opens up for our individual (and it is more likely to do so for a leader than for the average person), then it is not surprising that he should be tempted to take it. The surprising thing is how often altruism (plus, no doubt, other more earthy motives such as fear of sanctions) make a leader remain faithful.

At the level of the organization and movement, the phenomenon of "selfishness" is equally widespread. It ranges from the lack of desire of the AFL, in the 1930s, to concern itself with the unskilled in the new manufacturing industries, to the judgments by historians of so many peasant uprisings that their failure to show much interest in parallel movements in neighboring areas played a significant role in their defeat; from the German Peasant Wars of 1525 to Zapata's uprising in Morelos.

Even more apparent is the kind of "parochialism" (we have no desire to condemn; we regret the phenomenon, but understand it) shown when Mexican peasants, once they were endowed with land through a land reform program, were cool toward any efforts to organize those who were less fortunate than they, and had remained landless laborers (Landsberger and de Alcantara, 1971). In the case of black farmers' cooperatives, a similar hard line is generally shown by cooperatives already functioning toward new groups attempting to get organized. A systematic and more extensive treatment of this and other problems as found in the Latin American context is contained in Landsberger and de Alcantara (1970).

The Analysis of Goals

As a final exercise in the application of the three principles of formal analysis we recommended at the beginning of this paper, let us schematize very briefly the goals of working class and peasant organizations, illustrating the ideas of distinguishing levels (organizational from individual); distinguishing time-spans; and employing multi-dimensional continua instead of "types."

Using Smelser (1963) once again as our starting point, let us consider his ingenious division of collective behavior into panics, crazes, hostile outbursts, norm-oriented movements, and value-oriented movements. It seems to us, at least insofar as the movements of low status persons are concerned, that there is a logical break between the first three and the last two. The first three are distinguished from the others at the very least by the fact that they refer to types of *behavior* of individuals over a rather limited *time-span*, while the last two refer to the longer range nature of the *goals* of a movement.

"Hostile outbursts" and "panics," for example, are highly specific incidents and events which may occur as part of the evolution of a working-class or peasant movement which is, however, fundamentally oriented toward certain broad goals of a totally different nature. The movement as a whole, seen nationally, may have the goal of organizing workers and improving their working conditions. In the course of reaching that goal, violence of very different types may occur. Often, it is in fact the opposition which engages in it, so that "hostile outbursts" should often really be classed as part of Smelser's "social control." Even if the movement itself engages in violence, it may be an instrumental and not at all a subjectively unreasonable act: to frighten the opponent, or to call forth counter-violence and thus perhaps a martyr, in order to strengthen loyalty. (Once again, we see that the label of "irrationality" should not be applied too hastily.) A single act and a movement as a whole (for a short time or over a long period) may contain "irrational" and "rational" elements, and may be both expressive and instrumental.

But however complex the hostile outburst, it is usually at an entirely different level of analysis than the movement as a whole, much as the quality of a single sentence in a group interaction process is different from the quality of the member's contribution of which that sentence is a part, and even more different from the nature of the group seen as a whole. In sum: "hostile outbursts" and "panics" can occur together rather than being mutually exclusive; they may contain quite rational, instrumental elements; and they certainly do not preclude the movement's being, basically, norm or value oriented. If Smelser's five "types" were to be seen not as such but rather as analytical qualities, some (but not all) of our objections would be nullified.

We propose that the following distinctions be made, and the following dimensions used at least in the analyses of low status movements.

1. The goals of the movements should be separated clearly from the means employed to reach them.
2. Allowance needs to be made for analyses at different levels, and different time spans, both of means and of goals. The long-range goal of a peasant movement may be to get the government to change the land tenure system. But within a narrower time span, the goal may be to frighten local officials. (This is the usual analysis of intermediate goals being means to longer range goals).
3. The Parsonian distinctions between the expressive and the instrumental (seen as qualities of acts, not describing concrete acts in their totality) are appropriate. The burning of a landlord's house in rage is one thing; burning it to frighten is another: both motives may be present simultaneously.

4. We believe that the distinction between "norm-oriented" and "value-oriented" movements is perhaps better covered by *two* continuous dimensions describing the *breadth* and the *depth* of the goal respectively.

By *breadth* we mean the range of societal sectors with which the movement concerns itself. Thus, the British labor movement had very substantial programs in the fields of education and land use, while the American trade union movement has given these areas distinctly secondary treatment.

By *depth* we mean the extent of the changes envisaged in any one area. This dimension probably comes closest to Smelser's "norm-value" distinction.[1]

5. Means can be scaled in a roughly comparable manner according to their breadth and depth.

By *breadth* we mean the range of means used: a labor movement may use economic, political and cultural (elevating the education of its members) means, or it may confine itself to one or other of these.

By *depth* we mean something roughly equivalent to degree to which "un-institutionalized" means are used: to what degree are means utilized which have not been used by this group before (perhaps regarded as "non-legitimate" by some groups, especially opponents). Or is it contemplated to use only already customary means, such as petitions to the czar?

Figure 9-3. Dimensions of Goals (and Means) of Movements of Low Status Groups

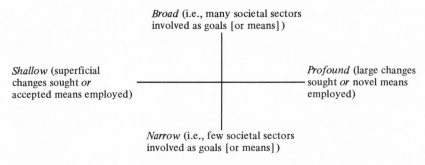

Summary

As we reflect on Smith's et al. definition involving voluntariness, coercion and economic benefit; distinguishing autonomous from non-autonomous;[a] and

---

[a]We have not dealt with the issue of "autonomy" in this chapter both for reasons of space and because we will deal with it in a chapter in the second volume of this series, where we will analyze problems concerning the environment of our organizations. Suffice it to say that the tension between the autonomy of trade unions and their subordination to or domination of relevant political parties has been in Europe and in most of the developing nations, a main thread in their histories.

formal from informal; we recognize that these do, indeed, constitute crucial issues. In the context of the social movements in which we are interested—those of the collective reaction to their low status of working classes and peasants— these characteristics, and others referred to by Smelser (1963), are often present simultaneously and the life of these movements is determined in part by the manner in which they resolve the immense tensions resulting from their simultaneous presence.

Note

1. For further elaboration of these dimensions, and for hypotheses dealing with them, see Henry A. Landsberger (1969, especially pp. 31-38 and 54-55).

References

Blumer, Herbert
1951 "Collective Behavior." In A.M. Lee (ed.), *Principles of Sociology*. New York: Barnes and Noble.
Johnson, Chalmers
1962 *Peasant Nationalism and Communist Power*. Stanford, California: Stanford University Press.
Kerr, Clark; John Dunlop; Frederick H. Harbison; and Charles A. Myers
1960 *Industrialism and Industrial Man*. Cambridge, Mass.: Harvard University Press.
Killian, Lewis M.
1964 "Social Movements." In Robert E.L. Faris (ed.), *Handbook of Modern Sociology*. Chicago: Rand McNally, chap. 12, 426-55.
Landsberger, Henry A., (ed.)
1969 *Latin American Peasant Movements*. Ithaca, New York: Cornell University Press.
Landsberger, Henry A.
1970 " 'Maximum Feasible Participation': Working Class and Peasant Movements as a Theoretical Model for the Analysis of Poverty and Race." Paper presented at the 33rd Annual Meeting, Southern Sociological Society, Atlanta, Georgia, April 9-11, 1970.
Landsberger, Henry A. and Cynthia H. de Alcantara
1971 "From Violence to Pressure Group Politics and Co-operation: A Mexican Case Study." In Peter Worsley (ed.), *Two Blades of Grass: Rural Co-operation in Developing Countries*. Manchester, England: Manchester University Press.
1970 "Ten sources of Weakness and Cleavage in Latin American Peasant Move-

158

ments." In Rodolfo Stavenhagen (ed.), *Agrarian Problems and Peasant Movements in Latin America*. New York: Doubleday-Anchor Books.

Lipset, Seymour Martin
1961-62 "Trade Unions and Social Structure: I & II." *Industrial Relations* 1 (1 and 2): 75-89, 89-110.

Maslow, A.H.
1954 *Motivation and Personality*. New York: Harper and Row.

Murray, Henry A.
1938 *Explorations in Personality*. New York: Oxford University Press.

Olson, Mancur, Jr.
1965 *The Logic of Collective Action*. New York: Schocken Books.

Palisi, Bartolomeo J.
1968 "A Critical Analysis of the Voluntary Association Concept." *Sociology and Social Research* 52: 392-405. Included as chapter 3 in the present volume.

Parsons, Talcott
1951 *The Social System* Glencoe, Ill.: Free Press.

Seidman, Joel; Jack London; Bernard Karsh; and Daisy L. Tagliacozzo
1958 *The Worker Views his Union*. Chicago, Illinois: University of Chicago Press.

Smelser, Neil J.
1963 *Theory of Collective Behavior*. New York: Free Press of Glencoe.

Smith, David Horton
1967 "A Parsimonious Definition of 'Group' : Toward Conceptual Clarity and Scientific Utility." *Sociological Inquiry* 37:141-167.

Tannenbaum, Arnold S.
1964 "Unions." In James G. March (ed.), *Handbook of Organizations*. Chicago, Illinois: Rand McNally and Co., chap. 17, 710-63.

Tannenbaum, Arnold S. and Robert L. Kahn
1958 *Participation in Union Locals*. Evanston, Illinois: Row, Peterson and Company.

Thompson, E.P.
1964 *The Making of the English Working Class*. New York: Pantheon.

Turner, Ralph H.
1964 "Collective Behavior." In Robert E.L. Faris (ed.), *Handbook of Modern Sociology*, Chicago: Rand McNally and Co., chap. 11, 382-425.

10 Types of Voluntary Action: A Definitional Essay[a]

DAVID HORTON SMITH, RICHARD D. REDDY, AND BURT R. BALDWIN

This chapter is concerned with arriving at a set of reasonably precise and empirically useful definitions for the phenomena of volunteer participation and voluntary action in general. Our procedure will be one of *explicating* existing terminology in order to make it more precise, rather than introducing a series of neologisms that refer to types of phenomena which seem similar only in the authors' view. The definitions will not simply be based on common sense, however. They involve theoretical assumptions and postulates about what are the most essential aspects of the phenomena to be dealt with. Thus, in the longer term there will be two concrete tests for the utility of the definitions and classifications offered here. First, they will be useful to the extent that other scholars and researchers find them to be helpful for organizing their own thinking and research on voluntary action phenomena of all kinds. Second, they will be useful to the extent that the elements of the empirical world that the present definitions highlight turn out to be the most important analytical or theoretical aspects of voluntary action phenomena over the long run.

There are many levels of system reference at which we could begin to discuss voluntary action—the international level, the national or societal level, the level of sectors within society, the community level, the organizational level, the role level, the individual level, or even the level of individual acts and situations. Because we believe the individual level of voluntary action to be especially important in the realm of definitions, we shall begin at this level in our present exposition. Perhaps most social scientists would begin instead with the organizational or even the societal levels. Yet our beginning with the individual level of voluntary action in no way denies the tremendous substantive and practical importance of *collective* voluntary action, as manifested in voluntary organizations and voluntary communities and societies. Our starting point is dictated by *definitional considerations* (and perhaps also personal predilections) rather than by any sense of the substantive preeminence of individual voluntary action over collective voluntary action of various kinds.

---

[a]The present chapter is a substantially revised version of an earlier paper by the same title that was presented to the Seminar Session on "Voluntary Action Theory and Research" organized by the authors at the 1970 American Sociological Association Convention.

Voluntary Action and Individuals
(Personal Systems)

Before getting involved with any definitions or technical terms at all, let us ask the basic question: "What are the phenomena of interest that we are attempting to define and classify?" If we cannot agree on what it is we are talking about, we can have no hope of ever reaching agreement on definitions or classifications. When we ask this question we are in fact asking for a *denotative* definition of our subject; we are asking for someone to point out the kinds of events or objects in the natural world that are to concern us. From a non-systematic survey of past treatments of the subject of volunteer participation and voluntary action, we would say that the phenomena of interest to us here may include the following kinds of human behavior: participating without pay in some organization concerned with human welfare and social betterment (e.g., the Red Cross); volunteering for some special task or arduous duty, with or without corresponding special remuneration (e.g., participating in a survey); working for low pay for some kind of organization (e.g., VISTA, a foundation, etc.) concerned with human betterment; contributing money, goods or services to some "cause" or social movement (e.g., donations to the United Fund or Common Cause); unremunerated or only partly remunerated activity in behalf of some political candidate, party, bill, etc.; voting; participating in church or other religious activities; participating without remuneration in some kind of club or organization *not* dedicated to general human betterment, but merely dedicated to the interests or welfare of its members (e.g., a hobby club or fraternal organization); stopping to help someone who is being attacked or robbed; picking up a hitchhiker; altruistic behavior in general, so long as it is not dictated by external force (as when a wealthy businessman meets a ransom demand for his captive wife, or when a surrounded army unit's commanding officer surrenders to the enemy in order to save his men from needless death) whether physical, legal, customary or economic; leisure time behavior in general, whether motivated by selfish or altruistic motives (or some combination of both) and whether in the context of some formal organization, an informal group, or solitary.

Doubtless some readers will disagree that we should be talking about *all* of the foregoing types of phenomena under the same rubric as voluntary action phenomena. Yet most readers will probably agree, at least, that the foregoing list of phenomena *includes* most or all of the general kinds of phenomena that they have in mind when they think of voluntary action. Any who find *nothing* in the foregoing list relevant to what they are referring to when they speak of voluntary action phenomena are operating in some other realm of discourse than the rest of us. However, the foregoing list is intended to be open-ended and tentative, in the sense that other types of phenomena might be added and certain types of activities now included in the list might be subtracted.

Some will now ask, "What is left out of that list; doesn't it include all of human behavior? And if it includes all of human behavior, then there is nothing distinctive about our present realm of discourse in contrast with any other realm in the social sciences." Our answer is that indeed there *are* a number of kinds of human behavior left out of the foregoing list. These other, omitted aspects of human behavior that are not seen here as voluntary action phenomena may be grouped into three broad clusters.

1. *Bio-socially determined behavior* is one broad class of essentially "non-voluntary" behavior. In part we include here the various kinds of behavior that are primarily determined by reflexes or by physiologically-based compulsions, albeit with an overlay of social learning regarding the expression of (both conscious and unconscious) *physiological needs and compulsions.* Such compelled behavior has at its roots the biological nature of man—the need for food, drink, sleep, air, sex, expression of aggression (and other emotions), excretion, pain avoidance, appropriate levels of sensory stimulation, etc. The conscious decision-making processes and motives of an individual affect the style and timing of the expression of these biologically based needs, but the needs themselves have a pre-social (and often pre-conscious) necessity of their own in normal human beings. Bio-socially determined behavior as we view it here also includes certain kinds of *personal and social maintenance activities* that are not so directly *compelled* by man's biological nature, but are still fairly directly related to it. In addition, these kinds of activities are the focus of strong social sanctions, usually in a family and kinship context. Some examples of this kind of behavior are personal grooming, adornment, bathing and dressing; child care, care of the elderly, and care of one's spouse or other members of the family; dieting, exercise, therapeutic and rehabilitative activities related to physiological well-being; socialization of the young; and engaging in some minimum of social interaction. All of these forms of bio-socially determined behavior help to define *man as a bio-social being.*

2. *Socio-politically compelled behavior* is another broad class of essentially "non-voluntary" behavior. We do *not* include here *all* kinds of socio-political behavior, but only that social behavior which is primarily *coerced by physical force*, coerced by the direct, high-probability *threat of the use of physical force*, or primarily motivated by the *fear of strong social-legal-political-economic sanctions* for failure to perform or act in a certain manner. Hypnotically induced behavior might also be placed in the present category, since it involves yielding one's will to an external social or political agent. For both bio-socially determined behavior and socio-politically determined behavior, the individual is primarily subjected to a particular kind of force that operates in large part to compel the behavior in question. The compelling force is essentially biological for bio-socially determined behavior; while the compelling force is largely socio-political for the present class of "involuntary behavior." In both types of "involuntary behavior," the latitude of individual action and the role of conscious individual choice is severely constrained. An individual has very little freedom to

ignore permanently either biological necessity or socio-political necessity. A great deal of human social behavior has this property of being severely constrained by the mores (strong customs) and/or by law. These latter areas of constraint in part define *man as a socio-political being.*

3. *Economically determined behavior* of certain kinds comprises still a third class of human behavior that we wish to omit from the class of "voluntary action." Specifically we wish to omit from the category of voluntary action all of those kinds of human behavior that are primarily motivated by the *desire for direct, high-probability economic benefits* (salary, fees, share of the profits or bounty, avoidance of expenses, etc.) *at existing market values for the goods or services produced or exchanged.* Though not "*in*voluntary" in the sense of the preceding two categories, the present category of human behavior is by our definition "*non*-voluntary." The present category of economic behavior includes most of the usual kinds of "work" done for pay, fees, etc., as well as including the more "primitive" forms of productive economic behavior such as hunting for food or growing it; hunting for shelter or constructing and maintaining it; obtaining skins for clothing and preparing them for use or making cloth and then clothing to wear; shopping for goods and services; barter and exchange; etc. Economic behavior is thus seen here to include both the direct production and exchange of economic goods and services for oneself and one's family as well as production and exchange for the market system. In a modern industrial society, most paid occupations fall into the present category of non-voluntary activity, as do various kinds of informal personal or family economic activity like "do-it-yourself" home maintenance pursued for essentially economic reasons (rather than enjoyment, etc.) and family shopping and economic exchange relationships. These kinds of activities serve to define *man as an economic being.*

Thus, when we speak of voluntary action at the level of individual behavior we are not talking about human behavior that is primarily motivated by physiological needs or personal-social necessity, nor about what one does because of coercion or socio-political necessity, nor again about what one does mainly to earn his living or to gain direct, immediate economic benefits. What we *are* talking about is human behavior that is *essentially motivated by the desire for other kinds of psychic benefits of one kind or another.*

Perhaps our scheme can be made clearer by suggesting the similarity between the present classification scheme and that of Maslow (1954). Maslow, in quite a different context, has classified human motivation in terms of a hierarchy of needs, arguing that the more basic needs in the hierarchy have to be satisfied before an individual is motivated by the higher level needs. In his scheme, physiological needs come first, as the most basic ones, followed by needs for physical protection, and then for security and love. Higher level needs are cognitive needs (curiosity, learning, exploration, interest) and then self-actualization needs (self-expression, realization of fullest personal potentialities for action and relationships in society). *In terms of the present scheme, voluntary action is (individual or collective) human behavior primarily motivated by the cognitive and especially the self-actualization needs of Maslow's hierarchy, while non-voluntary action is human behavior primarily motivated by the three more "basic" levels of need in his hierarchy.* This is at best a crude approximation of the relationship between his scheme and ours, of course, but we hope it may be helpful.

The context of voluntary action, like that of any other kind of behavior, may or may not be a formal organization. The motives involved in voluntary action may or may not be altruistic (oriented toward helping or satisfying others). The essential notion is that *individual voluntary action, as defined here, is what we do not because we have to but because we want to in view of the higher level psychic benefits it may give us and in view of some commitment to a larger goal.* Voluntary action need not always be rewarded with psychic benefits for the individual, even though it is often engaged in with the belief and hope that such benefits will be forthcoming. In fact, much voluntary action does not even have "psychic benefits" as its primary conscious motivation. More frequently, the individual sees himself as acting out of a commitment to help someone or to change some external situation. Psychic benefits play a more important motivational role in self-expressive voluntary action than in the instrumental forms of voluntary action—service-oriented, issue-oriented, and occupational self-interest voluntary action.

Individual voluntary action is that which gives personal meaning to life. It is that which one freely chooses to do either for enjoyment in the short term and/or from commitment to some longer term goal that is not merely a manifestation of bio-social man, socio-political man, or economic man. Voluntary action is human behavior rooted in man's capacity for enjoyment, in his compassion with the sufferings of others; in his imagination and curiosity; in his desire for the betterment of his own, his family's and his fellow workers' economic, political, and social situation; and in his desire for a more rational, just, and humane society. These kinds of motivations and the activities that follow from them help to define *man as a voluntary being*—man as a conscious, willing agent who can in part help to shape his own destiny and his own satisfactions in life—*voluntary man.* Voluntary action is *not* that which an individual does mainly because he is compelled by physiological needs, coerced by threat of physical-legal-social-political sanctions of a substantial nature, or spurred by the expectation of direct economic benefit for himself (or his family and friends) as a high-probability result of the activity.

In sum, we are suggesting that individual human behavior can be classified into four major heuristic categories in terms of the prime motivating forces operating upon an individual at any point in time: bio-socially compelled behavior, socio-politically coerced behavior, direct economic behavior, and voluntary behavior. The meaning of each of these four categories has been explicated earlier. It is important now to point out that *all of this is a matter of degree*, and that any given individual can be acting at a given point in time under the influence of all four kinds of motivation. In our earlier formulations we have emphasized that individuals or individual actions may be distinguished in terms of their *primary* or *essential* motivation. This phrasing was chosen because it readily permits theoretical and empirical gradations and combinations of motivations.

More specifically, we are most definitely *not* suggesting a dichotomous, "either-or" approach to defining voluntary action. Like nearly everything else in the world, voluntary action has many gradations and it is difficult (if not impossible) to state with finality where economic behavior or socio-politically coerced behavior shades into voluntary action. This does not mean that the polar ideal types of each of these kinds of behavior is unclear, nor does it mean that attempts to define any of these kinds of behavior are fruitless. Thus, *whenever we speak of "voluntary" action in contrast with all kinds of "non-voluntary" action or behavior, we are using the latter term as a shorthand for a much longer and more detailed explanation and description of the classes of activity that are not included under our technical term "voluntary action." "Voluntary action" represents an "ideal type" of behavior, a heuristic device.*

We further recognize that there are many alternative ways of conceptualizing and categorizing human behavior and human motivations—some schemes with many more classes of motives and some with fewer. It is our contention, however, that the present scheme of classification of motives is likely to prove most useful (or at least *more* useful than other existing schemes) for the study of voluntary action. When one begins to engage in empirical work on individual behavior, we strongly advocate that each of the four major types of motivation we distinguish be separately measured (as continuous variables) at several points over a period of time for each individual. On the basis of information from such a study one will be in a position to determine whether a given individual is engaging primarily in voluntary action, economic action, etc., at these different points in time. An individual's behavior at a given point in time may most accurately be expressed, in terms of the present scheme, as a position in a four-dimensional space representing the strength of each of the four major types of motivation. It may be useful at times to express individual behavior in terms of a greater number of dimensions, or then again it may be useful at times to express such behavior in terms of a single dimension from voluntary to non-voluntary. When the latter is done, we must realize that this is a simplification of a more complex reality, to be justified only on the basis of producing more fruitful or easily understood results in a given context.

Another way of expressing the above concerns about multi-dimensionality is to state that in reality we expect to find very few "purely voluntary" actions, just as we expect to find very few "purely economic" actions or "purely socio-politically coerced" actions or "purely bio-socially compelled" actions. Real behavior of real individuals has a complex motivational pattern and one that varies greatly over time and across situational contexts. What begins with one primary motivation may end with another. Yet this does not diminish the necessity for having a reasonably clear and operationalizable definition of voluntary action as an ideal type. Nearly any human action may have *some* aspects of bio-social compulsion, of socio-political coercion, and of direct economic benefit expectations. Yet this does not deny that certain actions are primarily motivated by considerations other than these—by expectations of psychic benefits and by commitment to other kinds of larger goals (helping people, changing society, etc.). Such actions are here defined as voluntary action. *The existence of biological, political, and economic man does not deny or preclude the simultaneous existence of voluntary man.*

Thus understood, voluntary action overlaps substantially with what is commonly called "leisure behavior," yet there is no complete correspondence between the two realms. Voluntary action can involve working at a poorly paying job simply because one believes in the work being done, whereas such behavior would *not* be called leisure behavior. Similarly, one may raise minks for profit or repair one's house in one's spare time, but this would not be called voluntary action *if* the primary motivation were economic rather than the psychic benefits of the activity itself or its results.

Similarly, voluntary action as here defined overlaps substantially with efforts to bring about social change. Yet there is much more to voluntary action than simply seeking social change, either individually or collectively. To define voluntary action narrowly as collective activity directly aimed at stimulating or controlling social change (as does Theodore in chap. 8 of this volume) is to ignore the vast majority of voluntary action that is directed at less socially innovative (but still important) goals of service, enjoyment, self-expression, and occupational self-interest.

Perhaps the area of most disagreement will be in regard to whether we should include *non*-altruistic ("self-oriented") activities in the category of voluntary action phenomena. The traditional view of voluntary action has emphasized mainly "altruistic" behavior. Warriner (in chap. 16 of this volume) has provided us with an "up-dated" statement of the approach, spelling out clearly the relations between altruistic behavior and voluntary action. We will argue that voluntary action phenomena definitely *should* include *non*-altruistic behavior, even though the altruistic versus non-altruistic distinction is an important one to be made *within* the broader category of voluntary phenomena. Few will argue against the inclusion of altruistic behavior as voluntary action. Perhaps the most important reason for including *non*-altruistic behavior as voluntary action phenomena is that there are more basic similarities than differences between altruistic and non-altruistic voluntary action phenomena. This statement, of course, is a theoretical assumption. It argues that, in the long run, more fruitful theory and research will result from considering both altruistic and non-altruistic voluntary action as falling into the same broad theoretical category. Only time will tell, but we can at least point out why we think this assumption is a good one.

For one thing, perhaps most kinds of voluntary action have both self-oriented and other-oriented components; human beings are complex and usually tend to engage in voluntary action for some combination of types of expectations. At the extremes, the distinction may be clear, as in the case of someone who sacrifices his life to save a stranger (altruistic, other-oriented) versus the case of someone who goes fishing alone simply because he likes to fish alone (non-altruistic, self-oriented). Yet in most cases people engage in voluntary action *partly* because they want to help others or achieve some larger altruistic goal, and *partly* because they enjoy directly the activity involved, the thought of possible results of the activity, the thought of themselves doing something for the general good of society, etc.

Another reason for including both altruistic and non-altruistic behavior as voluntary action is simply past social scientific usage. In dealing specifically with voluntary associations, sociologists have long considered as similar both altruistic organizations such as the Red Cross and non-altruistic organizations such as fraternal orders. If we exclude *non*-altruistic behavior from our denotative definition of individual voluntary action phenomena, therefore, we shall be doing violence at the collectivity level to the interests and theoretical perspectives of numerous social scientists in eliminating from consideration hobby clubs, fraternal organizations, leisure and recreation organizations, as well as eliminating from consideration people who are active in altruistic organizations for essentially *non*-altruistic reasons (e.g., the woman who joins the Red Cross for the prestige it might give her rather than because she is strongly committed to the organization's goals). Further, if we eliminate non-altruistic behavior from consideration, we shall become immediately involved in all sorts of difficult discrimination problems, attempting to distinguish what kinds of behavior are altruistic relative to whom and for whom, who decides what is good for whom (what people actually want vs. what is "good for them"), what is good and what is bad, do ends justify means (*all* means, or just some means), which is more important—short- or long-term benefit, etc.

Thus, we suggest that although the notions of psychic benefits and commitment to larger goals are crucial to both a denotative and a connotative definition of voluntary action, we further suggest that the notion of altruism or other-orientation in contrast with self-orientation is not a crucial *defining* element, even though it may be of great interest as a variable quality once voluntary action has been defined. For the moment, then, we are willing to include in the class of voluntary action behavior performed by individuals essentially for psychic benefits or for non-coercive, non-remunerative goals, whether that behavior be almost completely altruistic in the best sense of this word, or whether it be competely selfish (egotistical), in the worst sense of that word. To determine whether an act is voluntary we do *not* ask whether it is performed out of duty, guilt, paternalism, a desire for prestige, religious fervor, a sense of self-expression or demonstration of personal competence, a sense of justice, a view of long-term personal gain (even in a financial sense), social pressure from significant others, or the purest sense of altruism and love of mankind. All of these motivations are relevant kinds of psychic benefit and commitment to larger goals that would lead us to define an act as voluntary in the present sense. *Voluntary action directed at the long-range betterment of society and the general welfare may be the "best" kind of voluntary action in the eyes of most people, yet there are many other important kinds of voluntary action worthy of study and inclusion in the class of voluntary action phenomena, even if not clearly aimed at the general welfare*—for example, riots, wildcat strikes, fraternity hazing, shoplifting for "kicks," bingo parties, "social drinking," and perhaps even watching TV.

There are a number of further important points to be made by way of elaborating our definition of voluntary action so far. First, it is concerned only with individual behavior. (Separate definitions will be offered for voluntary action at the level of groups and societies.) Note also that the definition attempts to indicate how to determine whether or not a given *act or set of acts* by an individual are voluntary action. No attempt has yet been made to designate individuals as "volunteers" or "non-volunteers" on the whole (although this could now easily be done in a rough way by specifying some role or set of acts and then determining the proportion of voluntary actions involved). As defined here, voluntary action can be component of many different kinds of roles and types of activity. A business executive may engage in voluntary action one hour per year, while the leader of some social movement may engage in voluntary action fourteen hours per day every day of the year, or vice versa (the executive every day and the social movement leader one hour per year).

Second, it should be noted that there is no ideal "natural language" term available to refer to the kind of phenomena in which we are interested here. Both the term "volunteer participation" and the term "voluntary action" have their own drawbacks. By depending mainly on the term "voluntary action," we are attempting to avoid the creation of a neologism while at the same time trying to make it clear that we use this term in a special way. It is especially important, for instance, to be clear that our use of the term "voluntary" in the present context is quite a bit *narrower* than the common use of the term.

As commonly used, "voluntary" refers to the quality of having been chosen freely and consciously from among two or more alternatives without any substantial compulsion or coercion being applied. In this common sense of the term, voluntary acts are acts essentially under one's own conscious control; involuntary acts are acts essentially under the control of external forces (whether physical or social) or of one's own unconscious psychological or physiological drives. In either case, individual actions are viewed as determined by prior events, not as random actions unrelated to prior events. Palisi (in chap. 3 of this volume) has dealt with this problem on a more extensive basis. However, we disagree with his proposal to drop the concept of "voluntary" and replace it with a number of types of social forces. We believe the term "voluntary," as explicated here, to be still useful (especially if one assumes that *all* behavior is determined by prior and present states).

Our present definition and usage of the term "voluntary" differ essentially from the usual philosophical meaning of the term in that we *also* exclude from the category of "voluntary action" behavior that is to a substantial extent freely chosen but that is directed at personal maintenance, at compliance with strong social-legal-economic sanctions, or at direct high-probability remuneration as a result of the activity. Thus, we use "voluntary action" as a technical term. Its major drawback is that it will tend to be confused by some with the common sense or philosophical use of the term "voluntary act."[1] Such a confusion can be easily recognized, in most cases, since it leads to viewing the opposite of voluntary action solely as "involuntary action" rather than as "non-voluntary action," which would be the preferred usage under the present approach (even though involuntary—coerced or compelled—action is an important sub-type of non-voluntary action).

The possible alternative term, "volunteer participation," has its own virtues and disadvantages. Its virtue is that it avoids confusion with the common sense use of the term "voluntary" by emphasizing the "volunteer" aspect of voluntary phenomena. The term "volunteer participation" suggests acts chosen not only without compulsion, but also chosen out of positive commitment to larger goals and the possible psychic benefits of such acts. The drawback of the term "volunteer participation" is that it commonly suggests too narrow a range of phenomena, just as "voluntary action" tends to be taken too broadly. The term "volunteer participation" as commonly understood will not serve as the most general term because our definition includes as voluntary action many kinds of acts that are not in fact performed by "volunteers" per se. As we have defined the term, "voluntary action" can easily refer to the actions of people who are partly or even fully paid for their activities. The essential distinguishing characteristic of voluntary action, as we have defined it, is not the lack of direct remuneration (acting as a volunteer), but rather the primary emphasis on psychic rewards and commitment to larger goals, whether or not there are also monetary rewards. The emphasis is on the lack of primary concern for direct high-probability economic benefit.

As we define it, voluntary action *may* be directly remunerated. Clearly, actions that are *not* directly remunerated at all and that are performed essentially for psychic benefits or from commitment to larger goals are included within the proposed definition of voluntary action. But wherever there *is* direct remuneration for a role or action, the discrimination problem for the analyst is heightened. *In the usual case, if an individual is remunerated at all for acts that fall into the defined category of voluntary action, he is not fully remunerated. That is, the direct economic benefit he receives is not equal to the market value of the services rendered.* For example, someone with a college degree or an established craft skill may forego a regular "commercial" occupation in order to join the Peace Corps or take on a similar quasi-volunteer occupation (e.g., become one of "Nader's Raiders"). The pay received for his Peace Corps activities will be significantly less than he might otherwise make if he simply sold his services to the highest bidder on the open market. *This differential between the market value of one's services and the actual amount of economic benefits received (if anything at all) is a good, though not infallible, indicator of voluntary action.*

The differential in remuneration works well as an *exclusive* indicator of voluntary action (excluding all non-voluntary action), yet it is a bit too narrow in that it excludes those people who happen to be paid the full market value of their service, even though their essential motivation in the job is psychic benefit and commitment to larger goals, rather than the economic benefit itself (e.g., dedicated professionals). For those people who are fully paid for their jobs or activities, the crucial question is probably this, "Would you still want to be doing what you are doing even if you were *not* paid for it, or were paid much less for it?" If the answer is truthfully affirmative, then that person is really engaging in voluntary action *even though* he is fully paid for it. Of course, such cases are probably the exception rather than the rule in fully remunerated occupations. Voluntary action is probably much more common among persons who are *not* fully remunerated or not remunerated at all for their services and participation.

One of the virtues of the present way of looking at voluntary action is that it permits us to speak precisely and meaningfully not only about the fully paid voluntary action of individuals but also about individuals for whom their paid occupations in voluntary action agencies are *not* voluntary action in our technical sense of the term. Just as an individual in business or industry may be primarily motivated by the desire for psychic benefits and commitment to larger goals, so also may an individual in a nonprofit, non-governmental organization be primarily motivated by the desire for direct high-probability economic benefit. Put more simply, there are businessmen who love their work and its contribution to society, just as there are people in the "voluntary sector" who don't love their work and do it just for the salary involved.

It is an empirical matter to find out the proportion of voluntary action involved in any sector or organization of a given society at a given point in its history and development. And it is an empirical matter to find out whether a given act or role for a particular individual is in fact voluntary action or not. The same overt acts may be performed in the same setting by two different individuals, with those actions being voluntary action for one and just a job for the other.

For example, a business executive may be assigned to work for a period of time for the United Fund campaign as part of his paid job. This executive may perform the same sort of acts as some unpaid volunteer member of the United Fund campaign. If the executive is doing the work mainly because it is just an assigned task, while the unpaid volunteer is doing it mainly because he believes in it, the executive is *not* engaging in voluntary action by our definition while the unpaid volunteer is. To make the distinction even more clear, we may point out that a fully paid staff member of the United Fund is engaging in voluntary action by our definition *only* if he is mainly doing the work for psychic benefits and commitment to larger goals. If simply doing a job and getting paid is his main concern, then he is not engaging in voluntary action any more than the paid business executive just mentioned. And finally, if the paid business executive gets so wrapped up in the United Fund work that the next year he does the same work as an unpaid volunteer (rather than as a part of his paid job in a business organization), then his work the first time would be largely classified as voluntary action because of the shift in his concerns toward psychic benefit and larger goals rather than direct remuneration for the task at that time.

This last example brings up another point of interest that we alluded to briefly earlier. People's motivations for a given role or activity change over time. What begins as voluntary action in our terms may end up as no more than a paid job; and conversely, what begins as merely a paid job can become voluntary action if there is the appropriate shift in motivations. *This means that the reasons why an individual gets involved in an activity or role in the first place may be quite different from the reasons why he continues to perform that activity or role.* In every case this matter is an empirical question, not something to be inferred with perfect accuracy from the type of task or role itself (though *on the average*, inferences from the type of task or role may be quite accurate).

Some elaboration is in order regarding the earlier point about the differential between the full market value of an individual's services and the amount of actual remuneration. The technical term in economics that best refers to this differential is "opportunity cost"—the monetary value of the opportunities that are foregone. To use another term from economics, this differential constitutes a "grant" to the recipient. This calculation can only be a very rough one, since it must take into consideration not only the general and specific job markets but also the specific skills, education, personality, experience, and background of the individual. Important also is the distinction between short-term and long-term "opportunity cost" differentials for an individual. The long-term opportunity cost is much more difficult to calculate, since it takes as a base what an individual *might* have become in the long term, given his personal developmental potentials, intelligence, personality, family background, etc. Yet many of our life decisions have permanent effects on our subsequent short-term opportunities.

A bright youth from an upper-middle-class family who early decides to enter the ministry or social work as a career, and seeks the training for such a career, has rather permanently affected his later chances to become a highly paid business executive. This is one kind of *long-term opportunity cost* to him. The *short-term opportunity cost* refers to how much remuneration he foregoes by choosing one role or job for which he is *currently suited* as contrasted with other higher paying possibilities. In the field of social work, for instance, he might have the opportunity and choose to become a well-paid university professor. If this is about the best-paying job he could possibly get, given his current level of personal capacities, training, personality, and experience, then there is no *short*-term opportunity cost to him if he chooses this job, even though there still will be a large *long*-term opportunity cost relative to the economic benefits he might have received if he had chosen to become a business executive or physician. On the other hand, if he chooses instead to become a poorly paid caseworker in the rural South, helping people that most need help in his view, there is both a *short*-term *and* a *long*-term opportunity cost. Not only has he foregone a probably quite highly paid business (or other) career to become a social worker, but he has also foregone the best paying job in the short term in order to perform some other role that he believes to be more personally satisfying and socially important. Similar examples of long- and short-term opportunity costs could be given for a variety of other types of tasks, roles or occupations.

What is important in terms of the present definition of voluntary action is *consciously* foregone opportunity costs, not *un*consciously foregone opportunities. It is an indicator of voluntary action to forego a higher paying job in favor of a lower paying job that is expected to be more interesting, exciting, physically rewarding, helpful to society, etc. Yet once the choice has been made, the actual behavior on the job may or *may not* involve more voluntary action. On the other hand, it is not voluntary action to forego a better paying job simply because one is unaware of its existence or is mistaken in the relative economic benefits of various job or role opportunities.

As a final point by way of elaboration of the present definition of voluntary action, we must once again state explicitly that voluntary action is a matter of degree. There are no sharp and clean edges or boundaries where voluntary action suddenly becomes coercion or personal maintenance or just a job, etc. Our definition of voluntary action refers to behavior *primarily* motivated by the expectation of psychic benefits and commitment to larger goals, emphasizing one end of a complex continuum. Yet there is usually some component (however small) of psychic satisfaction and/or commitment to larger goals in *each* of our actions. What distinguishes voluntary action from these other actions is the *magnitude* of the psychic satisfaction/commitment to larger goal components. Where it will be generally most fruitful to make a "cutting point" on the continuum is a matter for future research to investigate. Perhaps there is some clear point at which expectation of psychic benefits and commitment to larger goals suddenly become paramount and associated behaviors change markedly, or conversely, a point at which these motivations become secondary and economic remuneration, coercion, or some other factor becomes critical, with associated behavior changing markedly.

To sum up briefly, voluntary action as defined here includes all behavior (whether individual or collective) that is primarily a product of commitment to values other than sheer, direct economic benefit, self-preservation, physical force, physiological need, and psychic or social compulsion. Voluntary action may involve helping others, helping oneself, or both. In any event, voluntary action tends to include all of those activities which most serve to give meaning and satisfaction to life from the standpoint of the individual.

Although we have not placed much emphasis on designating individuals as "volunteers," we may now define this latter term for the sake of completeness. *A volunteer may be defined broadly as a person engaging in voluntary action with little or no direct economic benefit being received as a result of this activity.* This is probably the most common case of voluntary action by individuals. However, a person can engage in voluntary action, not be remunerated at all, and still not commonly be considered a "volunteer"–when he votes, goes fishing, goes to a party or informal discussion group, etc. Hence a volunteer may be defined more narrowly as a person engaging in voluntary action in a formally organized social context. *A quasi-volunteer would be someone engaging in voluntary action with some significant direct economic benefit being received, though not the full market value of the services performed* (i.e., with at least a short-term opportunity cost present from the standpoint of the individual). In these terms, Peace Corps and VISTA volunteers are *quasi-volunteers*.

A *non-volunteer* would be someone who is receiving essentially full economic benefits for his services performed; such a person might or might not be engaging in voluntary action. We lack any really good term to refer to non-volunteers who are engaging specifically in voluntary action, as defined here. Contradictory as it may seem, the term *"voluntary non-volunteer"* might well be used to refer to persons who are fully remunerated for engaging in voluntary action (e.g., paid professionals and leaders in the voluntary sector). All other persons who are fully paid for their services but who are *not* engaging in voluntary action would then have to be called *"non-voluntary non-volunteers."* We grant that the latter two suggested terms leave much to be desired. Nevertheless, their meaning is clear and they are consistent with the other definitions offered here. Lacking any better ideas or suggestions for the moment, we offer these tentatively for what they might be worth to the reader.

Voluntary Action and Social Systems

So far we have been concerned with voluntary action as a characteristic of individual acts or as a description of individuals themselves. Yet it is also important to consider the definition of voluntary roles, voluntary groups, voluntary organizations, voluntary communities, the voluntary sector of society, and even a voluntary society. *The most important forms of voluntary action tend to be collective.* Since we shall be defining these terms in accord with the degree of voluntary action empirically present in each case, the occurrence of voluntary roles, etc., will always be relative to a particular time, place, social setting, culture and set of actors.

First let us consider the smaller types of social systems and social roles. When we term a role, group or formal organization "voluntary" we have in mind basically the amount of voluntary action that usually tends to be engaged in by members of that role, group or organization while acting essentially as members. This method of defining voluntary social systems emphasizes building definitions of higher level phenomena out of clearly defined lower level phenomena. Such an approach is a consciously "psycho-sociological" one, in contrast to the more usual sociological approach that might define voluntary social systems solely on the basis of the official or inferred goals of the system.

If the usual sociological approach is taken, one is hard pressed to deal with the situation where the goals of the social system in question are voluntary and yet the members of the system are not generally engaging in voluntary action as we have defined it. An example would be a large foundation or welfare organization that *claimed* to seek the general betterment of society, yet whose members mainly were motivated by economic interests rather than psychic benefits. Similarly, the sociological approach to definition is hard pressed to deal with the reverse situation where an organization with official economic goals actually is made up mainly of members who love their jobs or their results and are committed to larger goals (other than profit and coercion), hence actually engaging in voluntary action. An example would be a profit-making cooperative or corporation set up by a religious sect, most of whose members were mainly interested in preserving and demonstrating the validity of their faith rather than being interested in economic benefits per se. In fact, they might all draw only subsistence pocket money, allowing their "earnings" to accrue to the cooperative or corporation itself.

The psycho-sociological approach, on the other hand, has no difficulty in defining and classifying the foregoing examples. The first example would clearly not be classified as a voluntary action organization while the second example would, because of the nature of the motivations of the members. Another way of indicating the value of this approach to defining voluntary social systems is to *consider the very nature of the term "voluntary." This term really makes sense directly and concretely only when referring to the behavior of individuals. To start out at the level of social systems and try to define a voluntary group without reference to the behavior of individuals is a most difficult task and probably not feasible. For these sorts of reasons, therefore, we have chosen to define voluntary social systems primarily in terms of the relative amount of voluntary action engaged in by their members, irrespective of what the official goals and type of group may be.*

Landsberger (in chapter 9 of this volume) has argued that organizations and groups should not be classified solely on the basis of the motivations of participating individuals. Moreover, he argues that the organizational level should be considered in its own right as a starting point for the classification of organizations. We agree that, in dealing with some problems, the organizational level may be the most fruitful to begin with. This is the case in the example given by

Landsberger where the organization itself functions to constrain the behavior of its members regardless of the nature of their motivations for belonging to and participating in the organization. There are, of course, many fruitful typologies and classification schemes that might be used to describe types of organizations and social systems. Further, the system level at which one starts is bound to vary from one researcher to the next, and even for the same researcher when dealing with different problems. However, the problem of definitional consistency between system levels remains when we switch from one problem to the other. We are arguing that the *most fruitful* approach, taking account of the problem of definitional consistency, is to be found at the psycho-sociological level. Only time and future research and theory will tell if we are correct.

A *social role* has been defined (Smith, 1967, p. 152) as a "set of norms (normative expectations for behavior, both covert and overt) associated with a particular social identity." A social identity is a commonly recognized category or type of persons having importance for other persons because of some attributed distinctive characteristics. For instance, social identities are such naturally occurring types as woman, American, college professor, friend, etc. The roles corresponding to these social identities are the sets of normative expectations for behavior associated with being a woman, an American, a college professor, a friend, etc.

In line with our general psycho-sociological strategy of definition, then, a *voluntary role* may be defined as any role the majority of whose normative expectations involve engaging in voluntary action when performing the role. In the usual case, a voluntary role is also a role the majority of whose incumbents are *actually* engaging voluntary action when performing the role. If the latter is *not* the case, in spite of specification by norms that it *should* be the case, then we have an example of a voluntary role deteriorating (or, less pejoratively, changing) into a de facto non-voluntary role.

Not all voluntary roles are also volunteer roles. The latter comprise a sub-set of the former. A *volunteer role* may be broadly defined as a voluntary role for which participating role incumbents are not expected to receive any significant direct economic benefit as a result of their activity. A more narrow definition would stress that volunteer roles take place in a formally organized context, in addition to lacking any significant remuneration. A *quasi-volunteer* role may then be defined as a voluntary role for which participating role incumbents are expected to receive *some* significant, direct economic benefit (e.g., reimbursement of expenses, subsistence allowance, a small stipend or honorarium), but who are *not* expected to receive direct economic benefits corresponding to the *full* market value of services rendered. All other roles that are not volunteer or quasi-volunteer roles may be termed *non-volunteer roles.* Some non-volunteer roles are still voluntary roles (because voluntary action is involved)—the roles of minister or priest or rabbi, for instance, or the role of social worker. But *most* non-volunteer roles are also non-voluntary roles—occupational roles that have only secondary or minor components of voluntary action, for instance.

Note that these definitions do not require that *entry* into the role be a voluntary act. We already have an adequate psycho-sociological terminology for distinguishing roles whose entry is a voluntary act from those whose entry is not a voluntary act. *Ascribed roles* are those whose *entry* is non-voluntary, while *achieved or contingent roles* are those whose entry is a voluntary act in the present terms. Thus, it makes more sense in our view to reserve the term "voluntary role" for roles whose norms specify voluntary action and whose whole performance tends to be voluntary action for most incumbents. So defined, *most* roles in such organizations as the Peace Corps, the Red Cross, and the Black Panther party would be voluntary roles, while *most* roles in General Motors and the United States government would be non-voluntary, even though *all* of these roles would also be contingent rather than ascribed (i.e., subject to voluntary entry and exit).

The term *group* has been defined (Smith, 1967, p. 141) as *"(1) the largest set of two or more individuals who are jointly characterized by (2) a network of relevant communications, (3) a shared sense of collective identity, and (4) one or more shared goal dispositions with associated normative strength."* So defined, "group" is a very broad term, synonymous with "social system," and encompassing small informal groups, large and complex formal organizations, as well as whole societies. From the present perspective, a *voluntary group* may be defined as a group whose goals primarily involve voluntary action and most of whose members are engaging in voluntary action when they act as group members.

From this definition follow similarly the definitions of *informal* voluntary groups and *formal* voluntary groups. Groups may be divided into two major types—formal and informal. A *formal group or organized group* has been defined (Smith, 1969a, p. 2) as "a group that has an *explicit leadership structure* (at least one recognized leadership role whose incumbent has the right under specified conditions to make binding decisions for the whole group), a *natural proper name* (a unique, idiosyncratic label that is conventionally applied to the group in question and essentially only to them), and *clear group boundaries* (an explicit and precise conventional way of determining who is and who is not an analytical member of the given group)." *Informal groups* are all groups that are not formal groups.

Obviously, however, formalization is a matter of degree. Since the foregoing definition of "formal group" hinges on the meaning of the term "analytical member," it is important to define this term. Analytical members of a group have been defined (Smith, 1969a, p. 5) as "persons or groups who conventionally provide services primarily aimed at accomplishing one or more of the group's goals." In turn, an *organization* may be defined as "the largest set of analytical group members of an organized (formal) group having essential sovereignty and policy control over their own objectives and modes of accomplishing them" (Smith, 1969a, p. 5). Organized groups that exist as sub-units of a larger organization are termed "part organizations" to indicate their dependence on the larger whole. Particular branch offices of General Motors are thus organized groups and part organizations but not organizations in themselves, since they lack essential sovereignty. Similarly, local chapters of the Red Cross are part organizations, as are local parishes of the Catholic Church.

Informal voluntary groups would then be defined as informal groups whose goals primarily involve voluntary action and the majority of whose members are engaging in voluntary action when they act as group members. An example would be a clique of girls who frequently spend their leisure time together listening to records and talking about boys, or an informal group of army officers who are plotting to depose their president, prime minister, or king. *Formal voluntary groups* would correspondingly be defined as formal groups whose goals primarily involve voluntary action and the majority of whose members are engaging in voluntary action when they act as group members. And *formal voluntary organizations* or simply *voluntary organizations* would be defined as organizations (rather than simply groups) whose goals primarily involve voluntary action and the majority of whose members are engaging in voluntary action when they act as group members. One troop of the Boy Scouts would be a formal voluntary group, while the whole Boy Scouts of America would be an example of a formal voluntary organization (since the latter has essential sovereignty). The Peace Corps of the United States would also be an example of a formal voluntary *group*, but *not* a formal voluntary *organization*, since it is not autonomous and its ultimate policy is determined by the U.S. government. Thus, all formal voluntary organizations are also formal voluntary groups, but not all formal voluntary groups are also formal voluntary organizations. *To be termed a formal voluntary organization, a formal voluntary group must be essentially autonomous* (see Smith, 1969a, p. 5f).

It should be noted that the foregoing definition of formal voluntary organization is broader than the usual one, just as the present definition of voluntary action in general is broader. Moreover, there are special difficulties in keeping the foregoing definition of a formal voluntary organization clearly separate from a definition of formal *volunteer* organizations. We freely admit that it may be more trouble than it is worth to attempt to distinguish between these two, but consistency of definition and clarity of empirical, denotative reference demand it. "Formal *voluntary* organization" is the broader term while "formal *volunteer* organization" refers specifically to those kinds of formal voluntary organizations whose goals primarily involve *volunteer* activity and where the majority of members are participating in the organization essentially as volunteers.

It is the latter kind of organization that is usually called a "voluntary association" by sociologists. The first author of this chapter has also for some years been terming such organizations "FVOs." The present approach gives no reason to abandon the term "voluntary association" or to stop using "FVO" as an abbreviation specifically referring to formal *volunteer* organizations. Instead, the present approach would simply point out that voluntary associations or FVOs must be seen as but one sub-type of formal voluntary organizations in general. The terms "FVO," "voluntary association," and "formal voluntary organization" may all be loosely applied to part organizations, even though they are most properly applied to autonomous organized groups existing through time. The terminology suggested above applies correspondingly to organized groups or formal groups, just as with organizations per se (i.e., we may speak of *organized voluntary groups*, and *organized volunteer groups* as a special sub-type of the latter).

A few examples might help to make the foregoing terminology clear. A local troop of the Boy Scouts would be a formal *volunteer group*, and the Boy Scouts of America would be a formal *volunteer organization*, since it is autonomous, its goals primarily involve volunteer activity, and its members are mainly volunteers. On the other hand, the branches of the Peace Corps in various countries, *as well as* the national headquarters group, might best be termed a formal *voluntary group* (part organization) but *not* a formal *volunteer group* (at most a formal *quasi*-volunteer group) since most members are at least partially remunerated for their services, and the whole group is not autonomous of the U.S. government. Some but not all organized *voluntary* groups (formal voluntary groups) are *also* organized *volunteer* groups (formal volunteer groups), depending on the goals of the group and on the proportion of volunteers within their membership. Some organized voluntary groups, thus, are *not* organized volunteer groups, because they have mainly a paid staff as members and their goals do not involve primarily volunteer activity.

A *voluntary community* is a special kind of human settlement that emphasizes collective voluntary action by all members for the mutual benefit of other members of that settlement. Unlike the ordinary local community, the members of the voluntary community have some kind of special ideology or belief-value system that guides the development and operation of the settlement. Also unlike ordinary local communities, a voluntary community has a strong sense of group identity and its goals commit its members to joint activity both in work and in leisure to further the community's special goals, with an attempt to minimize contact with "outsiders." Finally, entry into and exit from the voluntary community (in its pure form) are voluntary action on the part of members of the community. Examples of voluntary communities include kibbutzim in Israel, earlier Shaker communities in the United States, so-called "hippie communes" in contemporary America, and various monastic religious orders all over the world.

Having now defined what we mean by voluntary roles, (formal and informal) voluntary groups, (formal and informal) volunteer groups, formal voluntary and formal volunteer organizations, and voluntary communities, it remains only for us to define the voluntary sector of society and the voluntary society. Economists and other social scientists and social observers often view society as consisting of two major "sectors"—the public and the private, or the governmental and the commercial (or business) sector. When used in this sense, the term "sector" refers to a broad class of groups and organizations. Richard Cornuelle (1970, p. 46) has suggested that the remaining groups and organizations of society be termed the *independent sector*. On the basis of our foregoing discussion, we would prefer the term *voluntary sector* for these remaining groups and organizations.

We would also suggest that these "sector classifications" are very rough, at best, so that *voluntary groups* (in our terms) may also be found in the government sector (e.g., the Peace Corps, VISTA, etc.) or in the commercial sector (e.g., a profit-making corporation or cooperative run by a religious sect; a corporate volunteer program). To an even greater extent one might find individual voluntary action or voluntary roles in the government sector or the commercial sector, wherever people are performing their roles mainly for psychic benefits and commitment to larger goals rather than mainly for other reasons. Conversely, there may be many groups, organizations, persons or roles broadly categorized into the voluntary sector that do not involve voluntary action. This imperfect exclusiveness of the three broad sectors, relative to the various kinds of individual and social system voluntary action we have previously defined, should not be particularly troubling. The broad, if rough, categorization by sectors still has value for summary purposes. The sector labels refer to three important aspects of society that may be viewed as equivalent to "forests"; and the earlier definitions presented allow greater precision when dealing with specific "trees" (individuals, groups, organizations, roles) in these "forests."

Finally, the *voluntary society* may be defined as a society in which the majority of members are engaging in voluntary action most of their waking hours. This is an ideal type of society that probably exists nowhere in the world today, yet it may be an important goal for all societies in the future. In primitive societies there is very little voluntary action simply because so much time must be taken up with the pressing business of working to keep oneself and one's family alive. Peasant or pre-industrial societies give little improvement, for most people, in the opportunities for voluntary action. It is only in modern industrial society that we really begin to see increased opportunities on a broad scale for the discretionary use of time, so that voluntary action becomes a viable possibility for large numbers of people for a substantial portion of their waking hours. But note that the voluntary society is not the same as a leisure society, since voluntary action is not synonymous with leisure behavior. The voluntary society might well involve the majority of people working hard at jobs they believe in and that give them substantial psychic benefits and a sense of commitment to larger goals, rather than merely plugging along to make a living and following a coercive set of social expectations and laws.

Major Sub-types of Individual
Voluntary Action

The foregoing two sections of this chapter serve to define some of the major aspects of voluntary action at both the individual level and social system level.

Still, it will be useful to begin again here with the category of all individual voluntary action (as defined earlier) and ask what are the most analytically useful sub-types within this broad category. As with any abstract category having numerous elements classified within it, individual voluntary action covers a multitude of types of phenomena. How we sub-classify these phenomena depends to an important degree on what we are trying to do. The present purpose is to suggest some small number of sub-types of individual voluntary action that will generally make sense for placing in context our review and synthesis of the literature in Part Two of this volume.

Our classification of individual voluntary action into sub-types is based on *three theoretically and empirically important dimensions of voluntary action: level of direct economic benefits received for the activity, level of formalization of the setting, and degree of autonomy of the setting.* These three dimensions define a table with six major cells in it, as in table 10-1. Only six cells result, rather than eight, because the autonomy dimension becomes relevant mainly for the formally organized settings rather than for the informal settings.

The typology of the voluntary action of individuals is not intended to be "revolutionary." It may be useful mainly in pointing out that there has been a tendency in the past for scholars, researchers, and professionals to focus on no more than one of the cells as voluntary action. This chapter and the typology itself aim at suggesting the possibilities of relating and integrating diverse perspectives and orientations toward individual voluntary action.

It must be noted that the typology does not itself define individual voluntary action. Instead, it locates some major contexts and settings within which individual voluntary action can be found. While providing examples of each type, the typology serves to stress that voluntary action may be found in *in*formal settings as well as in formal settings, both autonomous and non-autonomous in nature. Further, the typology makes clear that participation in voluntary action does not preclude economic remuneration, although true *volunteers* are, by definition, found only in the upper half of table 10-1, where the voluntary action is essentially unremunerated. Types of voluntary action in the lower half of table 10-1 involve either quasi-volunteers or dedicated professionals, in general, since activity is partly or fully remunerated.

The examples given in table 10-1 for each type of individual voluntary action (each cell) are meant to be illustrative rather than definitive or exhaustive. With a little reflection, the reader will easily be able to supply numerous other examples for each cell. Finally, we must note as before that *levels of remuneration, formalization, and autonomy are all really matters of degree*, so that the cells represent ideal types, rather than empirical types with perfectly clear differentiation among each other. Nevertheless, this classification scheme may help place the major "natural types" of voluntary action into typological perspective—including Peace Corps "volunteers," "Nader's Raiders," "garden variety" volunteer organization activity, volunteers in the courts, donating money to a charity, or volunteering for a special mission in the armed forces.

There is some evidence, especially within the non-remunerated cells of table

Table 10-1
Major Analytical Types of Voluntary Action of Individuals

Level of Economic Benefits Received	Level of Formalization of the Setting		
	Informal Setting	Formal (Organized) Setting	
		Autonomous	Non-Autonomous
Unremunerated or Nearly Unremunerated (Low Level of Economic Benefits)	Miscellaneous leisure, altruistic, charitable, service, and self-expressive activity (sports, donations, voting, picking up a hitchhiker, TV viewing, rioting, dancing, playing music with others, card playing, etc.)	Volunteer roles in regular FVOs or voluntary associations (Common Cause members, Red Cross volunteers, Boy Scouts, etc.)	Volunteer roles associated with the courts, prisons, hospitals, schools, etc. (volunteer teacher aides, hospital volunteers, court volunteers, etc.)
Partly or Fully Remunerated (High Level of Economic Benefits)	Volunteering for special remunerated tasks (surveys, experiments, arduous missions, etc.)	Voluntary Occupational Roles (Visiting Nurse Association, "Nader's Raiders," Association Executives, etc.)	Voluntary Occupational roles (VISTA, Peace Corps, Citizen Participation Boards, Volunteer Administrators, Social Workers, etc.)

10-1, that higher levels of activity in one aspect of one cell covary with higher levels of activity in other aspects of the same cell. That is, if an individual is a member of or is active in one voluntary association, he is more likely to be a member of or be active in other associations. Or if an individual is active in his informal relations, he is more likely to vote in elections, make donations to charities, etc. Moreover, there is also some evidence (Smith, 1969b; Ahtik, 1962; Allardt, et al., 1958) that levels of individual participation in voluntary action covary *across* sub-types. That is, people who are engaged in one sub-type of voluntary activity in table 10-1 (as represented by one cell of the table) are more likely to engage in some other sub-type of voluntary activity (represented by another cell). At the present time, this has been demonstrated most clearly for only a few specific cells (the non-remunerated cells, again).

For instance, individuals who are active in mass media exposure and in informal interpersonal relations (types of voluntary action included in cell 1 of table 10-1) are likely to be active in formal volunteer organizations (the type of voluntary action included in cell 2), according to Smith's (1969b) data for a sample of townspeople from eight Massachusetts towns and cities. Those who are active in voluntary associations (once more cell 2) have also been found to be more likely to vote (cell 1) in a large number of studies (Payne, Payne, and Reddy, chapter 11 in the present volume). This tendency for covariation among the different analytical types of individual voluntary action may be termed the *General Activity Syndrome* or perhaps the *Voluntary Action Syndrome*. Whatever it is called, it deserves a good deal of empirical investigation. *It suggests, among other things, a broad similarity in the psycho-social roots of individual participation in a variety of types of voluntary action, thus justifying the treatment of these various forms of voluntary action within a common conceptual framework.*

Major Sub-types of Voluntary Action
Across System Levels

In the previous section we highlighted three dimensions or continua that are especially useful in identifying and understanding some important "natural types" of individual voluntary action. That exposition in no way denies the theoretical relevance or empirical utility of *other* analytical dimensions or continua in the study of individual and/or collective voluntary action. For example, an important literature has developed over the years that identifies various types of voluntary associations according to internal characteristics, external characteristics, goals and aims, etc. However, virtually without exception, these typologies focus on and are directly applicable only to *one system level*, usually that of the voluntary association or formal voluntary organization.

The question thus arises, "Are there any analytically useful dimensions or continua that, with appropriate modifications, are relevant to understanding and application across the full range of system levels: act, role, informal voluntary group, formal voluntary group, voluntary community, and society?" That is, "What differentiating elements are common to voluntary action of all system levels?" Put yet another way, *"To what extent can voluntary action be described and analyzed at any or all system levels using a limited number of dimensions or continua?"*

In the discussion that follows, some clusters of major differentiations, dimensions, or continua are identified, described, and applied across the range of system levels. Far from believing this scheme to be complete, we simply hope that this presentation will serve to stimulate critical response, suggestions for alternative approaches, additions, deletions, and reclustering of the materials that follow. At the same time, we hope that we are offering some new perspectives on voluntary action and posing some new research problems for this field.

A review of prior definitional and typological efforts reveals myriad dimensions proposed and applied. Eliminating those dimensions that are of use only at some system levels and combining those dimensions with considerable overlap among themselves, a total of twenty-one continua that may be grouped into six clusters were deduced. The clusters thus arrived at are as follows: (1) control-separateness, (2) motivation-compliance structure, (3) social structuring of the situation, (4) timing of activity, (5) goals and aims of the activity of the entity, and (6) economic inputs-outputs.

Let us first examine the nature and content of each cluster, and then apply the continua with examples to each system level of voluntary action.

1. Control-Separateness

The control-separateness cluster includes five sub-dimensions: (a) *autonomy* (vs. linkage to other existing systems), (b) *secrecy* (vs. publicity), (c) *exclusivity* (vs. inclusivity), (d) extent of *responsiveness to the social environment*, and (e) extent of *responsiveness to the physical environment.* The cluster as a whole describes, defines, and investigates the permeability of the voluntary activity in terms of power, information, and people, as well as the responsiveness of the entity to vital dimensions of its environment.

The *autonomy dimension* aims at identifying the nature and extent of independence of voluntary action—the degree to which the power to make the full range of policy and implementation decisions is located in the "actor" or unit at the given system level. The *secrecy-publicity dimension* focuses on the extent to which information on the voluntary action is intended to be available—whether the action is intended to be essentially secret or whether it is intended to be highly open, public, and publicized. The *exclusivity-inclusivity dimension* probes the degree to which the voluntary action is or is not open to others (in general or according to some specific set of criteria). *Responsiveness to the social environment* refers to the influence of the social environment on the voluntary action— the degree to which the entity or unit is aware of, sensitive to, and takes the social environment into account in its voluntary action. This dimension looks at broader aspects of the relation to the social environment than does the autonomy dimension (which focuses solely on power and influence relations). *Responsiveness to the physical environment* focuses on the corresponding sensitivity of the voluntary action to aspects of the physical environment.

2. Motivation-Compliance Structure

A second cluster, dealing with *motivation-compliance structure,*[2] is comprised of four sub-dimensions: (a) *level of remuneration,* (b) *degree of voluntariness,* (c) *degree of altruism* (vs. self-interest), and (d) *level of psychic involvement.* Taken as a whole, the cluster is concerned with the nature of the motivation of the voluntary action and on the impact of whatever these motivational forces are on the actor's level of involvement. *Levels of remuneration* may vary on the individual level, for example, from neither direct nor indirect remuneration, to token remuneration, payment of expenses, subsistence remuneration, subsistence plus a small allowance, and then to full sustaining salary, bonuses and other short- or long-term economic benefits over and above a fully sustaining salary. It will be remembered that accepting remuneration need not *necessarily* prejudice the "voluntariness" of the action. As noted on the individual level in our definitional discussion above, although the "pure" volunteer will typically not even have expenses met, an individual may be paid a full and equitable salary and still be engaged in voluntary action. In analogous fashion, we distinguished between volunteer organizations and voluntary organizations, according to the importance of remuneration in the compliance structure of the group. Conceivably, following this same logic, it might also be possible to distinguish between volunteer societies and voluntary societies.

The *degree of voluntariness* (vs. coercion) is a second dimension within the motivation-compliance structure cluster. In this context, "voluntariness" is placed in polarity with coercion, whether the coercion arises out of physical threats, actual physical prodding or physical restraints, or fear of strong social, legal, and/or economic sanctions. In addition, coercion is seen as including the effects of physiological compulsions on the individual actor. The *altruism versus self-interest dimension* highlights the extent to which voluntary action is directly aimed at serving and satisfying other entities as opposed to the extent to which the voluntary action is intended to serve and satisfy mainly the "actor" or "unit" engaging in it. This understanding of the altruism-self-interest continuum does not deny that even altruism will still be significantly rewarding, if indirectly, to the actor or unit involved (serving, for example, to enhance self-esteem or image in the eyes of others). No value judgment is intended when this distinction is made.

Finally, the *level of psychic involvement* is yet another relevant dimension, focusing on the intensity of commitment to the voluntary action on the part of the "actor" or "unit." This dimension becomes extremely important in understanding how an apparently inconsequential manifestation of voluntary action can have tremendous effects on a society or the world at large, as the deepest of human commitment is communicated from one person to others, from one group to others, from one nation to others. Most of the important social movements of our time or previous times (e.g., from Christianity to communism) can ultimately trace their origins to the powerful commitment and involvement of one (or a few) charismatic leader(s) in some form of voluntary action.

3. Social Structuring

Still another cluster details the *nature and degree of social structuring of the situation.* There are two basic component dimensions here. Voluntary action settings may range in *sociality* from being essentially non-social or solitary to being very highly social. Voluntary action settings may also vary in terms of their clarity and degree of *normative structuring:* from essentially non-normative settings to informal settings to formally organized and highly structured normative settings. Voluntary action can be highly normative and structured even in non-social settings, just as voluntary action can be very unstructured normatively in highly social settings. Normative structuring refers to the extent of constraint by the social obligations and expectations of reference individuals or groups that *may or may not* be physically present when voluntary action takes place. By contrast, the degree of "sociality" of a setting refers to the *physical presence* of other individuals or groups in the immediate setting when the voluntary action usually takes place.

4. Time and Activity Dimensions

The elements involved in measuring *the time dimensions of voluntary activity* also form a cluster. Three continua come to the fore. *Time span* refers to the length of anticipated commitment by an actor or unit to a given voluntary activity. Such time spans may range from very short (a one-shot, momentary activity) to very long (a "life-long" commitment to a given activity, or a commitment by an organization over centuries). However, within a given time span, *periodicity* measures the frequency of occurrence of the voluntary activity. That is, although a given time span may include all manifestations of a given type of voluntary action, there will be varying levels of activity *within* that time span, and at times, perhaps, no activity. Many kinds of voluntary action have their own "natural periodicity"–daily, weekly, monthly, annual, etc. Action also varies in *intensity*. Even when an activity is taking place, it may be casual and relaxed in pace or range to very high intensity levels during a given time period, depending on circumstances.

5. Goals and Aims

Another cluster centers around *the goals and aims of the activity*. Five dimensions are identified here: *Change orientation* refers to the extent a voluntary activity may or may not be oriented toward change at any one or a number of system levels. Secondly, *goal multiplicity* refers to the extent voluntary action has multiple major goals or is focused primarily on a single goal. Thirdly, *substantive goal type* refers to the institutional type of goal that is the focus of voluntary action, since activities may range across a myriad of types of substantive goals (service, issue advocacy, occupational self-interest, entertainment, etc.). Fourth, a given voluntary activity may be rated along the *instrumental-expressive continuum*, according to the degree to which its goals focus on objective task accomplishment vs. enjoyment, self-expression, and interpersonal relations. Finally, voluntary action can be distinguished in terms of its *sector linkage*, according to whether its goals and aims primarily make it a part of the voluntary sector, the government sector, or the business sector of society.

6. Economic Inputs-Outputs

The analysis of *economic inputs and outputs* comprises the sixth cluster. Voluntary action will vary markedly in terms of the nature and extent of economic *inputs* and the nature and extent of economic *outputs*. A bridge club, for its basic activity, requires little more than a place to meet, tables, chairs, decks of cards, pads of paper, and pencils to keep score. In most instances, then, the playing of bridge costs little in itself and there are also virtually no outputs or products of economic value. On the other hand, the defense of the America's Cup in yachting costs various members of the New York Yacht Club (and members of challenging clubs) literally millions of dollars in design expenses, building expenses, transportation, maintenance of crews, tenders, etc. Despite this high level of economic input required, there is comparatively little output of direct economic value to the principal participants (merchants and innkeepers in the Newport, Rhode Island area do well, however). The sole tangible products, the twelve meter yachts, are often sold after the races at a very minor fraction of the total cost of their development and of the racing activity itself. The yachts themselves are basically suited only for racing and require extensive refitting for all but competitive day sailing, requiring in any case a sizeable crew. Thus, in this instance, input costs are high and the output is, in economic terms, low.

In the case of a major health voluntary association (e.g., the National Foundation, the American Heart Association, etc.), both inputs and long-run outputs promise to be large in economic terms. The research they sponsor is expensive, requiring a great deal of highly specialized equipment and highly trained and skilled personnel. Mass fundraising campaigns are undertaken annually. As with any research and development operation, the major output or product is the work being done until a "breakthrough" is achieved. Thus, there is prior to the "breakthrough" some, but not major, economic output. However, once a breakthrough is achieved, research costs (input) may be cut dramatically while the breakthrough itself can have major long-term economic effects by maintaining life and productivity for numerous persons who might otherwise have died or been disabled. Along this line of reasoning, many groups and programs aimed at "habilitation" and "rehabilitation," especially for the young, can have relatively low levels of economic input and high levels of economic output when a longer range time perspective is introduced.

The foregoing clusters of dimensions by no means exhaust the relevant dimensions that can be fruitfully used to distinguish among various kinds of voluntary action. Any combination of these dimensions can be used to develop a typology for a specific purpose. Table 10-1 is but one example of such a typology, intended to illuminate specifically the nature of individual voluntary action. Future research will have to determine which of the voluntary action distinctions suggested here really "make a difference" in the way voluntary action works. Our aim here is accomplished simply by laying them out for discussion and possible future research.

We do not feel, however, that the foregoing presentation of the major dimensions is quite adequate by itself to demonstrate the potential utility of each dimension. Therefore, in Table 10-2 we attempt to give a variety of examples at different system levels regarding how the dimensions just noted apply to concrete situations, though the placements must be viewed as quite impressionistic. There are several different system levels of reference to which the dimensions just discussed may apply: (1) the voluntary act of an individual, (2) voluntary roles (of individuals or groups), (3) informal voluntary groups, (4) formal voluntary groups, (5) voluntary communities, (6) the voluntary sector of a society, and (7) voluntary societies. In Table 10-2 we give examples only for the first five system levels, since they are the ones most commonly addressed and to which the dimensions best apply.

The contents of the table attempt to suggest at least three important points beyond simply illustrating how the various dimensions may be applied to types of voluntary action at different system levels. First, we are trying to make clear how certain apparently very *different* kinds of voluntary action at a given system level have much in common *analytically* in terms of their placement on some of the dimensions we have suggested. For instance, at the level of *the informal voluntary group*, we have chosen three examples that look very different indeed: a group of rioters (a newly formed clique of young men, and in some cases their girlfriends, who are participating together for a few days in various shouting, rock throwing, fighting, and eventually arson activities); a group of neighbors who (over a period of a few months, working evenings, weekends and days-off) help to rebuild the burned-down house of another neighbor family; and a group of men from the same plant/corporation who from time to time go on weekend or week-long fishing trips together over a period of years. However different these forms of voluntary action seem at first glance, Table 10-2 makes it clear that they are nevertheless substantially similar analytically in all involving high degrees of autonomy, high levels of responsiveness to the physical environment, low levels of remuneration, high degrees of voluntariness, and high levels of psychic involvement. This does *not* deny, for instance, the very important differences in altruism, time span, change orientation, instrumental orientation, and economic outputs of the three kinds of informal groups. It merely points out that there are more elements of analytical similarity than might have been thought at first. In a way, we are trying to suggest that certain types of activities that are analogous to "mice" have some important characteristics in common with "elephants" and "humans" when all are seen as "mammals."

The second purpose of the table is to show, by contrast, how certain apparently quite *similar* kinds of voluntary action at a given system level turn out to be quite varied in their placement on many of our analytical dimensions. For instance, at the level of *the formal voluntary group or organization* we have chosen three examples that tend to look rather similar: a corporate volunteer program (where company employees who desire to participate are placed in "big brother" or "big sister" roles with young delinquents, with a combined goal of helping and self-expression); an ad hoc environmental action volunteer organization (formed to use legal and political action to stop corporations from using or "developing" a certain wilderness area); and the United States' Peace Corps volunteer program. However similar in various respects these three formal volunteer groups might seem, they differ markedly in terms of degree of autonomy, exclusivity of membership, responsiveness to the physical environment, level of remuneration, voluntariness, change orientation, goal multiplicity, instrumental orientation, societal sector linkage, and level of economic inputs and outputs. There certainly *are* still many analytical areas of similarity, to be sure, but many important differences as well. The appropriate analogy here might be that there are "whales" that have been classed with the "fish" too long and that should instead be seen as "mammals" because of their analytical characteristics.

A third purpose of the table is to attempt to convince by demonstration that the proposed set of analytical dimensions, while far from complete, *does* at least pick up analytically a number of the important similarities and differences that most strike the eye among types of voluntary activity on various system levels.

Table 10-2

Examples of the Application of the Analytical Dimensions of Voluntary Action to Five Different System Levels of Voluntary Action

		System Level: *The Individual Voluntary Act*	
Analytical Dimensions of Voluntary Action	Donating a Pint of Blood to the Red Cross	Participating in a Police-organized Search for a Child Lost in the Woods	Joining the Association of Voluntary Action Scholars
I. Control-Separateness			
A. Autonomy of Social Setting	medium	medium	high
B. Secrecy (vs. Publicity)	medium	low	medium
C. Exclusivity	low	low	medium
D. Responsiveness to Social Environment	medium	high	low
E. Responsiveness to Physical Environment	low	high	low
II. Motivation-Compliance			
A. Remuneration Level	low	low	low
B. Voluntariness	high	high	high
C. Altruism	high	high	low
D. Psychic Involvement	medium	high	low
III. Social Structuring			
A. Sociality (vs. Solitariness) of Setting	medium	medium/low	low
B. Normative Structuring	high	medium	high
IV. Time and Activity Factors			
A. Time Span	short (1 hour)	medium (1 day)	short (5 minutes)
B. Periodicity Within Time Span	continuous	continuous	continuous
C. Intensity of Activity Within Time Span	low	high	low

System Level: *The Voluntary Role*

Analytical Dimensions of Voluntary Action	Volunteer U.S. Weather Bureau Observer	Participant in Anti-war March on the White House	Volunteer Member of a Church Choir
V. Goals and Aims			
A. Change Orientation	low	low	medium
B. Multiplicity of Goals	low	low	medium
C. Substantive Goal Types	health/service	health/welfare	scientific/economic/service/social/political
D. Instrumental (vs. Expressive) Orientation	high	high	medium
E. Societal Sector Linkage	voluntary sector	government sector	voluntary sector
VI. Economic Inputs-Outputs			
A. Inputs	low	medium	low
B. Outputs	low	low	medium
I. Control-Separateness			
A. Autonomy of Social Setting	low	medium/high	low
B. Secrecy (vs. Publicity)	high	low	medium
C. Exclusivity	medium	low	high
D. Responsiveness to Social Environment	low	high	medium
E. Responsiveness to Physical Environment	high	medium	low
II. Motivation-Compliance			
A. Remuneration Level	low	low	low
B. Voluntariness	high	high	high
C. Altruism	high	high	medium
D. Psychic Involvement	low	high	medium

Table 10-2 (cont.)

Analytical Dimensions of Voluntary Action	Volunteer U.S. Weather Bureau Observer	System Level: *The Voluntary Role*	
		Participant in Anti-war March on the White House	Volunteer Member of a Church Choir
III. Social Structuring			
A. Sociality (vs. Solitariness) of Setting	low	high	medium
B. Normative Structuring	high	medium	high
IV. Time and Activity Factors			
A. Time Span	long (years)	medium (1-3 days)	long (year)
B. Periodicity Within Time Span	cyclical (daily)	continuous	cyclical (semi-weekly)
C. Intensity of Activity Within Time Span	medium	high	low
V. Goals and Aims			
A. Change Orientation	low	high	low
B. Multiplicity of Goals	low	high	medium
C. Substantive Goal Types	service	political/social/ health/welfare/ economic/religious	religious/social/ expressive
D. Instrumental (vs. Expressive) Orientation	high	medium/high	low/medium
E. Societal Sector Linkage	government sector	voluntary sector	voluntary sector
VI. Economic Inputs-Outputs			
A. Inputs	low	medium	low
B. Outputs	low	low negative	low

Analytical Dimensions of Voluntary Action	System Level: *The Informal Voluntary Group*		
	Ad Hoc Group of Rioters	Group of Neighbors Helping to Rebuild a Burned-down House of Another Neighbor	Group of Fellow Workers Who Go Fishing Together from Time-to-time
I. Control-Separateness			
A. Autonomy of Social Setting	high	high	high

B. Secrecy (vs. Publicity)	high	medium	high
C. Exclusivity	low	low	low
D. Responsiveness to Social Environment	high	high	high
E. Responsiveness to Physical Environment	high	high	high
II. Motivation-Compliance			
A. Remuneration Level	low	low	low
B. Voluntariness	high	high	high
C. Altruism	medium	high	low
D. Psychic Involvement	high	high	high
III. Social Structuring			
A. Sociality (vs. Solitariness) of Setting	high	medium	medium
B. Normative Structuring	low	medium	medium
IV. Time and Activity Factors			
A. Time Span	medium (1-3 days)	long (months)	long (years)
B. Periodicity Within Time Span	continuous (except 12-8 a.m.)	cyclical (evenings, weekends, days off)	cyclical (irregular)
C. Intensity of Activity Within Time Span	high	high	medium
V. Goals and Aims			
A. Change Orientation	medium	low	low
B. Multiplicity of Goals	high	medium	low
C. Substantive Goal Type	political/economic/social/expressive	welfare/service/social	social-recreational
D. Instrumental (vs. Expressive) Orientation	medium	high	low
E. Societal Sector Linkage	voluntary sector	voluntary/economic sectors	voluntary sector
VI. Economic Inputs-Outputs			
A. Inputs	low	medium	medium
B. Outputs	high *negative*	high	low

Table 10-2 (cont.)

Analytical Dimensions of Voluntary Action		System Level: *The Formal Voluntary Group*	
	Corporate Volunteer Program (Working with Delinquents)	Ad Hoc Environmental Organization to Preserve a Wilderness Area by Volunteer Activity	United States Peace Corps Volunteer Program
I. Control-Separateness			
A. Autonomy of Social Setting	moderate	high	low
B. Secrecy (vs. Publicity)	medium	low	low
C. Exclusivity	medium	low	high
D. Responsiveness to Social Environment	medium	medium	high
E. Responsiveness to Physical Environment	low	high	medium
II. Motivation-Compliance			
A. Remuneration Level	low	low	medium
B. Voluntariness	high	high	medium
C. Altruism	medium	high	medium
D. Psychic Involvement	high	high	high
III. Social Structuring			
A. Sociality (vs. Solitariness) of Setting	low	medium	medium
B. Normative Structuring	medium	medium	high
IV. Time and Activity Factors			
A. Time Span	long (year)	long (years)	long (2 years)
B. Periodicity Within Time Span	cyclical (weekly)	cyclical (irregular)	cyclical (daily)
C. Intensity of Activity Within Time Span	medium	medium	high
V. Goals and Aims			
A. Change Orientation	medium/low	high	medium/low
B. Multiplicity of Goals	medium	low	high
C. Substantive Goal Type	social/service/ expression	environmental protection	health/education/ welfare/economic/ political/service/ expressive
D. Instrumental (vs. Expressive) Orientation	low/medium	high	high/medium
E. Societal Sector Linkage	corporate sector	voluntary sector	government sector
VI. Economic Inputs-Outputs			
A. Inputs	medium	low	high

Table title: System Level: *The Voluntary Community*

Analytical Dimensions of Voluntary Action	"Hippie" Farm Commune	Round the World Cruise Ship and Passengers/Crew	Trappist Monastery
I. Control-Separateness			
A. Autonomy of Social Setting	high	low	medium
B. Secrecy (vs. Publicity)	high	low	high
C. Exclusivity	medium	medium	high
D. Responsiveness to Social Environment	low	low	low
E. Responsiveness to Physical Environment	high	medium	low
II. Motivation-Compliance			
A. Remuneration Level	medium	low	medium/low
B. Voluntariness	high/medium	high	high
C. Altruism	low	low	low
D. Psychic Involvement	high	high	high
III. Social Structuring			
A. Sociality (vs. Solitariness) of Setting	medium	high	low/medium
B. Normative Structuring	low	medium	high
IV. Time and Activity Factors			
A. Time Span	long (years)	long (months)	very long (centuries)
B. Periodicity Within Time Span	cyclical (irregular)	cyclical (daily)	cyclical (daily)
C. Intensity of Activity Within Time Span	low	medium	low
V. Goals and Aims			
A. Change Orientation	low	low	low
B. Multiplicity of Goals	medium	medium	low
C. Substantive Goal Type	economic/social/political/artistic	social/esthetic/health/recreation	religious/economic
D. Instrumental (vs. Expressive) Orientation	medium	low	low
E. Societal Sector Linkage	economic/voluntary sectors	economic/voluntary sectors	voluntary/economic sectors
VI. Economic Inputs-Outputs			
A. Inputs	high	high	high
B. Outputs	low	low	low

We have a long way to go before we shall have a fully adequate set of analytical dimensions to permit high level theoretical and empirical analysis of the myriad kinds of voluntary action. Yet the codification process must be started and must be pursued vigorously, both theoretically and empirically, if the field of voluntary action research is to progress very far or very fast in its attempt to see as part of a whole a great many kinds of activities, collective and individual, that have for so long been seen as unrelated. We hope that our present primitive attempt to move toward better codification of the relevant dimensions of voluntary action across different system levels is at least a step in the right direction.

Conclusion

In this chapter we have tried to indicate the range of phenomena that might reasonably be considered under the rubric of voluntary action. We have tried to define fairly precisely a series of technical terms referring to the major *system levels* of voluntary action—from voluntary acts all the way up to voluntary societies. A simple typology of *individual* voluntary action was presented, hoping in part to make clear the focus of Part 2 of this book relative to the broader realm of voluntary action as a whole. Next we described briefly a series of twenty-one dimensions believed to be important analytical characteristics of *all* levels and kinds of voluntary action. No claim is made that this set of twenty-one dimensions is an exhaustive list of *all* important aspects of voluntary action—merely that these are some important aspects. Examples were then given in tabular form showing how the set of dimensions could be used to differentially characterize the "natural variety" of voluntary action at different system levels, bringing out otherwise unnoticed similarities and differences.

It is our hope that the present discussion and examples will, at a minimum, have three broad, long term effects: (1) We hope that other scholars will be stimulated to address some of the same definitional and typological issues we have touched on here. Much more theoretical work is needed before the field of voluntary action research can reach a level of really adequate theory development. (2) We hope that other scholars, researchers, and even practitioners will be inclined to take a somewhat broader and at the same time more refined view of voluntary action phenomena than they have in the past. In our view there is a great deal to be gained from such a perspective. (3) Finally, we hope that other scholars will begin to test empirically the utility and fruitfulness of both the definitions and the typological dimensions suggested here. If our discussion and examples here have any real value, they should help to make better sense of the bewildering variety of data that a complex reality presents us with in the field of voluntary action research. Specifically, the distinctions we have drawn should generally be associated with numerous other differences in the structure, functioning, and impact of voluntary action. Whether this is the case remains an open question to be dealt with by future comparative research.

Notes

1. An excellent discussion of the problem of "free will" and "voluntary acts" may be found in "The Freedom of the Will" by the University of California Associates, published in H. Feigl and W. Sellers, eds., *Readings in Philosophical Analysis* (New York: Appleton-Century-Crofts, 1949), pp. 594-615.

2. The notion of compliance structure was introduced by Etzioni. Further, although both somewhat different and broader than the definition of "normative-voluntary organization" suggested by Etzioni, the present definition of voluntary action nevertheless is based heavily on Etzioni's conceptualization. See Amitai Etzioni, *A Comparative Analysis of Complex Organizations* (New York: Free Press of Glencoe, 1961), chapters 1-3.

References

Ahtik, V.
1962 "Industrial Workers' Participation in Cultural, Social and Physical Leisure Activities." In *Evolution of the Forms and Needs of Leisure.* Hamburg, Germany: UNESCO Institute for Education, 102-110.

Allardt, E.; P. Jartti; F. Jyrkila; and Y. Littunen
1958 "On the Cumulative Nature of Leisure Activities." *Acta Sociologica* 3 (no. 4): 165-72.

Cornuelle, Richard
1970 "The Future of Independent Action in America." *Foundation News: Journal of Philanthropic Foundations* 11 (No. 2): 45-48.

Maslow, Abraham H.
1954 *Motivation and Personality*. New York: Harper and Row.

Smith, David Horton
1967 "A Parsimonious Definition of 'Group': Toward Conceptual Clarity and Scientific Utility." *Sociological Inquiry* 37: 141-67.

1969a "Organizational Boundaries and Organizational Affiliates." Paper presented at the American Sociological Association Convention, San Francisco, Calif. A revised version is being published in *Sociology and Social Research* (1972, in press).

1969b "Evidence for a General Activity Syndrome: A Survey of Townspeople in Eight Massachusetts Towns and Cities." *Proceedings*, 77th Annual Convention, American Psychological Association, 1969.

**Part Two: The Determinants
of Individual Participation
in Organized Voluntary
Action**

Introduction to Part Two

In Part Two we shall take up the question of individual participation in voluntary action. In particular, we shall focus on participation in formal voluntary organizations, voluntary associations, and volunteer programs. As the various chapters in Part One have made clear, there are many ways of looking at voluntary action, and many relevant system levels, from the voluntary society all the way to the level of individual acts. In the chapters that follow we shall be primarily interested in *individual voluntary acts*, as reflected in membership and participation in voluntary groups and programs. Relatively little attention will be paid to the character of the voluntary organizations or programs themselves. Instead, we shall be attempting to draw conclusions and generalizations about the individual as participant in most or all kinds of formal voluntary groups.

The focus on individual participation here is not meant to imply that this question or series of questions is intrinsically more important than various other substantive questions of voluntary action theory and research that can be asked and to some extent answered on the basis of an existing literature in several academic disciplines and professions. Practical considerations of the interest of the editors and other scholars have led to an initial focus on the individual participation question here. Yet, investigation of the determinants of individual participation in voluntary action is in a sense at the root of, or in the background of, most other questions regarding voluntatary action. Hence, even from a theoretical point of view, there is some justification for taking up the present substantive question early in this new series of volumes. Furthermore, a great many pieces of research have been performed and published on the present topic, making review and synthesis of these materials both a useful undertaking and a challenge.

Social Background and Social Role
Determinants

There is, however, still another standpoint from which we expect the focus of Part Two will be especially useful. It has been the conviction of the editors of this volume that, in many ways, the study of individual participation in voluntary groups and programs has been too narrow and in a way too "sociological." Specifically, we have felt that too much attention was continuing to be paid to the impact of social background and social role characteristics as "determinants" of individual participation in voluntary action, while not enough attention was being paid to other types of determinants (though perhaps in relation to social background and role characteristics). About a decade ago, the senior editor began a series of research studies based on this conviction, starting with his Ph.D. dissertation.

Unfortunately, this basic analytical criticism of the literature is still almost as true today as it was a decade ago. The number of references associated with each of the following chapters bears witness to the fact that even today a great deal more research has been focused on social background characteristics associated with individual voluntary action than has been focused on other kinds of determinants. We are not trying to argue here that social background and role characteristics are unimportant, nor that they do not differentiate in important ways between high and low participators, members and non-members. *What we are arguing is that this standard "sociological" approach is not sufficient.*

Psychological and Social Psychological Determinants

The usual approach to explaining individual voluntary action in terms of social background factors like age, sex, religion, socioeconomic status, etc., needs to be supplemented by at least two kinds of alternative and complementary approaches if a complete understanding of these phenomena is to be achieved. First, there must be more attention given to the *social psychological* and the more *strictly psychological* factors affecting individual participation. Specifically, this means there should be more focus on attitudes, personality traits, capacities, and related psychological characteristics of the individual as determinants of his participation. There should be more attention given to the perceptual and cognitive factors in specific situations that lead to a person becoming involved in voluntary groups and programs. There should be more focus on the kinds of learning experiences and socialization that are directly associated with individual participation in voluntary action. There should be more attention to the interpersonal dynamics and exchanges, the interpersonal pressures and influences that affect individual participation in voluntary action.

In the usual study of participation that focuses only or mainly on social background factors, the impact of social psychological and psychological factors can at best be inferred indirectly, and at worst cannot be dealt with at all. It is doubtless true, for instance, that differential class-based socialization experiences and differential class-based attitudes and personality traits help to explain why numerous studies have found socioeconomic status to be associated with individual participation in voluntary groups and programs. Yet this connection has seldom been directly demonstrated. One set of researchers tends to focus on social background factors as determinants of individual voluntary action, while another focuses on the relationships between socioeconomic status and personality, attitudes, and capacities.

Few researchers have gone to the trouble of *combining* the study of social background and social role factors with the study of attitudes, personality traits, capacities, etc., in attempting to predict and explain individual voluntary action. As a result, though we have a fair amount of information regarding the importance of various specific background, attitudinal, and personality characteristics in affecting individual participation, we have very little hard evidence (especially from large, intensive, and methodologically adequate studies) of how these broad classes of determinants are related to each other and of what their relative weights are in determining individual participation in various situations and contexts.

In part this situation has come about because of the compartmentalization fostered by the academic disciplines involved. Psychologists, including social psychologists trained in departments of psychology, are usually trained to be more interested in the attitudes, personality traits, capacities, habits, beliefs, and values of individuals than in their social background characteristics and roles. As a result, researchers with primarily psychological training are usually likely to ignore the important questions of relating psychological characteristics to particular social background characteristics and roles. Even if a psychological study of individual participation in voluntary action involves some sampling in terms of social background characteristics, there tends to be little attention to how the latter relate to psychological characteristics in a systematic way. And if there is such attention, its focus tends to be mainly on age and sex as the primary background characteristics of interest. The graduate training of a "good psychologist" tends to produce an aversion to social background and social role characteristics as objects of study, even in relation to more "primary" psychological characteristics.

Conversely, the graduate training of a "good sociologist" tends to produce an aversion to psychological traits and capacities as objects of study, even in relation to more "primary" social structural factors and the social background and role characteristics of individuals. Sociologists, including social psychologists trained in departments of sociology, are usually trained to be more interested in groups, organizations, and the social structural characteristics of societies than in the psychological aspects of individuals. Insofar as sociologists are trained to look at individuals, they are usually urged to focus on the social background and social role characteristics of individuals, since these characteristics are precisely the ones that permit some theoretical fit with higher levels of system reference (group, organization, community, society) in which the sociologist has primary interest. As a result, researchers with primarily sociological training are usually likely to ignore the important questions of relating social background and social role characteristics to psychological traits and capacities. Even if a sociological study of individual participation in voluntary action includes some "psychological measures" as well as the usual information on social background and social roles, the systematic relations between the "sociological" and the "psychological" are seldom fully explored in relationship to the dependent variables of participation.

By this point in our discussion, the good "social psychologist" or "psycho-sociologist" is probably exceedingly angry with the "stereotypes" just presented. In theory, social psychology was to be the linking "discipline" or field between the two established fields of sociology and psychology, eliminating or at least reducing the impact of the kinds of narrowness and academic bias just discussed. Similarly, "roles" and "attitudes" were to be primary kinds of linking concepts for the new field, being of interest to both "traditional" sociologists and psychologists. That was the way things were supposed to work, but *not* quite the way things have worked. Social psychologists *still* tend in most cases to be *either* psychologists *or* sociologists "under the skin," so to speak. Most social psychologists have a degree in sociology or psychology, not in social psychology. Most receive training mainly in a sociology department or mainly in a psychology department, not in a separate, balanced, and "integrated" social psychology department or program. Thus, many of the long-standing biases about what is "good research"—in terms of concepts, methods, topics, theory, etc.—are still absorbed by "social psychologists" either from the psychologists or the sociologists.

In addition, social psychology as an interdisciplinary field of study has developed some additional biases, or at least narrowing norms, of its own. The concepts of attitude and role, which were to become linking variables between the social system focus of sociologists and the personal system focus of the psychologists, have come to have theoretical and research "lives" of their own *without* at the same time being used very frequently as the linking concepts they were supposed to be. There is, of course, nothing unfortunate in social psychology having chosen to focus a great deal of its attention on roles and attitudes as central processes of interest in their own right. What is distressing is that in so doing, social psychology has often neglected a number of important questions about the *linkage* of social and psychological systems.

In particular, social psychologists (using this term broadly) have been deficient in spelling out both the theoretical and empirical interrelationships of social background and role characteristics, attitudes, beliefs, values, personality traits, capacities, and related processes as determinants of individual participation in voluntary action. "Traditional" sociologists and psychologists have been even more deficient in this regard, of course, but social psychologists deserve more criticism since they are the ones who should lead the way if they are to live up to their pretensions.[a]

---

[a]At this point, the present author should confess his own training and sense of academic self-identity, so that the reader can bear *these* biases in mind when interpreting the present argument. I took my undergraduate degree training almost equally in psychology and sociology and received an A.B. with majors in both. My graduate training was also in both fields, but with heavier emphasis on sociology, and my graduate degrees were specifically awarded in the latter field, although from a formally interdisciplinary department. I think of myself as a social psychologist and/or psycho-sociologist, according to the situation.

The editors hope that Chapters 11, 12, and 13 of Part Two of this volume will make clear the kinds of social background and social role characteristics, attitudes, personality traits, and capacities that have been and might be found important in explaining individual voluntary action. But even more importantly, we hope that these chapters, together with the present introduction and the concluding chapter, will stimulate a great deal more research (by social scientists of various backgrounds and academic self-identities) on how these various social and psychological factors combine and relate in diverse ways to explain individual participation in different kinds of voluntary action settings. *At a minimum, we hope the present review will serve to highlight the fact that, in addition to social role and background characteristics, there are numerous kinds of psychological and social psychological characteristics that are relevant and important to explaining individual participation in voluntary action.* This will seem obvious to the psychologist, but many other types of social scientists have yet to accept this proposition.

Contextual and Social Structural Determinants

All of the determinants of individual participation so far considered have been to some degree essentially "internal" to the individual, or at least attributable to the individual without intensive focus on his particular milieu or environment. However, some social background and social role characteristics grade over into what might be called contextual or social structural characteristics. Sex, age, race, health, physiognomy, and other physically-based background and role-indicative characteristics require relatively little attention to an individual's particular context, since their meaning tends to be quite similar for most individuals within any society. Other social background characteristics like nationality-ethnicity, religion, socioeconomic status, and organizational affiliations tend to require more careful examination of the individual's milieu in order to interpret their meaning. Still, for all of these types of background and social role characteristics one can generally view them as somehow "internal attributes" of the individual, as individual "memberships" in various kinds of socially recognized groups and categories. The sense in which they are "internal" may be more psychological than physiological, but nevertheless we have no difficulty in seeing a particular person as a husband, middle class, a salesman, a Roman Catholic, an Italian-American, etc. All of these kinds of social background and social role characteristics seem clearly to be "internal": to be useful primarily as indicators of internal states and dispositions to act, think, feel, and react in certain ways.

By contrast, contextual and social structural determinants of individual participation in voluntary action refer to factors essentially "external" to the individual, factors that are primarily attributable to the social and physical environment of the individual rather than to the individual himself. "Contextual factors" is the broader term, referring to *all* aspects of the settings of individual action, while "social structural factors" is a narrower term referring specifically to those contextual factors having to do with social structure and organizational structure as they may impinge on individual voluntary action. The physical world we live in at present is perhaps the broadest relevant example of a contextual factor. The *physical-ecological context* becomes a differential determinant of individual voluntary action when we inquire into the impact of a particular bio-physical environment on a certain kind of individual voluntary action.

Another very broad kind of contextual factor is the *socio-historical context* in which individual voluntary action takes place—from an ancient and isolated preliterate society to a contemporary industrial society. At lower levels of generality, we may find more specific social contextual factors that can be of great importance in understanding individual voluntary action: the cultural values of a society; the kind of religious and political traditions present; the degree of totalitarianism vs. freedom of association in the society; the degree of economic development and related aspects of societal modernization; the size and population density of the society; the region of a country in which the voluntary action is taking place; characteristics of the local area (city, town, rural area, etc.), even characteristics of the neighborhood. Historians, demographers, political scientists, economists, geographers, sociologists, and various other types of scholars have major contributions to make in understanding the relevance of such contextual characteristics to individual voluntary action. However, this work has barely begun, as Chapter 14 of Part Two of this volume will try to make clear.

An even more specific kind of contextual factor to be considered (in Chapter 14) among the determinants of individual voluntary action comprises some important organizational and social structural factors of the settings in which such action takes place. Focus here is placed on how individual participation is affected by such factors as the degree of bureaucratization and formalization of the setting, the general goals and activities of the voluntary group or program, the amount of influence that members are allowed to have on the policy decisions and administrative decisions within the voluntary action setting, the requirements or obligations for participation that are part of the voluntary action setting, etc.

In part, we may expect contextual factors to have their impact on individual voluntary action through the *mediation* of psychological traits and social background and role characteristics of the individual participants. Yet contextual factors may also have their own substantial impact without doing more than touch the periphery of the personal systems of the individual voluntary "actors" involved. Thus, contextual factors can have a crucial role, for instance, in defining *opportunity structures* for individual voluntary action of various kinds; in affecting recruitment and selection processes; in affecting the reward-punishment structure for voluntary action; in determining how effective a given kind of voluntary action is going to be, which in turn affects how many individuals are going to be attracted to that kind of voluntary action and how much they will participate; etc. Even though we are focusing in Part Two of this volume on why *individuals* participate, higher system level, external, contextual, and social structural factors must not be left out of the picture if we are to understand fully voluntary action phenomena. Naturally, when one begins to focus instead (in later volumes of this series) on how voluntary groups, voluntary organizations, social movements, and voluntary societies operate, social structural and contextual factors shift from being part of an important *secondary* approach to being integral to the *primary* approach, with matters of individual psychology and social role behavior taking a secondary (but still important) position.

Finally, we must point out by way of introduction that the relevant overall theories are lacking that can do justice to the whole range of empirical data, both illustrative and systematic, anecdotal and comparative, that is available on the matter of individual participation in voluntary action. We noted this to be a problem earlier within the set of "internal" determinants of individual voluntary action; it is all the more true for "external" or contextual determinants of individual voluntary action, covering as they do such a broad range of factors. And there is next to nothing that attempts to weave both "internal" and "external" determinants of individual action into a coherent, empirically-based theoretical system. The most we can do in this volume is to take a few furtive and hesitant steps in that direction in Chapter 15 of Part Two.

11

Social Background and Role Determinants of Individual Participation in Organized Voluntary Action[a]

RAYMOND PAYNE, BARBARA PITTARD PAYNE, and
RICHARD D. REDDY

Introduction: Formal Voluntary Associations and Social Background Factors

Formal organizations and associations are those which have (usually) written constitutions and/or bylaws, specifically designated leaders, explicitly stated goals and objectives, clear group boundaries, established procedures for inducting members, and the like. Voluntary formal organizations are those which a person may or may not join depending upon his own choices and decisions, even though in given situations there may be considerable pressures toward joining. That is to say, one becomes and remains a member by virtue of some action on his own part, not simply by birth or other factors over which the person has no control. It is understood also that a member has some control over the *amount* or *intensity* of his participation in such organizations, with the consequence that his degree of involvement aside from simple membership is also voluntary and depends upon his actions (Payne, 1954; Teele, 1965; Smith, et al., chap. 10 in this volume).

The importance of formal voluntary organizations in human society need not be dwelt upon here since this consideration is treated extensively elsewhere (Smith, 1966). However, it may be pointed out that such associations have become an integral part of our way of life and have developed or assumed primary responsibility for numerous basic social functions. This is not to say that our society could not possibly survive without formal voluntary associations. It does indicate, however, that the larger social structure contains numerous formal substructures, and that these have come to serve society's members as instruments for meeting a wide variety of needs, ranging from broad general social maintenance to highly individualized personal satisfaction (Rose, 1954; Katz, 1966; Hausknecht, 1962; Barber, 1950; Young and Larson, 1965).

[a]Raymond Payne died on January 5, 1971, before the manuscript was revised. The revision has been made by his wife and co-author, Barbara Pittard Payne, and by Richard D. Reddy.

Donald J. Shoemaker, Assistant Professor of Sociology, University of Southern Mississippi, assisted in the collection of the articles used in the initial version of the paper, which was presented to the American Sociological Association Seminar Session, "Voluntary Action Theory and Research: Steps Toward Synthesis," 1970.

These statements lead to the basic theoretical and research question at hand: what types of people join and participate intensively in many voluntary organizations, while other types join few, or none at all? By way of approaching this question, we have examined many studies in which social background factors have been found to be associated with rates of individual participation, and have attempted a summary and synthesis of the results of those studies. The studies selected to support this general relationship do not exhaust the research on social background factors and voluntary action. There was an effort to select a cross-section of studies from the wide variety of types of research published during the past two decades in leading journals, monographs, and books. The review of these selections is limited generally to voluntary participation in formal organizations and associations, and largely to the situation in the United States, although some exemplary studies from other countries are included.

Because participation varies so much within the population, the need arises to predict participation, and such prediction has been found to be difficult. The following analysis of social background factors reflects one effort to approach the problem of prediction in scientific research.

For clarity in presentation we will group the social background factors into seven clusters:

1. *Life cycle stage*, which includes age, marital status, number of children, age of children, and the life cycle stage as a complex.
2. *Socioeconomic status*, including income, education, occupational status, family or lineage status, home ownership, and combined measures of socioeconomic status.
3. *Socio-physical characteristics*, including sex, race, ethnicity, personal health, and physical abilities.
4. *Formal organizational affiliations and roles*, including occupation and work, religion, politics and school affiliation (if attending).
5. *Interpersonal roles and experiences*, including "significant-other" influences and informal relations with parents, neighbors, friends from various contexts, relatives, spouse, children, etc.
6. *Other social relationships and quasi-solitary activities*, including mass media behavior and leisure behavior of a non-organized sort.
7. *Residential mobility and length of time resident in a given community*.

Before detailing and summarizing the literature currently available on the relationship between these background factors and membership, participation, and leadership in formal voluntary organizations, a few general comments on the nature of the studies done are in order.

Most of the findings reported herein are the results of survey research designs, and the analyses are more often descriptive than causal. With only a few exceptions, the research on this topic has been cross-sectional. Babchuk and Booth

(1969) provide the only longitudinal data known to the authors relating background factors with membership, although Hyman and Wright (1971) also report some national trend data for the United States. Virtually all the studies used some standard form of probability sampling, including uses of area, block, simple random, and stratified sampling. Sample sizes rarely exceeded 1,000 persons. Although there have been studies from most areas of the U.S., there have been few relevant national area probability samples, perhaps the most notable being those in the United States by the American Institute of Public Opinion (AIPO) in 1954 and by the National Opinion Research Center (NORC) in 1955 and, in Germany, the study by Reigrotsky (1956). The results of the two major American studies are reported in Wright and Hyman (1958), Hausknecht (1962), and Orum (1966). Almond and Verba (1963) report on probability samples of four other countries, in addition to the United States.

Statistical analyses have only begun in recent years to go beyond simple measures of assocation. Multivariate designs including regression analysis and discriminant function analysis are regrettably rare, though increasing slowly in numbers in the past five years or so. Formal participation measures have typically been fairly simple, although more sophisticated (complex) scales were employed in some instances. The number of voluntary organization memberships was the most widely employed measure in the studies we reviewed. This was sometimes refined by the addition of information on the number of meetings attended in a specified time period, the offices held, and committeeships and committee chairmanships held, along with a variety of related items.

With this over-brief sketch of the methodological nature of the studies reviewed, let us turn now to the first important cluster of social background variables we have distinguished.

Life Cycle Stage

The life cycle stage cluster includes factors such as age, marital status, number of children, and the age of the children. The literatures relating these factors to membership, participation, and to leadership in voluntary associations will be reviewed, followed by a review of the life cycle stage as a whole.

Age. Age is, of course, a critical dimension of the life cycle. In this section we will treat age independently from other life cycle factors, especially those involving marriage and the family, while in one final section on life cycle stage as a complex, all of these related factors will be included together.

There are generally few or no opportunities for children from infancy to about age eight to participate in formal voluntary associations. However, at about eight, children become eligible for various kinds of scouting, athletic, and recreational association memberships. As they mature, an ever wider range of activities becomes available. However, ordinarily these youth organizations are under adult guidance and control. They are often linked to the major non-familial institutions that the child has contact with, notably churches and schools. As youths reach their mid-teens, they may become eligible for junior memberships in fraternal associations as well as other youth groups not directly linked to churches and schools (e.g., scouts, YMCA and YWCA groups, Boys' and Girls' clubs, etc.). *Unfortunately, these groups and the membership and participation patterns of children and youth have rarely been systematically studied.* Although relatively little is known about young adult (age eighteen to thirty) membership and participation, in part due to the lower rates of both, we know even less about voluntary participation between ages eight and eighteen. The latter is a period during which available evidence (e.g., Dotson, 1951) points to relatively high rates of membership and participation and during which youths have their first, and perhaps most significant, contact with the voluntary sector. Studies such as those of Gordon (1957), Coleman'(1961), and Barker and Gump, et al. (1964) point to the associational richness of high school life in America as well as the importance of these associational patterns to the life of the school as a whole and to its students. Theodore's review in a later volume of this series sheds light on college participation. Baeumler (1965b), in a study of small town high school students, noted that there were no significant differences between middle- and working-class adolescents in terms of membership and general attendance at meetings. However, he found that middle-class students were more likely to assume leadership and officership. Hollingshead (1949) and Coleman (1961) have also noted this tendency of the middle-class adolescent toward leadership in school voluntary settings.

In an excellent study, perhaps the best done relating age and participation, Mayo (1950) studied participation rates for each person over ten years of age in the farm families of a South Carolina county. Mayo noted an increase in participation from age 10-14 to age 15-19. However, as with others, including Argyle (1959), Schuyler (1959), and Wilensky (1961a, 1961b), Mayo notes a sharp decline in participation rate in the years between twenty and thirty. Indeed, Mayo found participation rates in this age range to be the lowest of all the age ranges he studied.

From these lows, participation rebounds in the middle years of life, when people are generally at their peak. Although the exact point of highest membership and participation has varied by the study in question (generally centering on the middle forties with a ± factor of ten years), most researchers noting an effect of age on participation have found membership and participation increasing throughout the middle years. (Goldhamer, 1942; Anderson and Ryan, 1943; Mayo, 1950; Bottomore, 1954; Foskett, 1955; Reigrotzky, 1956; Pressey and Kuhlen, 1957; Scott, 1957; Rose, 1960; Wilensky, 1961a, 1961b; R.V. Smith, 1964; D.H. Smith, 1972; and Curtis, 1971).

For the most part, these same authors note a decline from the peak in the middle-aged period. Others, focusing more directly on those approaching their later years have also noted a decline in participation after the middle years (McKain, 1947; Cavan, et al. 1949; Goldhamer, 1942; Mayo, 1950; Freedman and Axelrod, 1952; Hunter and Maurice, 1953; Fichter, 1954; McCann, 1955; Taietz and Larson, 1956; Havighurst, 1957; Douglah, 1965; and Babchuk and Booth, 1969). There are some indications that males retain their membership and participation patterns for longer periods of time than do women. (Mayo, 1950; Webber, 1954).

Many of the memberships retained by older people tend to be those held in the middle years (Rose, 1960). The disengagement of participation that takes place may be mainly with formal voluntary organizations related to work, although continued "emeritus" or "retirement benefit" memberships exist in many professional, business, and labor union organizations. Yet there has been, it would seem, a substantial increase in the number of voluntary organizations concerned with the aged in the United States in recent decades, reflecting in part greater numbers and a greater proportion of older and retired persons in the population.

Rose identifies three special kinds of relations older people have with voluntary associatons: (1) older persons participate in most of the kinds of voluntary associations that are found throughout American life; (2) older persons participate in organizations by and for the special benefit of older persons (i.e., for purposes linked to the special character, problems, needs, and interests of the aged in society); and (3) there are various other special benefit groups that may include younger people interested in helping the aged (Rose, 1960, p. 666).

Low rates of voluntary participation among older people may be due to several factors, such as declining energy levels, declining interest and involvement in occupations professions, and declining interest in community processes (Payne, 1960). Rose believes that a major factor causing the decrease in participation with age is that the changing of location and role at the onset of old age often pulls the individual out of his earlier social participation, and he is less motivated to go into new groups (Rose, 1960, p. 670). Unfortunately, past research does not demonstrate conclusively the relative weights of these various possible influences in causing a decline in participation with advancing old age.

Marital Status. Marriage is virtually normative in our society for those of sufficient age. It is also an important measure of social integration. Almost without exception, studies of membership and participation in voluntary associations have shown married persons to have higher rates of both membership and participation than those who are widowed, separated or divorced (Goldhamer, 1942; Hunter and Maurice, 1953; Bell and Force, 1956b; Scott, 1957; Wright and Hyman, 1958; Devereux, 1960; Hausknecht, 1962; Babchuk and Thompson, 1962; R.V. Smith, 1964; Douglah, 1965; Spiro, 1968; Rothrock, 1968; and Booth and Babchuk, 1969). Where measured separately in those studies, widows and widowers have generally had higher rates of membership and participation than those who are single or divorced or separated. Curtis (1971) found in a cross-national survey that these marital status effects are more pronounced in the United States and Canada than in other countries.

The only instance in the literature known to the authors where married persons did not in general show higher participation rates was Beal's study (1956) of participation in an agricultural cooperative (a marginal type of voluntary group). Conceivably the marketing functions of this group distinguishes it in this instance from patterns to be found in most other voluntary associations. However, Scott (1957) noted higher rates for the single among younger persons although these did disappear dramatically with increments of age.

Within specific organizations and when the single are younger, patterns may differ. For example, Babchuk and Thompson (1962) found that the married and those married for longer periods of time were more likely to be affiliated with groups in the population they studied. However, of those who were members, more of the non-married belonged to four or more organizations. In addition, Babchuk and Gordon (1962) noted a positive relationship between being unmarried and the assumption of leadership roles. Also, Kievit (1964) found that married college students participate less in *campus* organizations than non-married students, but the married students participate more in *community* organizations.

Although the foregoing kinds of results regarding marital status and individual voluntary participation have indicated that there is often a significant relationship, the explanations of such a relationship have been less satisfying and less well explored. The general explanatory model advanced—the integration hypothesis—argues that being married draws one more into the various kinds of formal and informal relationships of social life, voluntary organization memberships among them. There has been little direct evidence on the precise way in which this mechanism works over time (again we lack longitudinal studies), but what evidence there is lends some support to the proposed model. Harry (1970), for instance, found that spouse's participation in voluntary organizations had more positive effect on one's own attendance than did the presence of children in the family. This latter point, however, leads us to our next type of life cycle factor.

Number of Children. The evidence is not entirely clear on the relationship between the number of children in a family and the parents' rate of membership and participation in voluntary associations. But in general, the more children a parent has, the more likely it is that he or she will join associations and participate in them (Whetton and Devereaux, 1936; Mangus and Cottam, 1941; Goldhamer, 1942; Schmidt and Rohrer, 1956; Scott, 1957; Wright and Hyman, 1958; Devereux, 1960; Babchuk and Gordon, 1962; Douglah, 1965; and Spiro, 1968). However, there are some indications that memberships may decline gradually when the number of children exceeds two (Scott, 1957; Lazerwitz, 1962a). There is also some question as to whether being childless favors membership and participation or not. For, while Lazerwitz (1962a) found that the childless participated less than those with one child, Scott (1957) found that the childless participate more. Finally, some research indicates no relationships between the number of children a parent has and his or her participation (Ploch, 1951; Lazerwitz, 1961; Babchuk, 1965; and Rothrock, 1968).

Age of Children. More studies have investigated the relationships between the membership and participation rates of parents and the number of children they have, than between those rates and the age of these children. However, what evidence there is indicates that having *all children of school age* favors higher membership and participation rates (Schmidt and Rohrer, 1956; Lazerwitz, 1961; Spiro, 1968; Harry, 1970). Having pre-school children has a greater influence on wives than on husbands (Schmidt and Rohrer, 1956; Harry, 1970), serving most often to *reduce* levels of associational involvement. Kievit (1964) found that families in the first few years of marriage and childbearing have low involvement in formal voluntary organizations, perhaps the lowest of all age groups between childhood and adult years.

There is some evidence of a curvilinear relationship, for both husbands and wives, between membership and attendance rates and the age of the youngest child (Harry, 1970). That is, more participation occurs when the youngest child is of school age rather than younger *or* older. This finding may reflect other aspects of the life cycle stage, notably influences linked to increasing age. Or it may reflect the tendency for school aged children to draw their parents into advisory and leadership volunteer roles with youth and school related groups.

There are also indications that for women (at least, for women college graduates) the progression through having only pre-school children to having only school-age children is associated with increasing membership and participation in "community welfare" (comprising largely voluntary associational) activities and decreasing "home centered" (most often non-voluntary associational) leisure activities (Angrist, 1967). However, Angrist did not find major differences in the total amount of *leisure* (voluntary associational *and* non-voluntary associational) activity during this phase of the life cycle.

Life Cycle Stage as a Complex. In general, membership and participation in voluntary associations and in voluntary action agencies are formally possible and begin after about age eight. Typically, children participate in adult directed and dominated groups. Few, if any, leadership opportunities are open. Heavy emphasis is commonly placed on expressive activities such as sports and recreation. In adolescence, youths become eligible for membership (and leadership) in auxiliaries of adult fraternal and secret societies, etc. Especially for those attending school, an even wider range of activities and clubs is available. Although evidence is somewhat scanty, it seems that rates of membership and participation grow steadily from age eight until after graduation from high school or college. (It should be noted that little information currently exists on patterns and rates of membership and participation and leadership among graduate students or students in professional schools. However, it would seem that most "student" activities and organizations in universities are aimed at and intended for undergraduates.)

After individuals have left school, there appears to be a notable decline in individual membership and participation, especially for those who marry and are in the process both of starting their families and their occupational careers. Thus, during this period between age twenty and age thirty, membership and participation fell to a relatively low level (though rates seem to be lowest in *absolute* terms for those under eight and for those in extreme old age). From this period on, married individuals tend to exhibit higher rates of involvement than the non-married. Having children and especially having children of school age seems to increase these rates of adult membership and participation. Rates of membership, participation, and leadership once more reach a peak in the middle years (50-60 years old), but begin to decline steadily and with generally increasing rapidity as age increases, as children reach the later stages of adolescence and young adulthood, and as retirement approaches and is reached. It would seem that the highest rates of *instrumental* voluntary action are especially likely to occur during this high participation ("middle-age") stage of the life cycle.

Finally, as membership, participation and leadership rates in organized (and instrumental) voluntary action decline in later stages of the life cycle, religious and other expressive (and especially sociability) activities come to predominate. These expressive/consummatory voluntary activities tend to occur increasingly in informal rather than formally organized contexts.

Socioeconomic Status

The factors grouped under socioeconomic status include income, education, occupational status, family or lineage status, home ownership, and combined measures of socioeconomic status.

Income. Higher income is markedly associated with greater membership, participation, and leadership in voluntary associations. The findings are consistent in studies in the United States (Mather, 1941; Komarovsky, 1946; Reid and Ehle, 1950; Uzzell, 1953; Reissman, 1954; Foskett, 1955; Axelrod, 1956; Freedman, et al., 1957; Wright and Hyman, 1958; Devereux, 1960; Spinrad, 1960; Wilensky, 1961b; Babchuk and Thompson, 1962; Hausknecht, 1962; Lazerwitz, 1962a; Erbe, 1964; Douglah, 1965; Hodge and Treiman, 1968; Hyman and Wright, 1971; and Spiro, 1968). Hardee's study (1961) of a rural Australian town and Reigrotzky's national sample (1956) in Germany confirm this finding in other cultures and settings. Curtis (1971) found similar results in Canada and in the five countries of the Almond and Verba (1963) study.

In general, higher participation rates, in terms of both numbers of memberships and intensity of involvement, are found to be associated with higher income levels, particularly among persons with more education. However, there is some indication that participation rates may drop off somewhat at extremely high income levels.

Higher income is seen as the means with which persons can afford membership fees and other costs of joining and participating. Even more significantly, higher income *usually* implies eligibility for a wider variety of special and general interest groups, as well as being associated with higher educational and occupational status, which in turn tend to affect participation. An additional important relationship between income and participation in voluntary organizations suggested by these studies is that participation may itself directly or indirectly enhance income by providing contacts with potential customers, clients, and associates. Hence, there are some suggestions that higher income may be both a cause, a consequence, and a correlate of individual participation in organized voluntary action. There are no longitudinal studies we know of to settle this matter of causality.

Education. Participation in voluntary formal organizations is strongly related to level of education, with higher levels of education being associated with both more extensive and intensive involvement. This relationship has been reported in a wide range of samples in the United States since 1938 (Anderson, 1938; Bell, 1938; Mather, 1941; Warner and Lunt, 1941; Goldhamer, 1942; Komarovsky, 1946; Kaufman, 1949; Ploch, 1951; Freedman and Axelrod, 1952; Brandow and Potter, 1953; Reissman, 1954; Foskett, 1955; Axelrod, 1956; Nolan, 1956; Scott, 1957; Wright and Hyman, 1958; Zimmer and Hawley, 1959a; Devereux, 1960; Tumin, 1961; Wilensky, 1961b; Babchuk and Gordon, 1962; Babchuk and Thompson, 1962; Hausknecht, 1962; Lazerwitz, 1962a; Erbe, 1964; R.V. Smith, 1964; Douglah, 1965; Orum, 1966; Hagedorn and Labovitz, 1967, 1968a; Hodge and Treiman, 1968; Rothrock, 1968; Spiro, 1968; Hyman and Wright, 1971; and D.H. Smith, 1972). The limited number of foreign studies known to the authors indicate a similar relationship (Reigrotzky, 1956; Allardt and Pesonen, 1960; Hardee, 1961; Almond and Verba, 1963; and Curtis, 1971).

Major national surveys of voluntary associations membership in the United States like the AIPO (American Institute of Public Opinion) and the NORC (National Opinion Research Center) of 1954 and of 1955, respectively, revealed that three-fourths of the respondents having a college education held memberships in associations compared with three-fifths of those who had attended high school only and about two-fifths of those with an elementary education (Hausknecht, 1962). Subsequent studies have found broadly similar differences in participation by educational levels.

Such relationships have called forth explanations of various kinds, including hypotheses that more educated people participate more because of (a) greater access to voluntary associations at their higher socioeconomic levels, (b) greater ability to understand and be committed to abstract goals, (c) greater understanding of and familiarity with organizational operation, (d) greater self-confidence and social-confidence, etc. (D.H. Smith, 1972).

Differences in the *types* of organizations to which persons belong are also related to the extent of formal education (Hagedorn and Labovitz, 1967; Scott, 1957; Axelrod, 1956; Foskett, 1955). More educated persons tend to participate more in professional, business, civic, educational, scientific, cultural, social service, and political groups. Less educated persons tend to participate more in labor unions, sports and recreational groups, hobby clubs, fraternal lodges, and other kinds of groups with rather concrete and immediate goals, whether instrumental or consummatory.

Occupational Status. Urbanization, when accompanied by increases in the division of labor, functional specialization, and the elaboration of class structure, often results in a social class variation in membership and participation in formal voluntary organizations (Cousens, 1964). Higher levels of occupational status have been found to be positively related to higher rates of membership and participation across the range of sample types from rural community studies to national sample surveys in the United States (Lynd and Lynd, 1929, 1937; Anderson, 1938; Bell, 1938; Chapin, 1939; Warner and Lunt, 1941; Goldhamer, 1942; Komarovsky, 1946; Kaufman, 1948; Brown, 1953; Reissman, 1954; Foskett, 1955; Axelrod, 1956; Freedman and Freedman, 1956; Nolan, 1956; Freedman, et al., 1957; Scott, 1957; Wright and Hyman, 1958; Graham, 1959; Devereux, 1960; Spinrad, 1960; Babchuk and Gordon, 1962; Babchuk and Thompson, 1962; Hausknecht, 1962; Lazerwitz, 1962a; Erbe, 1964; Stark, 1964; Adams and Butler, 1967; Hagedorn and Labovitz, 1967, 1968a; Hodge and Treiman, 1968; Rothrock, 1968; Spiro, 1968; Schwirian and Helfrich, 1968; Hyman and Wright, 1971; and Smith, 1972).

Similar results have been attained in Latin America (Dotson, 1953) and Australia (Hardee, 1961). European studies confirm this same relationship (Bottomore, 1954; Reigrotsky, 1956; Svalastoga, et al. 1956; Gallagher, 1957; Hofstee, 1957; Rokkan, 1959; Zetterburg, 1960-1961; Allardt, 1961; Hardee, 1961; Ahtik, 1962; TenHave, 1962; and Curtis, 1971).

Virtually all studies report that individuals in lower socioeconomic groups tend to have few or no affiliations. However, religion is often one of the principal ways in which the poor participate. Religious groups may also provide a means by which migrants cope with the urban environment. The adult social-athletic clubs are the other major form of voluntary organization participation in the slum areas (Suttles, 1968, p. 107 ff.).

The political involvement of residents of poverty communities which have received federal government assistance in recent years is just beginning to be reported. Membership and participation in voluntary community and block organizations by the poor may drastically change their organizational participation patterns in the next decade (Kramer, 1969).

The working class or blue-collar worker is likely to belong to one and no more than two formal organizations (Cousens, 1964; Wright and Hyman, 1958; Hausknecht, 1964; Lynd and Lynd, 1929). Cohen and Hodges' 1963 study found that 70 percent of the working class held no memberships.

Working class individuals usually belong to different *types* of organizations than do members of the middle and upper classes. They are most likely to participate in those organizations that stress practical and personal benefits, and direct action. This is in contrast to most formal organizations whose goals are abstract and intangible. "When lower class individuals affiliate, it is with different types of associations from those favored by their middle-class counterparts; the former respond mostly to appeals which are direct and concrete and which can be more easily internalized" (Cousens, 1964, p. 230).

Many working-class persons may have sufficient income and not have access to certain formal voluntary organizations nor interest in many that are open to them. For example, Cousens (1964) reported in the area he studied that in school-related organizations open to all parents, only 17.5 percent belonged. They valued education, wanted good education for their children, but had no desire to participate in school clubs for the following reasons:

1. Because of their own limited education, they are unable to translate, without help, their concern, interest, and aspirations for their children into the type of abstract program and activity provided by the school clubs;
2. Because of their limited exposure and experience with formal associations, they are reluctant or inadequate to assume the initiative in seeking out the school club in order to become a member;
3. Attendance at school meetings may be frustrating and unrewarding if the program is above their level of understanding or if they are not received with much warmth, interest, or cordiality at the school;
4. The club leadership may be inadequate in meeting the needs of the membership through the activities which are sponsored.

Cousens concludes that organizations which are oriented to the local community and function to cope with community problems, and which are sufficiently uncomplicated, are the ones most attractive and appealing to lower-class working individuals (Cousens, 1964, p. 230).

The middle-class person is *expected* to have more memberships in voluntary organizations. They provide occupational and professional development opportunities. Where income is higher, so is eligibility for a wider variety of special and general interest groups. Participation in certain types of organizations is also a part of the style of life of middle and upper income people, particularly, perhaps, those persons newly arrived in these income groups. As such, the pattern can be expected to repeat itself partially from the force of custom alone.

Socioeconomic status (class) has been found to affect the social participation of the upper class professional and managerial couples. They most closely approximate the popular notion of "togetherness" by their frequent participation in church and recreational organizations (Adams and Butler, 1967, p. 501-507).

One national study of married urban women found participation in voluntary associations to differ by socioeconomic class, with the definition of the role of wife being the significant variable. The working class wife was more likely to have a conflict between housework and active membership. In the upper middle class the role of "wife" appears to be more compatible with voluntary group membership (Slater, 1960, pp. 616-619).

There are other considerations, however. Higher status persons are likely to belong to higher status (prestige) organizations. Payne's study (1954) in four Kentucky counties showed that local organizations did, indeed, exist in prestige hierarchies, and that the members of higher prestige groups were likely to have higher incomes, more education, and higher status occupations, and vice versa. These findings are similar in fact and implication to those of Pope's study (1948) of religious denominations in which higher status churches such as the Congregationalist and Episcopalian were found to contain predominantly (but not exclusively) upper class persons, whereas lower status churches (denominations, cults, etc.) contained predominantly non-upper class members.

Organizational participation may be recognized by many as the means of verticial social mobility. At the same time, membership in certain organizations may identify persons as belonging to given social classes, thereby serving a labeling or stereotyping function. As a consequence, certain memberships may be sought for either of these purposes. Also, a given type of membership may be seen as an aspect of either achieved or ascribed status, although it is commonly not assumed to be the latter.

Ross (1972) points out that participation in FVOs or community groups may be required as company policy. Pellegrin and Coates (1961) studied a southern town and found "executives, in representing their organizations and in furthering their own careers, seek to protect the corporations' interests and foster and maintain conservative, business oriented values and policies. The executive has a variety of motivations for civic participation, and participation is part of his expected role. His behavior is controlled by the corporation he represents" (p. 413).

In summary, *type* of organized voluntary participation varies by socioeconomic class. Lower-class and blue-collar urban memberships are dominated by church, union, lodge, and athletic clubs, with upper income persons having fewer of these affiliations. On the other hand, middle and upper class persons tend to have more memberships in general interest, career-related, and community-oriented organizations (both of an issue-advocacy sort and an altruistic service sort).

Parental Family or Lineage Status. While both the individual's current socioeconomic status and his parental family or lineage status have been found related positively to higher individual rates of membership and participation, the former tends to be a better predictor (see, for example, Hodge, 1970). However, for children and for those youths and young adults not yet earning their own livings, parental family or lineage status is the only meaningful and available measure of the individual's own socioeconomic status.

Higher parental family or lineage status is, in general, positively associated with higher rates of organized voluntary group membership, participation, and leadership (Coleman, 1961; Baeumlerb, 1965; Bohrnstedt, 1966, 1969).

Home Ownership. Home ownership has consistently been found to be related to higher rates of membership and participation (Mather, 1941; Anderson and Ryan, 1943; Scott, 1957; Wright and Hyman, 1958; Devereux, 1960; Babchuk and Gordon, 1962; Babchuk and Thompson, 1962; and Spiro, 1968). Other measures of property ownership such as landlord status and farm ownership, when used, have also been found predictive of more membership and participation in organized voluntary action.

Part of the explanation probably lies in this factor's close association with other elements of socioeconomic status. But some of the explanation probably also is associated with *length of residence in the community*, since it has been shown that persons of longer residence are higher participators than very recent immigrants (Martin, 1952). The element of *residential instability*, as related to owning vs. renting, is perhaps also involved here. Renting makes for more residential mobility, which interrupts patterns of affiliation, and causes a person to spend more time as a newcomer to the community, thus reducing participation even if all other factors are held constant.

Combined Measures of Socioeconomic Status. In some instances researchers have used combined measures or else their measures are somewhat unspecified when relating membership and participation to socioeconomic status. The results once more show a strong relationship between socioeconomic status and membership and participation in voluntary associations in the United States (Lynd and Lynd, 1929, 1937; Lundberg, et al., 1934; Warner and Lunt, 1941; Goldhamer, 1942; Anderson and Ryan, 1943; Lazarsfeld, et al., 1944; Bushee, 1945; Anderson, 1946; Komarovsky, 1946; Hay, 1948, 1951; Almond, 1950; Dotson, 1951; Freedman and Axelrod, 1952; Martin, 1952; Brown, 1953; Lipset and Gordon, 1953; Zimmer, 1955; Beal, 1956; Bell and Force, 1956a and b; Freedman and Freedman, 1956; Nolan, 1956; Taietz and Larson, 1956; Freedman, et al., 1957; Scott, 1957; Obenhaus, et al., 1958; Vidich and Bensman, 1960; Lane, 1959; Devereux, 1960; Slater, 1960; Babchuk and Gordon, 1962; Erbe, 1964; Baeumlerb, 1965a; Kornhauser, 1965; Borhnstedt, 1966, 1969; Orum, 1966; Rothrock, 1968; Nie, et al., 1969; Hyman and Wright, 1971; and Smith, 1972). Foreign studies show similar results (for example, Collison and Cooney, 1960; Nie et al., 1969; Zetterberg, 1960; Curtis, 1971; and Hardee, 1961).

Moreover, scholars have generally found a notable relationship between socioeconomic status and membership in churches (Boisen, 1916; Niebuhr, 1929; Kaufman, 1948; Hostetlar and Mather, 1952; Fichter, 1954; Freedman and Freedman, 1956; Bell and Force, 1957; Dynes, 1957; Vidich and Bensman, 1960; Lazerwitz, 1961, 1962b, 1964; Stark, 1964; Demerath, 1965; Goode, 1966; and Adams and Butler, 1967). However, a number of researchers have noted that rates of church participation of members may be less affected by socioeconomic status than is membership itself (see, for example, Bultena, 1949; Argyle, 1959; Burchinal, 1959; Lazerwitz, 1964; and Dillingham, 1965, 1967). That is, although they may be less likely in general to join a church, lower status individuals, when members, may participate at very high rates (especially if the church they joined is a lower status one).

Occupational Mobility. The evidence from studies of the relationship between occupational mobility and membership and participation in voluntary associations is mixed. Curtis (1959a, 1959b, 1959c, 1960) as well as Vorwaller (1970) in general have found that mobility exerts little or no influence on membership and participation rates, except perhaps when mobility is rapid or extreme.

However, Sykes (1954) and Freedman, et al. (1957) note that upward mobility is associated with larger number of memberships. Lipset and Gordon (1953), Sykes (1954), and Curtis (1958) have found downward mobility associated with decreases of membership and participation. But, Bahr and Caplow (1968), in a study of lower-class and skid-row men which discovered less affiliation among those on skid row, found no evidence that skid row was directly associated with loss of affiliation. It is quite possible that those studies purporting to have found *mobility* effects were in fact finding simple *status* effects—people adjusting their voluntary action to the type and amount appropriate to their current status. Thus, it is not mobility *per se* that matters, but rather current status level.

Socio-physical Characteristics

The socio-physical characteristics cluster consists of variables which include sex, race, ethnicity, personal health, and physical abilities. We term them "sociophysical" because it is the social meaning of the physical characteristics involved that is usually most important.

Sex. Most studies relating sex to membership and participation in voluntary associations have found men to have more membership and participation in the United States (Lynd and Lynd, 1929, 1937; Brunner and Kolb, 1933; Bell, 1938; Warner and Lunt, 1941; Goldhamer, 1942; Komarovsky, 1946; Dotson, 1951; Freedman and Axelrod, 1952; Martin, 1952; Detroit Area Study, 1952; Zimmer, 1955; Bell and Force, 1956b; Scott, 1957; Wright and Hyman, 1958; Rothrock, 1968; and Babchuk and Booth, 1969). In other countries this relationship appears even more strongly (for example, Dotson, 1953, Almond and Verba, 1963; Curtis, 1971). However, Hausknecht's analysis and comparison (1962) of two major national surveys, the AIPO and the NORC, reports that men and women join associations in equal numbers. The AIPO survey (1955) found 54 percent of the men and 57 percent of the women members of associations and the NORC (1954) found 36 percent of each of the sexes members. Lundberg, et al., (1934); Mather (1941); Bushee (1945); and Mayo (1950) have also found that women participate as much or even more than do men. The conflict between the latter results and those presented earlier seems most likely to result from variations in definition of what types of groups are included as voluntary associations (e.g., inclusion/exclusion of unions, church and church groups, etc.).

Types of membership are consistently reported to vary by sex. Women belong to more religious or "do goodism" organizations (service-oriented voluntarism) (see, for example, Fichter, 1954; Argyle, 1959; Schuyler, 1959; and Lazerwitz, 1961). Some organizations restrict membership to one sex, many of these groups being church related. Hausknecht accounts for the variation as reflecting cultural definitions of what is appropriate for men and women respectively. Therefore a greater number of men than women belong to civic and service organizations which include Lions, Kiwanis, and certain lodges and fraternal organizations like the Shriners, because these organizations are functional for men's occupations and careers (Hausknecht 1962). Yet for college age men and women, women are reported to participate more and more intensely than men in college and community organizations (Kievit, 1964). A study of female college graduates by stage of the adult life cycle suggests that single working women and married women (over 28 years of age) without children and working half time participate more in religious and religious related groups, service groups and women's social groups. The single women spend more time in self-enrichment activities concerned with the fine arts. Married women with children participate less in church, but more in church auxiliaries, welfare type groups and women's social groups (Angrist, 1967).

The increases in urbanization, in the number of working women, in the impact of the women's liberation movement, and in civil rights legislation, can be expected to increase the rate of membership and active participation of women in those organizations avoided or not accessible to women in the past. In fact, Almond and Verba (1963) indicate that more widespread participation of women in voluntary organizations in the United States is what accounts for this country's generally higher level of adult participation (as compared to less highly developed countries like Italy and Mexico).

Race. Data on black and white memberships in voluntary organizations are complex and, at first glance, seemingly inconsistent. The AIPO and NORC surveys indicated a larger proportion of whites than blacks were members of more than one organization (Hausknecht, 1962). Wright and Hyman (1958) and Rothrock (1968) also report lower membership rates for blacks. But these results generally fail to control for socioeconomic status—an important matter since blacks in the United States tend to have lower status than whites.

Other studies have concluded that the blacks belong to *more* associations than whites (Drake and Clayton, 1945; Lundberg, et al., 1934; Myrdal, 1944; Mayo, 1950; Lane, 1959). Some studies have discovered no significant differences in participation between whites and blacks when other factors are held constant (Freedman and Axelrod, 1952).

Providing an important perspective in this view, Orum's re-analysis (1966) of the 1955 NORC data indicates that educational and social class variables have less influence on black membership participation rates than these variables have for whites. When educational and social class factors were controlled, blacks were especially likely to be more active participants than whites. Olson (1970) replicated Orum's findings and found that voluntary participation rates for American (Cincinnati) blacks on a wide range of indices rose substantially in comparison with white rates when socioeconomic status and age were controlled.

Argyle (1959), Babchuk and Thompson (1962), and Orum (1966) made special note of high rates of black participation in religious and church groups. Orum (1966), replicating Wright and Hyman's (1958) analysis, confirmed higher rates of black participation in political organizations, but also found equal rates of participation in civic groups. Babchuk and Thompson (1962, pp. 647-655) concluded that the restricted black access to status-lending organizations in the United States has inclined them to create their own social world in the form of organizations to which they have access.

Still other studies show that approximately the same patterns of participation prevail that might be found among whites of similar occupational and socioeconomic levels, etc., with blacks having perhaps a somewhat larger proportion of church and lodge memberships than whites would have and a smaller proportion of members of veterans, military, and patriotic organizations. Hausknecht interprets the type and degree of black participation as an indication of the centrality of organizations to the black community. If, as Hausknecht surmises, the bulk of these organizations are all black in membership and have as their "clientele" members of the black community, this would indicate that there is a considerable degree of community orientation among blacks (Hausknecht, 1962, p. 75). R.V. Smith (1964) provides provocative evidence along these lines noting that blacks have higher participation rates in the inner city (where presumably there are higher concentration of blacks) than elsewhere (where presumably, with lower concentration of blacks, a sense of "community" might be more difficult to attain or where blacks may find themselves informally excluded from predominantly or exclusively white organizations). Ross (1972) has argued from his work in Tampa that blacks participate more where they form an "occupational community" as well.

Although an increasingly large body of data exists on the membership, participation rates, and patterns of black Americans, little systematic work has been done on the rates and patterns of involvement of Orientals and of American Indians or of those with mixed racial backgrounds (such as, for example, many Mexican-Americans).

Ethnicity. Although historians such as Handlin (1951, 1959) have extensively studied the patterns of association and adaptation of American immigrant groups, and although sociologists such as Thomas and Znaniecki (1918) and Lopata (1964) have studied immigrants from Poland and their adjustment to America, and Warner and Srole (1945) did some pioneer work, there has been little systematic study of ethnic voluntary associations or patterns of membership and participation of ethnics. However, Palisi (1963, 1965) has noted slight but not significant differences between membership and participation patterns of first and second generation working-class Italian-Americans, favoring the latter. Women were less likely to participate, especially in the second generation.

Scott (1957) found no relationship between ethnicity and membership in his study of Burlington, Vermont. On the other hand, Spinrad (1960) noted that minority (both racial and ethnic) groups tended to show greater rates of active participation in unions.

Typically, voluntary associations of ethnics play a vital role upon immigration and during the initial stages of the assimilation process. However, as assimilation continues, general (i.e., non-ethnic) associations assume greater roles in, and have a larger proportion of, the ethnic individual's voluntary association memberships and participation. Also, factors specific to, or especially salient in, the new country loom as more predictive than ethnic status or patterns typical in the country of origin.

Personal Health and Physical Abilities. One factor with clear implications for membership, participation, and leadership in voluntary associations and voluntary action agencies is personal health and physical abilities (Smith, 1964). Nevertheless, by focusing on "normal" populations, social scientists have tended to ignore some of the minimal criteria defining the boundaries for social participation. To the authors' knowledge, little systematic work has been done on this topic, relating health status to participation.

Relatively short-term but incapacitating illness is likely to have temporary effects only on levels of participation. However, those experiencing patterns of ill health over longer periods of time may, even when not totally incapacitated, be reluctant to join new organizations, may decline or resign from leadership positions, may otherwise decrease participation or may even drop out of some or all of those associations they belong to.

Individuals experiencing total or near total incapacitation may at times be able to retain some *memberships*, but virtually all other more active forms of voluntary participation are either severely restricted or impossible. In a study of the aged, Taietz and Larson (1956) suggested health factors are especially related to leadership and participation, rather than affiliation.

Those who are institutionalized in prisons, mental hospitals, in hospitals for the chronically ill, in homes for the infirm, and those who are shut-ins in their own homes are effectively barred from virtually all forms of participation in associations, being cut off from whatever modes of participation they had experienced before (other than "pseudo-membership").

In like fashion those who are crippled, paralyzed, blind, deaf, who are unable to speak or who are severely retarded may also find participation possibilities markedly limited. Handicaps such as these in some measure affect the ability of the person to get to meetings, to interact effectively with fellow members (especially when the organization has an essentially normal membership), and to participate cooperatively in the work or activities of the group or organization. An exception here would be voluntary associations of and for the handicapped of one kind or another. Yet there again have been very few systematic studies, if any.

Although minimal levels of personal health or of physical abilities are rarely specified by voluntary associations as *formal* eligibility requirements, the informal requirements as well as the general policies and programs of most groups effectively exclude most who are unable to function and participate beyond minimal physical health levels.

However, it should be noted that the experience (be it personal or of family or friends) of certain types of ill health or of physical disabilities may at times lead to various kinds of support and participation (cf., for example, Sills, 1957). Franklin D. Roosevelt's interest in and support of the National Foundation for Infantile Paralysis (now named the National Foundation) is but one example of what takes place frequently on a smaller scale for victims of that malady and of other diseases and disabilities. Also, in some instances, these very diseases and disabilities form the prime common group of mutual support associations of fellow sufferers and/or fellow victims.

Formal Organizational Affiliations and Roles

The cluster of formal organizational affiliations and roles includes those affiliations and roles that center around occupation and work, religion, politics, and school affiliation (if attending).

Work and Occupations. Many voluntary associations center around work and occupational roles and interests (e.g., professional associations, unions, businessmen's groups and civic associations, etc.). As noted before, socioeconomic factors are associated with higher rates of membership and participation. However, rarely have studies investigated the relationships between work or occupational roles, and voluntary group membership and participation (Ross, 1972). Also, rarely has a systematic attempt been made to study rates and patterns of participation by and across occupations.

However, Lenski's variable of "status crystallization" (1956), which reflects a balance between occupational role, income, and education, and Wilensky's variable of "orderly careers" (1961b), which focuses on a normal, paced, and steady career pattern, have both been found to be associated with higher rates of voluntary group membership and participation (see also Ross, 1972).

Religion. Those studies which report differential rates of membership and participation by religious identification have been marked by a failure to control for other relevant variables, notably socioeconomic factors. Also, since there has been a tendency not to distinguish between the various denominations of Protestantism, as well as the various subgroups within Judaism and Catholicism, the basic independent variable measures are usually quite crude in and of themselves. Religious (church) memberships probably account for the greatest number of memberships in formal voluntary organizations in the United States and these are likely to be present even when other involvements are non-existent (Pittard and Payne, 1969a, 1969b; Hostetlar and Mather, 1952). But due to the prevalence of church membership, many researchers exclude church membership from their studies of formal voluntary organizations, but include *church-related* organizations.

Keeping these important analytical qualifications in mind, Catholics have usually been found to have lower *non-religious* voluntary group participation rates (Warner and Lunt, 1941; Goldhamer, 1942; Komarovsky, 1946; Scott, 1957; Wright and Hyman, 1958; Babchuk and Gordon, 1962; and Spiro, 1968). Douglah (1965) alone finds Catholics participating more in non-religious associations. Nevertheless, Catholics have been found to have higher rates of *religious* participation (cf., Cowhig and Schnore, 1962, for example). Jews have usually been found to have the highest rates of membership and participation in non-religious organizations (Goldhamer, 1942; Wright and Hyman, 1958; Borhnstedt, 1966). However, their rates of religious participation are commonly the lowest (cf., Cowhig and Schnore, 1962, for example). Hausknecht's interpretation of the AIPO and NORC data suggests that the main variation is in the type of other, non-religious organizations in which these three major religious groups' members participate. He reports that far more Catholics join veterans, patriotic and military associations than Protestants; that Protestants join civic and service organizations slightly more than Catholics; and that more Protestants than Catholics join economic, occupational, and professional organizations (Hausknecht, 1962, pp. 76-77).

We have already noted the significance of religious group affiliation in Suttles' (1968) study of a Chicago slum area. In that study the church served as a means of ethnic identification for the Italians. Most of the blacks were Protestant and the church served them as a base for political protest and development of political leadership. No single church was found to serve Mexicans and Puerto Ricans as the Italian churches did. The churches did, however, provide these mixed congregations with a basis for trust and association.

Suttles analysis of the role of the churches in the slum area is supported by Lenski's earlier observation that "religious groups in the modern metropolis are a much more complex form of social organization than has generally been recognized. Far too often, American sociologists have regarded them as merely one more type of special formal organization . . . except, of course, that the religious group is viewed as far less influential" (Lenski, 1961, p. 18). This view, Lenski contends, ignores the communal and socialization aspect of the religious organizations.

If studies of these relationships continue in the future, it would be imperative that researchers go beyond measuring identification with one of the three major religious traditions in the United States, to note the general salience of religious identification for the individual: Is religion important to the individual? Does the individual adhere to the doctrines and credo of his church? Does the individual express his religious beliefs by regular public church attendance? In addition, it would be helpful to specify the denomination, sect, or movement the individual subscribes to within the church of his general religious identification. Moreover, the use of relevant controls, especially in the socioeconomic status realm, would be quite desirable. Finally, it will be helpful to include generally both church affiliation per se as well as participation in church-related voluntary groups in future studies. *Both* are relevant kinds of organized voluntary action.

Political Affiliation. There is substantial evidence in studies both in the United States and in other countries that political activity is associated with membership and participation in non-political voluntary associations (Lazarsfeld, et al., 1944; Birch, 1950; Coser, 1951; Campbell and Kahn, 1952; McWilliams, 1953; Berelson, et al., 1954; Hastings, 1954; Rosenberg, 1954-1955; Buchanan, 1956; Wilensky, 1956; Agger and Goldrich, 1958; Allardt, et al., 1958; Maccoby, 1958; Lane, 1959; McCloskey and Dahlgren, 1959; Rokkan, 1959; Allardt and Pesonen, 1960; Jensen, 1960; Dahl, 1961; Dogan, 1961; Marvick and Nixon, 1961; Allardt, 1961; Campbell, 1962; and Milbrath and Klein, 1962). Although the temporal priority of this relationship has not been fully established, research such as Maccoby's (1958) shows that active participation in non-political associations, especially when the interests of the association can be furthered by political activity, leads to increased political activity.

Higher socioeconomic status has been found to favor Republican affiliation (Lazarsfeld, et al., 1944; Berelson, et al., 1954; Campbell, et al., 1954; Eulau,

1955; and Murphy and Morris, 1961). However, Murphy and Morris (1961) point out that an individual's occupational "situs"—the area of a person's occupational efforts—significantly predicts the person's party affiliation. Specifically, they found that work in the fields of finance, records, and commerce favored Republican affiliation, while work in manufacturing, building, and maintenance favored Democratic affiliation. Nevertheless, to the authors' knowledge, there is no evidence of a strong relationship between membership and participation in voluntary associations of a general sort (e.g., those involved in health, social service, etc.) and either specific party affiliation in the United States or with "independent" status. If such relationships were to be found, they might well disappear when social class factors were controlled. Nevertheless, general political orientations (liberal versus conservative) have been shown to affect patterns of membership and participation in types of groups reflecting those orientations. For example, liberal Republicans may be members of the Ripon Society or even of Common Cause, but they are quite unlikely to also be active in the John Birch Society. Conservative Democrats may find the John Birch Society quite attractive, but are unlikely to be active in the Americans for Democratic Action.

School Affiliation. Schools, notably junior high schools, high schools, and undergraduate colleges tend to encourage, provide, and sustain rich associational environments for their students (cf., for example, Gordon, 1957; Coleman, 1961; Barker, et al., 1964). Graduate and professional schools would seem considerably less disposed to this practice, although the evidence is currently only impressionistic.

As mentioned in our discussion of the life cycle stage, relatively high and increasing rates of membership and participation have been found during the years between ten and twenty. Although much research is yet to be done on the patterns of adolescent membership and participation, it would seem that, due to students' formal and informal ineligibility for membership and participation in much of the associational life of the community, most of their participation currently takes place within or under the auspices of a school or college. However, a new trend may be emerging with many schools and colleges presently creating (and stimulating students to participate in) entire school programs of community involvement and voluntary participation, especially in the social service and change-oriented realms.

In general, however, there are strong indications that those currently attending schools and colleges have more memberships and are more active participants than those of the same age who are not attending. Therefore, school affiliation seems to be an important social background factor affecting individual participation in organized voluntary action.

Interpersonal Roles

Interpersonal relationships and especially primary relationships have long been an important focus of sociological investigation. Following the general lead of

Katz and Lazarsfeld (1955), a number of researchers including Sills (1957), Gouldner (1960), Babchuk and Gordon (1962), Jacoby (1966), and Booth and Babchuk (1969) have found important associations between voluntary group membership or participation and various personal influence patterns and processes. These studies have found that most often people join and become involved in voluntary associations because they are personally asked and encouraged to do so rather than through more impersonal means, even though mass media may provide a responsive attitudinal background to be triggered by a personal request.

Very often children learn to participate and are encouraged to participate by their parents. Where parents are or were active members and participants, their children are likely to emulate those patterns (Anderson, 1943, 1947; Martin and Siegal, 1953; Hyman, 1957; Johannes, 1958; Putney and Middleton, 1961; Baeumler, 1965; and Smith, 1972). Although mothers may be especially influential (Anderson, 1947; Martin and Siegel, 1953; Payne, 1955), fathers are found to have notable influence on their sons (Anderson, 1943, Hodge and Treiman, 1968) and mothers on their daughters (Anderson, 1943; Hodge and Treiman, 1968).

Spouses are especially influential on each other's membership and participatory roles (Anderson, 1943, 1946; Johannes, 1958; Babchuk, 1965; Hodge and Treiman, 1968; Adams and Butler, 1967; Adams and Mogey, 1967; Harry, 1970; and Smith, 1972). However, Babchuk (1965) and Adams and Mogey (1967) note the special influence of the husband in settings where both spouses participate together.

Having a large number of friends and being subject to their influence (Scott, 1957, Devereux, 1960; Wilensky, 1961a and b; and Babchuk and Thompson, 1962), knowing a large number of neighbors (Smith, 1972), and being involved with fellow workers (Spinrad, 1960) have been found to be associated with higher rates of membership and participation in voluntary groups. However, the influence of relatives other than parents and children on these rates has not been firmly or systematically established, indeed not investigated so far as we know.

Mass Media Exposure

Along with various measures of informal participation patterns and rates, mass media exposure is another measure of the "general activity" of an individual. In European studies, Allardt (1961) and Ahtik (1962) found exposure to various forms of mass media related to higher FVO participation rates. In a recent study of voluntary participation in eight Massachusetts towns, Smith (1972) noted that attending movies and reading newspapers, periodicals (in general), and especially non-fiction periodicals, were significantly related to the number of FVO memberships an individual has. All of these findings suggest that participation in organized voluntary action is associated with what might be called "information leadership"–greater exposure to the mass media.

Migration and Length of Residence

Migration experience and length of residence in a given community (or at a given address) may have a direct influence on social relationships and social participation, since those moving to new neighborhoods, communities, or regions find themselves having to "start again" in establishing new social relations and in joining those local groups they are attracted to. This process takes time and the newcomer lags behind longer-time residents. Such is the rationale for the inclusion of measures of migration and length of residence in studies of voluntary participation.

For the most part, studies of communities have found that lower rates of membership and participation may be expected for newcomers to a community during the first five years of their residence (Lindstrom, 1936; Kaufman, 1949; Martin, 1952; Brandow and Potter, 1953; Zimmer, 1955, 1956; Zimmer and Hawley, 1959a; Devereux, 1960; Babchuk and Thompson, 1962; Jitodai, 1965; and Spiro, 1968). After that period of time, the rates of newcomers and of longer-time residents tend to become similar.

However, a few studies, such as Beal's (1956) of a farmer's cooperative, as well as Scott's (1957) study of Bennington, Vermont, and Wright and Hyman's (1958) national survey, find no marked differences between newcomers and longer-time residents (although Scott notes a slight increase after ten years of residence). Litwak's work (1961) is unique in that it is the only one to note that although too short a residence in a community favors lower participation rates, so does too long a residence. Smith (1972) finds similarly that long term residents of towns participate less than the more mobile moderate or short term residents.

Deviant cases may be expected, especially when an organization is the unit of analysis or when modes and extent of participation are distinguished. For example, Babchuk and Gordon's investigation of a neighborhood improvement council (1962) revealed that although longer residence favored membership, newer residents of the area tended toward more frequent attendance and were more likely to assume leadership roles. Newcomers also had membership in a larger number of other groups.

In general, future studies would profit by making more specific the nature of the person's move. As Smith (1964) suggests, those moving from greater distances may require more time to acquire memberships and participate than those whose moves involve less drastic changes (moves within a metropolitan area or even within a given city or town). Along these lines, Spiro (1968) found that length of residence in a *neighborhood* was a better measure of membership and participation than was length of residence in the city.

Another important consideration is the background of the migrant, Freedman and Freedman (1956) suggest that adjustment and social participation in urban areas is more difficult for those of rural origin. Spiro (1968) provides a general confirmation of those findings when he notes that those from farm backgrounds as well as those from the South take longer to engage in urban voluntary participation than do other groups. Hoyt's research (1954) identifies yet another group that is markedly affected by migration—the elderly. Having moved, the elderly rarely regain former membership or participation rates.

Although to the authors' knowledge, no systematic study on this question has been made, it would seem likely that membership in some organizations is more subject to the effects of length of community residence than others. Some voluntary associations recruit members on a national basis (such as, for example, national occupational, professional, and scientific and learned societies). Changes of residence within the United States would be unlikely to affect membership in these or similar groups. Other associations (such as labor unions, churches, political parties, political action groups, fraternal and veterans groups, civic and service groups, etc.) commonly have local branches or affiliates across the country. These memberships would seem likely to be carried over in a new community context. However, those associations drawing only on a local population base would seem to be most open to the effects of migration and length of residence except, perhaps, groups such as studied by Babchuk and Gordon (1962) aiming at community change.

Gans (1967) provides some evidence to support these hypotheses in his study of the growth of a new town. Virtually all residents of the Levittown area were new to the community. In some instances national groups themselves played a major role in organizing chapters and branches, but this was complemented by the expectations and hopes of former members of these groups in other communities joining these organizations and/or founding groups of their own without the stimulus of regional or national offices where these existed. Moreover, although the major reasons for moving to Levittown centered around getting better housing, for many the move to Levittown symbolized the broader and more extensive change in life style. Before moving to Levittown 55 percent looked forward to "having voice in community affairs" while 45 percent and 28 percent looked forward respectively to "being active in civic groups" and in "joining clubs." In a random sample of residents a majority reported participating more in Levittown than in the past. Thus, there is room to advance a hypothesis that those expecting and looking forward to participating when they move to another community may be more likely to overcome the effects of migration on voluntary participation than those with less pronounced expectations and desires.

Summary

As a summary of our review of the literature, we will list a series of propositions which have generally been confirmed in the research to date as well as a list of hypotheses and possible directions for future research.

The propositions are rated both in terms of the strength and direction of relationships and in terms of the consistency with which the relationship has been found. Based on an estimated or actual zero-order Pearsonian correlation coefficient, relationships will be labeled "negligible" if the zero-order relationships are less than ± .099; "weak" if the relationship is in the ± .100 to .199 range; "moderate" if the relationship is in the ± .200 to .399 range; "strong" if the relationship is in the ± .400 to .599 range; and "very strong" if the relationship is in the ± .600 or larger range. Findings will be termed "inconsistent" when there is no pattern of results across the studies done on the relationship. "Low consistency" findings are those where there is a slight preponderance of results in a given direction. "Medium consistency" findings are those where a clear preponderance of a given pattern can be found in the data, but where there remains substantial variation. If a large majority of the results are in line with the main pattern, the results are labeled as of "high consistency." "Very high consistency" is reserved for those instances where there is little variation from the main pattern.

1. Membership and participation tend to increase from about age eight through about age eighteen, then decrease markedly. Toward the end of the twenties, membership and participation increase to a peak during the middle years (40-55). With increasing age, membership and participation decrease gradually at first, but then with increasing rapidity after retirement age. (Moderate to strong relationship, very high consistency).
2. Except for the young, married individuals join more often and participate more extensively than the single or the divorced, widowed or separated. (Moderate relationship, high consistency).
3. Widows and widowers show higher rates of membership and participation than the single, divorced, or separated. (Moderate relationship, medium consistency).
4. Having children is associated with higher rates of membership and participation for parents. (Moderate relationship, low to medium consistency).
5. Having all children of school age favors higher rates of membership and participation. (Moderate relationship, high consistency).
6. Higher income is positively associated with higher rates of membership, participation, and leadership. (Strong relationship, high to very high consistency).
7. Those with higher levels of education are more likely to join associations, to participate actively in them, and to assume leadership roles. (Strong relationship, very high consistency).
8. Higher occupational status is positively associated with membership, participation, and leadership. (Strong relationship, very high consistency).
9. Membership and participation rates are positively associated with higher parental family or lineage status. (Moderate relationship, medium consistency).

10. Home ownership and other measures of property ownership are positively related to membership and participation. (Moderate to strong relationship, very high consistency).

11. Combined measures of socioeconomic status, just as the separate indicators, are related to higher rates of membership, participation, and leadership. (Strong relationship, very high consistency).

12. Upward occupational mobility is related to higher rates of affiliation and participation. (Negligible to weak relationships, inconsistent to low consistency).

13. "Orderly careers" and "crystallized statuses" are related to higher rates of membership and participation. (Moderate relationship, medium to high consistency).

14. Working class ("blue collar") urban memberships in voluntary associations are concentrated in churches, unions, lodges (fraternal-social groups), and sports clubs. (Strong relationship, high consistency).

15. Middle, and especially upper-middle class persons tend to have proportionately more voluntary association memberships in general interest, career-related business and professional, community oriented, service oriented, educational, cultural, and political groups or pressure groups. (Strong relationship, high consistency).

16. Males tend to join more associations and to participate more actively. (Weak relationship, low consistency—holds best for less developed areas or countries where equality of sexes is least).

17. Blacks join and participate more than whites in the lower socioeconomic statuses. (Moderate relationship, high consistency).

18. If parents have been joiners and active participants, their children are likely to be so also. (Moderate relationship, very high consistency).

19. The affiliation and participation rates of spouses are intercorrelated. (Moderate to strong relationship, high to very high consistency).

20. Newcomers to a community (a few years or less) are likely to show lower rates of membership and participation than those who have been residents for longer periods of time. (Moderate relationship, high consistency).

21. Higher rates of media exposure, of participation in informal social settings, and of membership and participation in various formal organizational settings is positively related to higher rates of membership and participation. (Moderate to strong relationship, high consistency).

22. The tendency for different kinds of voluntary associational activity, informal interpersonal activity, mass media activity, and other formal organizational activity to be correlated or covary in a population of individuals can be viewed as a "general activity syndrome." (Moderate relationship, high consistency).

Suggestions for Future Research

Although there have been some hopeful signs in the past decade that the practice is becoming more common, adequate distinctions between various analytical types of individual voluntary participation—such as for example the number of voluntary organizational memberships an individual has, his leadership activities in a number of voluntary settings, joining a given single association when and if he is formally and/or informally eligible, general internal participation rates (such as frequency of attendance at various functions, and other global measures of activity), and specific internal activity (performing various leadership tasks and committee functions, etc.)—have seldom been made.

Patterns of involvement and participation in organized voluntary action have been discerned along the lines of various background factors (blacks versus whites, men versus women, lower income individuals versus those of higher income levels, etc.). Continued research along these lines may yield fruitful insights into aspects of participation that may have been obscured by undifferentiated measures of the number of memberships an individual has or by concentration on a given type of association. Similarly, some attention to the nature of expected or normative participation within a given organization or association, and deviations from those norms, may again yield valuable insights into voluntary action.

A critical need exists in studies of individual voluntary action for multivariate and for longitudinal research. Although we have documented here a number of relationships between social background factors and aspects of membership, participation, and leadership in organized voluntary action, the precise weightings of any or all of these independent variables and their causal relationships with each other very much remain to be explored, both in general and for given types of organizations and for given types of individuals. Similarly, we have few genuine longitudinal studies and not many retrospective analyses. Investigations of the life cycle stages point toward "associational career patterns," but there is no systematic data on shifts in membership and participation for types of individuals over extensive periods of time, or on the reasons for such shifts.

Much research is yet to be done on the relationship between health and physical abilities and rates and patterns of voluntary activity. The section on this theme is based essentially on hypotheses. We know little of patterns and extent of membership and participation for Orientals and Chicanos/Puerto Ricans or of the precise patterns of immigrant adoption of national patterns of voluntary action at first in immigrant associations and then in the associations of the wider community. Extensive research efforts are also required for fuller and more precise knowledge on the effects of work and occupational roles, of religious affiliations, of school attendance, of political affiliations, of the various types of interpersonal relationships, and of mass media exposure on patterns of membership, participation, and leadership. And the effects of migration and length of residence cannot be adequately understood until more longitudinal studies are performed.

Some other more specific topics on which research is much needed are the following: What are the social or background factors of the *non*-joiner in modern society, especially the higher or middle socioeconomic status non-joiner? What changes are occurring over time in the voluntary associational patterns of blacks and other minority racial and ethnic groups as their situation in American (or other) society changes? For instance, are they being more effectively assimilated into business and professional groups? What impact on the larger national patterns of participation will such emerging voluntary movements as "women's liberation," "brown liberation," etc. have?

Finally, there is a great need for more careful attempts, both theoretical and empirical, to explain and understand *why* various social background factors and roles tend to be associated with individual participation in organized voluntary action of various kinds. Most of the studies reviewed here have offered only speculation on the lines of causality involved. After roughly thirty years of research on the general relationships involved, surely the time has come to begin to look more carefully at how social background factors are themselves interrelated through time and how they in turn interrelate with personality, attitude, and contextual/organizational factors, as dealt with in the subsequent chapters of Part Two.

References

Adams, Bert N. and James E. Butler
1967   "Occupational Status and Husband-Wife Social Participation." *Social Forces* 45 (June): 501-507.
Adams, Robert Lynn and John Mogey
1967   "Marriage, Membership and Mobility in Church and Sect." *Sociological Analysis*, 28: 205-214.
Agger, Robert E. and Daniel Goldrich
1958   "Community Power Structures and Partisanship." *American Sociological Review*, 23: 383-92.
Ahtik, Vito
1962   "Industrial Workers' Participation in Cultural, Social and Physical Leisure Activities." In *Evolution of the Forms and Needs of Leisure*, by the International Study Group on the Social Sciences of Leisure (Unesco Inst. for Education/Hamburg, German): 102-110.
Albrecht, Ruth
1958   "The Meaning of Religion to Older People—The Social Aspect." In

D. Scudder (ed.), *Organized Religion and the Older Person*. Gainesville, Fla.: University of Florida Press, 53-70.

Allardt, Erik

1961 "Community Activity, Leisure Use and Social Structure." *Acta Sociologica*, 6: 67-82.

Allardt, Erik; Pentii Jartii; Faina Jyrkila; and Vrjo Littunen

1958 "On the Cumulative Nature of Leisure Activities." *Acta Sociologica* 3: 165-72.

Allardt, Erik and P. Pesonen

1960 "The Participation of Citizens in Political Life in Finland." *International Social Science Journal* 12 (No. 1): 31-45.

Almond, Gabriel A.

1950 *The American People and Foreign Policy*. New York: Harcourt, Brace.

Almond, Gabriel and Sidney Verba

1963 *The Civic Culture* : Political Attitudes and Democracy in Five Nations. Princeton, N.J.: Princeton University Press.

Anderson, C. Arnold and Bryce Ryan

1943 "Social Participation Differences among Tenure Classes in a Prosperous Commercialized Farming Area." *Rural Sociology* 8: 281-90.

Anderson, Walfred, A.

1938 *The Membership of Farmers in New York Organizations*. Ithaca, New York: Bull. 695, Cornell Univ. Agric. Exper. Station.

1943 "The Family and Individual Social Participation." American Sociological Review 8:420-24.

1946 "Family Social Participation and Social Status Self-Ratings." *American Sociological Review*, 11: 253-58.

1947 *Some Participation Principles: Their Relations to the Programs of Rural Agencies*. Bulletin 731. Ithaca, New York: Cornell Agricultural Extension Service.

Anderson, Walfred A. and Hans H. Plambeck

1943 *The Social Participation of Farm Families*. Mimeo Bull. No. 8. Cornell Univ. Ithaca, N.Y.: Agric. Exper. Station.

Anderson, Walfred A. and N. Sibley

1957 *The Social Participation of Fringe Families:* A Second Study. Rural Sociological Public. No. 50. Ithaca, N.Y.: Cornell Agricultural Experiments Station.

Angrist, Shirley S.

1967 "Role Constellation as a Variable in Women's Leisure Activities." *Social Forces* 45 (no. 3): 423-31.

Argyle, Michael

1959 *Religious Behavior*. Glencoe, Illinois: The Free Press.

1952 *A Social Profile of Detroit, Report of the Detroit Area Study*. Ann Arbor, Mich.: University of Michigan.

236

Axelrod, Morris
1956   "Urban Social Structure and Social Participation." *American Sociological Review* 21:13-18.
Babchuk, Nicholas
1965   "Primary Friends and Kin: A Study of the Associations of Middle-Class Couples." *Social Forces* 43: 483-92.
Babchuk, Nicholas and Alan Booth
1969   "Voluntary Association Membership: A Longitudinal Analysis." *American Sociological Review* 34: 31-45.
Babchuk, Nicholas and C. Wayne Gordon
1962   *The Voluntary Association in the Slum*. Lincoln, Neb.: University of Nebraska Studies, New Series no. 27.
Babchuk, Nicholas and Ralph V. Thompson
1962   "The Voluntary Associations of Negroes." *American Sociological Review* 27: 647-55.
Babchuk, Nicholas and Charles K. Warriner, eds.
1965   "Signposts in the Study of Voluntary Groups." *Sociological Inquiry* 35 (Spring 1965): 135-24.
Baeumler, Walter L.
1965a   *Socialization Influences and Social Participation—A Study of Generational Continuity in Membership and Participation in Voluntary Associations*. Unpublished Ph.D. Dissertation. Lincoln, Neb.: University of Nebraska.
1965b   "The Correlates of Formal Participation Among High School Students." *Sociological Inquiry* 35 (No. 2): 235-40.
Bahr, Howard M. and Theodore Caplow
1968   "Homelessness, Affiliation, and Occupational Mobility." *Social Forces* 47: 28-33.
Barber, Bernard
1950   "Participation and Mass Apathy." In Alvin W. Gouldner (ed.), *Studies in Leadership*. New York: Harper and Brothers, 477-504.
Barker, Roger G., Paul Gump, et al.
1964   *Big School, Small School: High School Size and Student Behavior*. Stanford, Calif.: Stanford University Press.
Bauder, Ward W.
1956   "Objectives and Activities of Special-Interest Organizations in Kentucky." Lexington, Kentucky: *Agr. Exp. Sta. Bull.* 639 Mar.
Beal, George M.
1956   "Additional Hypotheses in Participation Research." *Rural Sociology* 21: 249-56.
Beegle, J. Allan and Widick Schrozder
1955   *Social Organization In the North Lansing Fringe*. Mich. State University, *Agr. Exp. Sta. Tech. Bull.* 251.

Bell, Howard M.
1938   *Youth Tell Their Story*. Washington, D.C.: American Council on Education.

Bell, Wendell and Maryanne T. Force
1956a   "Social Structure and Participation in Different Types of Formal Associations." *Social Forces* 34: 345-50.
1956b   "Urban Neighborhood Types and Participation in Formal Organizations." *American Sociological Review* 21: 25-34.
1957   "Religious Preference, Familism, and the Class Structure." *Midwest Sociologist* 9.

Berelson, Bernard; Paul Lazarsfeld; and William McPhee
1954   *Voting: A Study of Opinion Formation in a Presidential Campaign*. Chicago: University of Chicago Press.

Birch, A.H.
1950   "The Habit of Voting." *Journal of the Manchester School of Economic and Social Studies* 18: 75-82.

Blum, Alan F.
1964   "Social Structure, Social Class, and Participation in Primary Relationships." In Arthur B. Shostak and William Gomberg (eds.), *Blue Collar World*. Englewood Cliffs, New Jersey: Prentice-Hall, 195-207.

Bohrnstedt, George William
1966   *Processes of Seeking Membership in and Recruitment by Voluntary Social Organizations*. Unpublished Ph.D. Dissertation. Madison, Wisc.: University of Wisconsin.
1969   "Social Mobility, Aspirations, and Fraternity Membership." *Sociological Quarterly* 10: 42-52.

Boisen, Anton T.
1916   "Factors Which Have to Do with the Decline of the Rural Church." *American Journal of Sociology* 22: 177-92.

Booth, Alan and Nicholas Babchuk
1969   "Personal Influence Networks and Voluntary Association Affiliation." *Sociological Inquiry* 39: 179-88.

Booth, Alan; Nicholas Babchuk; and Alan B. Knox
1968   "Social Stratification and Membership in Instrumental-Expressive Voluntary Associations." *Sociological Quarterly* 9: 427-39.

Boskoff, Alvin
1970   *The Sociology of Urban Regions*. (Second edition) New York: Appleton Century Croft, 181-82.

Bottomore, T.
1954   "Social Stratification in Voluntary Organizations." In D.V. Glass (ed.), *Social Mobility in Britain*. London: Routledge & Kegan, 349-82.

Brandow, G.E. and A.K. Potter
1953   "An Application of the Linear Discriminant Function." *Rural Sociology* 18: 321-26.

238

Brown, Emory J.
1953 "The Self as Related to Formal Participation in Three Pennsylvania Rural Communities." *Rural Sociology* 18(4): 313-20.
Brunner, Edmund de S. and J.H. Kolb
1933 *Rural Social Trends*. New York: McGraw-Hill, 262.
Buchanan, William
1956 "An Inquiry into Purposive Voting." *Journal of Politics* 18: 281-96.
Bultena, Louis
1949 "Church Membership and Church Attendance in Madison, Wisconsin." *American Sociological Review* 24: 348-89.
Burchinal, Lee G.
1959 "Some Social Status Criteria and Church Membership and Attendance." *Journal of Social Psychology* 49: 53-64.
Bushee, Frederick A.
1945 "Social Organization in a Small City." *American Journal of Sociology* 51: 217-26.
Campbell, Angus
1962 "The Passive Citizen." *Acta Sociologica* 6: 9-21.
Campbell, Angus; Gerald Gurin; and Warren E. Miller
1954 *The Voter Decides*. Evanston, Ill.: Row, Petersen.
Campbell, Angus and Robert L. Kahn
1952 *The People Elect a President*. Ann Arbor, Mich.: University of Michigan, Institute for Social Research, Survey Research Center.
Cavan, Ruth S.; Ernest W. Burgess; Robert J. Havighurst; and Herbert Goldhamer
1949 *Personal Adjustment in Old Age*. Chicago: Science Research Associates.
Chapin, F. Stuart
1939 "Social Participation and Social Intelligence." *American Sociological Review* 4: 157-66.
Cohen, Albert K. and Harold M. Hodges
1963 "Characteristics of the Lower-Blue-Collar-Class." *Social Problems* 10: 303-34.
Coleman, James S.
1961 *The Adolescent Society*. New York: Free Press.
Collison, Peter and Edmund Cooney
1960 "Leadership in Community Associations." *International Review of Community Development* 6: 163-71.
Coser, Rose
1951 "Political Involvement and Interpersonal Relations." *Psychiatry* 14: 213-22.
Cousens, F.R.
1964 "Indigenous Leadership in Two Lower Class Neighborhood Organizations." In Arthur B. Shostak and William Gomberg (eds.), *Blue Collar World*. Englewood Cliffs, N.J.: Prentice-Hall.

Cowhig, James D. and Leo Schnore
1962 "Religious Affiliation and Attendance in Metropolitan Centers." *American Catholic Sociological Review* 23(2): 113-27.
Curtis, James
1971 "Voluntary Association Joining: A Cross-National Comparative Note." *American Sociological Review* 36: 872-80.
Curtis, Richard F.
1958 *Consequences of Occupational Mobility in a Metropolitan Community*. Unpublished Ph.D. dissertation. Ann Arbor, Mich.: University of Michigan.
1959a "Occupational Mobility and Membership in Formal Voluntary Associations: A Note on Research." *American Sociological Review* 24(6): 846-49.
1959b "Note on Occupational Mobility and Union Membership in Detroit: A Replication." *Social Forces* 38: 69-71.
1959c "Occupational Mobility and Urban Social Life." *American Journal of Sociology* 65: 296-98.
1960 "Occupational Mobility and Church Participation." *Social Forces* 38: 315-19.
Dahl, Robert A.
1961 *Who Governs? Democracy and Power in an American City*. New Haven: Yale University Press.
Demerath, N.J. III
1965 *Social Class in American Protestantism*. Chicago: Rand-McNally.
Devereux, Edward C., Jr.
1960 "Community Participation and Leadership." *Journal of Social Issues* 16(4): 29-45.
Dillingham, Harry C.
1965 "Protestant Religion and Social Status." *American Journal of Sociology* 70: 416-22.
1967 "Rejoinder to 'Social Class and Church Participation.' "*American Journal of Sociology* 73(1): 110-14.
Dogan, Mattei
1961 "Political Ascent in a Class Society: French Deputies 1870-1958." In Dwaine Marvick (ed.), *Political Decision-Makers*. Glencoe: Free Press, 57-90.
Dotson, Floyd
1951 "Patterns of Voluntary Association Among Working-Class Families." *American Sociological Review* 16: 687-93.
1953 "A Note on Participation in Voluntary Associations in a Mexican City." *American Sociological Review* 18: 381-86.
Douglah, Mohammed A.
1965 *Factors Affecting Adult Participation in Education Activities and Volun-*

tary Formal Organizations. Unpublished Ph.D. dissertation. Madison: University of Wisconsin.

Drake, St. Clair and Horace R. Cayton
1945 *Black Metropolis*. New York: Harcourt Brace.

Dynes, Russell B.
1957 "The Consequences of Sectarianism for Social Participation." *Social Forces* 35: 331-34.

Eitzen, S. Stanley
1970 "A Study of Voluntary Association Memberships among Middle-Class Women." *Rural Sociology* 35: 84-91.

Erbe, William
1964 "Social Involvement and Political Activity: A Replication and Elaboration." *American Sociological Review* 29: 198-215.

Eulau, Heinz
1955 "Perceptions of Class and Party in Voting Behavior: 1952." *American Political Science Review* 49: 364-84.

Fichter, Joseph H.
1954 *Social Relations in the Urban Parish*. Chicago: University of Chicago Press.

Foskett, John M.
1955 "Social Structure and Social Participation." *American Sociological Review* 20: 431-38.

Freedman, Howard; E. Novak; and Leo G. Reeder
1957 "Correlates of Membership in Voluntary Associations." *American Sociological Review* 22: 528-33.

Freedman, Ronald and Morris Axelrod
1952 "Who Belongs to What in a Great Metropolis?" *Adult Leadership* 1:6-9.

Freedman, Ronald and Deborah Freedman
1956 "Elements in the Nonfarm Population." *Rural Sociology* 21: 50-61.

Gallagher, Orvoell
1957 "Voluntary Associations in France." *Social Forces* 36: 153-60.

Gans, Herbert J.
1967 *The Levittowners*. New York: Pantheon Books.

Garbin, A.P. and Vivian Lucille Laughlin
1965 "Military Participation in Voluntary Associations." *Sociological Inquiry* 35: 227-34.

Goldhamer, Herbert
1942 *Some Factors Affecting Participation in Voluntary Associations*. Unpublished Ph.D. dissertation. Chicago: University of Chicago.

Goode, Erich
1966 "Social Class and Church Participation." *American Journal of Sociology* 72(1): 102-11.

Gordon, C. Wayne
1957 *The Social System of the High School*. Glencoe: Free Press.

Gouldner, Helen P.

1960   *The Organization Woman: Patterns of Friendship and Organization Commitment*. Unpublished Ph.D. dissertation. Los Angeles: UCLA.

Graham, Saxon

1959   "Social Correlates of Adult Leisure Time Behavior." In Marvin B. Sussman (ed.), *Community Structure and Analysis*. New York: Thomas Y. Crowell, 331-54.

Hagedorn, Robert and Sanford Labovitz

1967   "An Analysis of Community and Professional Participation." *Social Forces* 45(4): 483-91.

1968a "Participation in Community Associations by Occupations: A Test of Three Theories." *American Sociological Review* 33: 272-83.

1968b "Occupational Characteristics and Participation in Voluntary Associations." *Social Forces* 47: 16-27.

Handlin, Oscar

1951   *The Uprooted*. New York: Crosset & Dunlop.

1959   *Immigration as a Factor in American History*. Englewood Cliffs, N.J.: Prentice-Hall.

Hardee, J. Gilbert

1961   "Social Structure and Participation in an Australian Rural Community." *Rural Sociology* 26: 240-51.

Harry, Joseph

1970   "Family Localism and Social Participation." *American Journal of Sociology* 75: 821-27.

Hastings, Philip K.

1954   "The Non-Voter in 1952: A Study of Pittsfield, Massachusetts." *Journal of Psychology* 38: 301-12.

Hausknecht, Murray

1962   *The Joiners: A Sociological Description of Voluntary Association Membership in the United States*. New York: The Bedminster Press.

1964   "The Blue-Collar Joiners." In Arthur B. Shostak and William Gomberg (eds.), *Blue-Collar World*. Englewood Cliffs, New Jersey: Prentice-Hall, 207-15.

Havighurst, R.J.

1957   "The Leisure Activities of the Middle-aged." *American Journal of Sociology* 63: 152-62.

Hay, Donald G.

1948   "A Scale for the Measurement of Social Participation of Rural Households." *Rural Sociology* 13: 285-94.

1951   "Social Participation of Individuals in Farm Rural Communities of the Northeast." *Rural Sociology* 16: 127-35.

Hodge, Robert W.

1970   "Social Integration, Psychological Well-Being, and Their Socioeconomic Correlates," *Sociological Inquiry* 40: 182-206.

Hodge, Robert W. and David J. Treiman
1968 "Social Participation and Social Status." *American Sociological Review* 33: 722-40.
Hofstee, E.W.
1957 *Rural Life and Rural Welfare in the Netherlands.* The Hague, Netherlands: G.P.O.
Hollingshead, August B.
1949 *Elmtown's Youth.* New York: John Wiley.
Hostetler, John A. and William A. Mather
1952 *Participation in the Rural Church.* Agricultural Experiment Station Paper 1762. State College, Pa.: Pennsylvania State College.
Hoyt, G.C.
1954 "The Life of the Retired in a Trailer Park." *American Journal of Sociology* 59: 361-70.
Hunter, Floyd
1963 *Community Power Structure.* Garden City, N.Y.: Doubleday and Co.
Hunter, W.W. and Helen Maurice
1953 *Older People Tell Their Story.* Ann Arbor: University of Michigan, Division of Gerontology.
Hyman, Herbert H.
1957 *Political Socialization.* Glencoe: Free Press.
Hyman, Herbert H. and Charles R. Wright
1971 "Trends in Voluntary Association Membership of American Adults." *American Sociological Review* 36: 191-206.
Jacoby, Arthur P.
1966 "Personal Influence and Primary Relationships: Their Effect on Associational Membership." *Sociological Quarterly* 7: 76-84.
Jensen, Jack
1960 *Political Participation: A Survey of Evanston, Illinois.* Unpublished Master's thesis. Evanston, Ill.: Northwestern University.
Jitodai, Ted
1965 "Urban-Rural Background and Formal Group Membership." *Rural Sociology* 30: 75-83.
Johannis, Theodore B.
1958 "Participation by Fathers, Mothers, and Teenage Sons and Daughters in Selected Social Activity." *The Coordinator* 7: 24-25.
Katz, Elihu and Paul F. Lazarsfeld
1955 *Personal Influence: The Part Played by People in the Flow of Mass Communications.* Glencoe: Free Press.
Katz, Fred E.
1966 "Social Participation and Social Structure." *Social Forces* 45 (December): 199-210.
Kaufman, Harold F.
1948 *Religious Organizations in Kentucky*, Agricultural Experiment Station Bulletin 524. Lexington: University of Kentucky.

1949 *Participation in Organized Activities in Selected Kentucky Societies.* Kentucky Agric. Bulletin 528.

Kievit, M.B.
1964 "Social Participation and Some Demographic Variables." *Journal of Sociological Psychology* 64 (Dec.): 355-68.

Komarovsky, Mirra
1946 "The Voluntary Associations of Urban Dwellers." *American Sociological Review* 11: 686-98.

Kornhauser, Arthur
1965 *Mental Health of the Industrial Worker:* A Detroit Study. New York: John Wiley.

Kramer, Ralph M.
1969 *Participation of the Poor.* Englewood Cliffs, N.J.: Prentice-Hall.

Lane, Robert E.
1959 *Political Life: Why People Get Involved in Politics.* Glencoe, Ill.: Free Press.

Lazarsfeld, Paul F.; Bernard Berelson; and H. Gaudet
1944 *The People's Choice.* New York: Duell, Sloan and Pearce.

Lazerwitz, Bernard
1961 "Some Factors Associated with Variation in Church Attendance." *Social Forces* 39: 301-309.

1962a Membership in Voluntary Associations and Frequency of Church Attendance, *Journal for the Scientific Study of Religion* 2: 74-84.

1962b "National Data on Participation Rates Among Residential Belts in the United States," *American Sociological Review* 27: 691-96.

1964 "Religion and Social Structure in the United States." In Louis Schneider (ed.), *Religion, Culture and Society.* New York: John Wiley and Sons.

Lenski, Gerhard E.
1956 "Social Participation and Status Crystallization." *American Sociological Review* 21: 458-64.

1961 *The Religious Factor.* Garden City, New York: Anchor Books.

Lindstrom, David E.
1936 "Forces Affecting Participation of Farm People in Rural Organization." *Ill. Agr. Exp. Sta. Bull.* 423.

Lipset, Seymour Martin and Joan Gordon
1953 "Mobility and Trade Union Membership." In Reinhard Bendix and S.M. Lipset (eds.), *Class, Status and Power.* Glencoe, Ill.: Free Press, 491-500.

Litwak, Eugene
1961 "Voluntary Associations and Neighborhood Cohesion." *American Sociological Review* 258-71.

London, Jack and Robert Wenkert
1964 "Obstacles to Blue-Collar Participation in Adult Education." In

244

Arthur B. Shostak and William Gomberg (eds.), *Blue Collar World*. Englewood Cliffs, New Jersey: Prentice-Hall, 445-57.

Lopata, Helena Z.

1964 "The Function of Voluntary Associations in an Ethnic Community: Polonia." In Ernest W. Burgess and Donald J. Bogue (eds.), *Contributions to Urban Sociology*. Chicago: University of Chicago Press, 203-23.

Lundberg, George A.; Mirra Komarovsky; and Mary A. McInerny

1934 *Leisure: A Suburban Study*. New York: Columbia University Press.

Lynd, Robert S. and Helen M. Lynd

1929 *Middletown*. New York: Harcourt.

1937 *Middletown in Transition*. New York: Harcourt.

Maccoby, Herbert

1958 "The Differential Political Activity of Participants in a Voluntary Organization." *American Sociological Review* 23: 524-32.

Mangus, A.R. and H.R. Cottam

1941 *Levels of Living, Social Participation and Adjustment of Ohio Farm People*. Bull. 624, Columbus, Ohio: Ohio Agric. Exper. Stat.

Martin, H.T. and L. Siegel

1953 "Background Factors Related to Effective Group Participation." *Journal of Abnormal and Social Psychology* 48: 599-600.

Martin, Walter T.

1952 "A Consideration of Differences in the Extent and Location of Formal Associational Activities of Rural-Urban Fringe Residents." *American Sociological Review* 17(6): 687-94.

Mather, William G.

1941 "Income and Social Participation." *American Sociological Review* 6: 380-83.

Maves, Paul B.

1960 "Aging, Religion, and the Church." In Clark Tibbitts (ed.), *Handbook of Social Gerontology: Societal Aspects of Aging*. Chicago: University of Chicago Press, 698-749.

Marvick, Dwaine and Charles Nixon

1961 "Recruitment Contrasts in Rival Campaign Groups." In Dwaine Marvick (ed.), *Political Decision-Makers*. Glencoe: Free Press, 193-217.

Mayo, Selz C.

1950 "Age Profiles of Social Participation in Rural Areas of Wake County, S.C." *Rural Sociology* 15: 242-51.

McCann, C.W.

1955 *Long Beach Senior Citizen's Survey*. Long Beach, Calif.: Community Welfare Council.

McCloskey, Herbert and Harold Dahlgren

1959 "Primary Group Influence on Party Loyalty." *American Political Science Review* 53: 757-76.

245

McKain, W.C.
1947   *The Social Participation of Old People in a California Retirement Community*. Unpublished Ph.D. dissertation. Cambridge: Harvard University.
McWilliams, Robert O.
1953   *A Study of the Relationship of Political Behavior to Social Group Membership*. Unpublished Ph.D. dissertation. Ann Arbor, Mich.: University of Michigan.
Milbrath, Lester and Walter Klein
1962   "Personality Correlates of Political Participation." *Acta Sociologica* 6: 53-66.
Moore, Joan W.
1961   "Patterns of Women's Participation in Voluntary Associations." *American Journal of Sociology* 66: 592-98.
Morgan, Christine M.
1937   "Attitudes and Adjustments of Recipients of Old Age Assistance in Upstate New York." *Arch. Psychol.* No. 214, 1-131.
Morris, Raymond N. and John N. Mogey
1965   *The Sociology of Housing*. London: Routledge.
Murphy, Raymond J. and Richard T. Morris
1961   "Occupational Situs, Subjective Class Identification, and Political Affiliation." *American Sociological Review* 26: 383-92.
Myrdal, Gunnar; Richard Sterner; and Arnold Rose
1944   *An American Dilemma*. New York: Harper.
Nie, Norman H.; G. Bingham Powell Jr. and Kenneth Prewitt
1969   "Social Structure and Political Participation." *American Political Science Review* 63: 361-78 and 808-32.
Niebuhr, H. Richard
1929   *The Social Sources of Denominationalism*. New York: Henry Holt & Co.
Nolan, Francerra
1956   "Relationship of 'Status Groupings' to Differences in Participation." *Rural Sociology* 21: 298-302.
Obenhaus, Victor; Widick Schroeder; and Charles England
1958   "Church Participation Related to Social Class and Type of Center." *Rural Sociology* 23(3): 298-308.
Orum, Anthony M.
1966   "A Reappraisal of the Social and Political Participation of Negroes." *American Journal of Sociology* 72(1): 32-46.
Olsen, Marvin
1970   "Social and Political Participation of Blacks." *American Sociological Review* 35: 682-97.
Palisi, Bartolomeo J.
1963   *Ethnicity, Family Structure, and Participation in Voluntary Associations*. Unpublished Ph.D. dissertation. Lincoln: University of Nebraska.

1965   "Ethnic Generation and Social Participation." *Sociological Inquiry* 35: 219-226.

1968   "A Critical Analysis of the Voluntary Association Concept." *Sociology and Social Research* 52 (July): 329-405.

Payne, Raymond

1953a "Some Comparisons of Participation in Rural Mississippi, Kentucky, Ohio, Illinois, and New York." *Rural Sociology* 18 (June): 171-72.

1953b *Organizational Activities of Rural Negroes in Mississippi.* Cir. 192. Mississippi Agricultural Experiment Station.

1954   "An Approach to the Study of Relative Prestige of Formal Organizations." *Social Forces* 32: 244-47.

1955   Relative Interest of Fathers and Mothers in Their Children's Participation in Formal Organizations. Unpublished. Paper presented to the *American Sociological Association*, Washington, D.C.

1960   "Some Theoretical Approaches to the Sociology of Aging." *Social Forces* 38: 359-62.

Pellegrin, Ronald J. and Charles H. Coates

1961   "Absentee-Owned Corporations and Community Power Structure," *American Journal of Sociology* 69: 413-17.

Phillips, Derek L.

1967   "Social Participation and Happiness." *American Journal of Sociology* 72: 479-88.

Pittard, Barbara B. and Raymond Payne

1969a "Commitment to Religion and the Church: A Study Using a National Sample." Unpublished. Paper presented at the Society for the Scientific Study of Religion, Boston.

1969b "Religious Organization in a Heart City Area: a Profile of Churches and Ministers." Unpublished. Paper presented at the Religious Research Association, Indianapolis.

Ploch, E.

1951   *Factors Related to the Persistencies and Changes in the Social Participation of Household Heads, Howard Community, Pennsylvania, 1937 and 1949.* Unpublished Master's thesis. Penn. State College.

Pope, Liston

1948   "Religion and the Class Structure." *Annals of the American Academy of Political and Social Science* 256: 84-91.

Pressey, S.L. and R.G. Kuhlen

1957   *Psychological Development through the Life Span.* New York: Harper and Brothers.

Putney, Snell and Russell Middleton

1961   "Rebellion, Conformity, and Parental Religious Ideologies." *Sociometry* 24: 125-35.

Reid, Ira and E.L. Ehle
1950-51 "Leadership Selection in Urban Locality Areas." *Public Opinion Quarterly*, 14: 262-284.

Reissman, Leonard
1954 "Class, Leisure and Social Participation." *American Sociological Review* 19: 76-84.

Reigrotzky, Erich
1956 *Soziale Verflechtungen in der Bundesrepublik*. Tubigen: C.B. Mohr.

Rokkan, Stein
1959 "Electoral Activity, Party Membership and Organizational Influence: an Initial Analysis of Data from the Norwegian Elections Studies." *Acta Sociologica* 4: 25-37.

Rose, Arnold M.
1954 *Theory and Method in Social Sciences*. Minneapolis: University of Minnesota Press. Ch. 3, "A theory of the function of voluntary associations in contemporary social structure," 50-70.

1960 "The Impact of Aging on Voluntary Associations." In Clark Tibbetts (ed.), *Handbook of Social Gerontology: Societal Aspects of Aging*. Chicago: University of Chicago Press, 666-97.

Rosenberg, Morris
1954-55 "Some Determinants of Political Apathy." *Public Opinion Quarterly* 18: 349-66.

Ross, Jack
1972 "Work and Formal Voluntary Organizations." *Journal of Voluntary Action Research* 1: 42-45.

Rothrock, Kenneth Martin
1968 *A Study of Voluntary Association Membership*. Unpublished Ph.D. dissertation. Lawrence: University of Kansas.

Schaff, Alvin H.
1952 "The Effects of Commuting on Participation in Voluntary Organizations." *American Sociological Review* 17: 215-20.

Schmidt, John F. and Wayne C. Rohrer
1956 "The Relationship of Family Type to Social Participation." *Journal of Marriage and Family Living* 18: 224-30.

Schuyler, Joseph
1959 "Religious Observance Differentials by Age and Sex in Northern Parish." *American Catholic Sociological Review* 20(2): 124-31.

Schwirian, Kent P. and Margaret L. Helfrich
1968 "Economic Role and Community Involvement of Business Executives." *Sociological Quarterly* 9: 64-72.

Scott, John C., Jr.
1957 "Membership and Participation in Voluntary Associations." *American Sociological Review* 22: 315-26.

Seals, Alvin and Jiri Koloja
1962   "A Study of Negro Voluntary Organizations in Lexington, Kentucky."
       Phylon 25 (Spring): 27-32.
Sills, David L.
1957   *The Volunteers: Means and Ends in a National Organization*. Glencoe,
       Ill.: Free Press.
Slater, Carol
1960   "Class Differences in Definition of Role and Membership in Voluntary
       Associations Among Urban Married Women." *American Journal of
       Sociology* 65(6): 616-19.
Smith, David Horton
1964   *Psychological Factors Affecting Formal Voluntary Organization Partici-
       pation in Chile*. Unpublished Ph.D. dissertation. Cambridge, Mass.: Har-
       vard Univ.
1966   "The Importance of Formal Voluntary Organizations for Society."
       Sociology and Social Research 50 (July): 483-94.
1972   *Voluntary Activity in Eight Massachusetts Towns*. Draft. Chestnut Hill,
       Mass.: Institute of Human Sciences, Boston College.
Smith, R.V.
1964   *Areal Variation in Formal Association Membership in a Large Metropoli-
       tan Community*. Unpublished Ph.D. dissertation. Ann Arbor: University
       of Michigan.
Spinrad, William
1960   "Correlates of Trade Union Participation: A Summary of the Litera-
       ture." *American Sociological Review* 25 (Apr.): 237-44.
Spiro, Shimon E.
1968   *Effects of Neighborhood Characteristics on Participation in Voluntary
       Associations*. Unpublished Ph.D. dissertation. Ann Arbor: University of
       Michigan.
Stark, Rodney
1964   "Class, Radicalism and Religious Involvement in Great Britain." *Ameri-
       can Sociological Review* 29 (Oct.): 698-706.
Suttles, Gerald D.
1968   *The Social Order of the Slum*. Chicago: University of Chicago Press, 42,
       107-112.
Svalastoga, Kaarl; E. Hogh; M. Pedersen; and E. Schild
1956   "Different Class Behavior in Denmark." *American Sociological Review*
       21: 435-39.
Sykes, Gresham M.
1954   *Social Mobility and Social Participation*. Unpublished Ph.D. dissertation.
       Evanston: Northwestern University.
Taietz, Philip and Olaf F. Larson
1956   "Social Participation and Old Age." *Rural Sociology* 21: 229-38.

Teele, James E.
1965 "An Appraisal of Research on Social Participation." *Sociological Quarterly* 6: 257-68.
TenHave, T.T.
1962 "A Pilot Study on Work and Leisure in an Area of Amsterdam." *Evolution of the Forms and Needs of Leisure*. Hamburg, Germany: Unesco Inst. for Education. 35-63.
Theodore, Athena
1970 "Catalysts for Change: The Voluntary Participation of College Students." American Sociological Association Seminar Session on Voluntary Action Theory and Research: Steps Toward Synthesis, Washington, D.C.
Thomas, William I. and Florian Znaniecki
1918 "The Polish Peasant in Europe and America." Boston: Gorham Press.
Tumin, Melvin
1961 *Social Class and Social Change in Puerto Rico*. Princeton, N.J.: Princeton Univ. Press.
Uzzell, Odell
1953 "Institutional Membership in Relation to Class Levels." *Sociology and Social Research* 390-95.
Vidich, Arthur J. and Joseph Bensman
1960 *Small Town in Mass Society: Class, Power, and Religion in a Rural Community*. Garden City, New York: Doubleday.
Vorwaller, Daniel J.
1970 "Social Mobility and Membership in Voluntary Associations." *American Journal of Sociology* 75: 481-95.
Warner, W. Lloyd and Paul S. Lunt
1941 *The Social Life of a Modern Community*. New Haven: Yale Univ. Press.
Webber, Irving L.
1954 "The Organized Social Life of the Retired in Two Florida Communities." *American Journal of Sociology* 59: 340-46.
West, James
1945 *Plainville, U.S.A.* New York: Columbia University Press.
Whetton, N.L. and C.C. Devereaux
1936 *Studies of Suburbanization*, I, Windsor, A. Highly Developed Agricultural Area. Storrs, Conn.: Agr. Experiment Station Bulletin No. 212.
Wilensky, Harold L.
1956 "The Labor Vote: A Local Union's Impact on the Political Conduct of Its Members." *Social Forces* 35: 111-20.
1961a "Life Cycle, Work Situation, and Participation in Formal Associations." In R.W. Kleemeier (ed.), *Aging and Leisure*. New York: Oxford University Press, 213-42.
1961b "Orderly Careers and Social Participation: the Impact of Work History on Social Integration in the Middle Mass." *American Sociological Review* 26(4): 521-39.

Wright, Charles R. and Herbert H. Hyman
1958 "Voluntary Association Memberships of American Adults: Evidence from National Sample Surveys." *American Sociological Review* 23 (June): 284-94.

Young, R.C. and O.F. Larson
1965 "The Contribution of Voluntary Organizations to Community Structure." *American Journal of Sociology* 71 (September): 178-86.

Zetterberg, Hans L.
1960-61 "National Pastime: Pursuit of Power." *Industrial International*, Stockholm, 105-07, 156-68.

Zimmer, Basil G.
1955 "Participation of Migrants in Urban Structures." *American Sociological Review* 20(2): 218-24.
1956 "Farm Background and Urban Participation." *American Journal of Sociology* 61: 470-75.

Zimmer, Basil G. and Amos H. Hawley
1959a "Suburbanization and Church Participation." *Social Forces* 37: 348-54.
1959b "The Significance of Memberships in Association." *American Journal of Sociology* 65 (September): 196-201.

12

Attitude Determinants of Individual Participation in Organized Voluntary Action

CHARLES LEE MULFORD and GERALD E. KLONGLAN

Attitudes may be regarded as predispositions to respond, as anticipatory responses to people, organizations, and situations. The task of this chapter is to suggest specifically how attitudes are relevant for an analysis of participation in formal voluntary organizations. Many questions and issues could be considered. While reviewing the literature, the present discussion will focus in detail upon two questions central to an analysis of formal voluntary organizations (FVOs): (1) the correlation between attitudes and affiliation, and (2) between attitudes and participation in FVOs.

Before we turn directly to these questions and issues, one or two clarifications and statements regarding points of departure are in order. First, we will specify how the term "FVO" is presently being used. Booth and Babchuk (1969, p. 179) have defined FVOs as "formal groups embodying continuity, rules governing eligibility, goals, and prescribed rights and obligations of members." Thus, a government agency, a business organization one is required to join, or an informal group is not an FVO. Nor are all FVOs alike. Etzioni (1961) points out that the term includes at least two types: (1) one where continued participation and commitment are conditions for the functioning of the FVO, such as a religious FVO, and (2) a type that can function only so long as these conditions really do *not* exist (e.g., some labor unions, most political parties, and some stockholders' organizations). For the latter type of FVO, apathy may even have a positive function. Jones (1954) also has noted this point and even suggested "a defense of apathy." We shall focus in this chapter only upon those FVOs where continued commitment and participation are deemed desirable.

Our primary concern in this chapter will be concentrated upon the attitudes and behavior of lower participants who are members of FVOs. Etzioni (1961) has stated that the control of lower participants is more problematic than that of higher participants and that the largest differences between organizations are found at the lower ranks. The reader is reminded that we are primarily concerned with lower participants who are "members." Many terms have been used to describe lower participants, including employees, rank-and-file, members, clients, customers, and inmates. These terms reflect different positions on the three-dimensional paradigm Etzioni has developed: (1) degree of involvement in the organization, (2) degree subordinated to organizational powers, and (3) performance obligations. According to Etzioni's paradigm, lower participants who

251

are members are by definition highly committed, medium on subordination, and low on performance obligations.

Why do people become members of FVOs; what is the importance of FVOs? Babchuk and Edwards (1965) have noted that FVOs are often seen as "integrative" forces for the personality and social system in urban society, but state that few social scientists have adequately treated either the role played by or place of FVOs in the community. According to Babchuk and Edwards, instrumental (I) FVOs are organized to maintain or change the status quo, not to bring about immediate personal gratifications. Expressive organizations (E) pursue the objectives of immediate personal gratification. Integration of the personality system is stressed in (E) organizations. Instrumental-expressive (I-E) FVOs are thought to be integrative for both the social system and the personality system. In their study of FVOs in Lincoln, Nebraska, Babchuk and Edwards (1965) found that most are of the (E) type. Expressive (E) type FVOs are not centrally located in the community. Instrumental (I) type FVOs are more likely to be central to the community, while (I-E) FVOs are about equally likely to be central or not central. They reported fewer of the (I-E) type than the (I) and many fewer of the (I) than the (E) type FVOs. Mulford (1967) has stated that (I-E) type of FVOs are more central to the community's sociometric status and communication network.

The evidence suggests quite strongly that most adult Americans possess attitudes at least somewhat positive toward FVOs and their functioning. Babchuk and Booth (1969), in their recent longitudinal study of participation in Nebraska, noted that voluntary membership is a characteristic of most adults and remains stable until they approach age seventy. The structure and functioning of FVOs relates to the rate and change of affiliation (i.e., tenure is greater and turnover less in multi-purpose FVOs). Most adult Americans participate in FVOs, but not in the same types. Babchuk and Thompson (1962) observed that, contrary to popular belief, blacks are more likely to belong to FVOs than whites, especially to churches and other expressive groups. Their interpretation of this is that, because blacks are not allowed to be active in much other organized life, they have chosen this form of participation as an alternative. Orum (1966), too, states that blacks are more likely to participate in order to compensate for social deprivation. Orum found that lower-class blacks participate more than lower-class whites. Blacks in general participate more in church and political FVOs, and are at least equally likely to participate in civic FVOs. Booth, et al. (1968) have noted recently that all lower-class and working-class adults (including both blacks and whites) are more likely to participate in the (E) or the (I-E) type of FVOs, while middle-class adults tend to participate more in the (I) type of FVOs. These results have obvious implications in terms of the design and packaging of FVOs intended to involve the poor and will be discussed in detail in a later section.

Our knowledge of why people participate in FVOs is still quite modest. Beal

(1956) has noted that most variables utilized in participation research have been of a "static" nature, such as age, occupation, family status, and education. The amount of literature on such social background variables is clear from the preceding chapter. Beal referred to these variables as "static" because they could not be readily changed by a social action professional, a member, or a leader. Beal's study of participation in farmers' cooperatives was one of the first to emphasize *both static and dynamic variables*. Beal found that dynamic variables were more predictive of participation. He suggested in 1956 that causative models utilizing many variables should be developed and that analysis should focus upon linkages between these variables in predicting membership and participation in FVOs. As is clear from the data presented in this chapter, Beal's suggestions were unfortunately largely unheard or ignored. One major aim of the present and the subsequent chapter is to expand and reinforce awareness of the need for more dynamic research on FVO participation.

Attitudes as Correlates of Affiliation

Attitudes should be considered as possible crucial variables by their very nature. Sargent and Williamson (1958) have stated that most social psychologists agree that temperament, traits, and attitudes are three discriminable and broad aspects of personality. Sargent and Williamson view temperament in terms of variables such as alertness, energy level, and speed of reactions. Traits they view as more or less enduring tendencies like introversion, sociability, self-sufficiency, neuroticism, and so on. While temperament affects the manner of behavior (the "how"), traits affect both manner and content of behavior. *Attitudes are regarded as predispositions to respond to persons, objects, and situations and are more situationally linked than traits.* Sargent and Williamson indicate, however, that it is difficult to distinguish between general attitudes and traits. A general attitude is an attitude held with regard to a broad class of persons, objects, or situations (e.g., attitudes toward foreigners or people in general, compared with more specific attitudes toward the Irish). Many types of attitudes have been studied by those who would like to know why people affiliate with FVOs. The present chapter will consider the role of attitudes with regard to FVO participation, but will not consider the role of temperament or traits. The latter types of factors are considered in the next chapter.

Attitudes as Anticipatory Membership and Participation

Black (1957, p. 63) notes that being a member "means that the individual accepts the group ... We may speak of ... these feelings and attitudes as one type of participation, signifying by itself a certain type or degree of involvement or participation in the group." In other words, favorable attitudes, in actuality, are a type of anticipatory membership and participation. Black's scale of participation reflects this point, for it includes items measuring several types of participation: (1) attitudes indicating acceptance of the FVO, as a requisite to membership, (2) degree of social interaction within the FVO, and (3) responsibilities assumed as an officer, board member and so on, as determinants of participation.

Hodge and Treiman (1968) also have observed that attitudes must be taken into account. They found that intergenerational transmission of membership and participation practices was as strong as present social role factors in terms of explanation. It can be argued that this "transmission" is accomplished at least to a degree through socialization intended to convey attitudes toward participation. In addition, Booth and Babchuk (1969) have observed that the personal influence of friends and relatives has a great deal to do with people joining the (E) type of FVOs.

Early Research: Attitudes as Effective
Predictors

But specifically, what types of attitudes have been found to be crucial for affiliation? Martin and Siegel (1953), Wilson (1954), and Rosenbaum and Blake (1955) were among the first to relate attitudes with affiliation and participation in FVOs. Each of the three studies involved college students. Martin and Siegel (1953) found that statements by college students that suggested their mothers are active in FVOs were correlated with student participation in college FVOs. Martin and Siegel also pointed out that college students who had a previous history of participation before college were most likely to participate. This seems to indicate that favorable attitudes lead to participation and membership. Rosenbaum and Blake (1955) found that college students who assumed that other students were favorably inclined toward participation were most likely to participate; this indicates reference group attitudes are a positive factor in determining membership and participation. Wilson (1954) found that participation in voluntary discussion groups was related to: (1) attitudes favoring group discussions, (2) identification with the college community, and (3) concern for the community.

Beal's (1956) study dealt with farmers who affiliated with and participated in farmers' cooperatives, as did Harp's (1959) which attempted to build upon Beal's earlier efforts. Beal found that the following variables were *not* related to affiliation and participation: (1) urgency of need at the time of joining, (2) source of first information, (3) number and type of cooperative ventures, and (4) type of cooperative. On the other hand, the following factors *were* significantly related: (1) *understanding* of cooperative principles, (2) *knowledge* of the cooperative, (3) *satisfaction* with the cooperative, (4) *"having a say"* in cooperative affairs, (5) *feeling responsible* to the cooperative, (6) *identification* with the cooperative, (7) feeling the cooperative is "their agent," not just another business, and (8) feeling the cooperative is acceptable in terms of the group's general value system. Beal found that these dynamic variables were better single variable predictors than the static variables, which emphasized socioeconomic status. Attitudes are considered dynamic because they can be changed more easily than socioeconomic and other social background variables. Unfortunately, in this study, Beal did not report multiple correlation or regression data. Path analysis techniques now available for "causal" analysis were not as well known in 1956. It would seem that one worthwhile task would be to attempt to cast the Beal data into a causal model and test this model with currently available techniques.

Harp (1959) also was aware of the need to develop models and to go beyond simple, lower-order analyses. He developed three hypotheses that were then tested and supported with the original Beal data: (1) participation varies directly with satisfaction, (2) satisfaction varies directly with understanding, and (3) participation is directly related to understanding.

Studies completed prior to and since the Beal research in 1956 have attempted to relate a variety of attitudinal items to affiliation and participation for a variety of samples of people in a variety of situations, without much sense of direction and seemingly with little interest in codification and theory building or testing. Downing (1957) and Scott (1953) found that *attitudes indicating the necessity of an FVO* were correlated with participation. Downing also found that older citizens participate in social clubs if the clubs are felt to be needed. Scott, who used a national sample of adults in twelve metropolitan areas in the United States, found that those adults who felt a need to strengthen civil defense were most likely to affiliate, give two or three hours a week of their time, and organize people on their block. Furthermore, "having a say" as Beal (1956) put it, or in other words, *perceptions about one's power to influence the social order*, has continued to interest researchers. Cooper (1961) found that a person's perception of the power of his subgroup, both liberals and conservatives, was positively correlated with the intensity of affiliation with the Democratic or Republican party.

Attitudes Toward the Community

Attitudes toward the community in which FVOs are found have been studied by several researchers. Freeman et al. (1957) looked at several attitudinal statements that focused on the community. Using multiple regression techniques, Freeman and his associates found the following attitudinal statements to be the most important correlates of affiliation and participation: (1) "a future which looks bright," (2) *feeling that "leaders are capable,"* and (3) that "people are not stingy." Deveraux (1960) found that *identification with the community* and community evaluation were related to participation in FVOs and to political participation. Deveraux also noted that those who participate in many FVOs are most likely to state that they do this because it is a *"duty" to the community.* Low participators are more likely to state that they participate in FVOs for sociability and fun. Finally, Deveraux observed that high participators are more likely to be "cosmopolitan"; high participators are *interested in local and national affairs.* Low participators are more likely to be "localite" in their orientations to the world around them, often uninterested in either local or national affairs.

Because some corporations encourage their executives to contribute to their community, researchers have investigated the relationship between the *sense of community obligation* and participation. Schwirian and Helfrich (1968) found significant, but low, correlations between social participation and an executive's level in an economic organization, as well as between social participation and his *perception of his "community role."* Schwirian and Helfrich specifically asked the executives, "As a business executive, do you think there are any special obligations that you owe to the community additional to those of the average citizen or non-business executive?" Affirmative answers were positively correlated to participation in FVOs within the community. Nelson et al. (1969) reported that they had developed a scale to measure the attitude *"commitment to solve community problems."* Items included in the scale dealt with willingness to (1) serve on a committee, (2) give two hours' pay, (3) give spare time one evening a week, (4) sign a petition, and (5) give a half day of spare time on Saturday. The scores produced with this scale were significantly related to social participation in community FVOs.

Middle-class citizens who participate in FVOs tend to do so because of their favorable attitudes toward the community and because of their sense of obligation to their community. Evidence suggests that benefits of many kinds accrue for middle-class people who participate. Sills (1957) found that volunteers who participated in the March of Dimes stated they received: (1) satisfaction from being able to accomplish short-term goals they helped to set, (2) a chance to put into practice organizational skills possessed, and (3) satisfaction from creativity. Sills also noted that participation in FVOs was not a new experience for these volunteers. Providing an additional perspective, Jesser (1967) has found that *community satisfaction* is not significantly related to participation when "social-helping" professionals (teachers, clergy) are studied; the opposite, however, is true for "technical-helping" professionals (lawyers, doctors), who probably are more integrated into the community.

Working Class and Minority Participation

The studies discussed to this point have been predominantly concerned with the middle-class and upper middle class people and their attitudes conducive to affiliation. Attitudes of the working class and minority groups have also been studied. Spinrad (1960) reviewed and discussed the results of thirty-five published studies that focused on participation in trade unions. Spinrad found that those who participate have a lower estimate of their community "as a place to live," positive attitudes toward other workers, high job satisfaction, and relatively high mobility aspirations. Participation in the trade union often results in status not found in the job itself. Hagburg (1966) has found that union members participate to the degree that they feel the union to be a source of primary group (expressive) satisfactions.

Jacoby (1966) states that people who have the "need" for affiliation and interpersonal gratification belong to primary groups and expressive FVOs, *as well as* to instrumental FVOs. People who do not have this need are more likely to join only instrumental FVOs. Orum (1966) states that this may be especially true for blacks who do so to compensate for social deprivation. Babchuk and Thompson (1962) also have noted that blacks are more likely to join expressive FVOs than whites; this is perhaps because of a sense of deprivation. Writing even more recently, Morrison and Hundley (1970) expressed a concern for continued research that would indicate the degree to which relative deprivation and perceived structural blockage determine farmers' willingness to join a social movement in its early stages. Morrison and Hundley hypothesize that early participants are dissatisfied because they have come to want more but feel that structural blockages exist. In general, these studies focus on sources of social or economic deprivation. Other research suggests that deprivation may be of a social-psychological origin.

Anomia, Affiliation, and Participation

Attitudes reflecting feelings of personal anomia, alienation, and isolation have also been investigated by many, with fairly consistent results. Anomia is a social-psychological consequence of normlessness or anomie. The central facet and characteristic of anomia is an uncertainty about relevant and appropriate behavior, which results in general immobilization on the part of the individual. Anomia in this chapter is considered to be an attitude (i.e., the predisposition to refrain from affiliation and participation of all sorts, including FVOs). The authors propose to consider anomia as an attitude, since it is often assumed that changes in one's social situation (including the removal of structural anomie or normlessness) would make for a lessening of perceived anomia. If, however, anomia is viewed as a general, pervasive, and relatively unchanging phenomenon, then it is possible that anomia could be considered a personality trait. There are a number of other dispositions for which the distinction between attitudes and personality traits is hard to draw.

Bell (1957) and Meier and Bell (1959) were among the first to suggest that personal anomia would be negatively related to FVO participation. Nelson (1968) utilized four existing scales to tap the diversity of definitions generally ascribed to alienation: (1) "bewilderment and confusion," (2) "Need inviolacy," (3) Dean's (1961) "powerlessness items," and (4) Srole's (1956) scale measuring various dimensions of anomia. Nelson cumulated the four scales into one general index and used it in his research concerning small businessmen. He found that, in his sample, alienation was negatively related to participation and willingness to enlist in authoritarian FVOs for owners, but not for business managers. Marsh et al. (1967) utilized Srole's anomia scale finding that anomia is significantly negatively related to utilization of the U.S.D.A. Co-operative Extension Service, but not to contact with a second public bureaucracy, namely the Employment Security Commission. To explain this inconsistency, they suggest that the most anomic persons include those who are most often unemployed; this greater "need" of the chronically unemployed may offset their predisposition to avoid contact with the Employment Assistance Agency.

Erbe (1964) gathered data from interviews conducted with adults in three small Iowa communities, relating those data to participation. Erbe used the complete Dean (1961) scale, which includes items to measure "powerlessness" and "social isolation." In his research, Erbe found that alienation is significantly correlated (in a negative direction) with organizational membership in FVOs, but not with political participation when membership level is held constant. FVO membership, however, remains significantly correlated with political participation independently of alienation. The correlation between FVO participation and political participation was noted earlier by Maccoby (1958). Erbe concludes that alienation is caused primarily by socioeconomic factors, although he doesn't present data to support this tentative hypothesis. In a more recent study, Eitzen (1970) found the anomia scores of middle-class women to be significantly correlated (again negatively) with FVO participation, with anomia thus functioning as a barrier to participation. In this study, Eitzen employed the Srole (1956) scale to measure anomia.

In contrast to the several studies mentioned that have focused on psychological isolation, Hagedorn and Labovitz (1968) found in a recent study that, under some circumstances, actual physical isolation may be associated with relatively high degrees of participation in FVOs. They found that professionals who were physically isolated from other professionals in their work environment reported a higher degree of participation in community FVOs. They interpreted this in terms of a theory (among several being tested) that alienation could lead either to reduced *or* heightened participation.

The Relative Importance of General and
Specific Attitudes

In a study of membership and participation in associations in Santiago, Chile, Smith (1966) performed one of the few studies utilizing simultaneously socioeconomic, attitudinal, and personality dimensions. Moreover, Smith employed multiple regression techniques in analyzing his data, rather than simply using tables and zero order correlations. He obtained measures of general and specific FVO-relevant attitudes, while also probing a variety of personality dimensions (see the next chapter of this volume, *passim*) and socioeconomic data. Smith found that general and specific FVO attitudes were the most important discriminators of FVO members from corresponding (matched) non-members. Personality traits produced a multiple correlation of .54, compared with .65 for general attitudes, .77 for specific attitudes, and a non-significant correlation for socioeconomic variables (the latter mainly indicating that the matching operation had been effective). *General FVO-relevant attitudes* that discriminated between members and matched eligible non-members were: (1) *general obligation to participate in FVOs*, (2) *general FVO instrumental value*, (3) *formal group preference*, and (4) *service orientation to leisure time*. Members were also found to be more involved in informal relations and church attendance than non-members. *Specific FVO-relevant attitude scales* that discriminated significantly between members and eligible non-members were: (1) *commitment* to the specific FVO, (2) *perceived efficacy* of the specific FVO to achieve its goals, (3) *felt obligation to participate* in the FVO, (4) *attractiveness* of the FVO, (5) *significant outside personal support* for the FVO, (6) *perceived personal fit* with the FVO, (7) *friendliness with people* in the FVO, and (8) whether the person was *influenced or recommended to join* the specific FVO. Smith also sought data to discriminate between active and inactive members. This data will be discussed in our next major section where we will focus on continued participation in FVOs.

In a related study of eight Massachusetts cities and towns utilizing these attitudinal variables, Smith (1972) found the same general FVO attitude variables to be important. They discriminated between townspeople with many versus few or no FVO memberships, and also discriminated between a criterion group of town leaders with high average FVO activity and random townspeople with relatively low average FVO activity.

Figure 12-1. Attitudes and Participation in FVOs

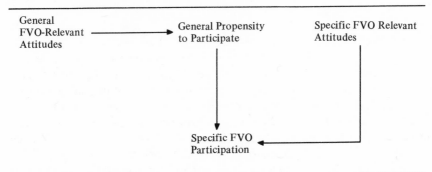

In general, socioeconomic variables utilized in empirical studies have often been shown to be modest predictors compared with some attitudinal variables. This is particularly true when background variables are first controlled in some manner, either by sampling or some statistical means. *While a great deal of research has been focused on the discrimination of FVO members from non-members, relatively little emphasis has been placed on the discrimination of active and presumably contributing members from the less active and unproductive, as will be noted in the next section.*

Attitudes as Correlates of FVO Participation Among Members

Admitting at the outset that the definition and measurement of effectiveness does represent major problems, it is still disappointing to us to observe the lack of attention researchers have given to this FVO dimension. Effectiveness has a number of facets. Effectiveness could mean the degree to which instrumental goals are accomplished. It also could include the degree to which the FVO is able to maintain itself over an extended period of time and secure scarce resources. It could also mean that continued participation and members' commitment are realized. In addition, it can be argued that an FVO is effective if participation in it leads to or encourages participation in others. We would suggest that a multiple measure of effectiveness based upon these and possibly other dimensions be utilized by researchers. Almost no variables, including attitudinal ones, have been systematically related to FVO effectiveness. At best, it seems that researchers have assumed that having and keeping members more or less guarantees at least a minimum degree of effectiveness. A number of interesting hypotheses about internal participation and activity as effectiveness have been developed and will be discussed in this section.

Attitudes Associated with Continued and Active Participation

Price (1968) has stated, but not tested, the hypothesis that organizations will more likely be active and effective if the ideology (attitudes) of the members is congruent with the dominant cultural values. Harp and Cummings (1968) and Davis (1961), who studied the activity and survival of small discussion groups, concluded that homogeneity may make for participation and continuity in expressive (E) type organizations; diversity of attitudes, however, probably makes for continuity in instrumental (I) type groups. Brooks et al. (1969) have stated that when attitudes exist that suggest that the FVO's goals are intangible and that members' roles are ambiguous, goal displacement is likely to occur. Intangible goals and ambiguous roles may lead members to leave the FVO.

Systematic analysis implies either multiple variable analysis of empirical data with such techniques as multiple correlation and regression techniques, or the development of complex and extensive logical models to test. Two studies of continued participation utilizing multiple regression techniques can be cited. Copp and Clark (1956), using static and dynamic variables, were able to account for 42 percent of the variance in their study predicting 4-H Club membership re-enrollment.

In the other study, Smith (1966) was able to account for 56 percent of the variance in discriminating active from inactive members of several FVOs in Chile by utilizing general and specific FVO-relevant attitudes, personality dimensions and socioeconomic factors. *General FVO-relevant attitudes* that significantly discriminated acitve from inactive FVO members were: (1) a *general obligation to participate* in FVOs, (2) a *general perception of the instrumental value* of FVOs, (3) *formal group preference*, and (4) a *service orientation to leisure time.* Smith found that eight *specific FVO-relevant attitudes* discriminated active from inactive members: (1) *perceived rewards for participation*, (2) *perceived social support within the FVO*, (3) *commitment*, (4) *perceived attractiveness*, (5) *felt obligation to participate*, (6) *perceived personal fit with FVO*, (7) *perceived efficacy of the specific FVO*, and (8) *outside significant-other support for participation in FVO.*

Smith proposed a "sequential specificity" approach suggesting first that proximity and social class variables act as "screens" with regard to participation, then general FVO-relevant attitudes, then specific FVO-relevant attitudes, followed finally by personality dimensions. Personality variables do discriminate best between actives and inactives in the Smith study. No longitudinal causal analysis was possible to test this model with his cross-sectional data, however.

Rose (1962) has also been interested in the attitudes of active versus inactive members of FVOs. He found that officers in statewide associations in Minnesota held somewhat different attitudes than a cross-section of the married population of the Twin Cities. Officers were also active in many other organizations. Officers score lower on a *"need inviolateness scale"* (i.e., they do not avoid social contacts). In addition, officers were less anomic and more *tolerant* of minority group members. Finally, the officers of statewide associations sampled were more *positive* toward the American government and more *active* in local politics and elections.

*Internal Communication and Decentralized
Power as Requisites to Activity and   Effectiveness*

A number of researchers have developed hypotheses about members' attitudes toward the internal functioning of FVOs. These researchers feel that *high de-*

grees of internal communication and *decentralized or shared power* will lead to active and effective FVOs. The League of Women Voters has served as the research setting for activity-effectiveness studies, with over one hundred local Leagues being measured by combining the ratings of national officers. Tannenbaum and Kahn (1957) stated that the more active and responsible leader is found in FVOs where he or she is controlled as well as controlling. They hypothesize that a smaller discrepancy between the actual and desired control structure will be correlated with more continued participation, involvement and loyalty in the FVO.

Likert (1961) found these attitudes to be present in active and effective Leagues of Women Voters: (1) pressure to participate comes from self or other members, not from officers, (2) feelings that members have influence, and (3) feelings that boards keep them informed and that officers are interested in them. Tannenbaum (1961) adds that attitudes suggesting *all* levels of personnel have control (members, board, and president) are positively correlated with FVO activity and effectiveness. These data support his hypothesis that leaders are controlled as well as control.

Smith and Brown (1964) have also studied the activity and effectiveness of local Leagues of the League of Women Voters. Their data indicate that decentralized control and total control are both correlated with activity and effectiveness. Decentralized control means members at each level feel they have power, while total control scores for each League were developed by adding the amount of perceived control across all levels. Attitudes that favor multi-directional communication (up and down the hierarchy) were the best predictors of member loyalty. Smith and Brown completed several multivariate analyses that resulted in these statements about attitudes and effectiveness.

More important than the amount of power a leader has is how he utilizes that power in FVOs. Smith and Tannenbaum (1965) have found that League members have favorable attitudes toward leaders who use their power to coordinate activities. Attitudes that suggest the League officers coordinate activities are positively correlated with League attendance and effectiveness. These studies with local Leagues of the League of Women Voters are quite important because efforts were made to measure both internal activity and effectiveness. We suggest that similar comparative research with other FVOs should be performed.

Copp (1964) states that the earlier emphasis on the relation of FVO knowledge and participation may no longer be appropriate to all FVOs. Copp points out, for instance, that many farmer cooperatives are so big and complex that the utility of knowledge about them and the opportunities for rank-and-file to participate have decreased. Copp feels that attitudes (especially loyalty) should be considered crucial to participation. Loyalty is considered to be members' willingness to remain in the FVO. Copp found that loyalty predicted these facets of continued member participation: (1) compulsion to recruit others, (2) influence a member feels he has in the cooperative, (3) acceptance of cooperative doctrine, and (4) satisfaction with cooperative doctrine. Loyalty was a better predictor of continued activity than knowledge or prior participation.

Inducements, Contributions and Continued Participation

As noted in the first section of this chapter, many people are led to affiliate with FVOs because they feel they may personally profit. One of the most promising theoretical developments is concerned with the implications of *inducements/ contributions hypotheses*. Early proponents of these inducements/contributions hypotheses included Barnard (1938), Simon (1957), and March and Simon (1958). Their primary focus, however, was on work organizations (governmental and business organizations) and not on FVOs. Phillips (1969) developed and tested two inducement/contributions hypotheses while studying FVO participation: (1) greater FVO participation will be associated with a greater number of positive feelings, and (2) the greater the extent of happiness (positive feelings minus negative ones), the greater will be the degree of participation and contribution in FVOs. Both hypotheses were supported. Phillips demonstrated that the correlation between the number of positive feelings and participation holds for all social classes. He states, however, that lower-class people may have to "invest" more in each instance of their participation since "they have fewer opportunities." Phillips hypothesizes that the participation and contributions of lower-class members will be correlated to both positive and negative feelings (i.e., to inducements and contributions), though this hypothesis has not yet been tested.

In work using a similar theoretical approach but with a more conscious inducement/contributions theory, Warner and Heffernan (1967) conducted a *benefit-participation contingency (B-PC) study*. They found the correlation between absolute number of benefits and FVO participation is not significant. The *ratio* of benefits to contributions, however, was correlated to participation in the voluntary farmer organizations studied. Warner and Hefferman feel that B-PC will allow them to explore part of an "exchange theory" of organizations and participation. They suggest that other researchers try to develop similar models including: (1) *non-benefit factors* (duties, coercion, commitment, etc.), (2) *costs of participation*, and (3) *alternatives available to members*. They stress that these factors should be analyzed from both the members' and the organizations' point of view.

Further, two points should be made with regard to the emergence of attitudes. First, as observed by Tannenbaum and Backman (1966), those who are most active in FVOs are likely to hold attitudes that are uniform. They argue that *attitude uniformity* is one measure or aspect of "groupness" (cf., Smith, 1967). In their study, officers tended to be most uniform in attitudes, then actives, followed by inactive members. Actives took more extreme positions when responding to attitudinal statements. Also, one may expect the emergent attitudes that develop to be consistent with other attitudes currently held. In addition, actives are likely to be most vocal about these emergent attitudes.

In summary, participation in a specific FVO may lead to emergent attitudes, such as the feeling that one has influence, one is kept informed, and so on. Participation also may lead one to evaluate positively the inducement/contributions ratio for participating in a given FVO. Specific FVO participation, emergent attitudes, and a significant inducement/contributions ratio are thought to lead to continued participation and commitment, which in turn are thought to be associated (other factors being equal) with other facets of organizational activity. Gouldner (1960), however, cautions us not to expect general commitment to all facets of an FVO. She has tested and found support for the hypothesis that commitment to the specific values of an organization is distinct from commitment to the organization as a whole. We suggest here that emergent attitudes may also have an effect on the FVO's structure and function.

A Summary of Types of Attitudes Emphasized

Our review of the literature indicates that a large number of attitudes have been measured by social scientists interested in FVO activity. At this time we will classify the types of attitudes studied and indicate which have been used relatively frequently and with relative success. In a sense, those types that have not been used represent research gaps that should be considered. Smith, et al. (1970) have suggested the paradigm of general and specific attitudes presented in Table 12-1. *General attitudes are thought to apply across a broad range of voluntary action settings and related social situations; and they are distinguished from specific attitudes concerning and centering on a particular FVO.* This classification is derived from one used earlier by Smith (1966). More types of attitudes have been related to affiliation (joining) than to active or continued participation in FVOs. Smith (1966, 1972) has utilized more types of attitudes than any other researcher cited in our review of literature. With the exception of some of the general and specific attitudes toward and involvement with Institutional Areas, Smith utilized nearly every type of attitude listed in Table 12-1 in his study of some FVOs in Chile and later in his study of FVO participation in eight Massachusetts cities and towns.

General FVO-Relevant Attitudes

Many of the suggested types of general FVO-relevant attitudes focusing upon FVO characteristics have largely been ignored by researchers. The general-FVO-

Figure 12-2. Attitudes, FVO Participation, and FVO Effectiveness

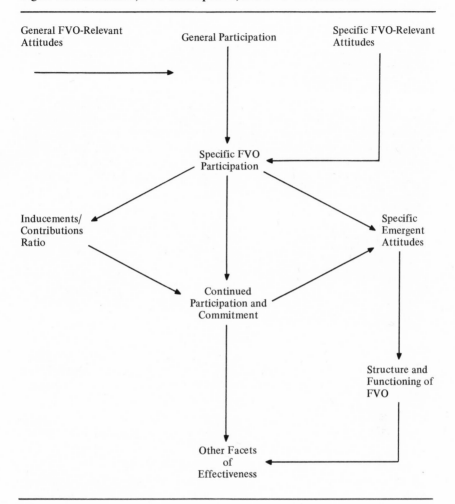

influence attitudes regarding one's "significant others" have seldom been explored in relation to participation. Also, personal experience with FVOs in
general as a focus has largely gone unstudied.

Several researchers, in addition to Smith (1966), have studied attitudes that
focus on a personal sense of relation to FVOs in general, and on an individual's
attitudes toward organized activities. Wilson (1954), Freeman et al. (1957),
Jesser (1967), and Schwirian and Helfrich (1968) report moderate to strong
relationships between FVO activity and attitudes indicative of a personal sense
of relation to FVOs in general, most often utilizing attitudes emphasizing a
general commitment to organized voluntary action or to the community. Wilson

Table 12-1

A Possible Framework for Grouping Attitudes Relevant to the Organized Voluntary Participation of Individuals

General Attitudes:

FVO Characteristics:
  general FVO instrumental value
  general FVO attractiveness, etc.

Others' General FVO Influence:
  perceived significant others influence
  perceived parental attitudes, etc.

Personal Experience with FVOs in General:
  social integration within various FVOs
  personal fit with FVO activities
  experiences with FVOs in general, etc.

Personal Sense of Relation to FVOs in General:
  overall obligation to participate in FVOs
  general commitment to organized voluntary action, etc.

Individual's Attitudes toward Organized Activity:
  formal group preference in general
  service orientation to leisure
  personal autonomy needs in general, etc.

General Attitudes toward and Involvement with Institutional Areas:
  Arts
  Economic
  Educational
  Familial
  Health
  Legal System
  Police
  Political
  Religious
  War and military
  Welfare and helping, etc.

Other General Attitudes:
  aspirations
  general interpersonal satisfaction and integration
  attitudes toward neighboring
  attitudes toward community
  role perception and investment
  anomia and alienation, etc.

Specific Attitudes:

FVO Characteristics:
  efficacy of FVO
  attractiveness of FVO, etc.

Others' Specific FVO Influence:
  significant others support for FVO
  parental support, etc.

Personal Experience with the Specific FVO:
  social integration within FVO
  personal fit with FVO
  experiences relevant to FVO, etc.

Personal Sense of Relation to the Specific FVO:
  specific obligation to participate in FVO
  commitment to organization, etc.

Individual's Attitudes toward Life and Activities of Specific Organization:
  formal group preference and experience re: specific FVO
  service opportunities and orientation re: specific FVO
  scope for personal autonomy in specific FVO, etc.

Specific Attitude toward and Involvement with Organization in Area:
  Arts
  Economic
  Educational
  Familial
  Health
  Legal System
  Police
  Political
  Religious
  War and military
  Welfare and helping, etc.

Other Specific Attitudes:
  Attitudes toward goals or activities involving the specific organization— e.g., liking fires and having interest in volunteer firemen; wanting to change the social order; civil rights; pollution, etc.

(1954), Sills (1957), and Deveraux (1960), in addition to Smith (1966), have found strong relationships between an individual's attitude toward organized activities and his affiliation tendencies.

As noted earlier, many people have been interested in the relationship between personal anomia and affiliation with FVOs. We defined anomia as the predisposition to refrain from affiliation of all sorts. As such, anomia may be considered an attitude that cuts across several general types outlined in Table 12-1. The research indicates a moderate to strong negative relationship between anomia and affiliation.

Specific FVO-Relevant Attitudes

A number of researchers have related specific FVO attitudes to FVO affiliation, with a moderate degree of success. Smith (1966), Beal (1956), Harp (1959), Downing (1957), and Scott (1953) found strong relationships between FVO characteristics (usually, stated need, effectiveness, personal fit, and attractiveness) and affiliation. Smith (1966) also found strong relationships between others' specific FVO influence and affiliation; other researchers have, in the past, largely ignored these kinds of attitudes.

Beal (1956), Smith (1966), Cooper (1961), and Larson and Cottan (1961) have found strong relationships between specific attitudes that focus on personal experiences related to the FVO and affiliation with that FVO.

Beal (1956), Smith (1966), Copp (1964), and Sills (1957) obtained strong relationships between FVO affiliation and specific attitudes which focus upon a personal sense of relation (commitment) to the specific FVO. Smith (1966), Sills (1957), and Deveraux (1960) reported strong relationships between the individual's attitudes toward his activities in a specific FVO and participation in that FVO. The other types of specific attitudes listed in Table 12-1 have largely been ignored or not systematically analyzed and reported.

The major affiliation research gaps (types of attitudes ignored or seldom utilized) include general and specific attitudes reflecting the influence of significant others, although Babchuk and Gordon (1962) and Tannenbaum and Kahn (1957) have touched on these issues with specific organizations. More research should consider further the role of nearly every type of general attitude presented in Table 12-1. With the exception of Smith's work (1966, 1972), these general attitudes have not received much attention.

Specific attitudes have received relatively more attention, especially those related to FVO characteristics and personal experience with the specific FVO. A major need at present is to build logical models in which the relationships between these general and specific attitudes can be studied. Smith (1966) is the only researcher cited who tried to systematically differentiate between active and inactive FVO members in studying the impact of various specific attitudes.

Smith found a strong relationship between eight specific attitudes and continued, active participation: (1) rewards for participation, (2) social support, (3) commitment, (4) attractiveness, (5) obligation to participate, (6) personal fit with FVO, (7) efficacy of specific FVO, and (8) outside significant-other support for FVO. Rose (1962) reported moderate to strong negative relationships between two general attitudes and active continued participation: (1) need inviolateness, i.e., need to avoid social contacts, and (2) anomia.

Warner and Hefferman (1967) reported a strong relationship between one specific attitude and degree of participation. They found that an attitude indicative of personal experience with the specific FVO (ratio of benefits to contributions) was more important for predicting participation than was absolute number of benefits.

Copp (1964) found that one specific attitude indicative of a personal sense of relation to the specific FVO (loyalty) was strongly related to four aspects of activity: (1) compulsion to recruit others, (2) influence a member feels he has in the FVO, (3) acceptance of FVO doctrine, and (4) satisfaction with FVO doctrine.

Summary of Major Findings

We will summarize the specific hypotheses that have been tested and supported by empirical data in this section. Hypotheses that have been suggested but not tested and hypotheses developed in this chapter will be presented in the last section as a guide for further research.

Hypotheses related to affiliation will be listed first, then hypotheses related to participation. The strength and direction will be described with the terminology used in other chapters of Part Two, namely, "negligible," ± .099; "weak," ± .100 to .199; "moderate," ± .200 to .399; "strong," ± .400 to .599; and "very strong," ± .600 or larger zero-order Pearsonian product-moment coefficients of correlation. In addition, terms indicative of the degree of consistency will be used for the hypotheses. These terms will include "inconsistent" for no pattern; "low consistency," slight preponderance of results in given direction; "medium consistency," clear preponderance, but substantial variation; "high consistency," large majority of results in line with main variation; and "very high consistency," little variation from main theme.

Propositions About Affiliation with FVOs

General FVO-relevant attitudes and specific FVO-relevant attitudes often predict FVO affiliation better than some socioeconomic or personality variables. The relationships between these attitudes and affiliation are strong and highly consistent.

Research has indicated that these *general* FVO-relevant attitudes are significantly related to more individual affiliation with organized voluntary groups:

1. General obligation to participate in FVOs. (Strong relationship with high consistency).
2. General perception of instrumental value of FVOs. (Strong relationship with high consistency).
3. Formal group preference; low degrees of need inviolateness. (Strong relationship with high consistency).
4. Anomia. (Strong and negative relationship with high consistency).
5. Service orientation to leisure time. (Strong relationship and high consistency).
6. Favorable attitudes toward participation in FVOs held by significant others. (Weak relationship with low consistency).
7. Friendly relations with people in specific FVO. (Strong relationship with high consistency).

Research has indicated that these *specific* FVO-relevant attitudes are significantly related to more individual affiliation with organized voluntary groups:

1. Commitment to specific FVO. (Strong relationship with high consistency).
2. Efficacy of specific FVO to achieve goals. (Strong relationship with high consistency).
3. Obligation to participate in specific FVO. (Strong relationship with high consistency).
4. Attractiveness of specific FVO. (Strong relationship with high consistency).
5. Outside significant-other support for specific FVO. (Strong relationship with high consistency).
6. Personal fit with specific FVO. (Strong relationship with high consistency).
7. Friendly relations in specific FVO. (Strong relationship with high consistency).
8. Influence by others to join the specific FVO. (Strong relationship with high consistency).

Propositions About Active and Continued
Participation in FVOs

Only a very few hypotheses have been tested with empirical data. The following *general* FVO-relevant attitudes are significantly related to continued individual participation in organized voluntary action:

1. General obligation to participate. (Strong relationship with high consistency).
2. General perception of instrumental value of FVOs. (Strong relationship with high consistency).

3. Formal group preference. (Strong relationship with high consistency).
4. Service orientation to leisure time. (Strong relationship with high consistency).
5. Need inviolateness. (Moderate to strong negative relationship with medium consistency).
6. Anomia. (Moderate to strong negative relationship with medium consistency).

These *specific* FVO-relevant attitudes are significantly related to active and continued individual participation in organized voluntary action:

1. Loyalty to specific FVO. (Strong relationship with high consistency).
2. Ratio of benefits to costs for participation in specific FVO (Medium relationship with medium consistency).
3. Perceived rewards for participation in specific FVO. (Strong relationship with high consistency).
4. Social support within specific FVO. (Strong relationship with high consistency).
5. Commitment to specific FVO. (Strong relationship with high consistency).
6. Obligation to participate in specific FVO. (Strong relationship with high consistency).
7. Personal fit with specific FVO. (Strong relationship with high consistency).
8. Efficacy of specific FVO. (Strong relationship with high consistency).
9. Attractiveness of specific FVO. (Strong relationship with high consistency.
10. Outside significant-other support for specific FVO. (Strong relationship with high consistency).

Conclusions

What about the future in terms of criteria for meaningful research? We already have suggested that additional new data may not be needed in some areas. Original data (static and dynamic), such as developed by Beal (1956) and Smith (1966), could be cast into a "causal" model and these models tested with currently available techniques. This would seem to be one prime research goal. Smith (1972) is currently undertaking this kind of analysis with his more recent data on eight Massachusetts cities and towns.

Perhaps a systems approach could be used that would allow us to incorporate existing data and knowledge with additional required data in a meaningful manner. Inputs could include: (1) socioeconomic variables, (2) attitudes, (3) personality dimensions, and (4) the degree of selectivity used to recruit members.

Etzioni (1961) has noted that FVOs differ in the degree to which "selec-

Table 12-2
Attitudes and FVOs

Inputs	Processes	Outputs
1. Socioeconomic factors	1. Communication	1. Affiliation
2. Attitudes	2. Socialization	2. Continued participation
3. Personality	3. Development of	3. Effectiveness of
4. Selectivity	emergent attitudes	FVO
	4. Development of	
	participation/contributions	

tivity" is used to recruit new members. He hypothesizes that if selectivity is low, additional socialization and communication may be required. Mulford, et al. (1968) have tested and found support for this hypothesis in one complex organization. Not only should this hypothesis be further tested in various FVOs, but also the different impact of high degrees of socialization and/or communication upon members' participation/contributions equations should be determined. Finally, it is essential that researchers concentrate more of their resources on determining how these input and process variables impact upon key output variables, including continued participation and FVO effectiveness.

Dillman, et al. (1970) have noted the importance of membership linkages for understanding community structure and related processes and have recently developed and tested a model of overlapping FVO memberships (membership linkages) with empirical data. Dillman and his associates noted that their overlap analysis revealed a substantial number of FVOs were linked in such a fashion so as to form clusters and these clusters were themselves linked by FVOs to other clusters. Future research which focuses upon interorganizational relations could consider the degree to which members of FVOs hold homogeneous attitudes with regard to themselves, the role of FVOs in their community, and attitudes toward their community.

References

Babchuk, Nicholas, and Alan Booth
1969 "Voluntary Association Membership: A Longitudinal Analysis." *American Sociological Review* 34 (February): 31-45.
Babchuk, Nicholas and John N. Edwards
1965 "Voluntary Associations and the Integration Hypothesis." *Sociological Inquiry* 35 (Spring): 149-62.
Babchuk, Nicholas and C. Wayne Gordon
1962 *The Voluntary Association in the Slum*. University of Nebraska Studies. New Series No. 27. Published by the University at Lincoln.

Babchuk, Nicholas and Ralph V. Thompson
1962 "The Voluntary Associations of Negroes." *American Sociological Review* 27 (October): 647-54.

Barnard, Chester I.
1938 *The Functions of the Executive*. Cambridge, Mass.: Harvard Univ. Press.

Beal, George M.
1956 "Additional Hypotheses in Participation Research." *Rural Sociology* 21 (September - December): 249-56.

Bell, Wendell
1957 "Anomie, Social Isolation, and the Class Structure." *Sociometry* 20 (June): 105-116.

Black, Therel R.
1957 "Formal Social Participation: Method and Theory." *Rural Sociology* 22 (March): 61-65.

Blau, Peter M. and W. Richard Scott
1962 *Formal Organizations*. San Francisco: Chandler Publishing Company, 77-86.

Booth, Alan and Nicholas Babchuk
1969 "Personal Influence Networks and Voluntary Association Affiliations." *Sociological Inquiry* 39 (Spring): 179-88.

Booth, Alan; Nicholas Babchuk; and Alan B. Knox
1968 "Social Stratification and Membership in Instrumental—Expressive Voluntary Associations." *Sociological Quarterly* 9 (Autumn): 427-39.

Brooks, Ralph M.; E. Walter Coward, Jr.; and George M. Beal
1969 "Some Effects of Intangible Goals on Extension Resource Development." Paper read at Rural Sociology Meetings, San Francisco.

Cooper, Homer Chassell
1961 "Perception of Subgroup Power and Intensity of Affiliation with a Large Organization." *American Sociological Review* 26 (April): 272-74.

Copp, James H.
1964 "Perceptual Influences on Loyalty in a Farmer Cooperative." *Rural Sociology* 29 (June): 168-80.

Copp, James H. and Robert C. Clark
1956 "Factors Associated with Re-enrollment in 4-H Clubs." *Wisconsin Agricultural Experiment Station Bulletin*, Madison, Wisconsin.

Davis, James A.
1961 *Great Books and Small Groups*. New York: The Free Press.

Dean, Dwight
1961 "Alienation: Its Meaning and Measurement." *American Sociological Review* 26 (October): 753-58.

Deveraux, Edward C., Jr.
1960 "Community Participation and Leadership." *Journal of Social Issues* 16: 29-45.

Dillman, Don A.; Gerald E. Klonglan; Paul Yarbrough; and Paul F. Schmitz
1970 "Voluntary Associations and Community Structure." Paper read at Rural Sociology Meetings, Washington, D.C.

Downing, Joseph
1957 "Factors Affecting the Selective Use of a Social Club for the Aged." *Journal of Gerontology* 12 (January): 81-84.

Eisenstadt, S.N.
1961 "Bureaucracy, Bureaucratization, and Debureaucratization." In Amitai Etzioni (ed.), *Complex Organizations*. New York: Holt, Rinehart and Winston, 276.

Eitzen, D. Stanley
1970 "A Study of Voluntary Association Memberships Among Middle-class Women." *Rural Sociology* 35 (March): 84-91.

Erbe, William
1964 "Social Involvement and Political Activity: A Replication and Elaboration." *American Sociological Review* 29 (April): 198-215.

Etzioni, Amitai
1961 *Complex Organizations*. Glencoe: Illinois: The Free Press of Glencoe, Illinois.

Freeman, Howard E.; Edwin Novak; and Leo G. Reeder
1957 "Correlates of Membership in Voluntary Associations." *American Sociological Review* 22 (October): 528-33.

Goffman, Erving
1956 *The Presentation of Self in Everyday Life*. Edinburgh: University of Edinburgh Press, 141-66.

Gouldner, Helen P.
1960 "Dimensions of Organizational Commitment." *Administrative Science Quarterly* 4 (March): 468-87.

Hagburg, Eugene
1966 "Correlates of Organizational Participation: An Examination of Factors Affecting Union Membership." *Pacific Sociological Review* 9 (Spring): 15-21.

Hagedorn, Robert and Sanford Labovitz
1968 "Participation in Community Associations by Occupations: A Test of Three Theories." *American Sociological Review* 33 (April): 272-83.

Harp, John
1959 "A General Theory of Social Participation." *Rural Sociology* 24 (September): 280-84.

Harp, John and Gordon J. Cummings
1968 "Discussion Groups and Public Affairs Education: and Analysis of Group Survival." Bulletin 70. Ithaca, New York: Department of Rural Sociology, Cornell University.

Hodge, Robert W. and David J. Treiman
1968 "Social Participation and Social Status." *American Sociological Review* 33 (October): 722-40.

Jacoby, Arthur P.
1966 "Personal Influence and Primary Relationships: Their Effect on Associational Membership." *Sociological Quarterly* 7 (Winter): 76-84.

Jesser, Clinton
1967 "Community Satisfaction Patterns of Professionals in Rural Areas." *Rural Sociology* 32 (March): 56-69.

Jones, W.H.M.
1954 "In Defense of Apathy." *Political Studies* 2: 25-37.

Larson, Richard F. and William R. Catton
1961 "When does Agreement with Organizational Values Predict Behavior?" *American Catholic Social Review* 22: 151-160.

Lefton, Mark and William R. Rosengren
1966 "Organizations and Clients: Lateral and Longitudinal Dimensions." *American Sociological Review* 31 (December): 802-10.

Likert, Rensis
1961 *New Patterns of Management*. New York: McGraw-Hill Book Company, Inc., 140-61.

Maccoby, Herbert
1958 "Political Activity in a Voluntary Organization." *American Sociological Review* 23 (October): 524-32.

March, James G. and Herbert A. Simon
1958 *Organizations*. New York: John Wiley and Sons, Inc.

Marsh, C. Paul; Robert J. Dolan; and William L. Reddick
1967 "Anomia and Communication Behavior: the Relationship Between Anomia and Utilization of Three Public Bureaucracies." *Rural Sociology* 32 (December): 435-45.

Martin, H.T. and L. Siegel
1953 "Background Factors Related to Effective Group Participation." *Journal of Abnormal and Social Psychology* 48: 599-600.

McClosky, Herbert and John Schaar
1965 "Psychological Dimensions of Anomy." *American Sociological Review* 30 (February): 14-40.

Meier, Dorothy L. and Wendell Bell
1959 "Anomia and Differential Access to Life Goals." *American Sociological Review* 24 (April): 189-202.

Morrison, Denton E. and James R. Hundley
1970 "Needed Research on Farmers' Movements." In Denton E. Morrison (ed.), Farmers Organizations and Movements. *Agricultural Experiment Station, Research Bulletin* 24, Michigan.

275

Mulford, Charles L.
1967 "Considerations of the Instrumental and Expressive Roles of Community Differentials and Formal Organizations." *Sociology and Social Research* 51 (January): 141-47.
Mulford, Charles L.; Gerald E. Klonglan; George M. Beal; and Joe M. Bohlen
1968 "Selectivity, Socialization, and Role Performance." *Sociology and Social Research* 53 (October): 68-77.
Nelson, Joel I.
1968 "Participation and Integration: the Case of the Small Businessman." *American Sociological Review* 33 (June): 427-38.
Nelson, Merwyn, Verl R.W. Franz; and D.G. Marshall
1969 "The Franz-Marshall Scale of Commitment for Community Action." *Rural Sociology* 34 (September): 396-401.
Orum, Anthony M.
1966 "A Reappraisal of the Social and Political Participation of Negroes." *American Journal of Sociology* 72 (July): 32-46.
Parsons, Talcott
1961 "Suggestions for a Sociological Approach to the Theory of Organizations." In Amitai Etzioni (ed.), *Complex Organizations*. New York: Holt, Rinehart and Winston, 39-40.
Phillips, Derek L.
1969 "Social Class, Social Participation, and Happiness: A Consideration of Interaction–Opportunities' and 'Investment'." *Sociological Quarterly* 19 (Winter): 3-21.
Price, James L.
1968 *Organizational Effectiveness*. Homewood, Illinois: Richard D. Irwin, Inc., 104.
Rose, Arnold M.
1962 "Alienation and Participation: A Comparison of Group Leaders and the 'Mass'." *American Sociological Review* 27 (December): 834-841.
Rosenbaum, Milton and Robert R. Blake
1955 "Volunteering as a Function of Field Structure." *Journal of Abnormal and Social Psychology* 50 (March): 193-196.
Sargent, S. Stanfeld and Robert C. Williamson
1958 *Social Psychology*, 2nd ed. New York: The Ronald Press Company, 52-56.
Schwirian, Kent P. and Margaret L. Helfrich
1968 "Economic Role and Community Involvement of Business Executives." *Sociological Quarterly* 9 (Winter): 64-72.
Scott, William Abbott
1953 "Attitudes toward Participation in Civil Defense." *Public Opinion Quarterly* 17 (Fall): 374-85.
Sills, D.L.
1957 *The Volunteers*. Glencoe, Illinois: The Free Press.

Simon, Herbert A.
1957 *Administrative Behavior*. 2nd ed. New York: The Macmillan Company.
Simpson, Richard L. and William H. Gulley
1962 "Goals, Environmental Pressures and Organizational Characteristics." *American Sociological Review* 27 (June): 344-50.
Smith, Clagett G. and Arnold S. Tannenbaum
1965 "Some Implications of Leadership and Control for Effectiveness in a Voluntary Association." *Human Relations* 18 (August): 265-72.
Smith, Clagett G. and Michael E. Brown
1964 "Communication Structure and Control Structure in a Voluntary Association." *Sociometry* 27 (December): 449-68.
Smith, David Horton
1966 "A Psychological Model of Individual Participation in Formal Voluntary Organizations: Application to Some Chilean Data." *American Journal of Sociology* 72 (November): 267-72.
1967 "A Parsimonious Definition of 'Group': Toward Conceptual Clarity and Scientific Utility." *Sociological Inquiry* 37: 141-67.
1972 *Voluntary Activity in Eight Massachusetts Towns*. (forthcoming).
Smith, David H.; Richard Reddy; and Burt Baldwin
1970 Personal communication from the editors of the current volume. November.
Spinrad, William
1960 "Correlates of Trade Union Participation." *American Sociological Review* 25 (April): 237-44.
Srole, Leo
1956 "Social Integration and Certain Corrollaries." *American Sociological Review* 21 (December): 709-16.
Tannenbaum, Arnold S.
1961 "Control and Effectiveness and Voluntary Association." *American Journal of Sociology* 67 (January): 33-46.
Tannenbaum, Arnold S. and Jerald G. Backman
1966 "Attitude Uniformity and Role in Voluntary Organizations. *Human Relations* 19 (August): 309-22.
Tannenbaum, Arnold S. and Robert L. Kahn
1957 "Organizational Control Structures." *Journal of Human Relations* 10: 127-40.
Warner, W. Keith and William D. Heffernan
1967 "Benefit-participation Contingency in Voluntary Farm Organizations." *Rural Sociology* 32 (June): 139-53.
Wilson, Everett K.
1954 "Determinants of Participation in Policy Formation in a College Community." *Human Relations* 7: 287-312.

13

Personality and Capacity Determinants of Individual Participation in Organized Voluntary Action

RICHARD D. REDDY AND DAVID HORTON SMITH

This chapter attempts to review the social science literature known to the authors that deals with the relationships between individual participation in organized voluntary activity and the class of determinants known as personality traits and capacities. Following our review, brief suggestions are offered regarding areas of future study and regarding appropriate methods and approaches.

Before turning to these tasks, however, we must first take up some preliminary conceptual matters. First, we must distinguish personality traits and personal capacities from other human phenomena. Second, we shall indicate how we have classified those realms of traits and capacities which have been our focus for this review. Finally, we shall comment on our typology of voluntary action, describing briefly the framework for our systematic review of the influence of these personality traits and personal characteristics on dimensions and aspects of voluntary action.

Personality Traits and Personal Capacities: Their Definition

Following Inkeles (1965), we shall distinguish between personal systems and social systems. The term "social system" refers to the specific socio-cultural context of and structure for interaction or, in Inkeles' words, (1965, p. 250) "relatively enduring systems of action shared by groups of people, large or small." The "personal system," on the other hand, emphasizes the individual actor. Thus, according to Inkeles, the personal system is "the system of action which characterizes a particular biological organism, notably a human being." The personal system, then, includes personality, capacities, attitudes, beliefs, social role characteristics, etc. Knowledge of both these action systems is, of course, essential for a well-developed and integrated understanding and interpretation of human interaction.

Since the essential focus of our discussion will be on two aspects of the personal system, personality and capacities, we shall now turn to defining them and distinguishing them from other aspects of the personal system. Personality can be understood and analyzed in terms of traits or dimensions, that is, in terms of relatively enduring, transituational dispositions which are relevant and salient in a large variety of situations. Seen in this fashion, *personality traits form a continuum with attitudes. The latter, though perhaps quite relevant and salient in their own realm, are more bound to a specific situation and are potentially less enduring.* Thus we may speak of a person's current attitude toward, and relationship with, a particular individual as being quite relevant and salient while dealing with him, or, perhaps, with those in some association with him. But this attitude or relationship would have to be generalized (be relevant and salient in and across a large number of individuals, contexts, and situations) before we would attempt, on this basis, to term the person either extraverted or introverted. A personality trait, such as extraversion, may be said to be a general disposition, lending flavor, character, or tonality to a number of significant aspects of a person's normal interaction across various situations. Finally, it is important to note that a specific attitude, or the behavior by which it is known or expressed, may or may not be directly or meaningfully related to any given personality trait.

As distinct from personality and the other aspects of the personal system, *capacities are probabilities of response and behavior of a certain kind, given the disposition to respond.* Thus, capacities, which include both physical skills and mental abilities, define the bounds within which personality may be expressed. One's disposition to act is limited and mediated by one's capacities to do so. An analogy drawn to the operation of a computer may be useful here: while a program (a capacity) defines and delimits the probabilities and patterns of response of the machine, an "execute" statement (the personality trait), an expressed command, is required to initiate these patterns of response. Evidence, including the work of Duncan (1969) on nonverbal communication and differences in such capacities, suggests that it is well to keep capacities theoretically and empirically distinct from personality traits per se. Indeed, in specific instances, without at least a minimal knowledge of an individual's capacities, it may be impossible to come to an adequate understanding of his personal expression and interaction.

"Beliefs" are most appropriately associated with attitudes and may be distinguished from attitudes by their greater cognitive component and lesser dispositional or active component. "Social role characteristics" may be seen as an interface between personality and social systems by limiting or defining the direction and extent to which personality may be expressed in various settings. Finally, physiological characteristics may be seen as operating in some instances as specific types of personal capacity—as a limit of what actions or how an action may or may not be performed.

Classification of "Personality Traits" and Personal Capacities

We made a brief review of the literature on the nature and measurement of personality traits and capacities, including works such as Eysenck (1955, 1960),

Guilford and Zimmerman (1956), Osgood, et al. (1957), Karson and Pool (1958), Hare (1960), Pawlik and Cattell (1964), Cattell (1965), Hundleby, et al. (1965), Guilford (1967), Duncan (1969), and Gibb (1969), as well as the summary and review sections on personality traits and capacities in the *Annual Review of Psychology* over the past decade. As the result of this review, nine commonly found realms or clusters of related kinds of personality traits and six capacities were chosen as being studied and discussed most often. We make no claim to their being exhaustive, but do believe them to be reasonably comprehensive.

The personality realms and dimensions thus derived and used in our analysis are:

1. Extraversion, sociability, friendliness, affiliation motivation, social confidence, socially desirable response tendencies, etc., *versus* introversion, interpersonal cynicism, distrust, etc.

2. Ego-strength, adjustment, satisfaction, self-confidence, optimism, positive self-image, impulse control, etc. *versus* anxiety-neuroticism, pessimism, emotionality, etc.

3. Assertiveness, aggressiveness, dominance, personal autonomy, etc., *versus* submissiveness, shyness, dependence, conformity, acquiescence, etc.

4. Achievement motivation, efficacy, competence, creativity, dependability, perseverance, etc., *versus* fatalism, alienation, powerlessness, apathy, etc.

5. Flexibility, adaptability, readiness to change, etc., *versus* rigidity, authoritarianism, need for consistency, compulsiveness, etc.

6. Empathy and relational closeness *versus* lack of empathy and interpersonal exclusion.

7. Morality and superego strength *versus* lack of interpersonal and group orientation and concern.

8. High energy levels, activity, and activation rates *versus* low energy levels, and activity and activation rates.

9. Planning and future time perspective *versus* lack of emphasis on planning and present orientation.

Capacities, for our purposes, are classified as:

1. Verbal abilities and general intelligence.
2. Spatial abilities.
3. Numerical abilities.
4. Mechanical-motor skills.
5. Social skills.
6. Other capacities: field dependence, psychic differentiation, awareness levels, defense mechanisms, tolerance of ambiguity, dissonance, or complexity, etc.

**Types of Individual Voluntary
Action**

Chapter 10 of this volume has served as our basis for defining, classifying, and analyzing the nature, settings, and contexts of voluntary action. Although some of the key concepts expressed there will be briefly summarized here, for a theoretical explication and placement of these concepts the reader is urged to consult that chapter.

The realm of voluntary action includes all human behavior that one is not forced to do, that one does not do purely as a job to earn one's living, and/or that one does not do because of physiological needs. Defined more positively, voluntary action is human behavior that is essentially motivated by the desire for psychic benefit of one kind of another—behavior we engage in not because we *have to*, but essentially because we *want to* in view of the psychic pleasures it will give us and/or in view of our commitment to some larger goals.

Simplifying somewhat the paradigm presented in chapter 10 (table 10-1) we distinguish here four major specific analytical types and one major general type of voluntary action for individuals. The four specific types (types 'A' through 'D') are derived by cross-classifying the level of economic benefits the individual receives from voluntary activity and the level of formalization of the setting in which that activity takes place. These types and some examples of activity associated with each type may be found in Table 13-1. The fifth and general type (type 'E') provides a means of analyzing the determinants of voluntary action across types. This latter type seems appropriate on the basis of an emerging literature on the "General Activity Syndrome"—a tendency for some persons to participate actively in a number of types of formal and informal settings of different types.

Although a substantial literature exists relating personality traits to aspects of informal, temporary, non-remunerated individual voluntary action (type 'A') and some literature relates personality traits to volunteering for special tasks, for experiments, etc. (type 'C'), our concern in this chapter will be for those studies that have investigated the relationship between either personality traits or personal capacities (or both) and individual participation in organized voluntary action (types 'B' and 'D') as well as in the overarching "general activity syndrome" (type 'E').

*Non-Remunerated Voluntary
Action in a Formal Permanent
Setting*

This category of voluntary action, while including the volunteer activity associated with formal volunteer associations (FVOs) such as membership and par-

Table 13-1

Types of Individual Voluntary Action

Level of Economic Benefits Received	Level of Formalization of the Setting	
	Informal, Temporary	Formal, Organized, Permanent
Unremunerated or Nearly Unremunerated (Lower Level of Economic Benefits)	A. Miscellaneous leisure, altruistic, charitable, service, and self expressive activity (sports, donations, voting, TV viewing, rioting, etc.)	B. Volunteer roles in regular Formal Volunteer Organizations or in non-volunteer organizations utilizing volunteer activity in some of their programs (fraternity membership. volunteer teacher's aide, etc.)
Partly or Fully Remunerated (Higher Level of Economic Benefits)	C. Volunteering for special tasks (surveys, experiments, arduous missions, etc.)	D. Voluntary occupational or quasi-occupational roles (work within Visiting Nurses Associations, with Nader's Raiders, in VISTA, in the Peace Corps, on Citizen Participation Boards, etc.)

E. The combination of all of the above within a single individual (the "general activity syndrome")

ticipation in fraternities, doing volunteer work for the Red Cross, etc., also encompasses volunteer roles associated with prisons, hospitals, schools, etc.

Because there is a more extensive literature known to the authors in this field and because a number of special issues have been treated in the literature, this review will focus on five aspects of volunteer participation in this realm: (1) The number of volunteer organizations an individual has membership in, (2) Leadership activities in various volunteer organizations, (3) Joining a volunteer organization (when and if either formally or informally eligible), (4) General internal participation (including frequency of attendance at various functions and other such global measures), and (5) Specific internal activity (performing various leadership tasks or assignments, etc.)

Since combined measures of membership and participation such as the Chapin scale tend to have the greatest amount of variance contributed by the number of memberships an individual has, studies using such measures as their dependent variable are listed and commented upon under the "number of organizational memberships" topic.

1. Number of Volunteer Memberships. Regarding our first trait, extroversion-sociability, Gough (1952), in a study of four high school senior classes in Minnesota, investigated the personality correlates of extensive memberships (the number of extracurricular activities in which the individual participated). Among the personality items (most of which were drawn from the MMPI) which proved to be related to extensive participation was a liking for social interaction. Further, Martin and Siegal (1953), with a group of 104 male undergraduate fraternity members at the State College of Washington, using a group participation scale to determine the correlates of effective group participation, found that "gregariousness"—a past history of group participation—was positively correlated with such effective participation. Finally, Smith (1972), in an investigation of volunteer activity in eight Massachusetts towns (N=302), found social confidence and sociability items to be significantly correlated with the number of memberships in volunteer organizations the individual has.

Concerning ego-strength—anxiety-neuroticism, Gough (1952) found a positive correlation between activity and self-confidence for high school seniors. Brown (1953), using a Chapin scale, in a study of three rural Pennsylvania communities (N=624), found membership and participation related to the individual's positive self-image. Mizruchi (1960), as part of an adult education survey in upstate New York (N=618), also using a Chapin scale to measure formal participation, found a marked and significant inverse association between formal social participation and anomie. Hausknecht (1962), using national sample survey data from the NORC (N=2317), found a positive relationship between optimism concerning the future—one measure of self-confidence—and the number of volunteer organization memberships the respondent had.

Bradburn and Caplovitz (1965), studying reports on happiness (yet another dimension of self-confidence and ego strength), found that the factor most significantly associated with high positive feelings of happiness is a high degree of social interaction and participation in the environment. Moreover, they found that while social interaction and participation items were quite often related only to positive feelings and not to negative feelings or even directly related to reported happiness, voluntary organization membership was an exception for it was related, in opposite directions, to both positive and negative feelings, and directly to reported happiness. In addition, Smith (1972) found a positive relationship between the number of volunteer organization memberships a person has and general ego-strength measures: optimism rather than pessimism, and a lack of psychosomatic symptoms indicative of stress or nervousness.

Concerning our third trait domain, dominance-aggressiveness-independence, Martin and Siegal (1953), in their study of fraternity members, found reported independence associated with group memberships. In the same vein, Smith (1972) found a positive relationship between items indicating dominance (having other people do things in the way the individual prefers, trying to strongly influence others' actions, etc.) and the number of organizations to which the individual belongs.

Gough (1952), in his study of correlates of participation in a number of high school extra-curricular activities, found a positive relationship between this measure of participation and a sense of poise and assurance, items associated with our fourth trait domain—achievement motivation—efficacy. Almond and Verba (1963), in their cross-cultural investigation of "the civic culture," found that a subjective sense of political competence was positively associated with an increasing number of memberships in volunteer organizations. Also, Smith (1972), in his study of volunteer activity in eight Massachusetts towns, found a positive relationship between achievement orientation and efficacy measures and the number of organization memberships an individual has.

In addition Smith (1972) found a positive relationship between measures of empathy and of relational closeness, our sixth domain, and the number of organizations to which the individual belongs. Gough (1952) likewise found a positive relationship between relational closeness, terming the phenomena "group centrality," and the extent of extra-curricular participation among the high school seniors he was studying. Finally, Gough also found positive relationships with "an indulgent and broad-minded social outlook" (our seventh trait domain—morality and superego strength) and with higher drive and energy levels, as well as a zest for life (our eighth trait—energy or activation levels).

Gough also found a positive relationship between extensive participation and two capacities we have identified: general alertness (general awareness levels) and poise, assurance, and social skills. Smith (1972) found a positive relationship between a high score on an "opposites test" measure of verbal capacities (general intelligence) and the number of organizational memberships a person has.

2. Leadership in Various Volunteer Activities. Jessie Bernard, et al. (1950) compared scores on the Bernreuter Personality Inventory and three indices of participation in college activities, one of which was general leadership activity, among 239 senior men and 172 senior women. Though results were not significant for the women in the sample, for the men general leadership activity was found to be associated positively with dominance (our third trait domain) and with self-sufficiency, a component of our ego-strength domain. However, in addition, Bernard, et al. found a negative relationship between "stability" (a component of our second trait domain), as measured by the Bernreuter, and general leadership activity.

3. Joining Volunteer Organizations. Jackson and Winkler (1964), with a random sampling of 184 freshmen entering the University of North Dakota, attempted to compare systematically the characteristics of those who pledge in fraternities or sororities and those who do not. Pledging for males was positively and significantly related to liking to work with and meet new people. Wood (1965) used Rorschach tests in a study of Pentacostal Holiness religious practice. He compared twenty-five Pentacostal members and twenty-four non-Pentacostals from the same communities. Wood found among the Pentacostals a strong expressed drive and need to feel close fellowship with others, our trait domain including extraversion-sociability. Smith (1966), when comparing members and matched non-members of volunteer organizations in Chile (N=171), found social confidence, another component of extraversion-sociability, to be significantly and positively related to membership. Also, Marx (1967) found social involvement positively related to being involved in a militant organization in the black community.

Wood (1965) found that participation in a Pentacostal Holiness sect is associated with a certain amount of anxiety (ego-strength vs. anxiety-neuroticism). Members indicated that they were able to respond to others, but that they were afraid they were incapable of establishing stable relations with others. On the other hand, Johnstone and Rivera (1965), in a massive study of volunteer participation in adult education programs, found that optimism about the future and a general readiness to accept change (two components of ego-strength) were associated with favorable dispositions toward learning and participation in adult education programs. Smith (1966), in his Chilean study, found that although components of ego-strength vs. anxiety-neuroticism (such as cynicism, optimism, satisfaction, and self-confidence) were associated with membership in volunteer organizations, their relationship was not statistically significant when other factors were controlled. Marx (1967) found a positive relationship between a favorable self-image and membership in militant groups in the black community.

Regarding aggressiveness-dominance, Jackson and Winkler (1964) found male pledges more dominant than non-pledges. Smith (1966) found a need for autonomy (a component of aggressiveness-dominance) to be negatively related to joining volunteer organizations.

As regards our fourth trait domain, achievement motivation-efficacy, Bell (1957), in an area probability sample of four San Francisco census tracts (N=701), established a positive relationship between anomia (powerlessness) and lack of memberships. Non-members of organizations had higher anomia (perceived lack of efficacy) scores than members. Levine and Sussman (1960) indicate that, in their sample, those joining fraternities were likely to do so because of a desire to be upwardly mobile (achievement orientation). Likewise, Jackson and Winkler (1964) found male pledges having a greater increase in personal power or renown. Neal and Seeman (1964), in a sample of 609 male residents of Columbus, Ohio, found that for both manual and non-manual workers, non-members of occupationally-oriented groups experienced the greater feeling of powerlessness (lack of efficacy) and this was especially true of the mobility-minded worker. Wood (1965) noted among his Pentacostal Holiness sect members a strong determination to defeat evil and become better or to consolidate gains already achieved (dimensions not only of efficacy but also of perseverance).

Seeman (1966), in a random sample of males aged 20-79 in Malmo, Sweden (N=558), found a high degree of powerlessness among unorganized workers. Smith (1966), in his work in Chile, found that achievement orientation and non-fatalism were related positively, but not significantly, to membership when other factors were controlled. Bohrnstedt (1969) replicated, with a sample of almost 2,000, the findings of Levine and Sussman as well as those of Johnson and Winkler with his report of a positive relationship between social mobility aspirations and fraternity membership. Sinha (1969), in a study of the motivation of Indian farmers who were involved in development programs (N=300) and those who were not (N=290), found that those involved in the development programs showed greater clarity in expressing their needs and were more realistic—both of which traits can be seen as being related to achievement orientation and efficacy.

Wilson (1954), while studying the determinants of participation in policy formation discussions in a college setting (N=c.100), found that participation was positively correlated with a democratic orientation, a trait very often juxtaposed to an authoritarian, rigid posture.

Concerning empathy and relational closeness, Jackson and Winkler (1964) found that both male and female pledges had less need to be empathic. Smith (1966), however, found a significant positive relationship between trust (a component of empathy and relational closeness) and membership in voluntary organizations. He also found a significant positive relationship between a moral orientation (morality and superego strength) and membership as well as a positive but not significant relationship between planning (planning and future time perspective) and membership. Wilson (1954) likewise found that participation was positively associated with a social service interest (a measure of morality and superego strength) as measured by the Kuder test. Wood (1965) similarly and not surprisingly found a strong moral orientation expressed among his members in a Pentacostal Holiness sect. Finally, Sinha (1969) noted, along with Smith, a positive relationship between planning and participation in a development program.

4. General Internal Participation. Smith (1966) in his study of Chilean volunteer organizations found that various measures of extraversion were positively correlated with active participation among volunteer organization members.

Bernard, et al. (1950), in their study of personality correlates of participation in college activities, found a small relationship between self-sufficiency (a component of ego-strength) and the hours per week spent in college activities. Smith (1966) found a significant relationship between optimism and active participation, and a non-significant relationship between the latter measure and self-confidence-satisfaction. Phillips (1967), in his study of 600 New Hampshire residents, found that active organizational participation was correlated (gamma=.27) with high positive feelings and happiness (trait 2, ego strength—extraversion-introversion).

Bernard, et al. (1950) likewise found a positive relationship between dominance and hours per week spent in college activities. Smith (1966) found a positive relationship between a lack of need for personal autonomy and active participation.

As regards efficacy and achievement motivation, Bell (1957), in his study of individuals in four San Francisco census tracts, found that among those of higher socioeconomic status inactive members of organizations had higher mean anomie scores. However, due in some measure to higher mean anomie scores among lower status people, there were no differences in that group between active and inactive participants. Almond and Verba (1963), in their five-nation study of "the civic culture," found a positive relationship between subjective political competence and the extent of one's voluntary participation. Smith (1966) found a positive significant relationship between achievement orientation/non-fatalism and active participation in volunteer organizations.

Wilson (1954), in his study of participation in college policy discussion sessions, found that those who actively participated in the discussions showed a positive community identification (morality and superego strength). Smith (1966) also found a significant relationship between moral orientation (and like measures) and active participation in volunteer organizations.

5. Specific Internal Activity–Leadership. Harned (1961), in a random sample of 41 ward committeemen in New Haven, Connecticut, investigated the relationship between authoritarian attitudes and party activity. She found no evidence that either high or low authoritarians are more likely to work for political parties. However, authoritarian committeemen were more likely to emphasize the importance of party organization per se, though they tended not to show interest in the issues.

Rose (1962) compared 71 leaders of Minnesota organizations with 195 individuals chosen in a random sample of the Twin Cities. Leaders tended to be more sociable (sociability-extraversion), they were more likely to take satisfaction from power and to feel free to take independent action (aggressiveness, dominance), and were more confident, having a greater sense of effectiveness (achievement motivation-efficacy).

Bordeau, et al. (1963) compared leaders and non-leaders from 96 members of the 4-H club in Florida. Leaders were found to have a better self-concept (ego-strength), to have more initiative (aggressiveness-dominance), and to be more dependable (a component of achievement motivation-efficacy).

Since a fairly extensive literature exists on leadership traits, including reviews by Hare (1960) and Gibb (1969), it is surprising that more work relating these traits to leadership in general in volunteer activity and to leadership within specific organizations has not been done. This would seem to be a promising area indeed.

Remunerated Voluntary Action in a
Formal-Permanent Setting

According to the typology of volunteer activity we have been following, the fourth specific type of activity is "formalized, remunerated." This mode of activity, then, is under the direction and sponsorship of some agency or organization or is formally and "routinely" established in some fashion. Though individuals at work in these settings are, in some measure, remunerated, that is, their essential subsistence and activity needs are met either by salary, in kind, or a combination of both, the primary motivation for joining and/or participating in this work of the organization is not the remuneration per se. Examples of this type of volunteer activity could (but in specific instances might not) include joining and working in the Peace Corps, VISTA, some church-related volunteer service organizations, some civil rights, peace action, and ecology groups, etc. Individuals may also be placed in this category when and if their role performance in a setting is such that it is either specifically or exceptionally "above and beyond the call of duty"—the more narrow prescribed role requirements. For example, lawyers are not commonly expected to so dedicate themselves to unpopular or largely unfought causes as have men such as William Kunstler or Ralph Nader. Also labor leaders need not perform their roles as has Cesar Chavez, etc.

It is difficult at present to do scholarly justice to this type of volunteer activity—and this, perhaps, is especially so when focusing on the personality traits and capacities of the individuals involved. For these traits and capacities are more often either ignored or assumed than they are scientifically analyzed and studied. Further, and correlatively, this type of activity may be only gradually becoming a focus of attention.

Perhaps the largest, though certainly not an extensive, literature on this type of volunteer activity deals with the United States Peace Corps. The results documented here on the Peace Corps may very well *not* be representative of possible findings for other groups or for individuals who might be placed in this category. The findings may not even hold for Peace Corps-like programs under the sponsorship of UNESCO, as well as those of countries such as Great Britain, France, West Germany, Canada, Denmark, Norway, Sweden, the Netherlands, and some of the "Communist bloc" countries. This, however, remains for either comparative and/or comparable studies to indicate and establish.

Turning to the evidence primarily on the Peace Corps itself, a number of contexts where personality characteristics have come to the fore should be distinguished: as general selection criteria for the acceptance or rejection of candidates, as specific selection criteria for admission to a particular program, as stated or implied motivations and self-evaluations of candidates derived from questionnaires, personality testing, and interviews, and lastly, as studies of the effects certain traits might have had on rated or evaluated performance criteria.

Hoopes (1961) lists some of the general requirements established as selection criteria. These included two components of our category of "verbal abilities and general intelligence": "above average intelligence" and "ability to communicate." Candidates were also screened for a number of personality traits including "emotional stability"—"adequate normal personality integration plus a margin of personal strength" (ego strength versus anxiety-neuroticism); "ability to establish effective relations with fellow workers, "friendliness," and "interpersonal warmth," (interpersonal relations: extraversion, sociability, social confidence, etc.); "adaptability" (rigidity-authoritarianism vs. flexibility-adaptability); "gentleness," "patience," "sensitivity," "respect for and acceptance of others" (empathy and relational closeness); and, finally, "dedication to service of people" and "a sense of mission in the context of good judgment" (morality and superego strength). A review of the work of the British organization, Overseas Voluntary Service, by Wainright (1965), makes special reference to two personality traits as general selection critera: a "wish to help" and "do good" (morality and superego strength) tempered and specified by a "show of initiative" (achievement motivation, perseverance, efficacy).

Morris Stein (1966) has commented on differences between those selected and those not selected from a pool of approved candidates (N=c.80) for participation in a rural community development program in Columbia, South America. He found that those accepted for this program were significantly different from those rejected on only two measures: "anxiety" (the Taylor manifest anxiety scale) and "psychological well-being" (the Barron ego-strength scale of the Minnesota Multiphasic Personality Inventory). Both of these measures would be tapping our second trait domain (anxiety-neuroticism vs. ego-strength). However, Stein notes that, in absolute terms (as measured against criterion groups), those rejected could be considered low on anxiety and high on psychological well-being. There was no significant difference between those accepted and those rejected along an "authoritarian-democratic" dimension (rigidity and authoritarianism). Further, the pool of eligibles for this program were categorized into five types according to their general orientations: socially-oriented, intellectually-oriented, action-oriented, resourcefully-oriented, and unconventionally-oriented. No "statistically significant" differences between these types were found according to the numbers from each accepted or rejected for this particular program. However, all (N=10) of those classified as "action-oriented" (our trait domain dealing with energy and activation level) were accepted for the program, whereas between 21 percent and 35 percent of those from other categories were rejected.

Stein also reviews the "self-description" questionnaires of those accepted for this rural community development program. These individuals described themselves as "affiliative," "trusting others," "liking to be with friends," etc. (extraversion, sociability, trust); as "trying to overcome weakness and repress fears," as "not afraid of sexual feelings," as "not avoiding pain, physical injury, or illness," as "not avoiding situations in which they would be likely to encounter harm, or find embarrassing or humiliating," and as "not avoiding action for fear of failure" (ego-strength/self-confidence vs. anxiety-neuroticism); as "ambitious," "aspiring," and "trying to accomplish difficult things" (achievement motivation); "as *neither* aggressive or passive" (aggressiveness-dominance vs. acquiescence-dependence); and, finally, as "enjoying cooperation with others," being "nurturant or sympathetic persons who avoided hurting others" (empathy and relational closeness), and enjoyed aiding helpless people" (morality and superego strength). Colmen (1966) reviews findings on expressed reasons why people wished to join the Peace Corps, especially those found by Gordon and Sizer (1963). Central among these were "general moral and ethical considerations" and a sense of "duty to one's fellow man or to the country," and a "desire to work in a cause" (morality and superego strength). Also of importance was a desire to "do something," "to help," "to use skills and knowledge," and "to develop as an individual" (achievement motivation-efficacy).

M. Brewster Smith (1965, 1966) studied the relationship between personality traits and rated effectiveness criteria among Peace Corps teachers in Ghana. In his study published in 1965, Smith tested fifty-eight volunteers while in training in the United States on two measures of authoritarianism (a derived F scale from the SSRC S-A schedule and Levinson's F scale). For those forty-four volunteers who completed two years of teaching in Ghana, these scores on authoritarianism were correlated with overall evaluative ratings and with peer nominations. Authoritarianism, as measured according to either scale, was found unrelated to either of these two criteria. In his subsequent article (1966) based on the same data, Smith factor analyzed both performance and personality traits. He termed the resulting first principal component factors respectively "competent teaching in Africa" and "self-confident maturity," the latter drawing high loadings on measures related to self-confidence, dependability, responsibility, openness to experience, tolerance, intellectual formulation of situations, and problems, etc.—items primarily related to ego-strength versus anxiety-neuroticism. A varimax rotation of the personality variables was performed and six factors were described. The scores on the performance principal component factor were then correlated with scores on the six personality factors derived from the varimax rotation. The highest correlations between this principal component performance factor ("competent teaching in Africa") were with the first varimax factor (communality equals 27%) "interpersonally sensitive maturity" (r=.80) and the fourth varimax factor (communality equals 11%) "dependent anxiety" (r=-.76). Sizable correlations were also found for his second factor (communality equals 13%), "intellectualizing future orientation" (r=.48) and for his fifth factor (communality equals 11%) "controlling responsibility" (r=.46). Thus, in sum, for this sample, effective participation might be seen as being positively related especially to our ego-strength versus anxiety-neuroticism domain, but also to achievement motivation-efficacy and planning and time perspective.

The authors consider these findings on formalized, remunerative voluntary activity to be far more suggestive than conclusive. In particular, sampling of Peace Corps volunteers in special programs may not be representative of volunteers for the Corps in general. Also, changes in programs, policies, volunteer types, and motivations could be expected over time. Further, it is not clear why some people with similar traits/capacities join and others do not—why only some eligibles choose to volunteer. More especially, however, serious questions may be raised as to how representative the Peace Corps is of this general type of voluntary action. Hopefully future research in this area will serve to clarify many of these issues and questions. Research in this area may be all the more valuable and fruitful if some of the reported trends in motivation, especially among our youth are, in part, correct. For reports of some involved in placement activities indicate that many young people find *this* type of occupational activity appealing and, according to their standards, inherently more worthwhile than the more traditional types of job opportunities usually open to them.

The General Activity Syndrome

The final type of voluntary participation to be discussed is the general activity syndrome. Some researchers have focused less on the type or context of activity, placing more emphasis on the amount of interpersonal activity, both formally organized in volunteer organizations and in informal settings. The activities usually studied within this type are ordinarily non-remunerated, including both our informal and formalized types, but at times researchers have included more informal permanent relations in their studies: visiting friends and relatives, etc.

Mussen and Wyszinski (1952) studied 156 undergraduates at the University of Wisconsin. One hundred and forty-eight were volunteers from introductory psychology classes, eight were campus political leaders. The sample was divided into five groupings: those with active political interests, those with moderate but potentially active political interests, those with moderate political interests, those with little interest, and finally, those with no political interests. Placement in these categories was based not only on membership and participation in political groups and activities, voting when and where eligible, etc., but also on the basis of levels of political knowledge and general interest. The politically apathetic individual was found to be generally passive. This political passivity was found to be associated with basic insecurity and a sense of threat (the ego-strength versus anxiety-neuroticism domain), with submissiveness and conformity (dominance versus acquiescence), and with rigidity (authoritarianism-rigidity). In addition, the politically active individual was found to possess a stronger sense of social consciousness and social orientation (morality and super-ego strength).

Christiansen and Black (1954), in a study of 317 rural high school students in Utah, investigated the relationship between personality adjustment and participation in a broad range of activities: in the family, in social groups, in school, and in church activities. Overall, they found a positive relationship between general participation and confidence, self-acceptance, and overall personal adjustment (ego-strength versus anxiety-neuroticism). However, they noted that *some* of the most frequent participators had average to low personal adjustment scores.

Herbert Maccoby (1958) investigated the relationship between different kinds of participation patterns in a community self-help organization and participation in other, especially political, organizations and their related activites. He found that a "positive and non-fatalistic sentiment" toward one's social environment (achievement motivation-efficacy) was positively associated with extensive memberships and participation.

Arnold Rose (1959), with data on 110 recent migrants to the Minneapolis area, investigated the relationship between personality traits and differing combinations of amounts of formal and informal participation. Rose found positive relationships between general high participation rates (including formal and informal relations both together and taken separately) and a social confidence, sociability measure ("people like you when they first meet you") as well as ego-strength and adjustment measures such as "general satisfaction with your life" and "feel life is meaningful."

Bronfenbrenner (1960), using a random sample of 547 in a small community, employed a community participation scale which included typing according to influence, leadership, working on behalf of organizations, attendance in different settings, etc. He found activity as measured by this scale to be positively correlated with trust and expressiveness (extraversion, sociability, trust), and negatively correlated with conformity and rigidity. In addition, Bronfenbrenner found intelligence (mental ability) positively associated with participation. Further, he discovered a curvilinear relationship betweeen presence of psychosomatic symptoms (anxiety-neuroticism) and participation—both leaders and non-participants tended to be higher on psychosomatic symptoms than were the majority of participants.

While studying factors associated with authoritarian orientations, Harned (1961), in her study of forty-one ward committee chairmen in New Haven, found that although there was no difference between authoritarian and equalitarian committeemen with respect to the number of types of volunteer organizations other than political parties to which they belonged, there was a definite tendency on the part of chairmen with lower authoritarianism ratings to consider themselves active participants in more associations—72 percent of the equalitarians, but only 26 percent of the authoritarians reported participating actively in two or more non-political organizations.

Erbe (1964), with a general population sample (N=631) of three small midwestern towns, found that political participation was highly associated with membership and participation in both sociable and issue-oriented organizations, social participation being found to be essentially cumulative in nature. Alienation (here involving components of both sociability and efficacy) was found to be an important predictor of political participation (negative relationship). Erbe, though not presenting any data from his study in this regard, called for further research on personality characteristics of high participators, expressing the hypothesis that especially extraversion might be significant.

Phillips (1967), in a study of 600 adult residents of New Hampshire, found that self-reports of happiness (our second trait—ego-strength vs. anxiety-neuroticism) was positively and significantly related to an index of social participation which included contact with friends, number of neighbors known, and active organizational participation.

In connection with a study of individual charitable donations, Thiessen (1968) has found that self-reported religiosity (a component of morality and superego strength) as well as participation in church activities show the strongest correlations with religious contributions. Also, for those of low or middle income, rates of secular activity, including political activity and participation in volunteer organizations, is associated with higher rates of giving in religious organizations. Nevertheless, religiosity is unrelated to secular contributions in low- and middle-income groups and negatively related among high-income individuals.

Bradburn (1969), in his study on the *Structure of Psychological Well-Being* (N=2,787), found that general activity in organizations was positively correlated with positive affect (a positive sense of well-being) and negatively correlated with negative affect (a sense of ill-being).

Smith (1970), in a paper on personality and the general activity syndrome based on a study of volunteer participation in eight Massachusetts towns and relying on multiple regression analysis of twenty-four small personality scales against a sixteen item comprehensive general activity scale (dealing with interpersonal, organizational, and media activity), reported that, controlling for other traits, general activity is positively and significantly predicted by social confidence (trait 1), social dominance (trait 3), efficacy in public affairs (trait 4), and social inclusion (trait 5). Further, it was found that mental abilities as measured by an opposites test (capacity 1—verbal abilities) were a significant and positive predictor of general activity.

In view of this research, and in view of the relationships found between various types of participation and personality traits and capacities, it would seem that more research probing these relationships would be in order.

Summary

Although a substantial amount of valuable work has been done that relates personality traits and capacities to various types of voluntary action, many important questions remain to be explored and investigated. In this section, we will highlight those personality traits that have been more consistently and actively studied in relation to organized voluntary action, and will briefly summarize the findings. We will then note those traits and capacities that to date have received little or no research attention, even though they would seem to merit systematic consideration.

For those traits which have been consistently and actively studied we will note both the *strength* of the relationships commonly found and the *consistency* of the findings in those studies that have investigated the relationship between the variable and voluntary action. In noting strength of relationships, the range of the zero-order Pearsonian correlation coefficients will be stated. Correlations of ±.099 will be termed "negligible"; of ±.100 to .199, "weak"; ±.200 to .399 "moderate"; ±400 to .599, "strong"; and ±.600 or larger, "very strong." In describing the consistency of the findings, the term "inconsistent" will be used when there is no pattern; "low consistency," when there is a slight preponderance of results in a given direction; "medium consistency," when there is a clear preponderance, but substantial variation; "high consistency," when the large majority of results are in line with the main variation; and "very high consistency," when there is little variation from the main theme.

1. Traits in the realm that includes extraversion, sociability, friendliness, affiliation motivation, social confidence, socially desirable response tendencies, etc. (versus introversion, interpersonal cynicism, distrust, etc.) are found to have weak to moderate positive correlations with various modes of voluntary action. These findings are very high in consistency.
2. Traits in the realm that includes ego-strength, adjustment, satisfaction, self-confidence, optimism, impulse control, etc. (*versus* anxiety-neuroticism, pessimism, emotionality, etc.) are found to have weak to moderate positive correlations with various modes of voluntary action. The findings are very high in consistency.
3. Traits in the realm that includes assertiveness, aggressiveness, dominance, personal autonomy, etc. (*versus* submissiveness, dependence, conformity, acquiescence, etc.) are found to have moderate to strong positive correlations with various modes of voluntary action. These findings are very high in consistency.
4. Traits in the realm that includes achievement motivation, competence, creativity, dependability, perseverance, etc. (*versus* fatalism, alienation, powerlessness, apathy, etc.) are found to have moderate to strong positive correlations with various modes of voluntary action. These findings are very high in consistency.

Turning now to those traits and capacities which, being to date less studied or not genuinely investigated at all, do not currently afford a fully adequate basis for generalization, the following tentative statements can be made:

1. Traits in the realm that includes flexibility, adaptability, and readiness to change (*versus* rigidity, authoritarianism, need for consistency, compulsiveness, etc.) have not been studied sufficiently to establish a range in strength of correlation, and the findings to date have been inconsistent.
2. Traits in the realm that includes empathy and relational closeness (*versus* lack

of empathy and interpersonal exclusion) are found with high to very high consistency to be positively related to voluntary action, but there are insufficient studies to specify the range in correlation. However, correlations have *not* been in the strong to very strong range.

3. Traits in the realm that includes morality and superego strength (*versus* lack of interpersonal and group orientation and concern) have been consistent, when (infrequently) tested, and generally have ranged from weak to moderate in strength of positive correlation with individual participation in organized voluntary action.

4. Those traits that center around energy levels and that center around planning have been found positively related to individual voluntary action, but research does not currently provide a basis for adequate generalization either in terms of strength of relationship or in terms of consistency.

5. Capacities of all kinds remain virtually ignored in the literature on individual participation in organized voluntary action. There have been no systematic attempts to investigate the possibility of correlations between the full range of verbal, spatial, and numerical abilities, mechanical-motor and social skills, or other capacities to aspects of voluntary action. Where studied, verbal/social skills seem to be positively associated with individual voluntary action, however, with high consistency.

Two special comments seem to be in order regarding strategies for future research: First, much of our "hard" data has been the result of survey research approaches in various settings. However, certain traits and perhaps, especially, capacities may be quite difficult to measure with precision in a reasonably brief questionnaire or interview. Other systematic approaches, including participant-observation, situational testing (including laboratory and clinical testing), content analysis, and various types of unobtrusive measures (e.g., records) may be able in some instances to provide us both valuable insights into processes involving voluntary action as well as, hopefully, convergent validation of prior findings.

Secondly, and with a different thrust, many of the studies discussed have relied on relatively weak statistics and overly simple statistical techniques, typically on the bi-variate tabular or correlational level, and only rarely have used approaches to data analysis such as factor analysis, multiple regression analysis, and path analysis. Ultimately, it will be desirable to know the relative predictive contributions of personality traits and capacities, as well as of background factors, attitude factors, and contextual/social structural factors in order to develop a viable, coherent model of and for individual participation in organized voluntary action which would hold for important types and contexts of that action. A related problem is the almost total lack of longitudinal data and longitudinal research designs, so that we are far from establishing causal lines.

In conclusion, then, personality traits and capacities have frequently had low interest priorities for sociologists and other social scientists whose focus has often been mainly on the voluntary group or voluntary action, and only secondarily on attitudes. On the other hand, psychologists have tended to show greater interest in personality and attitudes, but only a secondary interest in relating these to participation in voluntary groups. A review of some of the literature relating personality traits and personal capacities to types of voluntary action indicates that personality and capacity dimensions hold great promise for fruitful and significant research. Hopefully that promise will be fulfilled by more intensive future research in these areas.

References

Almond, Gabriel and Sidney Verba
1963 *The Civic Culture*. Princeton: Princeton University Press.
Bell, Wendell
1957 "Anomie, Social Isolation, and the Class Structure." *Sociometry*, 20:105-16.
Bernard, Jessie; Carol Ann Hecht; Sylvia Schwartz; Sylvia Levy; and William Schiel
1950 "The Relationship between Scores on the Bernreuter Personality Inventory and Three Indexes of Participation in a College Community." *Rural Sociology*, 15:271-73.
Bohrnstedt, George W.
1969 "Social Mobility, Aspirations, and Fraternity Membership." *Sociological Quarterly*, 10:42-52.
Bordeau, Edwina; Ruth Dales; and Ruth Connor
1963 "Relationship of Self Concept to 4-H Club Leadership." *Rural Sociology*, 28:413-18.
Bradburn, Norman
1969 *The Structure of Psychological Well-Being*. Chicago: Aldine.
Bradburn, Norman and David Caplovitz
1965 *Reports on Happiness*. Chicago: Aldine.
Bronfenbrenner, Urie
1960 "Personality and Participation: The Case of the Vanishing Variables." *Journal of Social Issues*, 16:54-63.
Brown, Emory J.
1953 "The Self as Related to Formal Participation in Three Pennsylvania Rural Communities," *Rural Sociology*, 18:313-320.
Cattell, Raymond B.
1965 *The Scientific Analysis of Personality*. Baltimore: Penguin Books.
Christiansen, John R. and Therel R. Black
1954 "Group Participation and Personality Adjustment." *Rural Sociology*, 19:183-85.

Colmen, Joseph
1966 "A Discovery of Commitment." *Annals of the American Academy of Political and Social Science*, 365:12-20.
Duncan, Starkey, Jr.
1969 "Nonverbal Communication." *Psychological Bulletin,* 72:118-37.
Eysenck, H.J.
1955 *The Psychology of Politics.* New York: Frederick Praeger.
1960 *The Structure of Human Personality.* Second Edition, London: Methuen and Co.
Erbe, William
1964 "Social Involvement and Political Activity." *American Sociological Review*, 29:198-215.
Gibb, Cecil A.
1969 "Leadership." In Gardner Lindzey and Elliot Aronson (eds.), *The Handbook of Social Psychology*, Second Edition, vol. 4. Reading, Massachusetts: Addison-Wesley, esp. 218-28.
Gordon, Suzanne and Nancy Sizer
1963 "Why People Join the Peace Corps." Washington, D.C.: Institute for International Services.
Gough, H.G.
1952 "Predicting Social Participation." *Journal of Social Psychology*, 35:227-33.
Guilford, J.P.
1967 *The Nature of Human Intelligence.* New York: McGraw-Hill.
Guilford, J.P. and W.S. Zimmerman
1956 "Fourteen Dimensions of Temperament." *Psychological Monographs*, 70, No. 10, (Whole No. 417).
Hare, A. Paul
1960 *Handbook of Small Group Research.* New York: Free Press, esp. 169-75, 292-93.
Harned, Louise
1961 "Authoritarian Attitudes and Party Activity." *Public Opinion Quarterly*, 25:393-99.
Hausknecht, Murray
1962 *The Joiners: A Sociological Description of Voluntary Association Membership in the United States.* New York: Bedminster Press.
Hoopes, Roy
1961 *The Complete Peace Corps Guide.* New York: Dial Books.
Hundleby, John D.; Kurt Pawlik; and Raymond B. Cattell
1965 *Personality Factors in Objective Test Devices: A Critical Integration of a Quarter of a Century's Research.* San Diego: Robert R. Knapp.
Inkeles, Alex
1965 "Personality and Social Structure." In Robert K. Merton; Leonard

Broom; and Leonard S. Cottrell, Jr. (eds.), *Sociology Today: Problems and Prospects*, vol. II, New York: Harper and Row, 249-76.

Jackson, Ronald and Ronald C. Winkler
1964 "Comparison of Pledges and Independents." *Personnel and Guidance Journal*, 43:379-82.

Johnstone, John W.C. and Ramon J. Rivera
1965 *Volunteers for Learning: A Study of the Educational Pursuits of American Adults*. Chicago: Aldine.

Karson, S. and K.B. Pool
1958 "Second-order Factors in Personality Measurement." *Journal of Consulting Psychology*, 22:299-303.

Levine, Gene N. and Seila A. Sussman
1960 "Social Class and Sociability in Fraternity Pledging." *American Journal of Sociology*, 65:391-99.

Maccoby, Herbert
1958 "The Differential Political Activity of Participants in a Voluntary Organization." *American Sociological Review*, 23:524-32.

Martin, H.T. and L. Siegel
1953 "Background Factors Related to Effective Group Participation." *Journal of Abnormal and Social Psychology*, 48:599-600.

Marx, Gary
1967 *Protest and Prejudice: A Study of Belief in the Black Community*. New York: Harper and Row.

Mizruchi, E.H.
1960 "Social Structure and Anomia in a Small City." *American Sociological Review*, 25:645-54.

Moss, W.T.
1969 "Substitutability of Recreation Activities in Meeting Stated Needs and Drives of the Visitor, and Implications for Planning Recreation Sites." Paper presented at the convention of the Rural Sociological Society, San Francisco.

Mussen, Paul and Anne Wyszinski
1952 "Personality and Political Participation." *Human Relations*, 5:65-82.

Neal, Arthur G. and Melvin Seeman
1964 "Organization and Powerlessness: A Test of the Mediation Hypothesis." *American Sociological Review*, 29:216-26.

Osgood, Charles E.; George J. Suci; and Percy H. Tannenbaum
1957 *The Measurement of Meaning*. Urbana, Ill.: University of Illinois Press.

Pawlik, K. and R.B. Cattell
1964 "Third-order Factors in Objective Personality Tests." *British Journal of Psychology*, 55:1-18.

Phillips, Derek L.
1967 "Social Participation and Happiness." *American Journal of Sociology*, 72:479-88.

Rose, Arnold

1959 "Attitudinal Correlates of Social Participation." *Social Forces*, 37:202-06.

1962 "Alienation and Participation: A Comparison of Group Leaders and the 'Mass'." *American Sociological Review* 27:834-38.

Seeman, Melvin

1966 "Alienation, Membership, and Political Knowledge: A Comparative Study." *Public Opinion Quarterly*, 30:353-67.

Sinha, Durganand

1969 "Study of Motivation in a Developing Country: Concept of Happy Life Among Indian Farmers." *Journal of Social Psychology*, 57:89-97.

Smith, David Horton

1966 "A Psychological Model of Individual Participation in Formal Voluntary Organizations: Application to Some Chilean Data." *American Journal of Sociology*, 72:249-66.

1970 "Personality and the General Activity Syndrome." Unpublished paper, Institute of Human Sciences, Boston College.

1972 *Voluntary Activity in Eight Massachusetts Towns*, unpublished manuscript (forthcoming).

Smith, M. Brewster

1965 "An Analysis of Two Measures of 'Authoritarianism' among Peace Corps Teachers." *Journal of Psychology*, 33:513-35.

1966 "Explorations in Competence: A Study of Peace Corps Teachers in Ghana." *American Psychologist*, 21:555-66.

Stein, Morris I.

1966 *Volunteers for Peace: The First Group of Peace Corps Volunteers in a Rural Community Development Program in Colombia, South America.* New York: John Wiley and Sons.

Wainright, David

1965 *The Volunteers: The Story of Overseas Voluntary Service.* London: Macdonald.

Wilson, Everett K.

1954 "Determinants of Participation in Policy Formation in a College Community." *Human Relations*, 7:287-312.

Wood, William W.

1965 *Culture and Personality Aspects of the Pentacostal Holiness Religion.* The Hague: Mouton.

14 Contextual and Organizational Determinants of Individual Participation in Organized Voluntary Action

DAVID HORTON SMITH AND RICHARD D. REDDY

While other chapters in this section focus on differing "internal" or personal correlates of individual membership and participation in voluntary associations, our focus here is on a number of influences on, and correlates of, individual membership and participation which are essentially "external" to the individual. Specifically, we are considering various contextual, social structural, and organizational correlates of individual membership and participation in voluntary associations. Contextual and organizational variables form a matrix within which the social background, personality, and attitudinal characteristics of individuals originate, develop, and change. Indeed, more "internal" individual characteristics have their essential meaning and interpretation in light of and with respect to the complex set of social expectations, norms, structures, cultural patterns, human population and bio-physical environment comprising the category of contextual characteristics.

The contextual (or, broadly, the environmental) dimension of determinants of individual voluntary participation is seen as comprising four major classes of explanatory variables: (1) the bio-physical environmental variables, (2) cultural and sub-cultural variables, (3) social structural variables (including institutional, organizational, group, and role factors), and (4) human population variables.

1. The *bio-physical environmental variables* of a social system or an individual can be defined as all non-human biological or physical aspects of the world surrounding the given social system or individual. As such, bio-physical variables include such factors as the climate, topography, richness of the soil, presence or absence of mineral deposits and other natural resources, levels of pollution, nature and quantity of flora and fauna, including domesticated animals, etc. Also included are all man-made objects, buildings, constructions and conditions, from the Panama Canal to the smog over Los Angeles or other large cities.

2. Following Smith and Fisher (1971), *cultural variables* are viewed as including all of the socially transmitted and created content and patterns of values, ideas, and other meaningful symbolic system elements that are associated with membership in a given society, ethnic group, or very widespread social roles within such systems. This definition of culture isolates as "culture" certain abstract but pervasive and powerful ideas and values that are not generally

associated with particular specialized roles, organizations, groups or settings in a society. Norms, attitudes, and other aspects of more specific role behavior will be referred to as elements of *social structure* rather than as *culture*. We thus wish to define as cultural those very *basic* patterns of values and ideas that are an integral part of early childhood socialization and are taught mainly by one's parents and relatives, together with neighbors or family friends.

3. *Social structural variables* refer to those normatively patterned social and individual behaviors that are associated with and learned through specialized roles, social settings, organizations, groups, and institutional contexts and that may be learned generally at any stage of the life cycle (rather than being largely learned by most people in their childhood and early years). In general the content of social structure is more detailed, refined, and specific than the content of culture, but this is not always the case. The main distinguishing characteristic of an element of social structure, in contrast with an element of culture, is that the former does not apply to or get learned by all or nearly all members of a society or ethnic group. *Social structure is the "fine grain" of custom, one might say, while culture is the "coarse grain"; social structure includes the details while culture sets the broad trends and patterns of societies.* Culture tends to deal with broad values, ideas, and perspectives (worldviews), while social structure deals more with norms for specific kinds of behavior, both overt and covert.

While the overall structure of organizations in a given society (as well as other contextual variables) may be an important determinant of the rates of individual participation in a given voluntary association, the structure of the given organization itself may also have a significant role in determining individual rates of membership and participation. Among these relevant organizational factors are the degree of formalization of the organization, its type of compliance structure, its eligibility requirements, its actual membership rates and characteristics, its recruitment patterns and approaches, its socialization practices and procedures, its communication substructure, ideological substructure, its political and control substructure, etc.

4. The *human population* variables are those biological and physical characteristics of the total human population of the society or territorial area under consideration. In a sense, we add this class of variables here mainly for conceptual completeness, since we know of little or no research relating human population factors (in the present sense) to *individual* voluntary action. In fact, there are scarcely any hints of data on the relationships between the bio-physical nature of the population in an area or society and the general level of incidence-prevalence of voluntary *groups* and voluntary action characterizing that population. Smith and Fisher (1971) only barely touch on the matter when discussing the rise of health-related voluntary groups. In consequence, we shall not attempt to deal with human population variables in subsequent portions of this paper.

Now let us turn to those three kinds of contextual factors on which there is some body of relevant theory and/or research, however scanty.

Bio-physical Environmental Determinants
of Organized Individual Voluntary Action

The bio-physical environment can affect individual participation in organized voluntary action in many ways. We shall try to suggest here only a few of these possible lines or chains of influence, leaving to others with more specialized skills in this area the task of providing a comprehensive overview. Moreover, what we have to say here is more a sketch of aspects of a theory than a summary of prior research. To our knowledge, there has been little or no research at all on how bio-physical environmental factors affect individual voluntary action.

Starting at the most abstract and broadest level, the general harshness of a bio-physical environment relative to the usual needs of the human species is likely to have a major impact on the prevalence of individual voluntary activity. Until and unless the individual has achieved a modicum of physical protection (from weather, wild animals, and other natural phenomena that can endanger his physical survival and comfort), he is generally unlikely to engage in much voluntary action, either of an organized or unorganized sort. Very harsh physical-biological environments (e.g., in the high mountains, in the arctic or antarctic, in large barren desert areas, etc.) put a premium not only on protection but also on the matter of obtaining enough food for oneself, one's spouse and family to survive. The constant struggle to find food (and/or grow food) and protection from the natural elements thus is likely to interfere with the time and opportunity for most or all kinds of organized voluntary action. Under such harsh conditions, human settlement sizes are likely to be quite small until (or unless) a very high level of technology is introduced (by innovation from within or diffusion from without). Such small settlement sizes are hence less likely to facilitate the development of very many kinds of organized voluntary action, in turn making the opportunities for the individual to participate in organized voluntary action much fewer and more limited.

Another way that the bio-physical environment can affect individual voluntary action is through its impact upon the growth of specific kinds of voluntary organizations in the immediate environment of the individual. For instance, ecological and conservation voluntary associations are likely to become prevalent in an area only when the destruction, defacement, and pollution of the natural bio-physical environment become widespread and obvious in that area. As natural resources and natural beauty become scarce and approach low levels or non-existence, conservation-ecology voluntary associations are more likely to arise, holding cultural and social structural factors constant. Therefore, individual opportunities to participate in (and the individual urge to form or help build) conservation- and ecology-oriented voluntary associations and volunteer programs are much less where natural resources are abundant and natural beauty has not yet been marred significantly by the influence of human industrialization, mining, and where neither natural resources nor beauty are immediately threatened by internal or external human influences and groups.

One final example of the impact of bio-physical environmental factors, chosen from a wide range of examples that could be given, is the manner in which climate affects individual attendance at organized voluntary activities of various kinds. On beautiful, balmy summer or spring days, individuals are much less likely to wish to participate in most forms of instrumental voluntary groups, though they may well be willing to participate in expressive, recreational kinds of organized voluntary activities. By contrast, inclement weather of a severe sort (heavy rains, blizzards with large snow accumulations, tornado or hurricane weather, etc.) is likely to reduce the probability of individual participation in almost any kind of organized voluntary action, instrumental or expressive. These are obvious kinds of observations to make, yet so far as the authors know there are no systematic studies whatever in the literature dealing with even these simple aspects of the relationships between the bio-physical environment and organized social activity. Let us hope these large research lacunae do not go unnoticed and unattended to much longer. (A more extensive series of illustrations and hypotheses regarding the relationship between the bio-physical environment and voluntary action in territorial social systems may be found in Smith and Fisher, 1971).

Cultural Determinants of Organized
Individual Voluntary Action

Not surprisingly, more attention has been paid to how cultural values and ideas affect organized voluntary action than to how bio-physical environmental variables do so. Nevertheless, even this area of investigation is only in its earliest infancy, as far as the development of *comparative* research is concerned. There are numerous historical, socio-political, and anthropological case studies (as well as studies from related fields) that focus on cultural values and ideas and their change over time in a particular society. Some of these studies touch directly on the implications of culture for voluntary action of various kinds, while the rest of these studies can usually support hypotheses regarding such implications if we choose to draw them.

What are lacking are studies that consciously focus on the implications of cultural values and ideas for voluntary action *across* a series of different cultures or societies.

The closest we come to the latter kind of comparative cultural study is perhaps in the study of how sub-cultural variations affect participation in voluntary action within a given country. For instance, Handlin's study (1951) of immigrants in America includes a chapter on immigrants' participation in their own voluntary associations of various kinds. His work and the work of other scholars has made it clear that the "culture shock" of an immigrant group entering a quite different culture often results in the formation of special kinds of exclusive voluntary associations based on criteria of ethnicity, nationality, or culture. These associations are strongest during the primary assimilation period, when large masses of culturally different immigrants are being absorbed and assimilated into a given country. A generation or two after the immigration essentially stops or declines markedly in magnitude, the corresponding ethnic-nationality based voluntary associations tend to decline as well (cf., Schmidt and Babchuk 1971).

Banfield (1958) provides an excellent contemporary example of (sub)cultural values that produce a deficient collective action orientation and limited individual voluntary action in organized groups. In his study of a small town in southern Italy, Banfield identified an ethos that he termed "amoral familism," produced by a high death rate, some conditions of land tenure, and the absence of the institution of the extended family. The "amoral familists' " behavior may be interpreted as if they were aiming at maximizing the material, short-run advantage of their nuclear family unit and assuming that all others in the town and environs will do likewise.

Banfield's "Montegrano," a town with a population of about 3,400 persons, had but one voluntary association—an upper-class club of about twenty-five members that principally engaged in playing cards and chatting. The local population had virtually no interest in any organized voluntary group or in the community as a whole except as it involved their own short-run material advantage. Community gains or improvements were also valued only in terms of the short-run material advantage accruing to the individual. If others might share disproportionately in the potential gain, the activity was opposed (following the "logic of collective action" discussed perceptively by Olson, 1965).

Organizations of any kind, be they formal or informal, voluntary or non-voluntary, were difficult to achieve and to maintain. As Banfield (1958) notes, (pp. 86-87) "The inducements which lead people to contribute their activity to organizations are to an important degree unselfish (e.g., identification with the purpose of the organization) and they are often non-material (e.g., the intrinsic interest of the activity as a 'game')." With their focus on the selfish and the material, the townspeople were virtually unable to trust each other and to have anything but a superficial, temporary, and conditional loyalty to an organization or group. Power was and could only be self-serving and corrupt. No claim could be made that one's interest was only in and for the public good rather than private advantage. There were not (and could not be) leaders or followers, or even individual initiative, due to a pervading mistrust of others and of their intentions. Officeholders, professionals, and educators all lacked a sense of mission or calling. Even if a rare individual had these latter traits, he would not be trusted or believed. The cultural values and perceptions of the world thus effectively precluded nearly all individual participation in organized voluntary action.

When the nature of various cultural systems is considered, we find a number of broad values and ideas that are highly variable among cultures while at the same time having great importance for voluntary action, individual or collective. For example, the whole notion of pluralism, liberty, freedom of thought, speech, and association in a culture is crucial. Cultures that value pluralism in religion (Adams, 1971), politics, associations, etc., (Rice, 1962; Horn, 1956; Fellman, 1963) are much more conducive to individual participation in organized voluntary action than are cultures emphasizing total consensus, conformity, and monolithic control by one party, one religion, and a minimum of voluntary associations, feared as probable sources of countervailing power (Selznick, 1960).

Another important cultural factor that affects voluntary action is the place of efficacy, mastery, accomplishment, and aspiration in the worldview and values of a culture. Cultures that foster and support such values—a "doing" rather than a "being" orientation, a "mastery over nature" rather than a "subjugation to nature" orientation, to use Kluckhohn and Strodtbeck's terms (1961)—are more likely to produce individuals who are willing or even eager to get involved in organized voluntary action, especially in "instrumental" groups that aim at the accomplishment of some objective (if abstract), external goal. Conversely, cultures that emphasize fate, destiny, resignation, and acceptance of the way things are tend to produce proportionately fewer individual participants in organized voluntary action.

One final example, selected from many that could be given here, is the role of cultural values regarding organizations per se. Some cultures' values emphasize expressive values and informality in human relations or strict, kin-defined hierarchies insofar as there is any formal organization of human relationships in collective enterprises. Other cultures emphasize rationality and efficiency, the values of formal organization in collective enterprises. Robert Seidenberg, in *Post Historic Man* (1950), argues that Western culture has precisely the latter value deeply embedded within it. If true, this fact could help account for the proportionately larger numbers of voluntary associations in Western versus other countries and cultures (though the evidence for the latter statement can be challenged by illustration in some cases—cf., Norbeck, 1972).

Another, more specific manner in which cultural values can affect individual participation in organized voluntary action is through the impact of such values and ideas on *specific kinds* of voluntary groups and their goals. For instance, "social problems" are in large part culturally defined, and the cultural definitions of what constitutes a social problem have an evolutionary history which can be traced for any given society. Perhaps one of the clearest examples is the changing cultural perception of, and evaluation of, "poverty" as a social problem in Western culture since the advent of the industrial revolution (cf., Bremner, 1956).

In this case there has been a complex mutual feedback relationship between culture and social structure. The culture of Western Europe facilitated the industrial revolution, whose social structural changes in turn affected Western culture in various ways. The existence of poverty and major wealth differences were highlighted as wealth became less tied to hereditary and political power bases, and more responsive to individual entrepreneurship. A "noblesse oblige" cultural value grew to be common among the wealthier classes, followed by the development of various kinds of organized voluntary action aimed at remedying or at least alleviating poverty and its attendant problems of social welfare. Robert Bremner (1956) has written at length about this process of cultural value change and its impact on the development of social welfare organizations and the social work profession.

Similar examples could be given with regard to the impact of other kinds of cultural values upon specific kinds of organized voluntary action—the relation of cultural values regarding science and inquiry to participation in scientific and health-oriented voluntary associations, the relation of kinship or caste values to participation in clan or caste voluntary associations (cf., Little, 1965). A more extensive set of hypotheses and illustrations regarding culture and voluntary action can be found in Smith and Fisher (1971).

Social Structural Determinants of Organized Individual Voluntary Action

To some extent individual levels of voluntary action are affected by the internal structure of voluntary groups themselves and by the nature of the community and larger society in which the voluntary action takes place. We term such factors "social structural and organizational" because they focus more on the nature of the social system or organizational setting of individual voluntary action than upon cultural or bio-physical contextual factors or upon an individual's characteristics. Yet these social structural and organizational characteristics can have a major effect on general levels of voluntary action. There has been more empirical research focused explicitly on the impact of social structural factors upon individual participation than is true for the other kinds of contextual factors. Yet even here the amount of systematic research available is very meager. Let us consider social structural determinants in terms of two broad subcategories—territorial social systems and organizational structure.

Territorial Social System Factors

1. *The social structural openness of a whole society* to voluntary action is very important when a broad historical and cross-cultural perspective is taken. Some societies in history and even at the present time have generally suppressed

voluntary associations and programs, or else the government or a particular ruling party has taken over and controlled voluntary action so that it lost its autonomy and independence from the government sector. Particularly damaging to voluntary activities are those centralizing processes that result in most power being taken from the local community and concentrated in a totalitarian national level dictatorship. Also damaging are other governmental policies which seek to restrict and limit the activities of the associations themselves, restrictions on freedom of association and speech (dissent). Nazi Germany (Allen, 1965), Stalinist Russia (Fisher, 1959), and Maoist China (Chao, 1954; Schurmann, 1969) are all examples of closed societies with regard to free and autonomous voluntary action, although they do have a *controlled* kind of voluntary action. In relatively open societies like our own, voluntary action of all kinds tends to be more frequent, autonomous, strong, and effective. The United States Constitution and our national values support and encourage voluntary action (cf., Horn, 1956; Rice, 1962; Fellman, 1963; Knott, 1962). Hence, we have more voluntary association participation per capita than many other countries (Almond and Verba, 1963). However, most Western European countries and various other nations with relatively "open" social structures also have high levels of autonomous voluntary action.

2. *The level of modernization of a nation* has a major impact on how much people participate in voluntary action, quite apart from the openness of the society. Research data and theory indicate that, other things being equal, voluntary action tends to be more prevalent in modern, highly developed, industrial or post-industrial societies (Smith, 1970). Primitive, peasant, pre-industrial, traditional, underdeveloped and developing societies tend to have rather low rates of voluntary action, though the rates are not zero in most cases. In fact, Boulding (1968) has argued that there is a general "organizational revolution," including great increases in numbers of voluntary organizations, that accompanies and follows the industrial revolution in a society.

3. *The socioeconomic level of a community* is an important factor in voluntary action levels for individuals in that community. Higher status regions, towns, communities or neighborhoods tend to have higher rates of participation in voluntary action. Research studies show that this impact of the socioeconomic status of *one's community* occurs over and above the impact of *one's own* socioeconomic status. Thus, a lower status person who happens to live in a high status community may participate *more* than a high status person who happens to live in a lower status community. The explanation for this impact of community status levels can be found in the differences in voluntary action opportunities and in prevailing attitudes toward voluntary action in high versus low status communities.

Bell and Force (1956) provide perhaps the first empirical evidence of a relationship between the socioeconomic status of a neighborhood, area, or census tract and rates of individual membership in voluntary associations. Bell and Force chose four census tracts in the San Francisco area for their study. Two tracts were of relatively high socioeconomic status (based on measures of occupation and education) and two were of lower socioeconomic status. Males only were included in the sample. Those living in the two higher status neighborhoods belonged to more associations, attended associational activities more often, and held office more often than those living in the two lower status neighborhoods. When single measures of individual socioeconomic status (education, occupation, and income) were held constant, those living in the high status neighborhoods *still* had higher associational participation rates than those in the lower status neighborhoods.

Schwirian (1962), in his research exploring the relationship between an individual's place of residence and his social participation rates, found that the influence of neighborhood characteristics was at times significant even when single controls (the income, occupational or educational levels, the religious or ethnic affiliations of the individual) were introduced into the analysis. However, Schwirian noted that the reported neighborhood effects could be eliminated in some instances when combinations of individual characteristics were used as controls.

P.S. Mohapatra (1964), in an unpublished research paper based on part of a Detroit Area Study, found that, controlling for levels of individual income and of individual education, socioeconomic status levels of census tracts (especially income and education levels) had an influential impact on individual participation in voluntary associations. Indeed, in a multiple classification analysis which included tract income and tract education as well as five measures of individual characteristics, *both of the tract* characteristics (but especially tract income levels) were stronger predictors of voluntary participation than any of the *individual* characteristics.

In perhaps the most extensive study of the influence of contextual variables on individual memberships in voluntary associations, Spiro's secondary analysis of survey data (1968) found net neighborhood effects to account for between 1.5 percent and 16.7 percent of the variance in individual membership rates. The exact result in a given analysis depended on the size and heterogeneity of the "areal unit" (neighborhood), the indices of participation used, the population sampled, and the individual variables used, among other factors. Overall, Spiro found that the *net* effects of all individual characteristics were stronger than the *net* effects of all neighborhood influences included in the study. Education and income were the best predictors of membership and participation for *both* the individual characteristics and the neighborhood influences. Spiro also noted that "neighborhood" associations (those drawing only on local residents for their members and participants and not being supported or sponsored by at least a quasi-cosmopolitan institution) were more strongly affected by the characteristics of the neighborhood than were non-neighborhood associations.

Finally, Smith (1972) has examined the impact of living in one or another of eight carefully selected Massachusetts cities and towns upon voluntary participation of various kinds. Four of the eight towns were selected as having notably *high* prevalence levels of voluntary associations, while the other four were chosen for their correspondingly low prevalence rates (voluntary associations/1000 population). The eight towns also differed markedly in size and average socioeconomic status. Statistical data describing the nature of each town were obtained, together with interview data from town leaders and a cross-section of local townspeople. Multivariate analyses of the data were performed using the full range of individual characteristics discussed in the preceding three chapters of this volume (social background, attitudes, personality traits, and capacities). When such a complete set of individual "internal" characteristics are controlled or taken into account, the residual impact of the socioeconomic level of one's city or town of residence (as a factor affecting voluntary activity) is very minor (1-3 percent of the variance out of 30-60 percent of the variance explained). These levels of impact of the town are still statistically significant at times, if insubstantial.

Smith's study (1972) controlled a broader *range* of "internal" individual factors studied than did any of the other studies reviewed here. Most prior studies, in fact, control *only* individual social background variables (or specifically, socioeconomic status variables), without controlling for the impact of attitudinal and/or personality factors. Since most of these other studies found somewhat greater degrees of impact of the socioeconomic level of tracts, neighborhoods, or communities upon individual voluntary participation than did Smith, it is possible that attitudes and/or personality traits may be mediating influences between the nature of one's immediate social environment and individual voluntary participation. In any event, there is clear empirical evidence from several studies that the socioeconomic level of an individual's residential social surroundings have an independent impact on his voluntary participation, even controlling for "internal" individual factors. *Without* controls for individual factors (e.g., individual socioeconomic status), the apparent impact of socioeconomic levels of one's census tract, neighborhood or community is, of course, much greater.

4. *The degree of organizational development of a community* is a separate but related factor worth noting, as examined by Smith (1972) in the study just discussed. Holding socioeconomic status constant, some communities simply have greater *overall* levels of organizational development than do others—they have more stores, banks, government agencies, hospitals, libraries, motels, manufacturing plants, service businesses, etc. Such towns are likely to be either the largest city in their local area or at some distance from larger nearby cities. They tend to have a well-developed sense of local pride and town "identity." They care about themselves as a town. They tend to have a local newspaper that is published explicitly *for* the town itself. In such "organizationally developed" towns there tend to be more voluntary organizations as well, and generally more

individual participation in voluntary action, other things equal. Again, this is partly due to more opportunities for individual voluntary action and partly due to prevailing attitudes in the townspeople that are more conducive to participation (cf., Smith, 1971a).

5. *The population size of a city or town* has been studied by several scholars in relation to per capita membership rates in voluntary groups (e.g., Curtis, 1971). However, most of these studies have not controlled "internal" individual factors while looking at the impact of community size (population). Therefore, the main conclusion we can draw at present is that the per capita participation of individuals in FVOs is generally greater in small towns (less than 10,000 population) than in large towns or cities in contemporary America (Smith, 1971b). However, this conclusion may be in part an artifact of the more thorough fieldwork methods that can be and tend to be used in small towns or villages versus large cities or metropolitan areas. We need to accumulate a great deal more evidence before we can be sure of what is going on here with regard to the impact of size of a city or town.

6. *Other characteristics* of territorial social systems might well be studied in relation to individual participation in voluntary activity and voluntary groups. However, research in this whole field is just getting started. The factors chosen for review in this section are ones that stand out from a multitude of possibilities as most salient to the authors. Other types of scholars would doubtless emphasize alternative territorial social system factors such as political factors, religious factors, educational factors, kinship factors, economic factors, etc.

Organizational Structure Factors

1. *The eligibility requirements for membership* and participation in various voluntary associations and volunteer programs are obviously going to have a major impact on who participates and why. An individual may be characterized by *all* of the relevant "internal" individual factors (social background, attitudes, personality, capacities) conducive to participation and by *all* of the external territorial social system factors conducive to participation. Yet if a particular kind of voluntary group (or every voluntary group in his social environment) has restrictive eligibility requirements, he will be unable to join and participate. These eligibility requirements may be explicit and written in the bylaws or administrative rules of a voluntary group, or they may be implicit and covert, used by those who recruit members but not made clear to outsiders and not written down. Eligibility requirements may involve age, sex, physical capacity, race, prior group affiliations, socioeconomic status, or any of a host of other characteristics. Almost any major human characteristic one could think of is used somewhere by some group as an eligibility criterion. We are not trying to pass moral judgments here on such requirements or on the types of criteria used.

Rather, we are pointing out that they are an important determinant of individual participation in particular types of voluntary action.

Membership (official recognition of affiliation) and participation (activity or resources devoted to the organization) are both theoretically and empirically distinct. *Official membership* involves the formal recognition by the voluntary association or program of the individual's belonging to the group and of the group's obligations to the member. The member both informally and formally accepts certain duties and obligations as well as rights and privileges when he accepts membership in the group. However, *participation* in a voluntary organization or program may take many forms: financial contributions (dues, gifts, donations); donation of goods (clothes, food, equipment, etc.) or facilities (a meeting place, furniture, telephones, etc.); contributed time, efforts, and talents without official affiliation; attendance at meetings and other official activities of the group; assumption of specific or general leadership roles or service responsibilities; etc. Official membership is usually necessary for people who hold leadership roles, but for most of the other kinds of participation the voluntary group *may* or *may not* require official membership as a prerequisite to participation.

Associations and voluntary action agencies differ markedly in their attitudes toward and use of non-members, as well as in their willingness to accept those interested in the group as candidates for membership. Almost without exception, groups in the voluntary sector are willing to accept (and they frequently solicit) *financial support* from non-members in addition to the contributions (usually "dues") of members. Indeed, some mass-based groups with extensive fund-raising efforts call all who make a donation "members" (e.g., the American National Red Cross). However, the vast majority of such "mass donors" do not consider themselves actual members and they are quite unlikely (and often constitutionally unable) to participate in the affairs and operations of the group in any way. Their main *practical* claim is to be able to deduct their contribution to the group from their income taxes and sometimes they can claim "official membership" in the organization in question.

Most voluntary associations will accept *some* donations of time and talents by non-members, especially when the group in question lacks either the manpower or the specific technical skills necessary to carry out all phases of their programs or activities. The large majority of "non-autonomous" volunteer programs in prisons, hospitals, schools, etc., fall into this category. Although the volunteer may rightly feel he or she is a part of the institution's program, it is rare that either the full-time staff person or the volunteer will perceive the volunteer to be truly a "member" of the staff. Volunteers will not normally be represented in and/or play a role in decision-making and policy-making situations in the institution as a whole or even with regard to the volunteer program itself.

Perhaps some of the greatest differences among associations are in their willingness to permit *non*-members to attend and to participate in their meetings in various ways. Almost without exception, voting and taking an active role in discussion and debate are officially restricted to members (or, where classes of membership exist, to some classes of members). However, while some organizations have all of their meetings open to the general public, others permit only certified members or accepted aspirants for membership to attend any meetings. Many groups hold *both* types of meetings on different occasions, some even holding both types each week. Although some voluntary associations permit non-members to participate in committee work or in special advisory capacities, virtually without exception official leadership positions must be filled by group members.

a. *Formal Eligibility Criteria.* However, a mere interest in the organization's work or program is seldom either formally or informally *enough* for individuals to qualify for actual membership in any but a minority of mass-based associations. The majority of voluntary associations and programs have *formal eligibility criteria* which exclude some types of individuals from membership. Cub scouts must be male and neither too young nor too old. The League of Women Voters admits only women who are old enough to vote, although it lowered its age requirements just before the voting age in the United States was lowered. Members of the Disabled American Veterans must, prior to membership, have been male members of the Armed Forces of the United States who, during their period of service, suffered some disability. The American Medical Association grants membership only to those it considers duly qualified physicians in the United States. Other professional groups have analogous criteria for membership. Parents Without Partners requires its members to be parents of live children and to be either widowed, separated or divorced. The Daughters of the American Revolution accepts as members those females whose forefathers can be established to have fought for the Colonial forces in the American Revolution. Some groups require their members to have alcoholism problems, be former mental patients, former drug addicts, very tall, obese, etc. Membership in the Black Panthers is not open to Caucasians or to Orientals.

Such formal eligibility criteria for official membership in voluntary associations and programs have received almost no systematic comparative research attention. Case studies of particular voluntary organizations, of course, sometimes touch on these matters. What we lack is an understanding of the nature of formal eligibility criteria and how they are devised and change over time for a broad cross-section of voluntary groups. For the moment, all we can say with certainty is that formal eligibility requirements are quite important determinants of many kinds of participation in voluntary action, and, as such, are deserving of a great deal more research attention than they have been so far accorded.

b. *Informal Eligibility Criteria.* Virtually all groups have, in addition to formal requirements for (or barriers to) membership, *informal eligibility criteria* by which members tend to be chosen and/or accepted. Informal requirements are especially significant for those groups without extensive formal requirements but with systematic (though often implicit) *assumptions as to who will or should participate.* Exclusive social and/or recreational clubs generally are not formally explicit as to who they exclude, but nomination and selection procedures, as well as costs of membership and participation, effectively keep most, if not all, those of certain religious affiliations, races, or socioeconomic status levels from membership. Men and/or children would be quite unwelcome as members of some garden or bridge clubs, though not formally excluded, just as women and/or children would similarly be unlikely to gain membership in some political, business, or social clubs. Similarly, adults of either sex are not likely to become members of various youth organizations, even though not formally excluded.

Since these informal and often implicit eligibility criteria are usually more subtle and at the same time more important than formal criteria, the fact that such criteria have very rarely, if ever, been studied systematically and comparatively is a first class scientific tragedy. How do informal eligibility criteria relate to organizational goals? What factors determine changes in such criteria over time? What is the *overall impact* of such criteria on the national rates of voluntary participation by specific categories of people—low income people, minority groups, women, the aged, etc.? Let us hope that voluntary action scholars turn to such questions, among others, in the near future.

2. *Other organizational characteristics* also may have an important impact on individual voluntary participation, especially for persons who have already become affiliated with a voluntary group of some kind. These factors all refer to how the structure of a *specific* voluntary group or program affects individual participants, yet such factors may be cumulated across all the voluntary groups a person belongs to (if any) in order to get a picture of the *net* impact of organizational structure factors upon his participation.

Many voluntary associations and voluntary action agencies have *required minimum levels of participation* for retention of "good standing" membership. Most often this minimum involves payment of membership dues or fees. However, some groups set minimum levels of attendance at meetings, time spent in various activities, etc. Such norms, when agreed to or understood as a condition of membership, tend to foster higher "official" rates of individual member participation, though they may tend also to hold down group size (since many inactive or "pseudo-members" never enter, or leave soon after entry). Unfortunately, we know of no systematic research on this topic, so we cannot cite any solid evidence on these matters, only these impressions and hypotheses.

Tannenbaum and his associates have done extensive work with the concept of *organizational control patterns.* In essence, the amount of control, while subject to sizable variation within organizations, is not a limited quantum, with increases of control in one subgroup or organization level necessarily producing decreases of control in another subgroup. Instead, in some organizations, the amount of control may be quite low for all subgroups and levels; in some other organizations the amount of control may be high for all levels; and in still other organizations some subgroups and levels may be high in control while others are low. Tannenbaum and Kahn (1958) noted in a study of four labor unions that the two most effective, active, and powerful unions had the highest amount of control exercised *both* by members and by officers. The most powerful and the most active union had both influential members and influential leaders.

Warner and Heffernan (1967) have investigated the influence of *the benefit (or reward) system* of a voluntary association upon its rates of membership and individual participation. They hypothesized that the greater the extent a member thinks he must participate in order to receive the association's benefits, the greater his participation will be. Although there was a weak positive correlation between the absolute number of benefits and participation, the positive correlation between participation and the *ratio* of benefits to contributions reached statistical significance levels.

To extrapolate these findings, it would seem that individuals are more likely to join an association if it promises to provide certain otherwise unattainable benefits, be these benefits for oneself or for others (cf., Olson, 1965). The extent to which such benefits are attained by participation serves to stimulate active participation. From this perspective, membership and participation have their own costs. In an individual's "personal economy," time or money spent in one setting limits, restricts, or even eliminates other options. Thus, within this "economy," if rewards or benefits may be forthcoming *without* active participation, without membership, or even without support of any kind, the individual is unlikely to "spend" his scarce resources in seeking those rewards or benefits. However, when those rewards or benefits are likely to be attained principally or only through membership or through active participation of one kind or another, the likelihood of such membership and participation in voluntary groups increases. This is especially the case when the "costs" of such membership and participation are substantial.

While Warner and Heffernan studied a farm organization, their findings have been echoed in studies of political activity and of participation in labor unions. Researchers such as Cooper (1961) report that the individual's perception of his subgroup's power in a political party organization is positively correlated with the intensity of his affiliation (or put another way, people will in general like and feel more identified with a group which they feel better represents their views). Nevertheless, people are *more* likely to participate actively when their participation will make a difference, when they feel their efforts may help to influence a decision, establish a program, attain a goal, and, in general, bring about a state of affairs they want to gain (see, for example, Gordon and Coulter, 1969; Edelstein, 1967).

Warner (1964) notes another factor that stimulates participation in associations. In that study, Warner found that the proportion of members in attendance at organizational meetings was significantly correlated with *the proportion of association members holding office* as well as with the proportion chairing *both* permanent and temporary committees. However, there was no significant relationship between attendance and the proportion of members serving on *either* one or the other kind of committee or merely "holding some position" in the organization. In smaller organizations, office holding was especially correlated with attendance, while in larger organizations both chairing and serving on permanent committees proved to be especially important. In sum, those with officially recognized and visible positions of responsibility and influence are more likely to attend voluntary organization meetings than those members lacking any responsible special role in the group.

Both Warner and Hilander (1964) and Indik (1965) have found strong negative relationships between *the size of a voluntary association* and its rates of membership participation. Moreover, Warner and Hilander noted that some aspects of participation were more closely related to size than others. Attendance at regular and special meetings, active involvement, and project participation were more closely related to the association's size than were, for example, the performance of special assignments and financial contributions. Of all aspects of participation, rates of individual financial contributions were least related to the size of the organization.

Chapin and Tsouderos (1955, 1956) explored *the level of formalization (bureaucratization) in voluntary associations.* In general, they found that as organizations became more formalized, membership increases and the frequency of general meetings rises rapidly but then decreases, approaching quarterly meetings. However, the larger the membership, the smaller the percentage of members who attend general meetings. As membership participation decreases, the average hours of volunteer service by leaders, the number of paid employees, the number of executive meetings, and the number of standing committees increase. Income tends to increase with increases in membership, as does the amount of property owned by the association. In sum, while formalization increases the resources and perhaps even the financial power of the association, it markedly reduces the individual participation potential and possibilities for the large majority of members.

Summary and Conclusions

Contextual and organizational determinants of individual participation in organized voluntary action promise to provide valuable insights into the basis for variations in individual activity rates between and within cultures, between and within societies, between and within organizations. However, hypotheses and theories suggesting the scope and nature of the effects of possible contextual and organizational determinants on individual voluntary participation can currently be supported only by a very few available examples from systematic and quantitative empirical research. While individual participation in organized voluntary action is, of necessity, the participation of an individual who is in and of a given context and in a given organization (or series of organizations), the focus of research efforts to date has been on the individual and on specific "internal" personal characteristics of the individual as determinants of participation, rather than on the "external" context of his action or the organization he participates in as determinants of participation.

Because of the limited number of studies dealing with most of the "determinants" (perhaps it would be better, in this case, to use the term "possible influences"), no attempt will be made in this chapter to make a summary assessment of the strength of the relationships studied or the consistency of the findings to date.

Reviewing existing theory and the research, we have found that little or no work has been done to assess how *bio-physical factors of the human population or of the environment* affect individual voluntary action. Studies are also lacking that systematically focus on the implications of *cultural values* across a series of differing cultures and societies for individual participation. However, there is some evidence that organized voluntary action in general is more likely in cultures with higher levels of collective action orientation and of modernization as well as in cultures that value pluralism. Organized voluntary action is also more likely in societies that have *social structural* openness and that have developed or adopted widespread patterns of formal organizational acitivity.

On the level of *the community*, there are indications that organized voluntary action is more frequent in those communities with higher socioeconomic levels and with greater degrees of organizational development. The size of the community is one of a number of other possible factors affecting rates and patterns of organized voluntary action.

While virtually all organized voluntary action programs have both *formal and informal eligibility criteria* for membership in their programs, very little systematic empirical work has been done regarding this vital interface between the voluntary groups forming part of the individual's context and the individual himself. We need to know how these criteria are devised, sustained, and changed over time for a broad cross section of voluntary groups. And we need to know in detail how these criteria actually affect individual participation in various groups.

Within various voluntary groups, we have indications that *organizational factors* such as the amount and distribution of organizational control, the benefit system, the proportion of office holders in the organization, the size of the organization, and its level of formalization affect the levels of and types of individual voluntary activity in the group.

In conclusion, this chapter should be considered more as an invitation and as a challenge than as a comprehensive review of a substantial body of relevant research. Our current state of knowledge is only suggestive of possibilities and our research findings are meager and only tentative. Yet, what we *do* know clearly suggests that further work is well warranted and, indeed, vitally necessary for a fuller and more adequate understanding, assessment, and prediction of the rates and patterns of individual participation in organized voluntary action.

References

Adams, James Luther
1971 "The Voluntary Principle in the Forming of American Religion." In Elwyn A. Smith (ed.), *The Religion of the Republic.* Philadelphia: The Fortress Press.
Allen, Vernon L.
1965 "Situational Factors in Conformity." In Leonard Berkowitz (ed.), *Advances in Experimental Social Psychology* Vol. 2. New York: Academic Press, 133-75.
Allen, William Sheridan
1965 *The Nazi Seizure of Power.* Chicago: Quadrangle Books.
Almond, Gabriel and Sidney Verba
1963 *The Civic Culture.* Princeton: Princeton University Press.
Banfield, Edward D.
1958 *The Moral Basis of a Backward Society.* New York: Free Press.
Bell, Wendell and Maryanne T. Force
1956 "Urban Neighborhood Types and Participation in Formal Associations." *American Sociological Review* 21:25-34.
Boulding, Kenneth
1968 *The Organizational Revolution: A Study in the Ethics of Economic Organization.* Chicago: Quadrangle Press.
Bremner, Robert H.
1956 *The Discovery of Poverty in the U.S.* New York: N.Y.U. Press.
Chao, K.C.
1954 "Mass Organizations in Mainland China." *American Political Science Review* 48 (September): 752-65.
Chapin, F. Stuart and John E. Tsouderos
1955 "Formalization Observed in Ten Voluntary Associations." *Social Forces* 33:306-09.
1956 "The Formalization Process in Voluntary Associations." *Social Forces* 34:342-44.
Cooper, Homer Chassell
1961 "Perception of Subgroup Power and Intensity of Affiliation with a Large Organization." *American Sociological Review* 26:272-74.

Curtis, James
1971 "Voluntary Association Joining: A Cross-National Comparative Note." *American Socilogical Review.* 36, 872-80.

Edelstein, David
1967 "An Organizational Theory of Union Democracy." *American Sociological Review* 32:19-31.

Fellman, David
1963 *The Constitutional Right of Association.* Chicago: Univ. of Chicago Press.

Fisher, Ralph T.
1959 *Pattern for Soviet Youth.* New York: Columbia Univ. Press.

Freedman, Jonathan L. and David O. Sears
1965 "Selective Exposure." In Leonard Berkowitz (ed.), *Advances in Experimental Social Psychology*, Vol. 2. New York: Academic Press, 57-97.

Gordon, Glen and Philip Coulter
1969 "The Sociological Bases of Party Competition: the Case of Massachusetts." *Sociological Quarterly* 10:84-105.

Handlin, Oscar
1951 *The Uprooted.* New York: Grosset and Dunlap.

Horn, R.A.
1956 *Groups and the Constitution.* Stanford, Calif.: Stanford University Press.

Indik, Bernard P.
1965 "Organization Size and Member Participation." *Human Relations* 18:339-50.

Kluckhohn, Florence and Fred Strodtbeck
1961 *Variations in Value Orientations.* Evanston, Ill: Row, Peterson.

Knott, James E., Jr.
1962 *Freedom of Association.* Brussels: Union of International Associations.

Little, Kenneth
1965 *West African Urbanization: A Study of Voluntary Associations in Social Change.* Cambridge, England: Cambridge University Press.

Mohapatra, P.S.
1964 "Residential Areas and Politically Relevant Behavior." Unpublished paper, Ann Arbor: University of Michigan.

Norbeck, Edward
1972 "Japanese Common-Interest Associations in Cross-Cultural Perspective." *Journal of Voluntary Action Research* (1) no. 1:38-41.

Olson, Mancur
1965 *The Logic of Collective Action.* Cambridge: Harvard University Press.

Rice, C.F.
1962 *Freedom of Association.* New York: New York Univ. Press.

Schmidt, Alvin and Nicholas Babchuk

1971 "Formal Voluntary Organizations and Change over Time: A Study of American Fraternal Associations." *Journal of Voluntary Action Research* (1) no. 1:38-41.

Schurmann, Franz

1969 *Ideology and Organization in Communist China. 2nd Ed.* Berkeley: Univ. of Cal. Press, Publication of the Center for Chinese Studies.

Schwirian, Kent P.

1962 *Residence and Social Participation.* Unpublished Ph. D. dissertation, Ames: State University of Iowa.

Seidenberg, Robert

1950 *Post Historic Man.* Chapel Hill, N.C.: University of N.C. Press.

Selznick, Philip

1960 *The Organizational Weapon.* Glencoe, Ill.: Free Press of Glencoe.

Smith, David Horton

1970 "Modernization and the Emergence of Voluntary Organizations." Working Paper No. 6, *Institute of Human Sciences Working Paper Series*, Chestnut Hill, Mass: Institute of Human Sciences.

1971a "Voluntary Organization Activity and Poverty." *Urban and Social Change Review*, 5 (No. 1): 2-7.

1971b "Estimating the Total Number of Voluntary Associations in a Country, City, or Other Area." Unpublished paper, Wash., D.C.: Center for a Voluntary Society.

1972 *Voluntary Activity in Eight Massachusetts Towns.* Draft of unpublished monograph. Boston College, Institute of Human Sciences.

Smith, David Horton, with Allon Fisher

1971 "Toward a Comparative Theory of the Incidence and Prevalence of Voluntary Associations." Paper presented to the Panel on Voluntary Associations in South and East Asia, Association for Asian Studies Annual Meeting, Washington, D.C.

Smith, R.V.

1964 *Areal Variation in Formal Association Membership in a Large Metropolitan Community.* Unpublished Ph.D. dissertation. Ann Arbor: University of Michigan.

Spiro, Shimon Ernst

1968 *Effects of Neighborhood Characteristics on Participation in Voluntary Associations.* Unpublished Ph.D. dissertation. Ann Arbor: University of Michigan.

Tannenbaum, Arthur S. and Robert L. Kahn

1958 *Participation in Local Unions.* Evanston, Ill.: Row-Peterson.

Warner, W. Keith

1964 "Attendance and Division of Labor in Voluntary Associations." *Rural Sociology*, 29:396-407.

Warner, W. Keith and James S. Hilander

1964   "The Relationship between Size of Organization and Membership Participation." *Rural Sociology*, 29:30-39.

Warner, W. Keith and William D. Heffernan

1967   "The Benefit-participation contingency in Voluntary Farm Organizations." *Rural Sociology*, 32:139-53.

15 An Overview of the Determinants of Individual Participation in Organized Voluntary Action

DAVID HORTON SMITH and RICHARD D. REDDY

Individual participation in organized voluntary action is participation by an individual who is embedded in a particular culture, social structure, and historical context, as well as being an analytical member of one or more specified voluntary groups or programs. In the four previous chapters of Part Two, research related to individual participation in organized voluntary action has been reviewed according to a number of major types of variables and levels of explanation. Attention has most recently been given to a range of contextual factors that vary from broad cultural, sub-cultural, and historical factors, through general social structural and contextual factors on the societal level, to more specific social structural and contextual factors operating within the locality and the "personal space" of the individual, especially his community and his voluntary groups. Earlier, a major emphasis was placed on a number of so-called "internal" or personal factors that have been found related to individual rates of participation in organized voluntary action: social background and role factors, personality and capacity factors, general attitudes toward voluntary action, and specific attitudes toward given voluntary action programs.

To the best of our knowledge, there is no existing theory in the literature relating all of these factors to each other in a comprehensive model that attempts to explain various kinds of individual participation in organized voluntary action. Yet there is obviously a great need for drawing together these disparate kinds of influences into some coherent and testable explanatory framework. An initial attempt has been made to sketch such a framework here. The approach taken follows in broad outline the approach taken by Allport (1951,1954) in attempting to account for the phenomenon of prejudice. More specifically, the present approach elaborates the *sequential specificity model* suggested by Smith (1964, 1966), who is at present continuing to work out and test the model on his data from a cross-sectional sample of townspeople in eight Massachusetts cities and towns (Smith, 1972a).

What follows should therefore be viewed as highly tentative—a suggestion and set of hypotheses rather than a well-confirmed theory. The model is at present little more than an attempt to link together in a reasonable causal and time sequence the kinds of factors that the existing research literature points to as important independent variables for the prediction of individual participation in organized voluntary action. Broader social and psychological theory have also been brought to bear in thinking through the possible and probable lines of causality, but few other realms of social science are in a much better state as far as possessing adequate, well-confirmed theories of a comprehensive sort about the phenomena to which they are addressed.

Basic to the present model is the attempt to explain a type of individual behavior by means of a variety of levels of explanatory variables that range from *very general levels* of explanation to *very specific levels*. Each level makes its own contribution to the understanding, explanation, and prediction of the phenomenon in question, and each level tends to have some influence on the next level in the sequence. Each level has its own proper focus, orientation, general mode of influence, and special areas of impact. Taken together the several levels serve to provide a reasonably comprehensive basis for the understanding, explanation, and prediction of the behavior or action in question. Figure 15-1 presents a rough schematic overview of the various types of explanatory variables and their suggested causal ordering.

Nature of the Dependent
Participation Variable

The version of the model presented in Figure 15-1 is a highly general one, both in terms of independent and dependent variables. With regard to the dependent variable, undifferentiated individual participation in organized voluntary action, we have earlier made the point that future research and theory will have to be more specific about the *kind* of measure of individual participation used. The general term "participation" has commonly been used to denote (a) both joining and belonging to a given formal voluntary group, (b) the total number of formal voluntary groups belonged to, and (c) a wide variety of activities and roles usually taken on in one or another degree by members of formal voluntary groups.

This global approach treats as a single phenomenon many phenomena that may be quite varied in nature. Thus, it is vital to note that the meaning of membership for an individual and the demands on an individual due to his membership per se will vary considerably from one organization to another. Organizations differ in the strictness and specificity of their membership requirements, as well as in their ability to confer prestige. Moreover, some organizations routinely make heavy demands on the time and resources of their members as members; while in other organizations, membership itself involves in practice only minimal commitment of time and resources (for example, only the payment of token dues), resulting in what may be called "pseudo-membership" (Smith, 1972b). In general, it can be said that official membership normally is a minimum criterion for internal organizational participation.

Beyond membership per se, a number of possibilities for internal participa-

Figure 15-1. Schematic Sketch of a Sequential Specificity Model for Explaining Individual Participation in Organized Voluntary Action

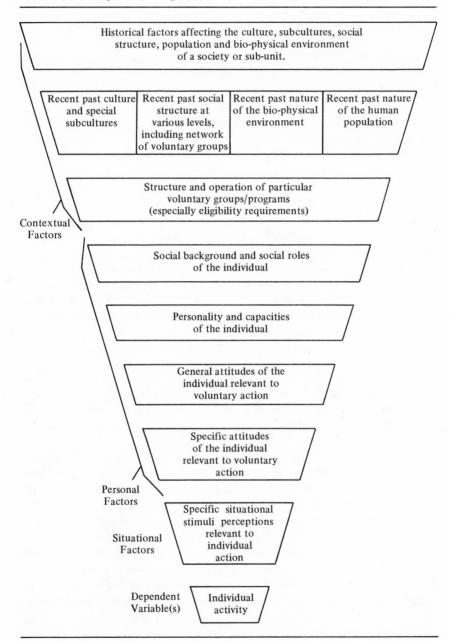

Source: David Horton Smith, *Voluntary Activity in Eight Massachusetts Towns* (unpublished monograph, 1972).

tion may exist, including attendance and participation in regular meetings and activities, attendance at special functions (parties, protests, work sessions, etc.), acceptance of positions of leadership and responsibility in the organization (including committee roles), and solitary pursuit of organizational goals (canvassing, letter writing, recruitment), etc. Indeed, in some organizations, certain types or levels of internal participation may be *required*, while in other groups payment of dues is the *only* requirement.

Actual member participation in the affairs and activities of an organized voluntary group may be considered and analyzed both *quantitatively* ("how much" attendance, leadership, etc.) and *qualitatively* ("what kind" of activities engaged in and roles taken). However, very little systematic attention has been given to the qualitative dimensions of participation *within* organizations, and relatively little attention likewise has been focused on individual membership patterns *across* organizations. Unfortunately, even the quantitative measures commonly used tend to focus on gross activity rather than tapping the kinds of personal concerns that are most related to that activity and measuring the detailed involvement of a person in the activity. For example, attendance at a function in and of itself may involve a relatively passive role in the related activities. What we really might wish to connote and denote by active participation may well be not only *extensive* attendance (or holding a number of roles) within a given organization or a series of organizations, but also *intensive* activity at the attended functions and in the specific roles. Attending an activity and holding an official role may tell us *something* about the quality of an individual's activity, but they are not sufficient indicators to capture the real variety usually present.

In sum, then, the model presented in summary form in Figure 15-1 seriously oversimplifies reality by including only a single, global kind of dependent variable dealing with individual participation in organized voluntary action. We recognize this fact, but believe the oversimplification is a useful beginning, both in terms of ease of presentation and in terms of the present state of knowledge about how the model might vary according to the particular kind of individual participation measure used. We shall return briefly later in this chapter to the theoretical matter of how the model varies with the type of dependent variable used, but a few words now are in order on why the foregoing chapters have made such a minor contribution to empirical refinement of the model presented, at least as regards how different measures of participation affect it.

The problem or deficiency can be put simply: Very, very few studies have taken the trouble to examine more than one index of individual participation as their dependent variable. Where data on a variety of aspects of participation have been gathered in a given study, they have almost invariably been combined into some overall index of participation. Moreover, even in the few studies where different measures of participation have been used separately as dependent variables, the separate measures involved have not been sufficiently developed and tested to give us very much confidence in their reliability. Hence, even if all of the foregoing chapters had attempted to report results separately by the type of participation measure used (an approach rejected as unwarranted in view of the quantity and quality of the data in most chapters), the nature of the existing research literature is such that we would have learned little more to help refine the model.

**Nature of the Various Independent
or Predictor Variables**

The model represented in Figure 15-1 also oversimplifies the complex web of interconnections among the various independent variables involved. However, unlike the situation for various kinds of participation measures, we *have* been able to examine in some depth the variety of relevant independent variable measures in the foregoing chapters of Part Two. In this sense, then, the model sketched here is simply a shorthand way of referring to the larger complex of variables discussed earlier. It should also be carefully noted that the editors had the present general model in mind in planning Part Two, so that the model has not so much emerged from the research reviewed as it has *guided* the present review.

The independent variables of the model are roughly divided into three broad categories, according to their rough position in the hypothesized causal sequence and according to their degree of specificity with regard to the individual and his specific behavior being explained/predicted/understood. The first category of independent variables in the model comprises the *contextual factors*. This set of influences are basically non-individual in nature. There are four main classes of explanatory variables we have distinguished as contextual factors: *cultural and subcultural variables, social structural variables* (including general institutional, organizational, group, and role factors as well as specific factors pertaining to a given group or organized setting for voluntary action), *bio-physical environmental variables, and human population variables*.

Following Smith and Fisher (1971), "by cultural variables we mean all of the socially transmitted and created content and patterns of values, ideas and other meaningful symbolic system elements that are associated with membership in a given society, ethnic group, or very widespread social roles within such systems." Thus, our definition of culture isolates as "culture" certain abstract but pervasive and powerful ideas and values that are not generally associated with particular specialized roles, organizations, groups or social settings in a society. Norms, attitudes, and other aspects of more specific role behavior will be referred to as elements of *social structure* rather than as *culture*. We thus wish to define as culture those very *basic* patterns of values and ideas that are largely learned early as part of childhood socialization, mainly at the hands of one's parents and relatives, together with neighbors, family friends, and perhaps teachers. Then social structure can be distinctly seen as those refinements of customs and normatively patterned behavior that are associated with special roles, groups, organizations, and social settings, and that may be learned generally at any stage of the life cycle (rather than being largely confined to learning in the early years).

Thus, "social structural variables" are viewed as those normatively patterned social and individual behaviors that are associated with and learned through specialized roles, social settings, organizations, groups, and institutional contexts. In general the content of social structure is more specific than the content of culture, but this is not always the case. The main distinguishing characteristic of an element of social structure, by contrast with an element of culture, is that the former does not apply to all or nearly all members of a society or ethnic group. Social structure is the "fine grain" of custom, one might say, while culture is the "coarse grain"; social structure includes the details while culture sets the broad trends and patterns.

The bio-physical environment of human population can be defined as all non-human biological or physical aspects of the world surrounding that population. As such, the bio-physical environment includes factors like the climate, topography, richness of soil, presence of mineral deposits and other natural resources, nature and quantity of flora and fauna, including domesticated animals, etc. Also included are all man-made objects, buildings, constructions, and conditions, from the Panama Canal to the smog in Los Angeles, in short, all human artifacts.

The human population variables refer specifically to the bio-physical nature and size of the population in a given area of reference (which may be the whole world). Where cultural and social structural variables dealt with patterns of thinking, feeling, and behavior of the population, the present category focuses on those aspects of the human population that are largely shared in some degree with the rest of the animal kingdom—matters of health, size, reproductive rates, appearance, etc. By contrast, the bio-physical environmental variables deal with where the human population is located and the "natural" conditions under which it lives.

Within the category of contextual variables we also make some distinctions in terms of time sequence and degree of specificity. Thus, the history of all four classes of general contextual factors is seen as forming the broadest set of background determinants of present behavior. Or more accurately, the distant past historical factors of a contextual sort are seen as affecting the more recent past states of cultural, social structural, environmental, and population variables. The "recent past" can include every point in time from several decades ago to the last moment prior to the dependent variable behavior to be predicted or explained. The term "recent past" is used to single out more proximate effects of contextual factors from more distant and hard to assess influences.

At a level of still greater specificity, we include as contextual variables a variety of characteristics of the particular formal voluntary groups or programs in which an individual (or set of individuals) is participating. These structural and operational aspects of the formal context of the individual's voluntary action bring us down from the level of general social structure in a society to those specific settings "where the action is," so to speak.

The second broad category of independent variables in the model we term *personal factors* or "internal factors." All of these variables can be seen as characteristics that are in some sense "attached to" individuals rather than being part of the general background or context in which many individuals function. However, the various contextual factors we have discussed form a matrix within which the personal factors, as a unique complex of characteristics of the individual, originate, grow, change, and cease to be. Personal factors, indeed, derive their essential meaning and interpretation from the complex of expectations, norms, structures, conditions, and patterns supplied by the contextual factors.

We have highlighted four major kinds of personal factors in our model: *social background and role factors, personality and capacity factors, general attitude factors, and specific attitude factors.*

Social background characteristics involve important *individual* social positions, roles, relationships and experiences. They provide the dynamic interface between the individual and larger contextual factors we have just discussed. Background characteristics give important indications of who the person is in a social sense and what kinds of formative, socialization experiences he is likely to have been exposed to (e.g., age, sex, race, status, life cycle stage, interpersonal role characteristics, etc.), as well as what he does (occupation, personal health and physical abilities, formal organizational affiliations, etc.). When we are investigating individual participation in organized voluntary action, background characteristics in part serve to mediate between the individual and the range of contextual factors which influence him. But in addition, due to the general importance and salience of social background factors in defining role expectations and eligibility for participation in various voluntary action programs, social background factors also play an important role in mediating between the individual and specific organized voluntary action programs or groups.

Personality factors and personal capacities describe the individual's enduring transituational orientations toward action and toward social relationships, as well as defining the limits of individual abilities to respond. While social background factors serve to identify a number of roles and statuses, personality factors indicate in broad terms the personal style or manner in which an individual's whole complex of roles and statuses are performed. Personality factors and capacities highlight the most generalized and enduring dispositions the individual has toward himself, toward others, and toward the rest of his actual or symbolic environment. Personality factors tend to highlight the "how" and "why" of a given behavior or action, whether or not that behavior is viewed as voluntary action.

General attitudes, as they are important for the present model, involve individual perspectives on and orientations toward leisure, toward voluntary action in general, and toward broad types of and contexts for voluntary action. General attitudes indicate tendencies toward (and away from) organized voluntary action in general or broad aspects of voluntary action. They serve to indicate if organized voluntary action in any form is familiar to and attractive to the individual, as well as what kinds of voluntary action (if any) are most likely to appeal to the individual. General attitudes are distinguished from personality traits largely by being *less* generalized and transituational dispositions than the latter. One must always talk about an attitude toward or about something (an object, person, situation, etc.), while personality traits are more general. One does not have to speak of "personality traits about" something.

Specific attitudes, as they are a part of the model, involve individual perspectives on and orientations toward specific voluntary action groups, programs, or organizations and toward their various specific aspects and dimensions. For individuals whose general attitudes dispose them toward voluntary action and toward given broad types of voluntary action, and for individuals who, further, are eligible both formally and informally for a specific kind of participation, specific attitudes indicate what activities, programs, groups, or organizations an individual is likely to get involved in, as well as the individual's probability of continuing that participation over a period of time. An individual may have general attitudes favoring participation in voluntary action, while his specific attitudes toward most of the voluntary groups in his social milieu are unfavorable (or conversely).

The third broad category of variables of the model outlined in Figure 15-1 comprises *situational variables*. This is perhaps the least studied and least well understood kind of variable of all those in the model. By situational variables we mean those characteristics of the immediate situation in which an individual finds himself just prior to and during the voluntary action being focused on as a dependent variable. In fact, so little do we know about the influence of such factors that this whole topic was dealt with only very briefly in the interpersonal roles section of the chapter on social background (Chapter 11), rather than giving the matter a chapter of its own as it theoretically deserves.

The Sequential Specificity Model
as a Set of Hypotheses

Having now reviewed briefly once again the major elements of the model, it will be worthwhile to turn to the structure of the model itself. At the moment, the structure is an extremely systematic one and simple to comprehend if complex to portray (fully) graphically and to describe in detail. The various major elements or classes of variables of the model are arranged in Figure 15-1 in a very special order, as guided by the model. Those classes of variables whose influences are believed to occur earliest in time are at the top of the Figure, with variables whose main influence is hypothesized to come later being placed lower down in the figure, in sequence, all the way to the last event/activity in the model—the dependent variable behavior to be explained/understood/predicted on the basis of all the relevant classes of prior variables in the model. Doubtless there are also important classes of variables not represented in the model even in summary form. The determination of the nature of such "residual variables" is a task for all of us in the future.

Another basic aspect of the model is the matter of increasing specificity, as noted earlier. Not only do the major influences of the classes of variables toward the top of Figure 15-1 occur earlier in time, according to the model, but such classes of variables are also more general in scope than the classes of variables occurring lower down (later) in the model. In this sense, the whole sequential specificity model can be viewed as analogous to a great funnel or set of ever finer filters, attempting to explain why a given individual at a given point in time in a given situation participates in some particular form(s) of organized voluntary action. At every stage of the filtration process some portion of the total human population, past and present, is eliminated from contention (actually, this is a probabilistic matter, not all-or-nothing, in most cases—though the relevant matters of being formally eligible or not and being alive or dead are certainly dichotomous states).

A third major aspect of the model, and the part that is complex to portray or to describe, is the assertion that *all* classes of variables prior in time to a given class of variables in the model can have an influence on the given class of variables. In terms of path analysis, this is usually termed a "complete model." This is the sort of model one begins with lacking any good empirical evidence that one or more of the possible lines of influence so hypothesized does not in fact occur or is not sufficiently important to be included. And since this *is* a beginning, the model is presently and tentatively stated as a "complete" one, pending evidence to the contrary.

Our argument in detail is that historical factors are the most basic variables, but also the most "indirect" variables, affecting individual participation in organized voluntary action. The most clearly discernable impact of historical factors is largely upon the recent past state of the culture and the total social structure of society. Yet historical factors can also be traced as influences on the sub-cultures and social structures of particular regions, geographic areas, and communities. When very detailed case histories are performed, historical factors can also be seen direct influences on particular voluntary organizations. Historical factors are also seen as influencing the recent past state of the human population and the environment in bio-physical terms. A very simple though tragic example would be the impact of the Viet Nam War upon the present or recent past human population and environment of Viet Nam.

The recent past of a human population, its environment, and its culture and social structure all tend to have a mutual influence on each other, but such factors can also be seen as having a direct influence on the structure of particular voluntary groups—affecting their goals, membership composition, financial status, eligibility requirements, impact on the larger society, etc.

All of the foregoing levels of contextual factors can have an influence on the social background and social roles characterizing a particular individual. The historical, cultural and social structural factors (as discussed in Chapter 14) are especially important as determinants of the opportunity structure for an individual—the variety and number of formal voluntary groups that will be available in an individual's immediate environment. These same kinds of factors also determine a great many things about an individual's educational, occupational, religious, residential, kinship, political, and interpersonal roles. In some cases (e.g., where wars kill off a large proportion of a male age-cohort and destroy places of residence and work), human population and environmental factors may even have an influence on sex roles, work roles, education, etc. The structure of particular voluntary groups influences the individual here largely by making persons with *some* social background characteristics eligible for participation while others are excluded (either totally or probabilistically).

At the next level of the model, all of the foregoing factors have an impact on individual personality and capacities, largely mediated through socially structured learning experiences. The individual's social background and social role characteristics are especially important here, for they largely *mediate* the impact of the more general contextual factors, especially the cultural and social structural factors. An individual's personality and capacities are thus most importantly molded by those aspects of social structure and culture which characterize him, his parents, or his significant others as social roles. The bio-physical nature of the human population and the environment can also have an impact on personality, though probably only a weak one. Again the impact of specific voluntary groups at this stage of the model is likely to be largely in terms of selection effects, in this case usually *informal* selection effects rather than formal requirements.

Both social background and personality and capacities in turn are viewed as affecting the individual's general attitudes toward voluntary action. Then all of these—together with the actual nature of a particular voluntary group—affect the specific voluntary group-related attitudes of the individual. General attitudes are thus seen as influences on, but not the sole determinants of, specific attitudes relevant to voluntary action.

The last set of determinants are both the most specific and the most immediate—the stimuli impinging on the individual in a particular situation relevant to a particular formal voluntary group. Very little research has yet been done at this level (e.g., examining how an individual first learns of a particular voluntary group, how he perceives the situation when specifically asked to join by a neighbor, etc.). The individual's perception of the situation will not be determined solely by the *objective* nature of the given situation and the given formal voluntary group. His perception of situational stimuli will also be affected by his general and specific attitudes toward the group, as well as by his broader personality, capacities, and social role characteristics.

Finally, all of the foregoing factors can have a direct effect (and often multifarious kinds of indirect effects) on the voluntary action of a given individual in a given group context. When all of these kinds of determinants (as spelled out in detail in earlier chapters) are brought to bear simultaneously on predicting and explaining participation, we may expect to account for quite substantial portions of the variance in empirical studies of individual voluntary action, as will be seen in a moment.

A Synopsis of Relevant Empirical Findings

Our review of prior research relevant to the foregoing model has mainly given us evidence bearing on each major predictor class as a single cluster, without generally controlling for the impact of other classes. Nevertheless, the evidence is still relevant. Let us look at it briefly.

Very little systematic research has been done relating historical factors affecting the culture, social structure, and subcultures of a society or the current culture and special subcultures of a society with patterns of individual participation in organized voluntary action. What evidence we do have bears more on the different but related question of the incidence and prevalence of voluntary organizations *per se* rather than on individual rates and patterns of membership in and participation in those organizations. While a number of highly plausible factors have been identified (levels of modernization, levels of collective action orientation, development of patterns of formal organization, the acceptance and/or promotion of pluralism, etc.) and some consistent evidence supporting those factors has been gathered, we do not now know to what extent variation in one of these factors or in a combination of these factors has affected variations in rates of individual membership in voluntary organizations or variations in rates of individual participation in those organizations.

The best documented effects of the current social structure on rates and patterns of individual participation in organized voluntary action deal with the influence of the socioeconomic level of the local community on participation. While this evidence is not yet extensive, the studies to date are consistent in showing that there is a relationship (usually relatively small) between higher socioeconomic levels in a community and higher levels of individual voluntary action. While there are strong theoretical reasons to consider other social structural elements including the degree of organizational development of a community, the size of the community, etc. and some suggestive research has been done along these lines, we do not yet have full confirmation through a series of replications.

The dynamic interface between organizational factors and the individual are the formal and informal eligibility requirements devised by the organization. These requirements specify who *can be*, and of those who can be, in some measure, those who *will be*, members of the organization and participants in its activities. There is a marked lack of empirical evidence on the development, maintenance, and change of either formal or informal eligibility requirements.

In recent years a number of researchers have investigated various organizational factors related to rates of participation within voluntary organizations. However, the effects of factors such as organizational control, benefits, levels of formalization, etc. have only been probed in relatively few studies so that the amount of variance to be associated with each in determining individual participation rates is unclear. This emphasis on organizational factors seems highly promising with the thrust of the research to date indicating that the more the organization is structured to allow the individual to participate meaningfully in its affairs and the more the individual can benefit through his participation, the greater the likelihood of both membership and participation.

There is substantial evidence that factors associated with the life cycle (age, marital status, number of children, age of children, etc.) are related to membership and participation in organized voluntary action. While the strength of the evidence varies with the respective factors identified and at times the relationship may be inconsistent or curvilinear, it is clear that these factors are related to membership and participation. The degree to which these effects are direct or are indirect is not yet established in the empirical research, though it would seem that life cycle factors play a major role in eligibility criteria, in the development of significant-other influences, and in the amount and use of leisure time.

The overwhelming weight of evidence is that socioeconomic status has a positive influence on the number of memberships an individual has in voluntary organizations, the amount the individual participates in an organization, the likelihood of the individual taking on leadership roles, etc. The evidence is stronger for the more direct measures of the individual's current status (income, education, occupational status, home ownership, etc.) than for less direct measures (family or lineage status, occupational mobility, etc.). However, since socioeconomic factors are so often related to formal and informal eligibility requirements, which means that most voluntary organizations are more or less homogeneous regarding SES, thus restricting the amount of variation in SES within a given organization, socioeconomic factors tend to explain more of the variance in the number of memberships an individual has than in the amount an individual participates within a given organization.

Research to date on the relationship between socio-physical characteristics and participation in organized voluntary action leaves many questions unanswered. There has been very little attention given to the effects of either personal health or individual physical abilities. Further, while there is research that shows that factors such as sex, race, and ethnicity affect the type of organization an individual joins (through the effects of eligibility criteria), there is only mixed and inconclusive evidence on whether an individual of a given sex, race, or ethnic group, other factors being equal, is more or less likely to participate actively in a given voluntary organization.

Research data are currently insufficient on the relationship between general organizational affiliations and roles and individual participation in organized voluntary action. Data from work and from school settings hint at a "spill over" effect with traits, skills, interests, and orientations developed or used in those settings influencing patterns of membership and participation. However, currently there seems to be more evidence that work and school roles influence the *type of organization* joined than the *number of memberships* an individual has and the *amount he participates*. While there is evidence that religion may influence the type of organization an individual joins (especially for those organizations of a partially religious nature), there is little evidence that, when other factors are controlled, religious affiliations affect the number of memberships an individual has or his rate of participation. While there is substantial evidence that political participation and other forms of voluntary action are linked, there is no conclusive evidence that membership in a given political party or holding a given political philosophy affects rates of membership and participation in other forms of voluntary action.

Despite the theoretical importance of significant-other influences and of personal influence patterns on a wide range of behavior including individual voluntary action, surprisingly little research has been done to confirm and evaluate the nature and the extent of the relationships involved. While the number of memberships and the amount of participation of parents, of spouses, and of friends have been found to influence those rates for the given individual, sufficient research has not yet been done to indicate the strength of these relationships.

Research on the influence of mass media exposure on individual participation in voluntary action, while consistent, is still scanty. To date there appears to be a positive relationship between greater mass media exposure and higher rates of membership and of activity, but the extent of this relationship is unclear and undetermined.

There are indications that both migration and the length of residence in a given community influence membership and activity in voluntary organizations. While there are strong theoretical reasons for believing these factors are influential, the research to date has not effectively distinguished between these factors and other possible background influences that may affect ease of adjustment or tendencies to participate. However, studies noting the negative effect of migration on membership and participation find that effect to diminish rapidly and substantially with time. Length of residence seems to favor membership and participation for the most part, the exception being that very long periods of residence coincide with increasing age, and as age increases beyond middle age, membership and participation tend to decrease.

There is very strong evidence of positive relationships between membership and participation in organized voluntary action and two personality traits: achievement motivation, competence and efficacy on the one hand and ego-strength and adjustment on the other. While each is influential in determining memberships, they are more powerful predictors of activity.

Traits associated with extraversion, sociability, and trust as well as traits associated with dominance and assertiveness have also been found with some frequency to be positively related to membership and especially to participation.

Some evidence exists showing the influence of empathy and relational closeness and of morality and superego strength on increased rates of individual membership and participation in organized voluntary action.

The possible effects of personality traits such as flexibility, energy and activity levels, and planning and future time perspectives on rates and patterns of individual participation have barely been explored. What evidence we have indicates positive relationships.

Individual capacities, while of theoretical signifiance, have also been virtually ignored in the literature on the correlates of individual membership and participation. Factors such as verbal abilities and general intelligence, spatial and numerical abilities, mechanical-motor skills, social skills, etc. have either only rarely or never been included in studies investigating individual participation in organized voluntary action. Those few studies that have investigated the relationship between verbal measures of intelligence and rates of membership and participation have found a substantial positive correlation. The future investigation of capacities would seem to hold substantial promise.

Of the general attitudes, those attitudes toward the community, the overall sense of obligation to participate, and a preference for formal groups have the strongest confirmation as being positively related to membership and participation in organized voluntary action.

Attitudes toward leisure and those toward various characteristics of voluntary organizations in general as well as attitudes toward one's previous experience in voluntary organizations and one's sense of significant-others' attitudes toward voluntary action are to date relatively unexplored as are attitudes toward various institutional areas.

Attitudes toward various characteristics of the specific voluntary organization (e.g., its attractiveness, its efficacy, etc.) have been found to be highly related to individual membership and participation. The same holds true for significant-others' influences, as well as one's personal experiences within the specific organization (personal fit and personal integration).

There is some evidence of a relationship between attitudes such as an obligation to participate in the organization or commitment to the organization and rates of membership and participation.

Virtually no research evidence has accumulated relating the individual's attitudes toward the life and activities of the specific organization or his attitudes toward and involvement in various aspects of the organization's activities and his rate of activity or his continued membership.

There has been a lack of systematic research interest in those proximate situational stimuli that increase the likelihood of individual membership and participation in organized voluntary action. Some evidence exists, however, that focuses on the importance of personal influence (personal contact and interpersonal pressures) in inducing membership and encouraging member participation. When respected acquaintances or close friends are involved in these processes, there appears to be a greater likelihood of a decision being made and of membership and participation. The personal influence of significant-others as well as other situational stimuli serve to create and to form a vital part of the "decisional field" that confronts the individual about to make his choice of whether to affiliate or not with a given organization as well as a continual series of choices as a member regarding whether to continue activity and, if activity is to be continued within the organization, what forms or types it will take and how extensive it will be.

The Effects of Using Various Measures of Individual Participation

Only two published studies known to the authors have attempted to examine the relative and composite impact of several of the major classes of predictors in the model using a multiple regression analysis approach. Smith (1966) found in his study of various voluntary groups in Chile that he could account for *56 percent of the variance in the rated participation of individuals in specific organizations* using measures of four of the classes in the model: social background, personality, general attitudes, and specific attitudes. For this particular kind of dependent variable, he found that personality factors were the most powerful predictors (44 percent of the variance when used alone), followed in strength by specific attitudes (35 percent of the variance), by general attitudes (24 percent), and then by social background variables (12 percent). The relevant path analysis was not performed.

In the same study, Smith (1966) compared the members of a variety of groups with non-members who were roughly matched on several social background characteristics (thus reducing the natural variation in background characteristics within the sample, but putting the personality and attitude variables to a more stringent test as discriminators of membership versus non-membership). Moreover, the non-members were selected to be generally non-members of all kinds of voluntary groups, not simply non-members of the specific groups for which there were members in the sample. Using the same classes of predictors as above, *71 percent of the variance in membership/non-membership* could be accounted for. For this dependent variable, specific attitudes were the strongest single cluster of predictors when used alone (59 percent of the variance), followed by general attitudes (42 percent), and personality variables (28 percent). Because of the matching procedure, social background variables made no additional contribution to variance explained when the other three classes of variables were already included in the prediction equation.

Rogers' (1971) study of several farm-related voluntary groups in the United States replicated generally the "internal participation" aspect of Smith's study. His dependent variable was a composite of attendance, recruitment of new members, and policy support for the group. Unlike Smith, he used measures of only three of the four classes of predictors noted above (omitting any measures of the personality realm). A multiple regression analysis revealed that *38 percent of the variance in his composite participation variable* could be accounted for by his three predictor classes. Since the personality measures were omitted and appeared to be the strongest single cluster in Smith's study, the amount of variance explained by Rogers is roughly in line with what Smith found for a comparable dependent variable.

Perhaps more importantly, Rogers found that the *rank order* of predictor clusters in affecting participation was identical with the ordering Smith found: specific attitudes were most powerful (34 percent of the variance when used alone), followed by general attitudes (13 percent) and then by social background variables (only 4 percent). A detailed comparison of the other portions of the path model for these two studies is not yet available. Nevertheless, the two studies indicate two important points: (1) *A substantial amount of the variance in individual voluntary participation within organizations can be accounted for by the personal factors portion of the model. And* (2) *there appears to be some stability across both studies and countries* (with admittedly scanty evidence!) *in the manner in which a portion of the general model predicts participation within voluntary associations.*

The two separate portions of Smith's study itself confirm another important point, suggested earlier in this chapter: *The major variable clusters of the model will probably have different weights when markedly different kinds of participation measures are used* (e.g., membership versus participation once a member; membership/non-membership in a given organization versus number of memberships in various voluntary organizations).

Further analyses of these two sets of data, and re-analyses by multiple regression and path analysis techniques of earlier sets of data collected by others may shed further light on the value and validity of the proposed model. The forthcoming study by Smith (1972a) of voluntary activity in eight Massachusetts towns will also attempt to test the model in greater depth.

Needs for Future Research

A variety of needs for further research have been stated in the earlier chapters of Part Two, so that there is no need to recapitulate substantive research gaps area by area. By contrast, there are some methodological needs or gaps that perhaps cannot be stated too often. (The reader will please bear with us here if the partial repetition is bothersome.)

Some of the needs that have been brought out earlier are the following, in no particular order: more replications of all kinds, more longitudinal studies on all aspects of voluntary action research, broader and more representative samples both of individuals and of voluntary groups, greater attention to national and cultural variations, more attention to the personal meaning of voluntary action to individual participants, more focus on individual participation "careers" in voluntary groups, more attention to the possible variations in findings if different kinds of participation measures are used (use of multiple criterion measures), and more use of multivariate analysis techniques.

There are also some points that earlier chapters have not touched on. For instance, a great deal more attention needs to be given to testing the reliability and validity of the predictors and especially the participation measures used in the present kind of study. A great deal more variance can be explained with a reliable variable than with an unreliable one, as many of our currently used ones may well be. This raises the matter of multivariate analysis, which has been mentioned earlier. We feel strongly that more progress could be made in the present area of voluntary action theory and research if more investigators would take the trouble to use multiple regression analysis and specifically path analysis techniques, or at least *some* kind of multivariate technique that permits proportional-reduction-of-error-variance interpretations and that permits assignment of differential weights to a variety of predictors.

A related point is the need for more thorough study of the interrelationships *among* the various kinds of explanatory variables reviewed in the past four chapters. We are much clearer that certain kinds of variables seem to be important when taken alone, or with one or two simple controls, than we are clear about how important each variable is when a larger number of other confounding variables is controlled. And we need to know the *conditions* under which certain variables become important or unimportant for a given kind of dependent participation variable. One very obvious condition affecting the apparent importance of nearly every predictor variable studied is sampling. When a representative random sample of persons is studied the results should be different in specifiable ways from the results that would be found using matched samples of members and non-members, for instance. This does *not* mean that only general, representative population samples are relevant. It does mean that we need to draw conclusions from each piece of research that take into account the conditions under which the participation phenomena were studied. At present we cannot even begin to do this because of our limited understanding of how all of the various factors we have reviewed fit together and influence each other.

Perhaps our greatest need, then, is for more studies that include *several* classes of predictor variables from those represented in Figure 15-1. Most studies reviewed in Part Two of this volume have dealt with only one or at most two classes of explanatory variables. Only when more researchers begin to design more comprehensive research projects on the determinants of individual participation in organized voluntary action will we be able to move toward refinement of the proposed model and/or the substitution of more adequate models. Such refinement will, of course, include more detailed specification of how variables are interrelated *within* the broad clusters of variables we have so roughly portrayed. Another obvious major area of eventual refinement will be the creation of a truly dynamic model, rather than the primitive, static one suggested here. Still, we must crawl before we can walk, and walk before we can run. We hope the present book and this chapter in particular will help move us along the path somewhat faster.

References

Allport, Gordon
1951 "Prejudice: A Problem in Psychological and Social Causation." In T. Parsons and E. Shils (eds.), *Toward a General Theory of Action*, Cambridge, Mass.: Harvard University Press.
1954 *The Nature of Prejudice.* Reading, Mass.: Addison-Wesley Press.
Rogers, David L.
1971 "Contrasts Between Behavioral and Affective Involvement in Voluntary Associations: An Exploratory Analysis," *Rural Sociology* (36) no. 3:340-58.
Smith, David Horton
1964 "Psychological Factors Affecting Formal Voluntary Organization Participation in Chile," Unpublished Ph.D. dissertation, Cambridge, Mass.: Harvard University.
1966 "A Psychological Model of Individual Participation in Formal Voluntary Organizations: Application to Some Chilean Data," *American Journal of Sociology* 72:249-66.
1972a *Voluntary Activity in Eight Massachusetts Towns*, Draft of unpublished monograph, Boston College, Institute of Human Sciences.
1972b "Organizational Boundaries and Organizational Affiliates," *Sociology and Social Research* (in press).
Smith, David Horton, with Allon Fisher
1971 "Toward a Comparative Theory of the Incidence and Prevalence of Volun-

tary Associations." Paper presented to the Panel on Voluntary Associations in South and East Asia, Association for Asian Studies Annual Meeting, Washington, D.C.

Part Three: The Altruistic Impulse and the Good Society

16 The Altruistic Impulse and the Good Society

CHARLES K. WARRINER

Most men in this time and culture, as in any era, live out their lives in a nest of events constrained by the web of that particular history within which they are caught. For them, the world is given. When they recognize broad processes or basic principles guiding these events, they see these as fixed and immutable. And so, the problem of their lives is to live as best they can within this framework. Some are especially vulnerable to the inequities, the accidents, and the cruelties of their time, but even at best most men face crisis and catastrophes, stumble, fall, and suffer.

The curse of some few men is that they have a vision of a different and better world possible through human action. In this sense they are humanitarians for they believe that man is the source of his own salvation and that by amending the laws of their time, by altering the processes in which they are involved, by changing the forces which impose the painful particulars of their own and other's lives they can attain the good society.

Throughout history such men have attempted in one way of another to alter the web of history. And they have often been successful. For centuries men lifted and carried heavy loads, accepting the strain upon their backs as a necessary condition of their servitude to nature. For centuries men lived under the threat of cholera and other plagues, accepting these epidemics as a natural consequence of God's wrath or of nature's cruelty. At various times men have lived under the yoke of despots, accepting these political systems as the natural order of the social world.

Men of imagination changed all that by their invention of the wheel and the machine, by their creation of vaccines and innoculations, and by their recognition that social and political orders may be varied and diverse. They successfully changed the course of history.

Yet, for all that things have changed as a consequence of vision, of knowledge, and action, they remain the same. Although the wheel and the machine took the burden off of men's backs, they have brought their own new tyrannies. Although medical knowledge has removed the spectre of death from major diseases of the past, modern industrial society has created new problems of illness and infirmity. Every human problem solved is followed by new human problems.

And so today, most men, as they always have, live their lives of quiet desperation caught up in events which they have little capacity for controlling and which involve their own disasters, heartaches, and sufferings. Children still die, though now more often from the wheel than from disease; loved one's are still broken by the wheel of life, though now more often by mental than by physical stress; men still suffer from arbitrariness not of their own making, though now more often from impersonal bureaucracies than from absolute monarchs.

Despite this, it is in our era, of all times, that faith is strongest in the ability to bring about a better world. More men spend more time than ever before in attempting to alleviate general human sadness and suffering, to improve the human condition, to bring heaven down to earth. The chapters in this book have been in some part, at least, inspired by the faith that something can be done. At the same time, is it not remarkable that in this time so many men lose heart, become apathetic, or seek escape from the human condition because life has lost its meaning?

Does this imply that the efforts of the past were of little avail? Does it mean that we have merely changed things without improving human life? Does it mean that the humanitarian effort of voluntary action, in part the focus of the chapters in this volume and the series it begins will have little value in increasing human happiness?

Not at all! Progress has been real enough though men still suffer. Few persons would argue that the elimination of many physical burdens has not improved the lot of men, extended life expectancy, and made it possible for them to be more human and less brutish. That we have other, more sophisticated sources of suffering is merely the essential dilemma of human progress. It appears inevitable to me that as we become more human, as we cast off the yoke of brute history, our capacity for suffering—in contrast to merely feeling pain—increases.

But progress toward the good society involves two elements of which the amelioration of certain of men's conditions is only one. Whatever the sources of our pain and of the torments imposed upon us by our particular world, we can live with these and surpass them in a satisfying and even joyful human life only as others participate in our lives through empathy and sympathy. It is only as others, touched by the altruistic impulse, come to our side that life is fully worthwhile.

The material aid given by the altruistic impulse, directly and personally expressed, may have little affect upon the lot of the sufferer. His fate is unchanged. But what he gains, what both gain, is a reaffirmation of their humanness and the destruction of their isolation and loneliness. No matter what the nature of our material condition, no matter what the burden, it is tolerable only when we know that others care about us, only when we know that others feel what we are feeling, only when we know that ours is a shared and not a lonely burden. Men cannot long survive as humans without the kind of interpersonal relationships that break their isolation.

In our search for the good society we have emphasized the first of these elements of progress and have neglected the second. *We have been more concerned with the external material conditions of people's lives than with the subjective conditions of their lives*—their quality of life, to use a popular phrase. Our philanthropy has lost the human touch. If we are to make the most of our opportunities for effective altruism, if we are to make our voluntary associations and our volunteer activities effective means toward attaining the good society, we must learn how to improve the human touch.

There are at least four major expressions of the altruistic impulse. Each is necessary and each must be in some ways consonant with the others if we are to make real progress toward the better society. Each of these forms contributes in a different way to changing the circumstances of our lives and to our ability to bear the circumstances we cannot change.

Empathy and Personal Altruism

In every time and in every place some men are especially touched by the sufferings of their neighbors. By their empathy with others they are particularly attuned to and receptive of the altruistic impulse. Such men have helped to carry the other's burden, have offered sympathy and love in times of grief, have given their own, often meager goods to ameliorate another's greater need. They have walked with the other through the lonely hours and down the lonely miles, though their own paths called them other ways.

Such altruistic acts stem from the capacity to *be* for a moment the other person, to stand in his shoes not as one's self merely transposed, but as if he himself is standing there. And empathy is more than a product of communication in the sense of message sending, it is active communing. I have elsewhere argued that such communication is the unique attribute of humanness and is essential if men are to surpass the bounds of their isolation and alienation, and to create a society in which they are more than merely parts of the environment with little relationship to one another (Warriner, 1970, chap. 4).

The practice of this form of communication is at a low ebb in our modern urban, chaotic society and as a result this form of the altruistic impulse is stifled. Some would trace this loss to the kinds of personalities which we build and, as discussed by Reddy and Smith (chap. 13 in this volume), seek the personality traits and capacities which engender the altruistic impulse in its various forms. If, on the other hand, we recognize that humans may be continuously emergent and that their personalities are a function of the continuity of their experiences with others, then we must look to the forms and patterns of the society for an explanation of the loss of the human touch. Many such sources could be identified, but three appear to be of central importance.

a. The Death of Cultural Norms of Personal Altruism. At most times and in most, though not all societies—our own urban, heterogeneous, symbiotic society especially excepted—culturally established patterns of personal altruism have been apparent. The frontier custom of hospitality to the traveling stranger, the rural community custom of plowing and planting for a sick man or the new widow, and the neighborly food and presence at times of illness and death were such cultural patterns of personal altruism. These cultural patterns are important for they do not depend upon the altruistic impulse or the capacity for empathy that any particular person may have. One brought food to the wake, opened the door to the stranger, and lent a hand at the harvest even if burdened with the soul of a misanthrope. These normatively supported patterns not only ensure that those in need receive help, but through the self-fulfilling processes engender the altruistic impulse.

Although instances of personal altruism may be found in the crowded urban street and in the lonely institutional corridor, the normative sanction for these has been lost. Much more widespread are the opposing norms of avoiding involvement, staying out of other people's business, and leaving it up to the police or social workers, (an example being the fatal stabbing of Kitty Genovese in New York City while forty uninvolved citizens looked on). The older norms have been lost because the situations by which they were defined no longer exist. The objective conditions of life have changed and we have not developed new norms for the new situations.

b. The Increasing Rationalization of Activities. Ever since the industrial revolution, there has been a growing rationalization of work and other activities so that the paramount criteria for guiding action have become differentiation, specialization, and efficiency in the achievement of limited productive goals. Work has been ripped out of the context of interpersonal relations so that men at work become parts of productive machines rather than parts of a network of social relations. Our churches and our schools, affected by the same forces, have evolved out of the context of human interaction. Large congregations and large classes produce audiences rather than participants in an interpersonal system. Even the family has been stretched apart by the individuated claims upon the time of family members.

These patterns of the present world reduce for all of us the opportunities for communion with others and turn interaction into a superficial information exchange. Many persons are left in the backwash of society, isolated by secondary relations at work and in leisure. They have neither families nor other small associations in which their needs for communion can be satisfied.

That such interpersonal relations are not available to many is dramatically shown by the men and women who cry out for the human touch. The growth of the hippie communes, the appeal of the "Jesus-freak" community, the rapid adoption of "group-grope therapies," and in less dramatic form, the rising incidence of psychiatric needs all demonstrate that many are isolated and alone. The synthetic euphoria of the "trip," individuated, isolating, and lonely, cannot replace the practice of humanistic altruism.

c. The Growth of the Chaotic Society. Philip Hauser (1969) has described ours as a "chaotic society," as a result of the population explosion, implosion, and differentiation. Although there may be other causes, we do have a society in which collective patterns of action are crumbling, in which coordination of action is weak or coerced by either convenience or force (cf. Etzioni, 1961), in which our relations with most people is symbiotic and informed only by temporary expediency. We use language gestures as bludgeons, manipulating others, rather than as tools of communication and communion. In such a society the exploitive, self-serving, and self-aggrandizing attitude is the norm for men who are isolated, alienated, and alone. Empathy is seldom possible for we are not usually involved in the kinds of continuing interaction in which we are permitted or encouraged to identify with another's experience.

Throughout the years preachers and prophets, poets and philosophers, from the Chinese to the Egyptian, from the Mohammedan to the Judeo-Christian, from the pagan to the sophisticated, have seen the necessity for love. They have known that our lives are bleak, barren, and brutish without the communion with others that leads to the altruistic impulse. But love is not enough to build the good society. *Love does not change the human condition, it only makes it human.*

Sympathy and Cooperative Altruism

In every society there are occasions of crisis and catastrophe and painful yokes common to many men. Floods and fires, epidemics and pestilential invasions, subjugation, and poverty attack many men at once. Though these are common conditions, men will often treat them as unique individual problems and seek a solution for themselves alone, suffering not only from their problems but also from "pluralistic ignorance." These may be occasions when each seeks only his own small advantage.

However, sometimes, men recognize that their's is not a unique situation and that others too are suffering as they are suffering. Because they are able, as themselves, to stand in the other's shoes and know something of what the other feels they are able to sympathize with him. They know that they suffer in common and so they may be struck by the altruistic impulse to invite the other to join in a mutual search for some advantage in the situation.

Such cooperative endeavors are found in all societies and at all times. Some cultures have emphasized this approach to life problems and provide models and normative sanctions to promote such action. Other cultures treat life as a zero-sum game in which there is no increase in the total value to be obtained by cooperative effort. Sociologically, we are most aware of cooperative altruism when it is expressed in formal voluntary associations such as the Rochdale Cooperatives formed by the weavers in England in the last century, the mutual benefit societies of the American community, or the attenuated form of legally sanctioned benefit districts. However, the latter may lose their character as cooperative endeavors and become institutional agencies serving clients, their former members (cf., Warriner, 1961).

The essential element in the successful formation of cooperative altruistic efforts is the capacity for sympathy, the ability to stand in each others' shoes, the ability to play the role of the other. Without sympathy there is no possibility of subordinating one's own small advantage to the collective welfare. Thus, the scope of such cooperative organization is limited by both the commonality of the life situation and by the existing patterns of interaction and identity.

The obvious value and success of such organizations in improving the common conditions of life have often led to attempts to generate this form of altruism in similar situations. I am told that in Honduras officials in one government agency were particularly struck by the success of indigeneous cooperative farming by the peasants on a certain neglected banana plantation. These officials wanted to promote this form of self-help in other areas and persuaded others to take on the form of this endeavor. However, these subsequent induced cooperatives were beset by "selfish" patterns: individual farmers failed to put their effort into the common enterprise and managers absconded with the funds. The same failures can be found in the United States and in any other locale where the imposition of synthetic cooperative endeavors has been attempted. These failures stem, I believe, from the lack of a common recognition of a common problem among the members of the created group, and from the lack of sympathy and the altruistic impulse which it engenders. When sympathy is lacking, no matter how good the organization looks on paper, each man will use the organization for his own ends, exploiting it for his own purposes and small advantages.

The evidence (cf., Curtis and Zurcher, 1971) suggests that in our attempts to organize cooperative endeavors among the poor and the blacks today we are failing in the same way. The common situation is not sufficient condition for the emergence of sympathy and of the cooperative altruistic impulse and consequently we find apathy, self-aggrandisement, and the exploitation of the poor by the poor and the black by the black within what we hoped would be approaches to the better society. Saul Alinsky, attempting to promote a common recognition of a common situation, is starting with the more fundamental issue as is the Black Power movement, but it is questionable whether the hate for others engendered in these programs is conducive to sympathy within the group.

Cooperative altruism, when it does occur, makes three major contributions toward the good society. It changes the material situation and thus alters the process of history, for this particular group at least. The peasants on the banana plantations, the weavers in England, and the small farmers in America were economically better off through the success of their cooperative endeavors. Secondly, by involving coordinate action and patterns of interaction, it reduces for this group the impact of the chaotic, symbiotic society. And finally, by providing opportunities for communication and communion, it increases the opportunity for empathy and the human touch.

Anthropopathy and Philanthropy

Empathy occurs when men recognize their common feelings and attitudes and are thus able to sorrow *as one*. *Sympathy* occurs when men share a common situation and thus are able to sorrow *together*. *Anthropopathy* occurs when men are different but recognize the capacity for suffering in others, thus they sorrow *for* others.

Recognizing that others may suffer, some men are struck by the altruistic impulse to do something *for* them, and so they send aid or attempt to organize general programs of relief or assistance to make changes in the other's circumstances—they then express the philanthropic form of altruism.

In contrast to other forms, philanthropy is based upon and increases the separation between those giving and those receiving aid. *Where personal altruism serves primarily to maintain a common identity, and where cooperative altruism increases the strength of the interpersonal relationships, philanthropy serves to widen the gulf between people. Doing for is not doing with or being with.* The very nature of the aid, the fact that it does not necessarily fit the scheme of needs of the receiver, as well as the impersonal and chauvinistic way in which it is presented, often serve as a symbolic affirmation of the differences in situation and circumstances.

Although philanthropy may alter the objective situation of others, it often does so without understanding the nature of their sorrow, the sources of their discomfort, or the character of their conception of the good society. Because of our peculiar folk-psychologies and our implicit beliefs that the poor and others are in trouble because of some motivational or moral failure of their own, we often impose conditions to our philanthropy: to get soup one must first be converted, to secure aid for one's children one must avoid men, to get assistance for the elderly, one must sign away the home of a lifetime. At the very least, one must tug his forelock and bowing low offer humble thanks to his benefactor.

As a result philanthropy, directly or indirectly, often imposes new strands in the spider web of history in which people are caught. We add to the constraints, the forces and impositions over which they have no control. Is it no wonder then that the welfare mothers, the blacks in the ghettos and the natives on the other islands say "whitey (or Uncle or welfare worker) go home, leave us alone!"

I must admit to a jaundiced view of philanthropic efforts for I believe that, as Willie (1970) says, "the ideas and attitudes of the sub-dominants . . . [tend to be] ignored or forgotten." Unless touched by sympathy and empathy, anthropopathy leads to separation and differentiation between those in need and those who aid. The typical anonymity of philanthropy (as for example in giving to the

United Fund or Community Chest), is a means of avoiding interaction, of avoiding involvement and its consequences—sympathy and empathy. Most philanthropic efforts probably do more for the philanthropist than for those he purports to aid. The delusion of most philanthropy is that it does good for others. At the very least, we must admit that adequate evaluations are lacking to demonstrate the objective value of philanthropy to the recipients.

Not all philanthropy has been exclusively dominated by anthropopathy. When it has been touched by sympathy and empathy, when those giving aid have become in part those being aided, then such assistance takes on some of the elements of cooperative altruism. But most frequently our philanthropy has become organized and rationalized, bureaucratized and institutionalized. Welfare agencies become more concerned with their domains than with the character of their altruism; and thus become an extension of the problem rather than a solution. Even at best they have focused more upon the objective conditions of men's lives than on their human needs (cf., Stanton, 1970).

But, philanthropy is a necessary element in a society where men are more dissimilar in circumstance and point of view than they are alike. Some are more vulnerable than others to the special disabilities of their time and these disabilities become self-perpetuating and expanding without outside help. If so, then we must learn, more clearly than we have, the appropriate and necessary scope of philanthropy, and how such efforts can be leavened by sympathy and empathy, and how they can be tied to and generate the cooperative and personal forms of altruism.

The Altruistic Impulse, Social Change, and Collective Altruism

Altruism in most of its expressions has little impact upon the larger forces and processes that lead to men's sorrows. Personal altruism at best relieves only the very immediate and temporary conditions of men's lives, cooperative altruism can ameliorate broader situational factors and improve the relative advantage of the participants, philanthropy may help remove special disabilities and provide basic sustaining conditions, but none of these forms of altruism as we have described them attack or try to change the fundamental laws, the basic forces, or the global processes that constrain these situations. Although the peasant's lot may be improved through cooperative farming, it does not alter the economic, political, and social forces which produce peasantry. Although philanthropy may sustain life in the poor, it does nothing about the sources of poverty. In sum, much altruistic activity can only purport to deal with the *symptoms* of a problem rather than the problem per se.

In the person of imagination, the concern for others—whether stemming from empathy, sympathy or anthropopathy—takes on an especially poignant form, for he sees one man's catastrophe multiplied by all men. For him the despot's lash on the prisoner's back is a thousand lashes on a thousand backs; the death of a neighbor from puerperal fever is the death of thousands of women in childbirth; the starving child of the street is a million children of neglect.

The arms of such a person cannot succor all these lonely children of God and so he seeks to find a new world in which pain and suffering no longer exist. His altruistic impulse leads him to seek a change in the conditions of pain and sorrow for all, not just to alleviate the burden of those present or to share the sorrow of those he knows.

Some of these men remain dreamers and draftsmen, content to portray their vision of the world-that-should-be in poems and pictures. But other men of imagination seek more active expressions of their concern. They attempt to take action upon the sources of man's difficulties; such men seek to change the world by re-forming it, either by revolution or reformation.

When the gap between his vision of the good and the present condition of man is blatant, and when his world view is apocalyptic and cataclysmic, such a man will turn to revolution and attempt the total destruction of the present social world. He feels that only through the ashes of the present can the eden of the future be built.

Although this position may genuinely stem from the altruistic impulse, it is often difficult to see the altruism; for such a position requires the willingness to sacrifice many men today in order to hope for the future. It is a view that only the most alienated and impatient of us can afford to accept because it requires the rejection of empathy and sympathy.

There are others, however, whose vision and impatience for the good society are tempered by sympathy for the man who is living today. He is unwilling to pay the present cost for a dramatic new world tomorrow. He therefore seeks re-formulation of the world through less drastic processes. It is true that often such men would have much to lose by putting the present world to the torch for they are not without hope. And because they are hopeful, they can afford sympathy and empathy.

This form of collective altruism leads to a variety of movements, programs, and associations designed to change in some large or small measure the process of history for all men. Sometimes these efforts are misguided for lack of knowledge or for mistaken belief; sometimes they fail for lack of leverage and the means to achieve the ends sought. Success, furthermore, is often hard to perceive or lies only in a vision of the future. Despite these limitations, there appears to have been a significant increase in this form of collective altruism in recent years—the Zero Population Growth programs, the attacks on pollution, and Common Cause are among the more recent manifestations of collective concern leading to collective action. These collective actions often seem a long way from the altruistic impulse. Men may use such movements and organizations for their own purposes. Kooks, firebrands, and misanthropes may play out their own nightmares within the shelter of new movements. On the other side, programs may be caught up in bureaucratic forms and self-serving, self-sustaining practices which lose sight of the altruistic collective goals with which they started.

The frequent failure of such programs from lack of knowledge leads some to believe that we can achieve this part of the search for the good society only through improved knowledge of the basic processes and principles of the world. This often leads to the expression of the altruistic impulse by the turning toward science and the search for knowledge. I suspect that for many of the authors in this volume, as for myself, the humanitarian sentiment was at least one factor in our career decisions, as well as being a factor in writing the foregoing chapters.

It is often difficult to mobilize men to act in collective altruistic movements. The immediate improvement for their own and others' lives appears small and the future seems a long way off. More importantly, participation depends upon confidence in the knowledge which specifies the relation between the latent, hidden and abstract forces and the particulars which we wish to change. Most of all, there must be a vision of and confidence in the better society as emerging from the present.

But without effective, informed, and visionary collective altruism we shall be unable to get out of the constraint of the web of history. It is for this reason that we must learn how to organize and sustain such efforts, whether through already established institutions (whether voluntary, commercial, or of government) or through new organizations and new kinds of collective behavior.

Voluntary Associations and the Good Society

The altruistic impulse, at whatever level, is promoted by and is expressed through interaction with others. The kind of altruism generated is a function of the kinds of inter-human relationships involved. The association with others is an important consideration in any concern with altruism. In our social world the voluntary association is especially important. Professor Bode (in chap. 4 of this volume) identifies this relevance when he says: "Voluntary associations seem to represent a kind of filling and connecting tissue between major social structures and between individuals and their situations."

It has not always been so. In some societies all relationships and activities are organized by an encompassing kinship system. All persons, by birth, are caught up in a network of relationships which they cannot avoid. At other times, as in the earlier American society, the local community was the encompassing system and one was caught up in networks of relationships by residence. One could be isolated only by the exercise of considerable resistance to the importuning of the church, the school, the neighborhood system, the volunteer fire department, and the lodge. Although institutional agencies and voluntary associations existed, they were part of a single network of relations and each, including the family, served in that network. One's economic relations could not be divorced from his family associations, nor the family from the church, nor the lodge from the city government. Here such voluntary associations, if indeed in that context they could be called voluntary, were not filling and connecting tissue, but were the very fiber of the community.

Today, however, we have lost the sense of community by growth, by mobility and differentiation, and, especially, by the institutionalization of separate activities. Work takes place in one large institution, play takes place in another, personal maintenance (i.e., shopping, eating, and sleeping) in others. The school, the church, and the government have each developed large programs of activities encapsulated in their own organizations. But most importantly each has rationalized its activities to eliminate patterns of stable and continuous interpersonal relations (cf., Warriner, 1964). In this context, the voluntary association, whether formal or not, takes on a heightened significance. *In our society there are at least five important functions of such associations.*

1. For many people the voluntary association is the only source of communion with others, the only place where we can come to stable, common understandings about ourselves and the world or some small part of it. Because the family is no longer subject to strong institutional sanctions—even the marriage ceremony is losing its popularity—we must soon count it as just another voluntary association. It is often less able than other associations to provide a stable relationship for its members.

2. As societal maintenance and control activities became lodged in even larger bureaucracies—work, religion, education, government, and recreation—the client of these services becomes ever more powerless and the voluntary association, as a cooperative endeavor to control this aspect of one's circumstances, becomes ever more important. The labor union, the consumer organizations, the associations of welfare clients, the taxpayer associations, and the Reorganized Union of Mad Politicians become the only way that individuals can regain some control over their environment. Ineffective as they may sometimes be, they are often the only means available.

3. If, as Etzioni (1967, 1968) argues, the good society is an "active society," of which one necessary characteristic is consensus, then we must recognize consensus formation as one of the major functions of the voluntary association. In the stable kinship society, consensus comes out of the past and changes slowly by small accretion. In the small, local community, more active consensus was formed through the intensive discussion of events which took place within the very agency of the news—person to person communication. The "tree of knowledge" in every village square of early America was the news network and the news analysis in which everyone participated. Today, as individuated members of a mass audience for programed news and analysis,

we have little chance to participate in a consensus formation process except through voluntary associations (imperfect though this process may be even for voluntary associations).

4. Voluntary associations, because they are voluntary, and essentially private, have a capacity for introducing change that is not open to more institutionalized agencies. New patterns of life may be tried out. The hippie communes, the extra-legal marriage, the free universities, may not survive as organizations, but they are trying out patterns of action, modes of relationships and philosophies which may prove viable, indeed necessary in the present or future world. These are social experiments that institutional agencies often cannot afford to undertake if they are to perpetuate themselves.

5. Finally, voluntary associations, especially those deriving from collective altruism, may be an important if not a major element in long-range societal cybernetics and control. Institutional agencies, the government in particular, become captured in limited, non-transforming criteria for judgment. Voluntary associations may be the only means for providing transforming knowledge and using transforming judgments in the planning for our society (cf., Etzioni, 1967).

These functions, few of which are well-performed by any of our major institutional agencies today, are necessary in the search for the better society. It may be that the most effective way of satisfying these will be through voluntary associations and other kinds of voluntary action rather than through the major institutional structures. *In fact, some would argue that the very definition of the good society is the preeminence of voluntary associations and voluntary action based on altruism. If that is so, then voluntary associations must become the fabric of our society, not just the filling and connecting tissue, and we must learn how to make them so.* The series of volumes reviewing and synthesizing knowledge about voluntary action that we have begun here will, we hope, contribute to this learning as well as to the development and maintenance of the good society, the voluntary society.

References

Curtis, Russell L. and Louis A. Zurcher, Jr.
1971 "Voluntary Associations and the Social Integration of the Poor." *Social Problems* 18 (No. 3).
Etzioni, Amitai
1961 *A Comparative Analysis of Complex Organizations.* New York: The Free Press of Glencoe.
1967 "Toward a Theory of Societal Guidance." *The American Journal of Sociology* 73:15-50.

1968 *The Active Society: A Theory of Societal and Political Processes.* New York: The Free Press of Glencoe.

Hauser, Phillip

1969 "The Chaotic Society: Product of the Social Morphological Revolution." *The American Sociological Review* 34:1-19.

Stanton, Esther

1970 *Clients Come Last.* Beverly Hills, California: Sage Publications.

Warriner, Charles K.

1961 "Public Opinion and Collective Action: Formation of a Watershed District." *Administrative Science Quarterly* 6:333-59.

1964 "Social Integration and the Nature of Urbanization." Chapter 8 In Richard L. Stauber (ed.), *Approaches to The Study of Urbanization.* Lawrence, Kansas: University of Kansas Publications, Governmental Research Series, No. 27.

1970 *The Emergence of Society.* Homewood Illinois: The Dorsey Press.

Willie, Charles

1970 "Community Development and Social Change." Paper presented to the Seminar on Voluntary Action Theory and Research: Steps Toward Synthesis, American Sociological Association Convention, Washington, D.C.

Author Index

Subject Index

Accounting and voluntary action, 3
Acts of Toleration, 87
Ad Hoc Committee on the Triple Revolution, 111
Agriculture and voluntary action, 3
Alcoholics Anonymous, 7
Alienation, 111, 118, 129, 257–258, 345, 351
Alinsky, Saul, 348
Altruism: 6–7, 21, 129, 154, 160, 163
165–167, 183, 187, 343–354; collective, 350–352, 354
Altruistic impulse: the, 344–352; and empathy and personal altruism, 345–347; and death of cultural norms of personal altruism, 345–346; and increasing rationalization of activities, 346–347; and social change, 350–352
"Altruistic Voluntary Organizations", 30, 32, 33, 35, 37
American Automobile Association, 123
American Baptists, 85
American Cancer Society, 4
American Civil Liberties Union, 5, 34
Americans for Democratic Action, 227
American Federation of Labor (AF of L), 154
American Heart Association, 186
American Institute of Public Opinion (AIPO), 209, 215, 221, 222, 225
American Lutheran Church, 96
American Medical Association, 6, 65, 311
American Red Cross, 35, 160, 166, 175, 176, 281, 310
American Sociological Association, 9, 17
American Sociological Review, 54
"Analytic group members", 175
Anglican Church, 84, 87
Annual Review of Psychology, 279
Anomie, 130, 257, 267
Anthropathy: defined, 349; and philanthropy, 349–350
Anthropology and voluntary action, 3
Apathy: 143, 144, 290, 344; and voluntary action, 6, 40, 251
Architecture and voluntary action, 3
Area Planning Action Councils (APAC), 3, 8
Associations (see organizations)
Association of Voluntary Action Scholars (AVAS), 1, 10
Attitudes: defined, 251; related to participation in voluntary organizations, 253–271, 321, 327, 328, 330, 334–335;

general attitudes: alienation, 257–258; anomia, 257–258, 267, 269; concern for the community, 254, 269; formal group preference, 259, 261, 269–270; General FVO Instrumental Value, 259, 261, 269; obligation to participate, 259, 261, 269; identification with the community, 254, 255, 257, 269; obligation to the community, 269; service orientation to leisure time, 259, 261, 269–270; *Specific attitudes*: attractiveness of FVO, 259, 261, 269–270; commitment to FVO, 259, 261, 269–270; felt obligation to participate in FVO, 259, 261, 269–270; friendliness with people in FVO, 259, 261, 269; identification with organization, 255; loyalty to organization, 262; need for organization, 255; perceived efficacy of FVO, 259, 261, 269–270; perceived personal fit with FVO, 259, 261, 269–270; personal influence in organization, 255; presence of influence or recommendation to join FVO, 259, 261, 269; satisfaction with organization, 255; significant outside personal support for FVO, 259, 261, 269–270; understanding of organization's principles, 255
Authority structures, 90, 93, 96
Authority: charismatic, 90; rational pragmatic, 90, 96
"Autonomous, contributive cause organizations", 25–27, 29
Autonomy; 27, 176–177, 182, 187, 306; of organizations, defined, 26

Bernreuter personality inventory, 283
Berrigan brothers, 102
Big Brother organization, 122
"Bio-Socially" determined behavior, 161–165
Black caucuses, 3, 7
Black churches, 3
Black Muslims, 42
Black Panthers, 119, 175, 311
Black separatism, 94, 122
Black studies and voluntary action, 2, 3
Boy Scouts of America, 42, 176, 177
Bureaucratization, 1, 204, 314, 353
Bureaucracy, 111, 113
Business enterprise (see private sector)
Business and voluntary action, 3

Calvin, James L., 84

Psychic involvement in organizations, 183–184, 187
Psychic needs, 139
Psychology: discipline of, 201; and voluntary action, 7; of volunteering, 7
Public administration and voluntary action, 7
Public agencies (see governmental agencies)
Public opinion polls, 101, 117
Public sector (see also governmental agencies): 178, 185; and involvement in voluntary organizations, 36, 37
Puritanism, 84, 87, 103, 111

Quasi-voluntary organizations, 30–38, 86

Reference groups, 7, 31, 131, 184
Reformation, the, 83–85
Religion: associational-communal, 99; cultic, 101; confessional, 101; prophetic, 101; and voluntary action, 7
Remuneration, 72, 132, 152, 160, 168, 174, 175, 183, 187, 280, 286–290
Reorganized Union of Mad Politicians, 353
Republicans, 227
Republican party, 226, 255
Reuther, Walter P., 140
Revolutions, 3, 5, 23
Ripon Society, 227
Ritualism, 98
Rochdale Cooperatives, 347
Rockefeller, Nelson, 101
Roman Catholic Church, 88, 91, 93, 176
Roosevelt, Franklin D., 224
Rose Growing Society, 46
Rorschach tests, 283
Rotary, 120
Rural Sociology and voluntary action, 3

Sebastian, John, 114
Sects: 85–88, 90, 94, 101, 226, 284; and voluntary action, 7, 177–178
Secularization, organizational, 101
Senior Core of Retired Executives, 36
"Sequential specificity" model of participation in voluntary organizations: 261, 321–338; empirical testing of, 335–336
Service ideal: 25–38, 94; compartmentalization of, 30, 38; conflict with other organizing principles, 35
Settlement Houses, 8
Sierra Club, 34
Shriners, 221
Significant others, 7, 265
Simon, Paul, 114
Slave revolts and uprisings, 3
Social Change: 2, 8, 22, 127–133, 187; institutionalization of, 128

Social forces, 43–48, 58–59; and group norms, 44, 45, and interaction, 44, 45; opportunity structure, 44, 45
Social mobility, 136, 285
Social movements: 2, 4, 6–8, 22, 23, 27, 28, 73, 114, 130, 135–149, 184, 351; expressive, 136; instrumental, 136; and "irrationality", 150, 151, 155; norm oriented, 146, 151, 154–156; psychology of, 7; value oriented, 154, 156
Social psychology: discipline of, 202; and voluntary action, 7
Social systems: 109, 113, 132, 173, 175, 277, 299; "system breaks", 109, 113; territorial, 299, 305–308
Social work and voluntary action, 7
Socialization: 119, 161, 200, 300; and academic disciplines, 201
Society: industrial, 109, 113, 114, 117–122, 128, 162, 178, 204, 306; leisure, 5, 22, 109, 178; peasant, 21, 178, 306; pluralist, 100; post industrial, 1, 109, 112–115, 117, 118, 120–124, 306; transition to post industrial, 109, 114, 117, 118, 122; preindustrial, 82, 86, 119, 178, 306; voluntary, 5, 8, 21, 22, 25, 30, 37, 109, 113, 159, 172, 177–178, 182, 183, 186, 194, 199, 354; volunteer, 183
Sociology: discipline of, 51, 52, 58, 59, 202; and voluntary action, 8
"Socio-politically compelled" behavior, 161–165
Southern Christian Leadership Conference (SCLC), 34
Sports and voluntary action, 5
Status: achieved, 82, 175; ascribed, 42, 57, 58, 82, 175, 218
Synagogue Council of America, 92
Synanon, 7

Tax exemptions: and churches, 94, 102; and voluntary organizations, 35
Taylor, James, 114
Teacher Corps, 4
Technology: 112, 113, 301; and social change, 102, 128, 133; and social control, 111
Theological bases of voluntary action, 7
Theology and voluntary action, 7
"Total" institutions, 90
Totalitarianism, 122–123
Trade unions (see labor unions)

UNESCO, 287
United Church of Christ, 96, 98
Unitarianism, 88
United Automobile Workers (UAW), 123
United Fund, 6, 36, 160, 169–170, 350

About the Contributors

James Luther Adams, Professor Emeritus of Christian Ethics, Harvard Divinity School, and Distinguished Professor of Social Ethics, Andover Newton Theological School, is author of *The Changing Reputation of Human Nature, Taking Time Seriously, Paul Tillich's Philosophy of Culture, Science, and Religion*, and editor and translator of numerous volumes by Paul Tillich.

Burt R. Baldwin, Senior Research Associate in the Institute of Human Sciences and Instructor in the Department of Sociology at Boston College, is currently engaged in research on the problem of incidence and prevalence of voluntary organizations.

Jerry G. Bode, is Assistant Professor of Sociology at the University of Arizona; his published papers include "Status and Mobility of Catholics vis-a-vis Several Protestant Denominations," "The Silent Science," and "Protestant Churches as Voluntary Associations."

Phillip Bosserman, is Professor of Sociology and Director of Research for the Program of Leisure Studies at the University of South Florida, and author of *Dialectical Sociology* and *Mission and Public Education in Liberia*.

Richard Gagan, Assistant Professor of Sociology and a member of the Program of Leisure Studies at the University of South Florida, is currently engaged in research on post-industrial life-styles in the U.S.

Gerald E. Klonglan, Associate Research Professor and Associate Professor of Sociology at Iowa State University, is author and co-author of over 90 research monographs, articles, papers and books in community organization and change. Especially focusing on inter-organizational relations, social power, organizational effectiveness in bringing about change, instigated social change, adoption and diffusion of innovations, communication impact and social indicator measurement. Current empirical research activity in smoking and health, alcoholism and in community socio-economic development.

Henry A. Landsberger, Professor of Sociology and Research Professor in the Institute for Research in the Social Sciences at the University of North Carolina, has written widely in the fields of complex organizations and industrial sociology.

Charles L. Mulford, Associate Research Professor and Associate Professor of Sociology at Iowa State University, is author and co-author of over 30 articles, monographs and professional papers in community, power structure analysis, complex organizations and instigated social change.

Bartolomeo J. Palisi, is Associate Professor of Sociology at California State College; his articles include "Ethnic Generation and Social Participation," "An Approach to Using Social Relationships as an Independent Variable in Studying Urban Areas," and "A Critical Analysis of the Voluntary Association Concept."

Barbara Pittard Payne, Associate Professor of Sociology and Urban Life at Georgia State University, has published: *Meaning and Measurement of Commitment to the Church* and *The Protestant Parish.*

Raymond Payne (1919-1971), Professor of Sociology at the University of Georgia, wrote *The Community: A Classified Annotated Bibliography* (with Wilfred C. Bailey) and *Georgia Fact Book on Aging.*

Richard D. Reddy is a Ph.D. candidate in Department of Sociology at Boston College.

Ross P. Scherer, Associate Professor of Sociology at Loyola University of Chicago, is Managing Editor of *Review of Religious Research* and edited *The Lutheran Parish in an Urbanized America; The Church and Its Manpower Management* (with Theodore O. Wedel).

James M. Shultz, private management consultant specializing in educational, voluntary and non-profit organizations, is senior author of *Educational Development Officer: Catalyst for Change in Higher Education*, a monograph of the National Laboratory for Higher Education and has authored and coauthored various organizational studies.

David Horton Smith, Ph.D.: Director of Research for the Center for a Voluntary Society in Washington, D.C., Associate Research Professor at the Institute of Human Sciences, and Associate Professor of Sociology at Boston College, is Editor of *Urban and Social Change Review* and *Journal of Voluntary Action Research.*

Athena Theodore, Associate Professor of Sociology and Director of the Program in Community Affairs at Simmons College, Boston, edited *The Professional Woman* and has authored various articles and papers.

W. Keith Warner, Professor of Sociology at Brigham Young University, is a former editor of *Rural Sociology* and author of various articles, book chapters, and bulletins.

Charles K. Warriner, Professor of Sociology at the University of Kansas, is author of *The Emergence of Society* and numerous articles on various sociological problems, including the often-reprinted "Groups are Real: A Reaffirmation."